D1571855

RENEWALS
DATE DUE

GAYLORD			PRINTED IN U.S.A.

Yale Historical Publications

RYAN DUNCH

*Fuzhou Protestants
and the Making of
a Modern China
1857–1927*

Yale University Press
New Haven & London

Published under the direction of the Department of History of Yale University
with assistance from the income of the Frederick John Kingsbury Memorial Fund.

Set in Sabon type by Keystone Typesetting, Inc.
Printed in the United States of America by Sheridan Books, Chelsea, Michigan.

Library of Congress Cataloging-in-Publication Data
Dunch, Ryan, 1962–
Fuzhou Protestants and the making of a modern China, 1857–1927 / Ryan
Dunch.
     p. cm. — (Yale historical publications)
Includes bibliographical references and index.
ISBN 0-300-08050-6 (alk. paper)
1. Fuzhou Region (Fujian Sheng, China) — Church history — 19th century.
2. Protestant churches — China — Fuzhou Region (Fujian Sheng) — History — 19th
century.   3. Christianity and politics — China — Fuzhou Region (Fujian Sheng) —
History — 19th century.   4. Fuzhou Region (Fujian Sheng, China) — Church
history — 20th century.   5. Protestant churches — China — Fuzhou Region
(Fujian Sheng) — History — 20th century.   6. Christianity and politics — China —
Fuzhou Region (Fujian Sheng) — History — 20th century.   I. Title.   II. Yale
historical publications (Unnumbered).
BR1287 .D86 2001
280'.4'0951245 — dc21   00-011311

A catalogue record for this book is available from the British Library.

The paper in this book meets the guidelines for permanence and durability of the
Committee on Production Guidelines for Book Longevity of the Council on
Library Resources.

10 9 8 7 6 5 4 3 2 1

For Cynthia with love and gratitude and in fond memory of Lucille Gracey, who took a keen interest in this work but did not live to see its completion

Contents

Acknowledgments

The making of this book began with a paper written for a graduate seminar on the city in modern Chinese history in the spring of 1992. In researching that paper I was struck by the many references in mission sources to the involvement of Chinese Protestants in social and political activism in Fuzhou around the time of the 1911 revolution, and became interested in seeking more detailed corroboration of that involvement in Chinese-language sources.

That I was able to find such corroboration is in large measure owing to the efforts of the late Professor Chen Zenghui of the History Department, Fujian Teachers' University, who in conjunction with others in the 1950s and 1960s made efforts to collect and safeguard documentary materials relating to the history of the Protestant church in Fujian. Access to that collection, housed then in the History Department and now in the Institute of Religion of the university, was basic to my research, as were the materials in the Fujian Teachers' University Library, the Fujian Provincial Library, and the Fujian Provincial Archives, all in Fuzhou, and the library of the National Committee of the Protestant Three-Self Patriotic Movement and China Christian Council in Shanghai. My thanks go to these institutions and their staff, and in particular to Professor Tang Wenji, chair, and Professors Lin Jinshui, Xu Gongsheng, Xie Bizhen, and Zhan Guanqun, all of the History Department, Fujian Teachers'

University, who were gracious and generous hosts during the year I spent in Fuzhou in 1993–1994. Thanks are also due to Zheng Xi'an, president of the Anglo-Chinese College, Fuzhou, who helped facilitate many aspects of my family's stay in China, and to the individuals in Fuzhou, Shanghai, and the United States who kindly consented to be interviewed by me for this project.

Outside China, the peerless collection of mission-related materials in the Day Missions Library of the Yale Divinity School has been absolutely indispensable, and I extend my heartfelt thanks to its curator, Martha Smalley, and her associate Joan Duffy. I am grateful also for the assistance provided by the staff of the following institutions: the Special Collections division of the University of Oregon Library; the General Commission on Archives and History of the United Methodist Church, at Drew University in Madison, New Jersey, with special thanks to the associate archivist Mark Shenise; the Archives of the YMCA of the USA at the University of Minnesota, St. Paul, with special thanks to its curator, Dagmar Getz; the Archives of the Church Missionary Society, University of Birmingham, England; the Chinese collection of the Bodleian Library, Oxford University, England; and the Oriental and India Office Collections of the British Library.

Financial support for my research was generously provided by Yale University and the Yale University Council on East Asian Studies and by the Committee on Scholarly Communication with China. Especially significant was a travel grant from the Council on East Asian Studies in the summer of 1992 that enabled me to make contact with scholars in Fuzhou and alerted me to the sources and research potential there. Letters of introduction from Professor Zhang Kaiyuan of Huazhong Normal University, who was in New Haven as a Luce Scholar in 1991–1992, were also very helpful on that occasion.

Institutional support for the transformation of the dissertation into a book came from Calvin College and the University of Alberta. The inclusion of the photographs in the volume was made possible by a generous research grant from the Winspear Fund of the Faculty of Arts, University of Alberta.

The debts of gratitude I owe to my many teachers and colleagues in graduate school are more than I can cite individually. Daniel Bays, though never formally my teacher, has been generous with his help and interest ever since I first wrote to him in 1989 for advice on pursuing the study of the history of Christianity in China. Emily Honig and the members of her graduate seminar in 1991–1992 gave encouragement in the early stages of this project, as did Beatrice Bartlett, who oversaw my initial marshaling of bibliographic sources in her seminar the following year. Helpful comments on sections of the dissertation as it took shape were provided by Pat Giersch, Cynthia Gracey Dunch, Madeline Hsu, Sarah McElroy, and Ruth Rogaski. Most crucial were the consistent help and support of my adviser, Jonathan Spence, who went over every draft chapter promptly and with great thoroughness and never failed to offer insightful and constructive suggestions.

Many people have helped in large and smaller ways in the transformation of the dissertation into a book. Particular thanks are due to the four scholars who read through the whole manuscript at different stages and gave invaluable advice on it: Valerie Hansen, Beatrice Bartlett, Paul Cohen, and the anonymous reviewer for Yale University Press. Jianhong Li checked the quotations and translations in the text. The maps were drafted by Aidan Rowe and Ray Au of the Technical Resource Group, University of Alberta. Andrew Gow generously read and commented on the penultimate draft of the final chapter. Helen Siu energized me with her feedback during the Association for Asian Studies annual conference in 1999. At Yale University Press, I am indebted to Charles Grench for agreeing to consider the manuscript and to Mary Pasti, who has helped spare future readers many redundancies and inconsistencies through her diligence as manuscript editor. Needless to say, I am responsible for any errors of expression, fact, or interpretation that remain.

The process that resulted in this book has commanded much of my attention over the past decade, and the task could not have been accomplished without my family. My parents, Patrick and Lelia Dunch, and my parents-in-law, Cecil and Lucille Gracey, have provided support in many forms, for which I am grateful. My three children, Melanie, Kieran, and Jonah, all born since I began digging into the world of the Fuzhou Protestants, remain bewildered about what Daddy does, although Melanie likes the concept of writing books. My wife, Cynthia Gracey Dunch, on the other hand, knows only too well what is involved in writing books; none of this would have been possible without her patience, sacrifice, and encouragement, and to her the book is dedicated.

Note on Sources and Terms

Protestant missions in China have left behind an extensive array of source materials, but many of those materials do not readily yield the sort of information I was seeking, or do so only tangentially. Most of the findings in this study were possible only because I was able to juxtapose and compare mission sources with church sources and other primary materials in Chinese. Many of the crucial sources were located during research in Fuzhou in 1993–1994. Since some of the materials used in this study are not well known, I have noted the location of some items in the notes and bibliography.

Being able to identify references to the same individuals in different sources in many cases required knowing people's various alternative names (*zi* and *hao*), as well as their given names (*ming*) and the names by which they are known in mission sources in English (usually a romanization based on the pronunciation of one or more of their names in the Fuzhou dialect). In cases where knowledge of the variant names has been important in identifying the same person in different sources, I have listed that person's alternative names in parentheses after the given name (all in the standard *pinyin* romanization), along with the Anglicized dialect form found in the mission sources, if relevant, at the first mention of the individual in the text and in the glossary.

The *pinyin* spelling has been used for place-names except when quoting from or citing sources in which the older spellings are used.

Translations are mine except where otherwise specified.

Introduction

Over seventy years have now passed since the Reverend Nathan Sites of America began to lay the foundations of our church in Minqing in 1866. In those seventy years, first Burma and Siam ceased sending tribute to our country, then Korea, Okinawa, and Taiwan were annexed by Japan, Annam was ceded to France and Jiaozhou to Germany, and the Cassini Agreement [of 1896, which ceded railway and mining rights in Manchuria] was reached with Russia. On the heels of these events came the Boxer Uprising. Patriots (*you zhi zhi shi*), indignant at these constant setbacks in national affairs, at the repeated disasters of military defeat, national disgrace, loss of territory, and imposition of indemnities, turned to Christianity. In fact, to put it dispassionately, in these few decades the autocratic system built up over four millennia has been overturned, the national revolution has succeeded, and the intellectual monopoly of the Confucian tradition has been broken open, allowing European and American scientific and cultural thinking to penetrate. These varied and strenuous changes are what have made it possible for China not only to survive but also to retain its international status; and, directly or indirectly, they have all come about through Christianity.[1]

So runs the opening passage of a history in Chinese of the Methodist church in Minqing County, near Fuzhou, published in 1938.

The passage sums up a certain understanding of modern Chinese history, an understanding that is unremarkable in every respect but one: the role claimed for Christianity. For the Chinese Methodist author of this passage, as for most Chinese nationalists, China's recent history had been a story of territorial encroachment by aggressive foreign powers, under pressure of which the ancient imperial political order and its ideological basis had disintegrated, and China had become a modernizing republic, just in time to enable it to retain its sovereignty and its position in world affairs.[2] However, whereas most nationalist accounts in this vein would class Christian missions as one facet of the aggression of the imperialist powers, this writer presents Christianity as both a spiritual refuge for Chinese nationalists concerned about their country's future and the principal underlying catalyst of the positive changes in recent Chinese history. The dominant verdict of Chinese nationalists, both in the Communist period and earlier, has been that Chinese Christian converts were either pawns of foreign interests or an otherworldly minority of no political importance; in contrast, this writer claims that Chinese Christians, far from being denationalized, were motivated by their patriotism to embrace Christianity.

The question raised by juxtaposing this passage and the more customary narratives of modern Chinese history is a fundamental one: What is the place of Christianity, and in particular of Chinese Christians, in that history? Chinese Christians are a group about whom we know surprisingly little, particularly before the 1920s. Although there are many studies of Christian missions — Catholic and Protestant — in modern China, and several monographs on the Chinese intelligentsia's rejection of Christianity in different periods, few scholars have focused their attention on the perceptions and social impact of the many Chinese converts to Christianity.[3]

This situation is not unique to the field of Chinese history. Until recently it has been true of the study of Christian missions in modern history in general that more attention has been paid to missions and missionaries than to local converts. Now there is a growing recognition that Christianity is no longer only, or even predominantly, a Western religion, and a corresponding trend in scholarship toward shifting the focus of historical and anthropological research onto non-Western Christianity and non-Western Christians.[4]

This book represents an effort to uncover and describe the experiences and social role of Chinese Protestants in one part of China, the Fuzhou (Foochow) area of southeast China, from the time of the earliest conversions in the mid-nineteenth century until the Northern Expedition of 1926–1927 that unified China under Nationalist Party (Guomindang) rule. Although mission sources are important here, the chief focus is not on missionaries or on the missions as institutions but on how Chinese Protestants understood themselves, how that self-understanding changed over the period, and what difference the existence of the Chinese Protestant community made to Chinese society.

My attention was drawn to the Fuzhou region because Fuzhou was one of the earliest and in numerical terms more successful centers of Protestant missionary work in China, and the region has had less scholarly attention than some other parts of China (e.g. Guangzhou, Shanghai, or Tianjin). Also, sources for the history of Protestant Christianity in the Fuzhou area seemed in my initial investigation to be relatively abundant, as they indeed proved to be.

Catholics had been in Fujian Province far longer than the Protestants, but I confined my study to the three Protestant missions that worked in the area of the chief city, Fuzhou, and to the churches they founded. This limitation is justified practically by the fact that the sources for the Catholic church in Fujian, including the archives of the Dominican mission, located in Spain, are quite distinct, and intellectually by the fact that the Catholic and Protestant communities were institutionally, religiously, and culturally separate. I discuss this more in Chapter 1.

In giving primacy to the experience of Chinese church members rather than missionaries, I build up a picture of Protestant Christianity in China which is different from that in much previous work. The book consists of three major sections. The first chapter makes the argument that in converting to Christianity, Chinese Protestants did not cease to define themselves as Chinese, and that, conversely, they understood the Protestant message through the prism of Chinese cultural norms, which resulted in differences of perspective, and sometimes conflicts, between Chinese Protestants and the missionaries. This assertion would be quite unremarkable were it not that some works on missions in China have tended to present Chinese converts as denationalized or dependent figures, culturally or psychologically dominated by Western missionaries.[5] In developing this argument, the chapter looks at the ways the religious experience of Chinese Protestants echoed themes in Chinese popular religion, and at the ways the Protestant churches as communities borrowed from Chinese models of communal organization.

The second section, consisting of Chapters 2 and 3, shows how deeply and extensively involved Chinese Protestants were in the movement for political and social change in the Fuzhou area in the early twentieth century. They were positioned for such involvement by the process of Protestant social mobility in the late nineteenth century, which is sketched in the last part of Chapter 1. By 1900, Protestants were disproportionately represented in the emerging professional sector of urban society: the new Western-style bureaucracies (the Customs, the postal service), service professions like (Western) medicine and education, and the professional roles connected to international trade and finance.

Chapter 2 discusses the role played by Protestants in the new forms of political and social activism that developed in Fuzhou in the first decade of the twentieth century based on this professional sector. Chapter 3 extends that discussion by highlighting the Protestant role in the Fujian Provincial Assembly, which first met in the fall of 1909, and in the 1911 revolution itself. The late Qing provincial assemblies have generally been dismissed as elite-dominated and socially conservative, but by focusing on the actual legislation debated and passed by the Fujian Provincial Assembly and the role of the two Protestant members in it, this chapter shows that the Fujian Provincial Assembly, far from representing the last gasp of the traditional gentry, was an extension of the new political dynamism manifested in the burgeoning of voluntary associations in the city since 1900. These chapters together demonstrate that Chinese Protestants played an important role in the political changes of the 1901–1911 period in Fuzhou, and that their involvement as patriotic and progressive Chinese was accepted and welcomed by non-Christian elements within the progressive elite which brought about the overturning of the imperial political order in local society.

The question raised by these findings is why Chinese Protestants enjoyed such a high level of acceptance in Chinese society in the early twentieth century, when in the previous decades Christian converts had commonly been despised by elite Chinese, and later in the twentieth century the dominant rhetoric of Chinese nationalism defined Chinese Christians as tools of imperialist aggression. This question is addressed at several points in the book, but most directly in Chapters 4 and 5. Both secular nationalists and Protestants, I argue, tended in this period to see the process of building China into a strong, modern nation primarily as a matter of moral education, of molding the Chinese people into a nationally conscious and public-spirited citizenry. This shared agenda is one important reason why Chinese Protestants in the Fuzhou area were accepted as part of the informal progressive coalition in the early twentieth century. In fact, in the early years of the Republic (to 1922), Protestant Christianity enjoyed an unprecedented level of elite interest and political patronage in the Fuzhou area. The YMCA in particular became very popular in Fuzhou in this period, partly because of the facilities it offered, which were unmatched by any other public institution in the city, and partly because its stress on morality and Christian citizenship had a strong appeal amid the political confusion of the early Republic.

Beyond this shared perception of the requirements of modern nationhood, however, I argue that the Protestant churches were an important conduit by which elements of the symbolic repertoire of the modern nation-state became known in the Fuzhou area. Whereas we are accustomed to thinking of missions as agents of cross-cultural transmission in the relatively tangible areas of texts, ideas, vocabulary, scientific terminology, and so on, it is less common to associate missions and their Chinese adherents with the transmission of modernity as mundane practice on the local level. This is the subject of Chapter 4, which draws on the recent scholarly interest in the role played by public ceremonies and symbols such as national flags and anthems in the construction of nation-states in the modern world. These symbolic features of nationalism came into being along with the first wave of modern nation-states in the eighteenth century and were imitated by later nationalists seeking to replicate the model of the nation-state or national revolution in their own social and historical settings.

As this chapter shows, Protestants in the Fuzhou area made extensive and early use of the Chinese flag, patriotic hymns, and other ceremonial affirmations of Chinese nationhood in church settings. They also drew deliberately on the United States as a model for China, both before the establishment of the Republic of China in 1911 and after it. Consequently, Protestants in the Fuzhou area were predisposed to regard themselves as citizens of a modern nation well before those concepts were widely shared in China. Moreover, the evidence available suggests that Protestants in the Fuzhou area were regarded by their non-Christian political associates in the early twentieth century as possessing a special expertise on the use of symbols in the service of the nation. In short, in this chapter I argue that, in the Fuzhou area at least, some of the symbolic elements that were to become so important to Chinese nationalism in the twentieth century initially made their way into Chinese local practice through the Protestant churches.

The 1911 revolution and the Protestant influence in the new Republic sparked great optimism among Chinese Protestants in the Fuzhou area. Protestants expressed a confident hope that China, having become a modern republic, would soon also become a Christian nation. This hope was not realized, and the final chapter addresses the counterfactual question, Why did China not become a Christian republic? From most perspectives on modern Chinese history the question is so implausible that it scarcely warrants an answer, but for Chinese Protestants in the 1910s the conversion of the nation to Christianity seemed a real possibility. However, even at the height of this optimism, Chinese Protestants in the Fuzhou area faced considerable obstacles to the realization of this political-religious vision. These obstacles were compounded in the 1920s, when the ascendancy of a new rhetoric of nationalism influenced by the Leninist theory of imperialism placed Protestants once more on the fringes of Chinese nationalism. In Chapter 6 I discuss these developments as they were played out in Fuzhou, culminating in the assault on church institutions in the city in the wake of the Northern Expedition of 1926–1927, which, though not ending the presence of Protestant Christianity in Chinese society, did bring to an end the

Protestant synthesis of piety, patriotism, and progress which had been so influential in Fuzhou society in the decades since 1900. The concluding section of the chapter links that demise to the engulfing of civil society by the revolutionary state after 1927.

The making of this book began with my desire to trace the linkages between Protestants and society in one area of China in order to develop a better understanding of Chinese Protestants as a group and their role in modern China. Those linkages turned out to be more extensive than I had anticipated, resulting in a book that centers as much on the cultural and institutional undergirding of political change in local society as it does on the Protestants themselves. As with any local study, the question of typicality is inevitably raised: How applicable to China more generally are the portrayals and arguments developed here for the Fuzhou area? If, as I argue, Protestants in Fuzhou were vitally involved in shaping Chinese modernity, and particularly modern politics, in local society, should we expect to find a similar influence in other urban centers in China?

Clearly, Protestants were more numerous in Fujian than in most other parts of China. Also, not all Protestants were the same; as we will see, even within the Fuzhou region differences between the churches connected to the different missions resulted in Chinese members of the Methodist church being more heavily involved in politics than members of the other two churches were. However, while the Fuzhou region is no doubt distinctive in some respects, many of the findings for Fuzhou could well apply to other areas of China, or at least to the more cosmopolitan parts of the country. As Paul Cohen pointed out nearly thirty years ago, there were a number of Christian or Christian-influenced reformers active on the fringes of Chinese political life in the late Qing period, and many of the early participants in the anti-Qing revolutionary movement were Protestants.[6] Sun Yatsen and a number of his colleagues in the first Republican cabinet of 1912 were baptized Protestants, and recent research has highlighted the fact that Chinese Protestants in the United States "were considered political radicals and social progressives" in the overseas Chinese community.[7] The YMCA enjoyed great popularity not only in Fuzhou but also in many of the other principal cities of China in the early Republic. The matter of defining a basis and direction for the new nation was wide open all over the country, and the identification and popularization of symbols for China as a modern nation was a national issue, not simply a local one.

It may well be, then, that Protestants played influential roles in this period in other parts of China, as they did in the Fuzhou area. Moreover, even if Protestants per se were not as important in other locations, it is certainly true that the period from 1900 to the 1920s was a tremendously fluid time all over the country, during which multiple visions of China's future were being articulated and negotiated in complex and fascinating ways. To uncover more of this complexity, we need more studies which bridge the historiographical divide imposed by the 1911 revolution and which pay attention to the local textures and cultural underpinnings of political change.

The Chinese men and women who are the subjects of this book lived in troubled times, which forced them to deal with difficult and compelling issues. As I have studied and pondered their lives, I have not always agreed with their decisions, but I have on many occasions found myself gripped with admiration for their sacrifices and awed by the poignancy of their stories. I hope that my distillation of a few chapters does justice to their rich history.

*Fuzhou Protestants and
the Making of a Modern
China, 1857–1927*

Protestant Christianity in the Chinese Context

In the fifth year of Tongzhi (1866) the strange foreigner returned to Lujiao. The man had come in the heat of summer two years before, dressed in peculiar clothing all of white, and wearing a white hat, like some deathly apparition.[1] That time all had fled at the sight of him, except for Liu Xuebin, who had summoned up the courage to invite the stranger into his home. Later, hearing of the visitor and fearing that Liu was too poor to entertain him fittingly, the wealthy clan elder Liu Yaoyang had invited the foreigner to stay in his home, where he had remained for several days before departing.

This time, the foreigner, who went by the surname Xue and the given name Cheng'en, "inheritor of grace," came with two Chinese companions from the great metropolis of Fuzhou, two hundred *li* downstream. They came intending to rent a place for the preaching of their doctrine, but in this they were opposed by the relatives of their host, Liu Yaoyang, and signs were posted in the town, reading, "The outsiders seek to establish a religion, but their true intentions are mysterious." Accordingly, Xue and his companions left Lujiao for the nearby village of Banzhong, where they began to speak on the street about their doctrine, saying, "We come as representatives of heaven to proclaim the way." Hearing them, a scholar of the town rapped the foreigner on the head with his pipe and said, "Who are you that you dare to make yourself equal to Confucius?" Rather than retaliating, the foreign preacher apologized in a peaceable voice, saying, "Please forgive me if I have spoken wrongly." His humble attitude astonished the onlookers, and word about the visitors spread. Now, Huang Mingwang of Hufeng village was of an inquisitive disposition, and hearing of the foreign preacher and his companions, he walked over to Banzhong and invited them to his house, where they stayed, discussing the doctrine from dawn until dusk with all who came to listen.[2]

The main features of this account, based on a Methodist history published in the 1930s, could apply to the beginnings of Protestant mission work in countless other rural locations in China. In this particular setting, however — Hufeng village in Minqing County, Fujian — one of those who came often and listened with interest was a youth of seventeen named Huang Naishang. Huang's father was a carpenter in Hufeng, and Huang had had some schooling during the agricultural off-seasons. Writing of his conversion many years later, Huang stated that through his schooling he had developed an earnest desire to live according to the precepts of the sages, but had been puzzled by the "great contradiction between the words of those who read Confucius and Mencius and their actions."[3] Accordingly, when the foreigner and his friends told him that no one could attain total goodness by relying on his own power alone, but only by relying on the power of God to overcome all evil, Huang was interested in what they had to say. He was given two Christian books, one an account of the doctrine of creation, and the other the New Testament, and read through them several times. After some months of consideration, Huang "repented of [his] past mistaken beliefs (*mixin*) and the sins [he] had committed," and was baptized along with his lineage uncle Huang Fuju in the winter of 1866–1867; they were the first two Protestant converts in Minqing County.[4]

This young convert from a poor family in an average village of an undistinguished county became a major figure in provincial and national life, and an important participant in the developments traced in this book. His conversion and his early adult life provide useful points of entry for an overview of the development of Chinese Protestant communities in the Fuzhou area to 1900.

Chinese Religions and Protestant Conversion

The history of Christianity in Fujian Province dates back at least as far as the Yuan dynasty (1280–1368), when Nestorian Christian communities are known to have existed in the Quanzhou area in southern Fujian, as well as European missionaries belonging to the Franciscan order. These communities died out, however, and Christianity as an ongoing presence in Fujian began with the Jesuit mission in the province in the late Ming dynasty. The Jesuit Giulio Aleni, often dubbed the Apostle of Fujian, entered the province in 1625 and traveled extensively in it over the next twenty-five years, making many converts from the upper classes of Chinese society. Later, the Franciscans and the Dominicans took up work in the province, the latter in particular becoming very influential in Funing Prefecture, in northeast Fujian near the border with Zhejiang Province. The first Chinese to be made a bishop, Luo Wenzao (Gregory Lopez), consecrated in 1685, was from the city of Fu'an in that prefecture, and adherents to the Roman Catholic church remain very numerous there today.[5]

The Jesuit work in Fujian ended with the disbanding of the order in the eighteenth century, and the Franciscans also gave up work in the province, leaving the churches there under the oversight of the Spanish Dominicans based in Manila. When Protestant missions began work in Fuzhou in the mid-nineteenth century, therefore, not only did they come from a totally different religious and social milieu, the Protestant world of industrializing Britain and America; they also spoke a different language from the Catholic missionaries already working in the province. In addition, the Protestant and Catholic missionaries were theologically antagonistic to each other, and their missiological strategies and assumptions were quite different. For example, the Catholic missions in Fujian invested little energy in running schools until the Republican period (1911–1949), whereas the Protestants came to place a heavy emphasis on educational work by the 1880s. Moreover, the Protestant missions in China adopted terminology in Chinese for basic Christian doctrines that was not at all like the terminology in use in Chinese Catholicism since the seventeenth century. The result of all these differences, as well as very different modes of worship, was that the Protestant and Catholic branches of Christianity in Fujian, and in China more generally, developed in quite separate communities and often appeared to ordinary Chinese to be distinct religions; this gulf between the two in Chinese society continues into the present. In the Fuzhou area between 1857 and 1927, such contact as there was between Catholic and Protestant communities was in the main competitive or hostile.

Fuzhou was one of five Chinese ports opened for foreign residence under the conditions of the Treaty of Nanjing signed between Britain and China in 1842. The first Protestant missionaries to take up work there arrived in 1847, and by 1850 the three mission societies that were active in the Fuzhou area for the next century had missionaries working in the port. These three missions were the American Board of Commissioners for Foreign Missions, an interdenominational agency rooted in the old Congregational churches of New England; the

Board of Foreign Missions of the Methodist Episcopal Church (North), a church that had expanded swiftly in America since the early nineteenth century as white settlement spread westward across the continent; and the Church Missionary Society (CMS), which drew its personnel and support from the low church or evangelical wing of the Church of England and the Church of Ireland.[6] From the missionaries' perspective, Fuzhou was a difficult station. Health problems took a heavy toll, and results were many years in coming. The American Board mission baptized its first convert in 1856, after nine years of labor; the Methodists, the following year; and the CMS, in 1861.[7]

The early history of the Protestant missions in Fuzhou has been treated in detail by Ellsworth Carlson in his book *The Foochow Missionaries, 1847–1880.* As the title indicates, Carlson's book concentrates on the missionaries, and it gives a valuable analysis of the problems that their presence and activities posed for Chinese officials. However, while it acknowledges the important role played by Chinese "helpers" in the expansion of the Protestant churches in the Chinese countryside, Carlson's book says little about the lives and perspectives of the Chinese preachers and converts and tends to attribute little autonomous agency to them.[8] In this Carlson reflects the nature of the mission sources; missionaries in their correspondence with the home boards seldom gave much personal detail on their Chinese associates, and mission publications naturally focus on the doings of the missionaries themselves.

Nevertheless, it is possible to derive important detail about the Chinese side of the missionary-Chinese interaction from the materials available, and particularly from those few surviving sources in which Chinese Protestants wrote about their own lives. That Chinese side is the focus of this book. Missionaries appear only peripherally in it, because in most instances they *were* peripheral to the day-to-day life and religious practice of Chinese Protestants.

What motivated Chinese people to convert to Christianity, and what did Christianity mean to them? According to Huang Naishang's main account of his conversion, he found in Christianity the solution to two problems that had troubled him as a young man: finding the power to live out the moral precepts he encountered in the classical texts he had read in his studies, and finding a way to bridge the gulf he saw between the teachings of the ancient sages and the practices of those around him who appropriated their mantle. Huang's comments point us toward the continuing importance in the lives of individuals of the moral discourse of late imperial China. Thomas Metzger has argued that the classical texts of late imperial China held out the possibility of complete self-mastery and social harmony, but that both goals proved elusive, leaving individuals with a "sense of predicament" that could be resolved only with the entrance of new physical and social technologies from outside China in the nineteenth century. Other recent works have also helped uncover the importance of moral endeavor in the social life of countless individuals in late imperial China.[9]

During those intense months late in 1866 when Huang Naishang was grappling with Christian ideas, he tells us that he came to the opinion that Christianity and the teachings of the Chinese sages were similar in stressing reverence for heaven and love for humanity, but that Christianity supplied a spiritual dimension which the Chinese sages lacked. He admired the Christian principles of redemption from sin and salvation of the soul, which could cause even the most wicked to reform themselves, and the doctrines of heaven and hell, which could motivate people to do good and impart a dread of doing evil. Moreover, Huang was impressed with the Christian teaching of resting every seventh day to worship and hear instruction in the Scripture, which he saw as an excellent way to ensure the education of believers. This account, written in the summer of 1911, continues with a passage that reflects the iconoclasm and openness to new ideas of that revolutionary period:

> Therefore in Western countries all men and women, from kings and princes to commoners, adhere to this religion, without distinctions of wealth or rank. How different indeed from the teachings of the Confucians! They say, "All things are rooted in heaven," but know nothing of either the creation or the future end of all things. They refuse to discuss the afterlife and its rewards and punishments, saying, "Not yet knowing life, how can we speculate about death," yet they believe in ghosts and honor spirits, even offering sacrifices to gods of mountains and rivers, thunder and lightning, and letting themselves be led astray by the deceptions of every diviner and geomancer. They have an inflated opinion of themselves and look down on others, and respect the arts and learning of China simply because they are familiar, rejecting whatever comes from abroad.[10]

According to this account, Huang Naishang converted to Christianity because of his own sense of moral shortcoming, his perception that Christian teaching answered questions that the Chinese classical tradition avoided, and his contempt for the practices of Chinese popular religion. However, this account of his conversion and the briefer one in his autobiography were written many decades after the events they describe, when Huang was very much in the public eye. They were composed with an apologetic purpose, to suit an age in which both the Chinese scholarly tradition and popular religious practices were coming under increasing criticism from modernizing nationalists.[11] In addition, it is likely that Huang's memory of his conversion and his understanding of what it meant were influenced by his subsequent decades of study and living as a Protestant. In short, these statements written in 1911 and 1917 cannot be taken at face value as reflections of Huang's state of mind in 1866.

Nevertheless, Huang's description of his conversion exemplifies the bifurcated stance of Chinese Protestants in the Fuzhou area in the late Qing period toward the ethical teachings and religious practices of their society. Protestants generally expressed respect for the moral tenets of the Confucian tradition (albeit sometimes refracted through a Christian lens), while asserting that Christianity could "fulfill the Law."[12] By contrast, Fuzhou Protestants regarded Chinese popular religious practices and anything connected with Buddhism or Taoism as base, pointless, and idolatrous. In taking this attitude they drew on and echoed the long-standing hostility of the Chinese political elite for popular religion.[13] Thus, the most substantial attempt by a Protestant scholar in Fuzhou to reconcile Christianity and Chinese tradition consisted of an extensive compilation of quotations from Chinese classical sources, with commentary, marshaled to support Protestant moral positions and to legitimate Protestant critiques of Buddhism, Taoism, and popular customs; it was published in 1903. The same writer, Huang Zhiji (Uong De Gi, 1866–1928) later published an extensive work comparing the teaching of Christianity to that of the ancient Chinese philosopher Mozi, finding in the latter a Chinese precursor to, but not a substitute for, Christ.[14]

These attempts at intellectual synthesis belong to a later period, however. For most of the first-generation converts to Protestant Christianity in the Fuzhou area before 1900, and probably for Huang Naishang himself in 1866, the primary frame of reference within which they heard and responded to Christianity was not the personal struggle for sagehood, but the family and communal ritual practices summed up in the term "popular religion."[15] The term refers to the interlocking pantheon of "gods, ghosts, and ancestors" that constituted the unseen world which most Chinese inhabited and the interactions with that world which gave structure to the passage of time through the festivals and markers of the ritual year.[16] This was the world not of learned philosophical and ethical systems, but of incense and chanting; of dreams, mediums, and divination; of colorful gods, some fierce-faced, like the warrior Guandi or the gods of plague and pestilence, others merciful, like the bodhisattva Guanyin; of ancestors to be pleased and hostile ghosts to be appeased. It was this world in all its complexity and vitality that early Chinese Protestants inhabited and from which they converted.

With reference to Chinese popular religion, the central Protestant claim was that its gods were nothing but dumb idols with no power and that at the core of Christianity was the worship of the one true God. Thus the first Protestant church in Fuzhou, opened by the Methodists in the commercial suburb south of the city wall in 1856, was named Zhenshen tang, "True God Church."[17] Since the chief determinant of the popularity of different deities in Chinese religious practice was people's belief in the deity's *ling,* or "efficacy," referring to the power of the god to answer the petitions and fulfill the requests of worshipers, the Protestant message, in its blanket denial of the efficacy of all such deities, confronted popular religion at its core and pitted the God of Christianity against the local gods. Protestant preaching did not deny the existence of the supernatural world, however; the Chinese belief in evil or hostile spiritual forces was affirmed by Protestants, and deliverance from the power of those forces through faith in Christ became another core element of Chinese Protestant belief.

These points are illustrated in the most detailed conversion account of a Chinese Protestant in the Fuzhou area, the autobiography of the Methodist preacher Xu Yangmei (Hu Yong Mi, 1837–1893).[18] Xu Yangmei and his brothers Bomei (Hu Bo Mi, 1828–1907) and Chengmei (Hu Sing Mi, 1840–1898) were converted, along with their parents and other family members, in 1857 and 1858 and were soon working unpaid as part-time preachers ("exhorters") on Sundays. In 1869 these three brothers were among the seven men who became the first ordained Methodist preachers in Fujian.[19]

Xu Yangmei was of a serious disposition as a young man. He records how he avoided the temptations of gambling, wine, licentiousness, and opium before hearing about Christianity, and how he sought to practice the teachings of every religion with which he was familiar—Buddhism, Taoism, the ritual orthodoxy of the state, and popular religion: "I was constantly either reciting the name of the Amida Buddha and abstaining from meat, or contemplating the [Taoist] paradise and elixir of immortality, or making offerings to heaven and earth and revering the ancient sages and worthies, or serving the local deities. I was considered uncommonly devout. However, I dreaded ghosts and feared death, and on this account my heart was constantly disturbed."[20]

Xu's family lived close to the True God Church, and his father, who was an officer in the constabulary under the Min County magistrate, had become friendly with the missionaries who preached there. Thus, Xu Yangmei's elder brother Bomei met no opposition from his parents when he was baptized early in 1857. Xu Yangmei, however, opposed his brother's conversion, and argued with him at length before finally coming to agree with him that Christianity was good and converting to it himself.[21]

Xu Yangmei's religious anxiety ended with his conversion to Christianity, according to the autobiography, and he discarded his statue of Guanyin and images of other gods. In fact, since his parents and younger brother were baptized at the same time, the whole extended family discarded all their gods and began meeting together for daily devotions. Around 1872 or 1873, however, having been a full-time preacher for over ten years, Xu went through some kind of spiritual crisis during which he felt himself to be cut off from Christ and under attack by Satan. The autobiography indicates that this experience, which continued for several months, involved vivid images of the devil spirits of Chinese demonology and culminated in what Xu describes as a vision of hell, populated in Chinese fashion by "serpents, dragons, ghosts, and demons" and filled with terrifying sounds. As he stood petrified before this scene, Xu states, two men suddenly appeared on either side of him, placed their hands on his chest (*xiong,* here probably signifying the seat of the mind or soul), and guided him step by step through to the other side.[22] This vision of deliverance prefigured the reality, for his psychological turmoil ended and his peace of mind returned soon after the experience.

Similar emphasis on the supernatural is evident in the conversion account of another of the first Methodist preachers, Xie Xi'en (Sia Sek Ong, 1839–1897). Xie was a young teacher in a village school when he first came into contact with Protestants. As a boy, he had come across a Chinese morality tract "with pictures representing the punishment awaiting the wicked. One was snatched up at death by the Prince of Devils and sawn asunder, while others were roasted at a copper-pipe to which they were chained." These images stayed with him and gave him a desire to do good in order to avoid such dreadful retribution, and after his conversion he interpreted his encounter with this tract as a way God had predisposed him to believe in Christianity.[23]

Before Xie Xi'en converted to Christianity, he became a *dis*believer in the efficacy of the gods of his community. This became evident to him when his firstborn son became very ill. According to this account, "My relatives and friends tried to persuade me to worship idols in behalf of the child. But in this affliction I discovered that I had the root of the Truth in my heart. I firmly believed that men's lives were in God's keeping. The more they tried to persuade me, the firmer my heart was fixed. When the child finally died they heaped reproach upon me for doubting the power and efficacy of the idols. I heard all their severe words patiently and gained the victory." After struggling with himself for another month or so, Xie decided to embrace Christianity. He describes the point of decision this way: "I . . . determined to forsake all the cherished joys of this world . . . , knelt down, confessed my sins and prayed. I arose with my sorrow still resting upon me. My heart panted for mercy. . . . The thought occurred to me: I have heard much preaching and remained hard-hearted, maybe the Lord has cast me off forever." Some hours later, however,

"I was walking to and fro when a voice seemed to say to me: 'The Lord has heard your prayers and forgiven your sins.' It seemed to be above me, at my side and within me. My sorrow disappeared, I could not tell how, or at what moment, and peace and joy unspeakable filled my soul. . . . While alone in a benighted village in the year of our Lord Eighteen hundred and sixty-one, and in the Sixth month, I experienced God's pardoning mercy."[24]

Neither of these men was converted through the immediate agency of foreign missionaries, although they had had contact with them. And, as these accounts show, they found in Chinese religious life ample parallels with the world they saw in the Christian Scripture: concepts of sin and retribution, struggles against threatening evil forces, supernatural visions and voices, and the hope of immortality and salvation. At the heart of their conversion experience was the rejection of the efficacy of the gods of popular religion. Critiques of Buddhism and Taoism by the Chinese elite also, ironically, pointed people toward Christianity in some cases: Huang Qiude (Wong Kiu Taik, 1834?–1893), a close friend of Xu Yangmei and later the first Chinese Anglican clergyman in Fujian, was influenced to become a Christian by reading some of the Confucian polemical texts against Buddhism and Taoism, in addition to Christian books given him by Xu.[25]

The competition between the Protestant God and local gods took a literal form in the experience of Xu Bomei while he lived and preached in Gutian County, inland from Fuzhou to the northwest (in 1877; map 1.1).[26] According to a manuscript memoir written by Xu late in his life, there was a drought in Gutian while he was there, and the people of the city were all sacrificing to the god of the locality and praying for rain.[27] One of the church members was asked why the Protestant preacher was not also praying for rain. Hearing this, Xu let it be known that if the people refrained from praying to the local god, he would pray to his God for rain, "for if you and I pray at the same time and copious rains come to end the drought, the power of my God will not be demonstrated to you." The people agreed to stop praying for three days, during which time Xu would pray to the Christian God for rain. He and the small band of Protestants in the town assembled in the chapel the next dawn to fast and pray for rain. They broke to eat at 11 A.M. and resumed praying at 1 P.M. and again at dawn the following morning. At noon on the second day, the sun was still shining brightly, and there was no sign of rain. The church members were mocked when they went home to eat. When they assembled again for the afternoon, they all prostrated themselves and prayed even more earnestly. Around 1:30 that afternoon, Xu records, clouds suddenly gathered and rain appeared imminent. Seeing this, the people brought their "wooden idol" to the vicinity of the chapel and began to chant prayers and invite the god to

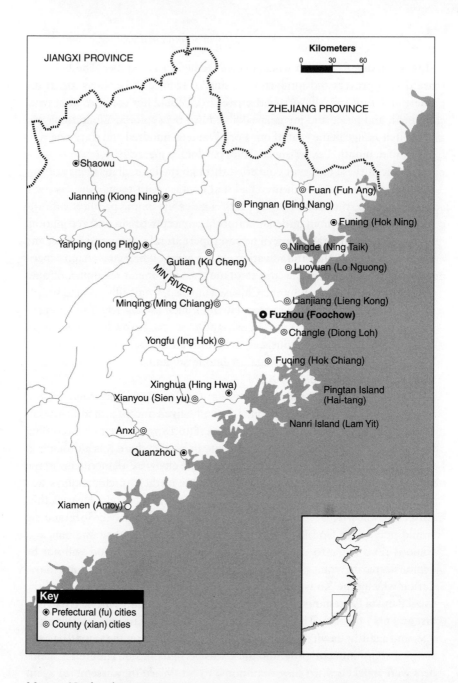

Map 1.1. North and east Fujian Province, around 1900. City names are in *pinyin*, with dialect names as commonly romanized in mission sources shown in parentheses. The inset shows the southeast coast of China.

enter a medium, making a great commotion.[28] Hearing the noise and realizing that "they wanted to take credit for God's work," the Protestants stopped praying and went to the door of the chapel to watch. After about an hour the clouds dispersed and the sun came out, and the crowd and the medium left, mortified, leaving the statue of the god and instruments of worship lying in the street until nightfall. The following dawn the Protestants assembled again and prayed, and early that morning the rain came.[29]

Xu does not claim that the town converted en masse after this event. On the contrary, he alludes to the words of Christ about those who saw without perceiving and heard without understanding.[30] For our purposes, what is important in this account is Xu Bomei's perception of a real spiritual competition between his God and the false gods of the local people. The account is also important because, as a narrative, it echoes the biblical story of the prophet Elijah praying to end a three-year drought in Israel, which also took place in the context of a competition with other gods (the prophets of Baal; see 1 Kings 18).

Interpretation of their own lives in terms of narratives taken from the Bible is another fascinating aspect of the early Protestant experience in the Fuzhou area. Xu Yangmei's autobiography contains several instances of this, including similar accounts of ending a drought by prayer on two different occasions.[31] Another instance is one of the most interesting episodes in the book. While stationed inland in Gutian in 1879, Xu had a dream in which he saw one of his fellow preachers, the former opium addict Lin Zhenzhen (Ling Ching Ting, 1825?–1879), looking healthy and dressed all in white, on a white horse. Lin rode into the church courtyard and told Xu he had come especially to invite Xu to follow him. Xu concluded (rightly) that Lin had died, and at first thought the dream meant that he would die too, but later he came to see the dream as meaning that he was to succeed Lin as minister in Fuqing County, south of Fuzhou (fig. 1.1).[32] This account echoes in some respects the dream of the apostle Paul of a man summoning him to preach in Macedonia, recounted in Acts 16:6–10, and it is mixed with other elements of New Testament imagery (the white clothes and white horse).

As these examples indicate, for early Chinese Protestants, as for Protestant converts in West Africa around the same time, the Bible furnished not merely doctrines but also "paradigmatic narratives," particularly of supernatural experience.[33] Furthermore, once the Bible was translated into Chinese and circulating in print form, its appropriation and interpretation were to a large degree out of the control of missionaries, who might have been uneasy with the literal way Chinese converts applied some of its supernatural elements.[34] This is indicated by the fact that the supernatural orientation of the early Chinese Protestants is more evident in writings in Chinese and in writings

Fig. 1.1. Grave of early Methodist preacher Lin Zhenzhen. The grave is in Chinese style, and only the text on it marks it as a Christian grave. The gravestone reads: "Qing, Guangxu 4 [1878/1879]. Jesus said, 'I am the resurrection, I am the life. All who believe in me, though they die, will certainly live.' Grave of Mr. Lin Zhenzhen of Nanri." Methodist Collection, Drew University, Madison, New Jersey.

translated from accounts by Chinese Protestants (as in the case of Xie Xi'en) than in the regular published mission sources in English.[35]

Many other examples of this supernatural orientation could be given, involving laypeople as well as preachers.[36] For instance, one of the early Anglican converts in Gutian County was an illiterate old carpenter who was fond of recounting an out-of-body experience in which he saw the glory of heaven, the model for which could well have been the apostle Paul's reference to such an experience in 2 Corinthians 12:1–4. This man did not have any contact with missionaries until well after his conversion, and by the time he was baptized in 1868 he was already a zealous lay evangelist. In later years he took to walking all through the region wearing the text of the Ten Commandments, the Christian Cross and an explanation of it, and the account of his own experiences on a banner sewn on his back.[37]

One of the CMS missionaries in Fuzhou wrote in 1880 of another person who had a supernational experience — a rural woman who "was possessed of an evil spirit" and was told in a dream that if she wanted to rid herself of this affliction, she should go to Fuzhou to learn the doctrine of Jesus. She showed up at the missionary's house with her husband and four children, begging to be taught "the doctrine," and was employed as a cook for the boys' boarding school. Some days later she had a "fit" (trance?), during which she was oblivious to those in the room and talked wildly about God and Christ and the Holy Spirit and said she believed in the Son of God, which struck the missionaries watching as very strange, since to their knowledge she had never been instructed in Christian teaching. The next Saturday night, she had a dream in which the evil spirit that afflicted her seized her by the neck and commanded her to leave Fuzhou at once or it would kill her. She woke up with a pain in her neck, but instead of leaving, she went and sat by herself in the church. While she was there, the pain in her neck left her, "and she experienced a strangely happy sensation, and since that day she has had no return of those strange attacks" that had plagued her for three years. She stayed in the mission school in Fuzhou for a year and studied with the missionary's wife, after which, having learned to read the New Testament and parts of the Old, she returned to her home area as an unpaid lay evangelist ("Biblewoman").[38]

Although these instances all date from the first twenty years or so of Protestant expansion in the Fuzhou area (1857–1880), similar experiences are recorded in later periods, particularly in places where Protestant teaching had newly penetrated. For example, in 1891 the daughter of a rural Protestant in Minqing was married to a man in another part of the county. Two of the villagers noticed some volumes of the Bible in her bridal trousseau, and their interest was piqued — as well it might have been, for not many rural brides carried books of any sort to their new homes. They borrowed the books and later went to the bride's home area and listened to the preacher there explain Christian doctrine. After returning home, one of these men dreamt of an old man who struck his head with a board and said, "Is there a teaching that will promote good relations with neighboring states?"[39] He then said, "Heaven has condescended to the people below, making rulers and teachers for them." Waking up, he told the dream to his companion, who said, "He did not strike the whole body, only the head; you and I are to serve as the heads." "From that time forth," the account continues, "they determined to bear the cross throughout their lives and read the Bible in the morning and the evening, and they thought nothing of walking a distance of over thirty *li* to the church to worship. In less than a month, friends and relatives were following their lead, and the next year they started a congregation in the village, called Huang Qixiang to be the pastor, and established a school for the instruction of the young."[40]

According to this account, then, the church in this area was begun by two laymen as a result of a vision received in a dream. Complicating the story considerably is the fact that the words of the old man in the dream are quotations from *Mencius,* one of the foundational texts of the Chinese classical tradition. In the passage in question (1B.3), King Xuan of the powerful state of Qi asks the sage how he can ensure peaceful relations between states. Mencius answers that being willing to serve other states, large and small, is the basis of peace and that the king who does so "delights heaven." When the ambitious king balks at this answer, Mencius goes on to discuss the role of rulers, quoting the Book of History (*Shangshu*) to show that rulers are sent by heaven as teachers of the people "to assist God on High in loving them" (*zhu Shangdi chong zhi*).[41]

What are the words of Mencius doing on the lips of a heavenly messenger in a dream in this Christian context? As we have already seen and will note again in later chapters, Fuzhou Protestant texts in Chinese regularly employ Chinese classical texts to validate Christian teachings. On this level, two main aspects of the passage make it amenable to Christian use. First, it uses the term *Shangdi,* by this time accepted among the Methodists as the appropriate translation for the Judeo-Christian God, and it ascribes to rulers a role as divinely appointed teachers acting as assistants to God in communicating his favor to the people; in this case what Mencius says of rulers is clearly being applied by analogy to leaders in the church. Second, the passage speaks of such rulers "bringing peace to the people of the world" (*an tianxia zhi min*); here an analogy to the potential of the Christian message and its bearers to bring peace is probably intended.

In putting these quotations in the mouth of a messenger of God in a dream, however, this story moves beyond a straightforward appropriation of a classical text. In announcing to these men their selection by divine mandate to become "heads" of the Protestant religion in the area, the angelic figure speaks with the voice of the Chinese classical tradition; the ancient Chinese sage Mencius becomes a vehicle for the revelation of the Christian God. Assuming, as seems reasonable, that the text gives us the substance of the origin story of the Protestant church in this part of Minqing as it was transmitted orally (noting that the time span between the event in 1891 and the publication of this book in the 1930s is relatively brief), we can suppose that this would have been an immensely powerful validation for Protestant belief for that church community. Certainly it shows very clearly that conversion to Christianity was not a simple repudiation of Chinese culture in the minds of Chinese Protestants.

Judging from these examples, we can see that although in some respects conversion did set Chinese Protestants apart from and in conflict with their society, in other ways Protestant belief drew on some important elements in Chinese culture. In particular, Chinese Protestants in the Fuzhou area drew on the supernatural beliefs and imagery of Chinese religion and popular culture, much as the Taiping movement had done.[42] Communication through dreams and visions; out-of-body experiences; contending gods — all were stock elements of Chinese culture, seen in vernacular fiction, local drama, religious iconography and mythology, and popular worship; and Protestants found analogues and counterparts to them in the world of the Christian Scripture.[43]

Moreover, Chinese Protestants in the Fuzhou area interpreted their new beliefs in the light of Chinese religious and ethical sensibilities, which also contained moral precepts and concepts of hell and guilt, of salvation and heavenly grace, of life after death, and even of incarnation. At the same time, in translating a foreign concept (God) using a term found in the Chinese classical canon (*Shangdi*), Chinese Protestants were simultaneously reinterpreting and laying claim to that canon, and indeed to a certain understanding of Chinese history, seen as a decline from the ancient monotheism found in the earliest texts. The full weight of a "purified" Chinese tradition lay behind the Protestant rejection of "idolatry." In several important ways, therefore, Protestant Christianity was comprehensible to Chinese listeners, and Chinese Protestants adapted elements in their culture as they appropriated it; most of this appropriation was done without direct reference to foreign missionaries.

The dominant themes in Protestant belief changed over the decades. Literacy, education, and knowledge of the outside world tended to follow Protestant belief, particularly for second-generation and later Protestants in any given locale. As a result, Protestants became more educated and more inclined to claim a place in Chinese elite society, and the stress on supernatural experience gave way to an emphasis on the association of Christianity with science, rationalism, and progress. An example of this transition is the Protestant doctor Xu Zeya, a son of Xu Bomei, who on occasion was called on to perform exorcisms. This he did, not by prayer and fasting, as his father probably would have done, but by the more prosaic means of holding an ammonia-soaked cloth over the nose of the patient whenever the evil spirit manifested itself.[44] After the turn of the twentieth century, when modernizing nationalists began assaulting popular religion under the new label of "superstition," Protestants aligned themselves with the new order, at least in urban society.[45] That modern alignment was not an inevitable consequence of conversion, however, and we would be mistaken to equate conversion with detachment from Chinese society and entry into a westernized, missionary-dominated, or modernist cultural reality.

Congregations and Communities

The months following their baptism at the close of 1866 were difficult ones for Huang Naishang and his uncle. Huang writes that he was scolded and harangued throughout the large walled compound that comprised his village. "Fortunately," however, "the 1,100 inhabitants of our village were all of a single lineage, and thus all related by blood to one another, so although we were slandered, insulted, and even struck, we did not meet with any greater harm."[46] The next year, three more men of the lineage, all brothers or close cousins judging by their common generational name, came to the Christian faith, along with an outsider who was living there. One of these men had been an ardent follower of the local gods and had served as a medium in the communal festivals. Another, by contrast, had lost belief in those gods some time before, after his young wife died of complications from childbirth despite his prayers and offerings for her recovery. These four converts were followed by the son of the medium, the younger brother of the widower, and others, until a group of a dozen or so men were meeting together regularly for worship and instruction.[47]

In the winter of that year (1867), the Methodist church in Fuzhou sent Xu Yangmei to live and minister in Minqing, where he remained for the next seven years. Finding that Huang Naishang was "endowed with zeal and wisdom, was diligent in study, and was helpful in evangelizing and entertaining visitors," Xu took him on as an assistant and later licensed him as an exhorter, the lowest rank of lay preacher in the Methodist system. Huang worked with Xu throughout the following year and a half, and Xu had a shaping influence on his later life.[48] Huang traveled with him on some of his preaching and visitation tours, which covered all twenty-four districts of Minqing and parts of the surrounding counties. Xu gave the young Huang intensive instruction in the Old and New Testaments, and Huang studied them so thoroughly that fifty years later he could still recite from memory many of the passages he had memorized at that time.[49]

Xu Yangmei was an effective preacher, and people came from near and far to hear him and invite him to preach in their villages. He also had a patient and courteous manner, which enabled him to overcome hostility and dispel rumors, so he came to be on good terms with the men of literary attainment and wealth in the area.[50] In the first year of his ministry in Minqing, forty to fifty people became probationary church members, and the next year Minqing was made a circuit under the supervision of the Fuzhou pastoral district (superintended by Xie Xi'en, whose conversion was discussed above).[51]

The pattern evident in this account is characteristic of the way the Protestant church spread throughout the Fuzhou region. An initial visit by a missionary or Chinese preacher would spark the interest of a handful of people, who would begin meeting together, usually in the face of clan opposition. In time, others, often related by ties of kinship or friendship to the first converts, would join them in their meetings and then convert. If the interest warranted it, a Chinese preacher would be stationed there, renting a home to serve as a chapel, initially as an outstation of an existing congregation elsewhere (fig. 1.2). He would travel in the surrounding area, preaching where he was welcome and often teaching literacy and the Bible to the converts and their children or perhaps taking a talented young man like Huang Naishang under his wing for on-the-job training. The preacher's wife would get to know the women of the place and perhaps teach them to read. Over time, the chapel would become a pastorate in its own right, with its own outstations in the surrounding region, in some cases served by one of the first converts of the

Fig. 1.2. Methodist chapel in a Chinese residence adapted for the purpose. Churches of this type were typical of the early phase of mission work in rural Fujian. Methodist Collection, Drew University, Madison, New Jersey.

mother church; thus, three of the initial six Minqing converts later served as preachers in other parts of the county.[52]

Although this pattern applies to all three of the missions operating in the Fuzhou area, the missions differed in important respects. Their varying denominational backgrounds resulted in very different beliefs about church government — differences that had practical implications for the degree of autonomy enjoyed by the Chinese preachers affiliated with each mission. The missions also differed in their willingness to resort to consular intervention in cases of conflict between converts and their neighbors and, more simply, in the ability of the Chinese preachers they attracted. All these differences affected their rates of expansion.

The American Board mission was by far the slowest to grow, having only 215 baptized converts and probationers in 1880–1881, after thirty-three years in the area (table 1.1).[53] To some extent, this was by preference. Of Calvinist and Congregational background, the American Board missionaries were wary of the swift extension of the other two missions and rather skeptical of the authenticity of their conversions (much as the New England religious establishment had been suspicious of the revivalist enthusiasm of new sects like the Methodists and Baptists in the United States in the early nineteenth century).[54] As Congregationalists they believed that each church should be governed and supported by its members, and they concentrated on developing a small number of congregations, composed of well-instructed converts, toward the point of being self-supporting and self-governing. In accordance

Table 1.1. American Board Mission Statistics for Fujian, 1881–1930

Year	Ordained Preachers	Total Chinese Employed	Communicant Members	Total Constituency	Number of Schools	Total Students
1880–81	2	27	215		10	172
1885–86	2	46	311		16	296
1890–91	2	56	546	860	31	452
1895–96	5	124	1,102	3,748	55	1,477
1900	9	241	1,959	4,349	92	2,058
1905	11	318	3,001	(3,875)[a]	132	2,424
1910	8	321	1,994	2,896	75	2,611
1915	14	302	2,761	5,832	104	3,453
1920	14	430	3,145	8,974	143	4,909
1925	18	429	4,305	13,900	129	4,746
1930	21	247	3,348	8,358	88	3,680

Source: Annual Report of the American Board, 1881–1931.

Note: Tables 1.1, 1.2, and 1.3 are organized to be as directly comparable as possible, but it should be noted that each mission defined the categories in somewhat different ways. "Ordained preachers" was a narrower category for the American Board mission and the CMS than for the Methodists; "total Chinese employed" includes schoolteachers for some of the missions but not for others; and communicant membership and total constituency (which generally includes members, probationary members or inquirers, and baptized children) were also variously defined. The geographical areas encompassed by the statistics are also quite different for the three missions. Nevertheless, these tables provide a good general indicator of the strength of the three churches in the Fuzhou area relative to one another.

[a] Figure for "average attendance at Sunday worship" rather than "total constituency."

with this emphasis, they made a guarantee of at least partial financial support of the pastor by his church a prerequisite for ordination and so did not ordain any Chinese clergy until 1876, well after the other missions did.[55] The same priorities led them to invest much energy in producing Christian literature, educational materials, and medical texts in Chinese (from which the other missions also benefited), and their mission was the first to open a permanent hospital in Fuzhou, in 1870.[56]

Looking back after many decades in China, Charles Hartwell, the veteran missionary of the American Board mission, recalled a conversation he had had "some forty years ago" with the redoubtable Scottish missionary William Chalmers Burns, who lived in Fuzhou for a time around 1860. Burns, a gifted linguist, was an unconventional missionary pioneer who insisted on wearing Chinese dress and living with the Chinese on Chinese terms. He translated *The*

Pilgrim's Progress into Chinese and also produced the earliest hymns in several Chinese dialects. In Fuzhou he lived in the Methodist chapel, where he became a close friend of and major influence on the Xu brothers just as they were embarking on their lives as full-time Methodist preachers.[57]

According to Hartwell, Burns had remarked that the Methodist system of church government, with its many grades of workers organized in a clear hierarchy with exact titles, was more attractive to the Chinese than the more democratic Congregational model. John Mahood of the CMS had agreed with this judgment, and said that the Anglican system was the next best adapted to the Chinese setting. Reflecting on these conversations toward the end of his life, Hartwell was forced to agree that the more authoritarian and hierarchical church polities of the Methodists and the Anglicans had proven more effective in Fuzhou than the Congregational system of self-governing and self-supporting congregations had, although he still believed the latter was the "most ideal."[58]

The CMS mission was distinguished by the Anglican beliefs in apostolic succession and the importance of the priestly office, which meant that only clergymen properly ordained by a bishop could administer the Eucharist, administer baptism, or pronounce absolution or the final benediction in worship services. The bishop alone could confirm the baptized converts and ordain clergy, and until 1906, when the Fujian mission became a diocese in its own right, it fell under the jurisdiction of the colonial Bishop of Victoria, who was located in Hong Kong, six hundred miles away. Since the bishop could only visit every few years, the rite of confirmation was downplayed in practice, and ordinations were rare.[59] Consequently, the great majority of CMS congregations were served by "catechists," who could not baptize or administer communion and were clearly in a subordinate and dependent position relative to the foreign missionaries. The position of Chinese ordained clergymen of the CMS was different, for they were in theory the equals of missionaries. They were few in number, however; the first Chinese Anglican minister in Fujian was ordained in 1868; four more followed in 1876, and one was ordained in 1880 and another in 1881.[60]

Despite these structural problems, the Anglican mission expanded more quickly than either of the other missions up to 1880, claiming a total of 113 stations and 3,556 converts (including candidates for baptism and baptized children) by 1880 (table 1.2). In 1881, while there were only seven ordained clergy, the mission employed a total of ninety-three catechists.[61] Much of this expansion was due to the personality of one man, the Reverend John R. Wolfe, the dominant missionary in the CMS mission from his arrival in 1862 until his death in Fuzhou in 1915. Wolfe was a complex figure. He was an

Table 1.2. CMS Mission Statistics for Fujian, 1871–1928

Year	Ordained Preachers	Total Chinese Employed	Communicant Members	Total Adherents	Number of Schools	Total Students
1871			271	633		65
1875			400	1,200		
1880		100	1,251	3,556		
1885		108	2,011	5,704	32	
1890	8	224	2,267	8,489	92	1,271
1895		157	3,062	13,111	169	2,399
1900		460	4,327	21,478	212	3,354
1905		483	4,806	12,824	224	3,356
1910		535	4,841	11,379	175	4,038
1915	20	714	5,167	12,910	194	4,896
1920	29	808	7,054	20,153	207	5,799
1925	37	745	7,220	17,599	197	6,054
1928	38	606	7,192	15,292	137	4,048

Source: Annual Report of the Church Missionary Society, 1871–1931.
Note: See table 1.1.

idealist who (unlike some of his missionary colleagues) genuinely liked the Chinese and believed that God could work at least as well through them as through European missionaries: "I believe in the Chinese, and above all in the power of God, who can use them as he can use us in promoting his cause in the earth," he proclaimed during one of the many stormy exchanges with the CMS headquarters that pepper his correspondence.[62] Since he believed the Chinese clergy to be "presbyter[s] equally with himself," he was admirably loyal to those he had nurtured in the ministry; however, this made him quick to credit their accounts of persecution and very slow to accept criticism of them when they failed to live up to the trust placed in them—as some of them did.[63] He was also impulsive, uncompromising, and domineering, and he clashed violently with successive generations of CMS missionaries who were sent out to work with him and in later years also with his own protégés among the Chinese clergy.

Largely because of Wolfe's dominance, the CMS put more emphasis on diffusion and extension than on organization or on deepening the Christian experience of converts, until increasing evidence of weaknesses in their work forced some reevaluation in the 1880s.[64] The CMS was also more aggressive than the American missions in insisting on the rights granted to Christian missions under the treaties between China and the Western nations to own property and pursue missionary work unmolested. The readiness of the CMS to invoke consular power was apparently one reason for its rapid growth, for it became known among the Chinese as more "powerful" than the other missions, with the result that it was more often plagued with people who were motivated to "convert" in order to avoid taxes or to seek help in their legal disputes.[65] The aggressive approach of the CMS missionaries culminated in the famous Wushishan incident of 1878, in which mission property inside Fuzhou was destroyed by a mob incited by city leaders. Dissatisfied with the compensation offered by the provincial government, the missionaries took their case to the consular court, but the court ruled in favor of the Chinese officials and against the missionaries, to their consternation.[66]

The Methodist system that the Presbyterian William C. Burns so admired was constructed around a complex hierarchy of pastoral divisions, conferences, and ministerial ranks — exhorter (*quanshi*), local preacher (*benchu chuandao*), probationary preacher (*shiyong chuandao*), deacon (*zhishi*), elder (*zhanglao*), and bishop (*jiandu* or *huidu*). Appointment to each rank required passing annual examinations in prescribed multiyear courses of study.[67] Congregations were grouped into circuits, each with a preacher in charge, and circuits were organized in pastoral districts, under the authority of a presiding elder (later called district superintendent), who visited each of the circuits on a quarterly schedule. At the apex of the system was the "annual conference," which referred both to the meeting, held over seven days in the fall of each year, and to the body of people who were entitled to vote in it: all the probationary preachers, deacons, and elders of the church. The conference was the governing body of the church, with the power to hear and approve reports and to decide appointments, promotions, salaries, and pastoral questions.[68] Membership in the conference implied a willingness to be appointed anywhere at the will of the conference, in line with the Methodist emphasis on itinerant ministry.[69] Those who wished to settle in a particular place resigned from the conference and were "located" as "local preachers." The whole system was spelled out in detail in the *Discipline* of the Methodist Episcopal Church, which was translated by S. L. Baldwin and Huang Naishang between 1869 and 1872 and updated in a new translation in 1892.[70]

The first Chinese Methodist preachers in Fuzhou were licensed to preach through the expedient of having them admitted in absentia as probationary members of annual conferences in the United States.[71] In 1866 the Methodist mission in Fuzhou began holding annual meetings at which the Chinese preachers were full participants and the minutes of which were published in Chinese as well as English.[72] In 1869 the first Methodist bishop to visit China ordained seven Chinese preachers as elders and deacons — among them Xu

Bomei, Xu Yangmei, Xie Xi'en, and Lin Zhenzhen — and in 1873 four of them were made presiding elders of districts.[73] Finally, in 1877, the Fuzhou Methodist church was constituted as an annual conference in its own right, equivalent in status to the annual conferences that made up the Methodist Episcopal Church in America; it consisted of thirty-five members, only five of whom were missionaries. This system laid the basis for a rapid growth of the Methodist church from the 1890s on; by 1900 its communicant membership had surpassed the combined total of the other two missions, and it remained numerically the strongest of the three throughout the Republican period (table 1.3).[74]

The structure of the three missions had practical consequences for the roles played by Chinese Protestants. Under the Methodist system, the Chinese preachers and the missionaries were of equal rank, both symbolically and actually (although the missionaries were sent out and paid by the mission board). New missionaries were admitted to the conference on probation, just as junior Chinese preachers were, and they went through the same examination process for advancement as their Chinese counterparts did.[75] The conference had real decision-making power, and the votes of the Chinese members were equal to those of the missionaries. The consequences of this became evident very quickly as the Chinese preachers pressed for a greater emphasis on education, particularly education for women and girls, and a higher grade of education, including English instruction for boys. They were supported by two of the missionaries, Nathan Sites and Franklin Ohlinger, but the other missionaries were opposed, particularly to English instruction, because they felt it imperative that education remain subordinate to evangelism. In 1881 a wealthy merchant and recent convert, Zhang Heling (Diong Ahok, d. 1890), offered ten thousand dollars to purchase a site for a college on condition that English would be taught there. With the backing of the Chinese pastors, Ohlinger accepted the gift, bought a site, created a board of trustees, and that fall opened what would become one of the premier mission schools in late Qing China, the Foochow Anglo-Chinese College.[76] Opposition to the school from other missionaries simmered over the next few years, and in 1883 the dispute came to a head when one of them, Nathan Plumb, was publicly excluded from communion by the Chinese pastors and Ohlinger on the charge that he had opposed the wishes of the conference and had "slandered" some of the Chinese pastors.[77]

The other missions in Fuzhou were not prepared to allow the Chinese to control church affairs to the extent of being able to outvote (let alone excommunicate) missionaries.[78] In the American Board mission, authority remained in the hands of the missionaries and a handful of older Chinese preachers until the early twentieth century. Large and festive annual meetings of preachers

Table 1.3. Methodist Episcopal Church Statistics for Fujian, 1870–1930

Year	Ordained Preachers	Total Chinese Employed	Communicant Members	Total Adherents	Number of Schools	Total Students
1870		91	931	2,139	6	129
1875			1,228	2,301		
1880	11	118	1,468	2,841	19	193
1885	40	159	1,869	2,002[a]	38	418
1890	62	275	2,626	3,364	81	1,271
1895	51		4,898	11,411		
1900	95	909	6,995	16,541	275	6,296
1905	91	1,134	9,264	25,702	155	4,479
1910	133	1,152	12,470	32,756	210[b]	4,834[b]
1915	137	1,543	15,455	61,102	252	7,349
1920	164	2,652	21,259	43,523		
1925	216		29,217	59,993		
1930			35,915	48,572		

Source: Annual Report of the Board of Foreign Missions, 1870–1930. The Foochow Conference split into the Foochow and Hinghwa Conferences in 1898, and the Yenping and South Fukien Conferences split off from those two in the Republican period, giving a total of four conferences; to keep the later figures consistent with the earlier ones I have aggregated the figures from all the relevant conferences for the later years.

Note: See table 1.1.

[a]Incomplete — not all districts reporting.
[b]Figures for Foochow Conference only.

and lay delegates were held from the 1890s, but they were purely inspirational in content, with no discussion of business or financial matters.[79] In 1911, influenced by the trend toward self-government in Chinese society from 1908, the preachers of the mission established a Preachers' Self-Governing Society, modeled on the Fujian Provincial Assembly. It was not until the beginning of 1913 that the American Board did the equivalent of what the Methodists had done in 1877, adopting a constitution under which the churches of the mission became the Fuzhou Congregational Church (Gonglihui), with Chinese and missionaries taking joint responsibility for its administration and finances.[80]

In 1883 the CMS in Fujian instituted a system of pastoral districts overseen by a Provincial Church Council made up of missionaries, Chinese clergy, catechists, mission school teachers, and lay delegates, which met annually under the chairmanship of J. R. Wolfe. In name, this body was the highest authority in the Fujian Anglican church, and it was clearly taken as such by the Chinese

church workers and members.[81] However, when long-standing tensions between the senior Chinese clergy and some of the younger missionaries came to
a head during the Provincial Church Council session of 1900, subsequent
events revealed that the real power remained in the hands of the missionaries
and the mission board.[82] Responding to the crisis, the CMS in London reiterated that the council was only deliberative, not legislative or executive. It also
stated, in a decision that was symbolically very important, that in the absence
of the chairman — Wolfe, whose seniority was undisputed among the Chinese
clergy and laity — its meetings should be chaired by the next most senior *missionary,* rather than the vice-chairman, who was a Chinese clergyman.[83]

It is clear, therefore, that the Methodist conference system was unique
among the Fuzhou missions in the symbolic equality and the degree of real
power that it afforded to the Chinese preachers. One set of statistics clarifies
the contrast: by 1881, when the American Board mission had two ordained
clergy and the CMS had seven, the Methodists had admitted a total of fifty-
three men to probationary or full membership in their annual conference.[84]
The Methodist mission was also unique in publishing not just works written in
Chinese by missionaries but also tracts and essays written by Chinese preachers, beginning in the early 1870s.[85] One reason for the difference is that the
Methodists had an exceptionally talented pool of Chinese preachers; at least,
this was the judgment of missionaries of the other societies in Fuzhou.[86] It is
also clear that the Methodist missionaries simply accorded more trust to the
Chinese than the other missionaries did, and this trust was institutionalized in
their church structure.

Although the balance of power between Chinese church workers and missionaries varied considerably from mission to mission, these differences are
less important than their similarities when we turn to the role of Chinese
church workers in local society. The Chinese preachers of all the missions were
in a position of leadership and honor relative to their congregations. They
were literate, educated men, playing the role of teacher to those under their
care. The titles by which they were addressed — *mushi* (literally "shepherd-
teacher," a neologism used to translate "pastor" or "Reverend" and reserved
for ordained men) and the classical Chinese term *xiansheng* ("sir" or "master,"
applied to American Board evangelists, Methodist local preachers, and CMS
catechists) — both carried connotations of the respect due to teachers. Moreover, there is evidence that the Protestant pastors sought to behave as men of
status in local society, or were expected by others to do so — and that this was
one of the major causes of the perennial conflicts between Protestants and
their neighbors.

Those conflicts have been the focus of a good deal of scholarly attention, usually concentrated on those more important instances that became the subject of international diplomatic negotiations, the *jiaoan,* or "missionary cases."[87] In the case of the Fuzhou Protestant missions, the earlier *jiaoan* (up to 1880) were well covered by Ellsworth Carlson in *The Foochow Missionaries, 1847–1880,* and there is no need to go over the same territory here. As with the history of Christianity in China in general, scholarship on the *jiaoan* has placed more emphasis on foreign missionaries and their deeds than on Chinese converts. With their Victorian attitudes and their tendency to rely on the strong arm of secular power, missionaries in late Qing China have provided easy targets for retrospective condemnation, whether for Chinese scholars seeing anti-Christian outbreaks as a manifestation of popular opposition to imperialism or for Western scholars critical of the missionary endeavor.[88] However, conflicts between Chinese Christians and others in their society included not only the *jiaoan* with their diplomatic ramifications but also a host of more minor disputes, many of them not involving missionaries directly.[89] These conflicts should be seen, I believe, as part of the everyday fabric of social life in the resource-strained environment of nineteenth-century China.

Chinese society in the nineteenth century was under great economic, demographic, and administrative pressure. The vast majority of the population lived at a slender margin above the subsistence level, a margin that could be swiftly jeopardized by natural disasters, war, excessive rents or taxation, or the petty legal disputes that occurred with increasing frequency over the course of the nineteenth century.[90] In Fujian, where population density was particularly high and arable land very scarce, the social mechanisms by which ordinary people scraped by included crop diversification, involvement in foreign trade, emigration, membership in secret societies, and piracy or banditry.[91] A fundamental feature of rural society in Fujian was an exceptionally strong system of lineages, frequently gathered in single-lineage fortified villages, like Huang Naishang's in Minqing, which competed for scarce resources with the surrounding communities.[92] This competition could be violent; Fujian was notorious (along with Guangdong, to the south) for frequent outbreaks of *xiedou,* or armed interlineage conflict, which could continue for years and include pitched battles with thousands of participants.[93]

Until recently, discussions of conflict between Protestant converts and Chinese society have not in general placed the phenomenon within this social context.[94] The topic is a large one, and what follows here is by no means an exhaustive discussion, but I will suggest ways Chinese Protestants in the Fuzhou area sought to defend their interests and manage conflict according to Chinese social norms, focusing on the role of the Chinese preachers as mediators, patrons, and protectors of their Protestant flocks. It is increasingly being recognized that local leadership in late imperial Chinese society took a variety of forms and was exercised in diverse ways.[95] With respect to their congregations, Protestant preachers in the Fuzhou area played a role that was in many respects analogous to that of men in local society who were acknowledged community leaders without being truly part of the scholar-official stratum — such as lower degree holders and lineage elders.

Christian preachers and converts were routinely vilified in the official discourse of the late Qing. Chinese officials, publicly at least, portrayed Christian converts as lowlifes and vagabonds who converted for personal gain, fomented trouble in local society, and tried to use their anomalous status under the treaties to impose upon decent people.[96] In evaluating this image, we need to remember that many other classes of people were similarly scapegoated in official documents, sometimes for the very same reasons (the allegation that they fomented litigation, for instance), and that these condemnations, based as they were on the priorities of the Qing state, obscure as much as they reveal about the actual workings of local society. To cite some examples, a whole generation of scholarship has uncovered the complexity and importance in late imperial China of religious sectarians, who were invariably portrayed as dangerous subversives in official sources, and recent work on the functioning of the Qing legal system (as opposed to its structure and regulations in the abstract) is forcing a reevaluation of the roles of litigation brokers and yamen underlings (clerks and runners), classes of people who were similarly pictured as no-good, unscrupulous troublemakers in official sources. In each of these cases, the reality has been shown to have been far more nuanced and ambiguous than official sources reveal.[97]

Instead of accepting the official images of Christian preachers at face value, then, we need to start with the concrete question of how they related to their congregations and communities. It is by no means clear that Protestant preachers were always suspect or ostracized in the social settings in which they ministered. Many of them were, like Xu Yangmei, cultured individuals who could relate on a par with the men of stature in the villages and county seats. Moreover, in their preaching they presented Christianity as having Chinese antecedents and according with Chinese ethical norms. Xu recounts a number of incidents that illustrate these points. Early in his time in Minqing, some people spread rumors that he desecrated printed paper, in violation of the Chinese respect for the written word. Incensed, the literary men of the village came to confront him, but their attitude was altered when he invited them in, served them tea, and entertained them with great attention to etiquette, showing himself to be a cultured man who could not have done what was reported of him. The ways Christian teaching and Chinese ideas could overlap is evident on another occasion, when Xu was mediating with some village elders to have the converts excused from participating in the annual festival of the village deity because they "worshiped God" (*bai Shangdi*). According to Xu, when he made this appeal, the elders responded: "Worshiping Shangdi is a good thing. We all agree with that" (*bai Shangdi shan shi ye, wubei wu bu shi zhe*); that is, they affirmed the worship of Shangdi in an inclusive sense as something sanctioned by Chinese culture, rather than in the exclusive sense of Christian monotheism.[98]

As literate men with a specialized knowledge and a public teaching role, Chinese preachers were seen as men of status and turned to for help in difficult situations. These situations did not necessarily involve Protestants directly; Xu Yangmei records that he successfully mediated a *xiedou* feud between Huang Naishang's clan and the neighboring Liu village, for instance. Or they could involve Protestants along with their neighbors, as when Protestant villagers on the Fuqing coast called on Xu Yangmei to intervene with the soldiers from the county yamen, who were threatening to levy a fine on the whole village for a piracy incident that had occurred nearby (Xu refused to intervene with the officials on this occasion but stayed with the people to pray until the danger was past).[99] Xu writes that this kind of incident occurred a great deal in the populous coastal county of Fuqing, which he describes as particularly lawless, racked with lineage feuds, banditry, and extortionate soldiers and tax collectors.[100] Xu states that illicit supplementary taxes levied by the district runners (subordinate officers of the county magistrate) responsible for tax collection (*liangyi*) were a frequent problem for the Protestants and villagers in general in Fuqing. He also recounts petty harassments that church members experienced in local society, such as compelling them to contribute for the annual procession of the local god, denying them access to the seashore (presumably in connection with bringing in their catch), or allowing their fields to be encroached on.

Xu's depiction of these situations and his response to them speaks volumes about the important role the preacher played in the lives of rural Protestant converts: "The church members are not educated and do not know how to manage when difficulties arise, so they consult with the preacher about everything," he writes. The preacher could not remain aloof, Xu felt; in fact, by taking pity on them and involving himself in their struggles, the preacher was imitating "the Savior, who, when he wanted to save sinners, did not come only halfway down from heaven, but left his heavenly palace for this dusty world [*chenshi*, a Buddhist term connoting the impermanence of the mundane world], became a man in contact with sinners, and was even called the 'friend of sinners.'" The forms of help the preacher could provide included "exerting himself to mediate if mediation was possible, or taking opportunities to remonstrate with the lawless elements in the locale (*xiangfei*), or, on occasion, petitioning the local magistrate with the facts of the matter when the tax collectors (*liangyi*) have taken too much, thus saving much complication." During his four years in Fuqing, Xu says that he often dealt with such situations and found the officials diligent and cooperative; in not one of these cases did he refer the matter either to the missionaries or to the U.S. consul.[101]

At other points in his narrative, Xu Yangmei is frank about the problems posed by people who converted in the hope of financial gain or help in legal disputes, and according to his own account, he consistently refused to cooperate in such schemes. Clearly, therefore, in his view there was a distinction between those who sought to use Christian conversion to escape or subvert Chinese law and genuine cases of suffering among his flock due to conflicts with neighbors or to abuses connected with tax collection. With the latter, Xu felt it was his duty to become involved, even to the extent of intervening in the relationship between the magistrate and his underlings. Under Chinese law, however, access to the magistrate's yamen was a privilege of degree holders above a certain rank.[102] Xu had no status other than that of a commoner; he certainly was not entitled to offer unsolicited advice to the magistrate on problems of local administration, and his doing so would doubtless have provoked the resentment of the yamen underlings whom he accused of wrongdoing.

It is clear from the archival record that Protestant preachers in the Fuzhou area frequently played this kind of role and considered themselves justified in doing so. This became very evident in the CMS mission in the early 1900s, when the home mission board and younger missionaries on the field tried to put a stop to the involvement of the Chinese church leaders in litigation. The mission board was concerned by reports that the involvement of the Chinese preachers in lawsuits had resulted in many nominal adherents in the church in Fujian, people who had calculated that by subscribing one dollar to the church they could get protection and avoid ten dollars in lawsuits, as one missionary characterized it.[103] In its determination to combat this problem, the CMS in London issued a blanket prohibition on church workers becoming involved in litigation and, in addition, stated that Chinese preachers had "no excuse for acting as arbitrators between Christians and heathen, or even defending Christians who, in common with their heathen neighbours, are exposed to tyrannical or unjust proceedings at the hands of the Government officials."[104]

The leading Chinese members of the Anglican church—clergy and laity alike—were unanimous in their opinion that "peace-making" or mediation had to be permitted and seen as distinct from litigation, and Wolfe and a minority of the other missionaries agreed.[105] As evidence of the distinction between the two, Wolfe included a document submitted to the British consul in Fuzhou by the Fuzhou Taotai, transmitting a commendation of one of the Anglican clergy in Fuqing County, Ye Duanmei (Iek Duang Me), by the county magistrate, who wrote that over the fifteen years of Ye's pastorate in the town he had exerted himself as a peacemaker and had not permitted any disputes between converts and others to become lawsuits.[106] As this official commendation implied, from the Chinese viewpoint mediation of disputes was indeed a substitute for litigation, not part and parcel of it.[107]

On the other hand, both mediation and "entering the yamen" (i.e., approaching the magistrate about legal matters) implied an elite status for Protestant clergy, and the majority of the CMS missionaries, who believed that peacemaking and entering the yamen could not be separated, were certainly correct in pointing out that the catechists and clergy of the mission had no such status under Chinese law, but only by virtue of their link to the foreign church.[108] In their view and that of the home board, the problem of people pretending to convert in order to gain protection as members of the foreign church could be stamped out only if the Chinese preachers refused to involve themselves *in any way* in disputes between converts and other members of society. From the perspective of Chinese local society, however, Protestant preachers did have the (de facto, though not de jure) status of church leaders — in Protestant terminology, they were shepherds — and, in consequence, the obligation to mediate disputes. Wolfe was no doubt right in stating that "the pastor or catechist who would refuse to do this would, I am sure, very soon lose influence among his people."[109]

The sources reveal other ways in which Protestant preachers had responsibilities thrust upon them by their status as leaders. In 1888, Wolfe asked the CMS to approve an increase in the salary of the Chinese clergy, on the grounds that their status required them to attend all the weddings and funerals of the church members in their large districts; because all guests at these events were expected to give gifts of 200–300 cash, this meant a significant expense for the clergy.[110] Earlier that decade, a Chinese priest in the county seat of Luoyuan got into major financial difficulties when he ran short of funds during the construction of a new church and preacher's residence there. Reading between the lines of the differing accounts of this complex case, the underlying cause (along with a lack of clear supervision of the mission funds) was this man's sense of the requirements of his status. He had the new house ornamented after the manner of wealthy Chinese, according to the bishop, rebuilding the outer gate of the courtyard in a more imposing style, not just once but twice.[111]

Finding the money running out, he became desperate lest he lose face before the church members, and went heavily into debt to raise money to finish the work. Wolfe, who supported him, says that part of the difficulty arose because there were mortgages on the purchased property that were concealed from the preacher until after the sale was concluded, and that he sold his own property in his home village to help pay off these mortgages.[112] Less friendly commentators report that he docked the pay of the catechists under his charge to cover his debts and began hiring out his services in lawsuits. According to one missionary, "Spiritual life died within him, [and] he became harsh, proud and exacting." He was transferred away from Luoyuan and eventually stripped of his clerical license for dishonesty, but he continued to insist that his debts had been incurred in the interests and work of the church, and some members of the Luoyuan church took his side, believing that he had been unfairly treated by the bishop and the mission.[113]

This was the most dramatic case, but not the only one, of CMS preachers going into debt. In 1886, Wolfe reported his shock and disappointment at discovering that "many of our most trusted helpers have gone deeply in debt and have nothing wherewith to pay."[114] How to interpret this is the important question. The clergy and catechists of the CMS were not poorly paid, earning between 48 and 180 Mexican dollars per year, or 32 to 119 Haikuan (Customs) taels.[115] Their salaries were thus on a par with those of village school teachers, who, according to Evelyn Rawski, earned a median annual salary of around 44 taels in the late nineteenth century; in fact, they were probably better paid on the whole, for only unmarried catechists earned the lowest salary, and their incomes increased with experience, to a maximum of 96 Mexican dollars, or around 63 Haikuan taels.[116]

Clearly, their jobs entailed expenses not faced by schoolteachers, such as extensive traveling and gift-giving obligations. In addition, however, there are hints in the Luoyuan case that some CMS preachers regarded themselves as occupying a higher social station than that allotted them under Chinese social norms and thus sought to follow a lifestyle higher than their salary would sustain. This impression is supported by scattered references to preachers wearing the formal clothing of degree holders, or not showing due deference to magistrates, or demanding that magistrates receive petitions from them (as in 1903 when a Methodist preacher in Minqing "came into [the] yamen in a most offensive and peremptory manner [and] demanded that a petition he had prepared should be presented to the magistrate").[117] Prominent laymen could also regard themselves as having status through the church that they did not possess under Chinese law. In 1905 a leading Anglican layman in Fuzhou was disciplined by the church for, among other things, being "rather too fond of helping in litigation" and having the title "English Provincial Council Delegate" printed on his calling card (the two charges are certainly related, since one procured an audience with officials by sending in one's calling card).[118]

Chinese Protestants in all the missions clearly felt that it was appropriate and necessary to receive important foreign visitors with all the customary Chinese accoutrements of status they could muster, for there are numerous references to visiting bishops, mission executives, and the like being welcomed well outside their destinations by large groups of Christians, "dressed in hired official robes" in one account, and escorted into the city or village in an official-style sedan chair or preceded by the ornate umbrella used in official processions.[119] In true Chinese fashion, banquets and large quantities of firecrackers were part of the festivities on these occasions. As with the other aspects of the corporate life of the Chinese Protestant communities, these welcomes were not engineered by missionaries and were often embarrassing to them. In my opinion, they can best be regarded as another way Chinese Protestants drew on Chinese social practice to construct an alternative social structure of status and meaning for their lives.

In his book on the Boxer uprising, Joseph Esherick writes of a recurring "pattern" in rural Shandong whereby Christians became "more obstreperous" as they grew in numbers through the 1890s, and began "abusing their power in lawsuits, or extorting fines and banquets from fellow villagers."[120] In developing this picture, Esherick relies heavily on interviews of former Boxers and villagers conducted in China in the ideological climate of the early 1960s; not surprisingly, these sources do not present the Chinese Christians in a favorable light. In the Fuzhou area at least, the relationship between the small clusters of Chinese Protestants and the surrounding society was much less clear-cut. In reviewing the evidence available in mission sources, particularly with respect to the role of Protestant preachers in local society, it becomes clear that they were indeed guilty of some of the behavior with which they were charged by late Qing officials, as Esherick asserts for Shandong. They did mediate disputes and sometimes involved themselves in litigation or presented appeals to the local magistrates, and in doing so they certainly exceeded their prerogatives under Chinese law. Some of them dressed or lived above their station according to Chinese social usage.

It is possible to interpret any and all such instances as a straightforward case of Protestants seizing on the treaty provisions to aggrandize themselves and impose on their neighbors, but it is also possible, and in my opinion more persuasive, to recognize that preachers were men of substance in local society, certainly in the eyes of their congregations and at least some of the time in the eyes of community leaders and even of officials. As men of stature, educated, and in a public leadership role, they had obligations that were culturally dictated, and faced pressures that missionaries and Western mission executives were not always able to recognize.

The ambiguity in this situation is, in my view, exactly parallel to the ambiguity in the relationship between local elites and the state in late Qing China. Local elites frequently assumed the role (or image) of protectors of the common people from the depredations of the "state" in the form of the yamen clerks and runners, and affirmed their own leadership status (and made money) in the process. Examples include elite attempts to regulate the customary fees charged in legal cases, and the common elite practice of acting as intermediaries in the collection and transmission of taxes (*baolan*).[121] The practice of *baolan* was viewed with particular hostility by the Qing state, for it encroached on the prerogatives of the local magistrate and could easily become a form of tax evasion; nevertheless, magistrates were seldom able to prevent it.[122]

The example of *baolan* is an appropriate one, because it seems that some CMS clergy and catechists in the Fuzhou region were exercising this function on behalf of their church members by 1902.[123] They defended the practice to the missionaries as necessary to protect Protestants from being squeezed by rapacious tax collectors; this is, of course, precisely the justification customarily offered by the influential families who engaged in it in Chinese society in general. By the same token, the involvement of Protestant clergy in mediating disputes, addressing petitions to the magistrates, and even aiding in litigation can be seen as an exercise of the protective functions that flowed from and were required by their leadership status, rather than an employment of their treaty privileges to encroach aggressively upon elite prerogatives and state authority. At the least, it is clear that the real situation was complex and that the way Chinese Protestants as corporate bodies operated must be understood from the perspective of Chinese society, not as if they were somehow separate from that society. Just as Chinese Protestants appropriated Christianity in ways that made sense in Chinese terms, Chinese Protestant communities operated in ways that reflected the patterns and modes of Chinese society and, consequently, often jarred with missionary expectations.

Protestant Social Mobility

At the Methodist annual meeting in the fall of 1868, less than two years after his baptism, Huang Naishang was appointed a probationary preacher on the recommendation of Xu Yangmei; he had successfully passed a two-day series of examinations which covered, in addition to Christian texts on a variety of subjects, an illustrated introduction to world geography.[124] He remained with Xu Yangmei in Minqing another year, then, in 1869, at barely twenty years of age, he was appointed the preacher in charge of the East Street chapel, the one Methodist church inside the Fuzhou city walls. Figures for 1869 are not available, but in 1868 this congregation had thirty-six members, plus twenty probationers and ten children; of that number, nine adults and three children had been baptized during that year.[125]

Huang says little about this experience, but we may infer that it was a daunting prospect for the youth from an inland village to be put in charge of a church inside the teeming metropolis of Fuzhou, with 300,000 inhabitants within the walls and as many more again without, its several government yamen, its proud scholars, and the sumptuous homes of the wealthy. It could not have reassured him to know that five years earlier in this very post his mentor Xu Yangmei had been attacked and Xu's wife and sister assaulted during a sudden riot in which the chapel, the CMS church, and other mission properties were destroyed.[126] As it happened, Huang did not remain in the post for very long, for in the spring of 1870 he became ill (possibly with tuberculosis), resigned from the chapel, and returned to Minqing to recover.[127]

The following year, 1871, was the year Huang Naishang found his calling. Many missionaries employed "language tutors" or literary assistants to handle tasks involving written Chinese — translations, correspondence, and so on — and although they usually remain shadowy in mission sources, they were crucial in allowing missionaries to function in Chinese society, for however good their spoken Chinese, few missionaries could write elegantly in the language. In 1871, Huang became the literary assistant to the Reverend S. L. Baldwin, and this move into full-time writing and study launched him on the course that would eventually bring him into regional and national prominence as a journalist, editor, political essayist, and revolutionary activist.[128]

Over the ensuing decades he worked with Baldwin and other missionaries on a great many translations on religious and secular topics, as well as writing essays and editing church publications on his own account.[129] In 1874 he and Franklin Ohlinger founded and edited the first periodical in Fujian, the monthly *Xunshan shizhe* ("Zion's Herald"; later *Minsheng huibao,* "Fukien Church Gazette"), which, in addition to church news, published national and international news and articles on scientific topics.[130] In 1875, hearing that the death of the young emperor the previous year had been due to smallpox, Huang wrote an essay in the magazine explaining the concept of vaccination, as a result of which the Methodist church led the way in promoting the practice in Fujian. He also wrote, with Mrs. Baldwin, five lengthy essays against the Chinese custom of footbinding, which, besides appearing in the magazine, were published as a tract, more than thirty thousand copies of which were distributed in the province.[131]

As he threw himself into this literary work, Huang became increasingly aware of the lack of higher-level scholars in the church and Christianity's consequent lack of credibility and influence in the higher echelons of Chinese society. Consequently, he decided to seek success in the classical civil service examination system and devoted himself to learning to write the specialized type of essay required for the exams. In 1877, at the age of twenty-eight, Huang passed the examination for the *shengyuan* (licentiate) degree, earning second place among the candidates. He was advised by some people to study English and by others to take up Western medicine, but he was unwilling to settle for either of these courses, preferring to aim at breadth of knowledge and urging that ideal on the brighter young men in the church. In 1894, Huang's persistence was rewarded when he passed the examination for the *juren* degree, thirtieth among the 134 graduates in Fujian that year.[132]

Earning the *juren* degree launched Huang on a new phase in his life. He moved out of church publishing and into broader spheres of reformist activism, pioneering journalism, and political involvement. His subsequent career will be touched upon in the following chapters. Here, the point to be stressed is that Huang's personal social mobility flowed from his conversion in 1866, which led first to his employment in church work, then his immersion in studying, writing, and editing, and ultimately to his examination success. The social mobility that Protestant conversion could open up is further illustrated by the careers of Huang's younger brothers and his children. Huang's presence in Fuzhou enabled his brothers to escape the cramped orbit and narrow opportunities of their inland village. One brother, Huang Naiying (1859–1893), was admitted to the Foochow Arsenal School, the path-breaking naval school specializing in "Western learning" founded by the statesman Zuo Zongtang as part of the reform efforts of the 1860s. He finished his studies in 1880 and secured a position paying thirty dollars per month, a very high salary. At his elder brother's urging, he gave up this job in order to help the Ohlingers get the newly formed Anglo-Chinese College off the ground, becoming a teacher in the college at a monthly salary of only six dollars. He later worked in the Telegraph Office in Fuzhou before his untimely death in 1893. Another younger brother, Huang Naimo (1863–1894), also had a naval education, graduating in the first class to go through Li Hongzhang's Beiyang Naval Academy, in 1884. Over the next decade he served as a naval officer and steadily rose in rank, but he went down with his ship when the Beiyang fleet was demolished by the Japanese in the war of 1894.[133]

Huang Naishang married in 1873, at the relatively late age of twenty-four.

His wife had been educated in the American Board mission's boarding school for girls, and after their marriage she ran a school for girls in their home for several years. She died young, in 1890, leaving two sons and two daughters, all four of whom received an extensive education in both Chinese and English.[134] In 1896 the eldest daughter, after traveling in England and America, was married to Dr. Lin Wenqing (Lim Boon Keng) of Singapore, a graduate of Edinburgh University and a well-known physician, reformer, and educator in the colony. A contemporary source describes her as "a refined, enlightened and well-educated gentlewoman" who took "a sympathetic and active interest in all the reform movements of this period, in which her husband played the chief role." A few years later, Huang's second daughter married another well-known British-trained doctor in the Straits Settlements, Wu Liande (Wu Lien Teh, Gnoh Lean Tuck), who became the most celebrated Chinese physician and medical historian of the early twentieth century.[135] Like his father, Huang's eldest son sought success through the Chinese examination system, becoming a *shengyuan* in 1894, the same year Huang Naishang earned his *juren* degree, and being selected as a *gongsheng* (senior licentiate) in 1897.[136] The second son studied medicine in Singapore and was practicing in Fuzhou in the 1930s.[137]

Huang Naishang's story is an extraordinary one, yet the mobility that it illustrates was a common experience among Chinese Protestants in this period. As is aptly symbolized by the early preachers studying world geography, Protestant conversion opened up, quite literally, a whole world of opportunities for young Chinese of ability. In general, conversion created for those who were not literate a desire or need to acquire literacy and for those who, like Huang, were literate when they converted, a desire to study Christian doctrine. With the desire came the opportunity, as new congregations formed and literate preachers were put in place to serve them; very often preachers taught converts to read, or used their chapels as schools for the local children. In time, the three Protestant missions created graded networks of schools that linked rural villages to boarding schools in the county seats and, from there, to the higher schools and seminaries in Fuzhou, providing a conduit for social mobility for rural dwellers that was without parallel in Chinese society before the Republican period and, arguably, until the 1950s. From the 1880s on, this educational system began opening up opportunities for transregional and international mobility, connecting young Fuzhou Protestants with the upper echelons of Chinese society in Southeast Asia and providing access to university education in America and (less commonly) Britain.

Education was one side of the mobility equation; employment was the other. With Protestant conversion came opportunities for some for employment in church work, or in Protestant publishing, or in educational and medical institutions. Over the generations, Protestants tended to move into education and medicine and into government service, particularly in the new Western-style bureaucracies that emerged in the late nineteenth century beginning with the establishment of the Imperial Maritime Customs in the 1860s. By the turn of the century, Chinese Protestants in the Fuzhou area had developed from an insignificant and low-status minority into an upwardly mobile and increasingly respectable cohort with a disproportionate presence in the modern professional sector in Fuzhou.[138]

The significance of the new educational and career paths opened up by the Protestant churches becomes evident when contrasted with the general picture of social mobility in Chinese society. In late imperial China the principal route to status, power, and wealth was through acquiring the classical learning needed to compete in the official examination system. Unlike in many other societies, there was no class barrier preventing commoners from acquiring elite status through examination success, and consequently the aspiration to acquire an education was widely shared at all levels of Chinese society.[139] However, in practice the system favored the wealthy, who could muster the resources to educate their young to the high level needed. It also favored those who lived near the cultural riches and teaching expertise found in major educational centers. In Fujian, over half of the *jinshi* graduates over the 267 years of Qing rule came from Fuzhou Prefecture, and 77 percent of those were from the two counties which the city of Fuzhou straddled, Houguan and Min.[140] Rural village schools such as the one Huang Naishang attended in his youth were fairly common in Qing China, but they were not linked systematically to higher rungs on the educational ladder, and success in the examinations required specialized skills far beyond those gained through a few years' study in such a school.[141] In sum, although the system created a near-universal aspiration for education and its rewards, "the content of the civil service competition clearly excluded over 90 percent of China's people from even the first step on the ladder to success."[142]

It is in this context that the alternative system provided by Protestant education must be seen. Protestant missionaries founded schools almost as soon as they arrived in Fuzhou, at first because it was the easiest way to acquire an attentive audience. As the churches spread, the aim of the schools became to train workers for the church and, in the case of the girls' schools, to produce educated wives for church workers.[143] In addition, in instructing candidates for baptism, the churches often provided literacy training in order to equip them to read the Bible and understand Christian doctrine. This was often at the initiative of Chinese preachers or in response to the wishes of local converts. For example, when Xu Yangmei moved in 1860 to the earliest Methodist outstation, the village of Niukeng, fifteen miles northwest of Fuzhou, he found that nobody in the village could read, and many did not even know which way up to hold a book. Xu began assembling the converts every evening and teaching them to read the Bible, character by character and line by line, and he reports that these poor farmers were delighted with what they were learning and "greatly revered the Bible."[144] Conversion for these people brought both the motivation and the opportunity to learn to read, and with literacy came an array of new opportunities that over time removed these converts or their descendants entirely from the subsistence life of rural China.[145]

The eagerness with which these rural converts seized the chance to study was not unique; many other instances can be cited of Protestant converts seeking basic education for themselves, their wives, or their children, as we have already seen. One of the single women missionaries who came to Fujian in increasing numbers in the 1880s and 1890s reports that new converts often asked that their wives be instructed in their new faith, which fueled the spread of literacy and Bible classes for adult women.[146]

During the last twenty years of the nineteenth century the Protestant educational effort became more formalized. All three missions developed an extensive series of small schools in rural villages (as well as in and around Fuzhou city in the case of the American Board), which were much like their traditional Chinese counterparts in having one teacher each and about twelve to twenty-five students, except that the teacher was a church member who had studied in a mission boarding school in Fuzhou, and the curriculum included the Bible and Christian variants of the elementary Chinese primers as well as the Chinese classics (fig. 1.3).[147] These schools could be in places with an established congregation or could be a prelude to making converts and establishing a congregation. In the CMS a period of service as a teacher was the first step toward becoming a catechist, which, for the most able, could lead to ordination.[148] From around 1890, as missionaries took up residence in increasing numbers in secondary cities in the region, mission schools in the villages fed their better students into boarding schools run by missionaries or Chinese preachers in the county seats, and these in turn fed into the higher-level schools and seminaries in Fuzhou itself (fig. 1.4).[149]

All three missions became extensively involved in operating schools, particularly from the 1880s on, and educational work came to absorb a significant proportion of mission funds and personnel (see tables 1.1–1.3). Over time, the rationale behind the schools changed. Whereas the initial rationale for running schools had been evangelistic, that is, to win converts and train church workers, by 1911 it "had been broadened to the characteristically educational one of fitting [people] for life under Christian auspices," as a

Fig. 1.3. Typical Protestant country day-school interior in the late Qing, showing pupil reciting texts to a teacher. Notwithstanding the biblical texts on the walls, in physical appearance, pedagogical style, and even to some extent curricular content, such schools were probably not far different from other basic Chinese schools. Methodist Collection, Drew University, Madison, New Jersey.

Methodist historian put it in the 1930s.[150] One explanation for this is that Chinese Protestants tended to see the mission schools more broadly than the early missionaries did, as part of the overall effort of the Christian church to convert, reform, and uplift China, and pressure from the Chinese church was an important reason why education came to figure so prominently in Protestant mission work in the Fuzhou area and in China generally.[151]

Pressure from the Chinese was also largely responsible for what was the single most significant change in mission educational policy, the introduction of education in English. This turning point came with the founding of the Anglo-Chinese College in 1881, which led to several years of bitter controversy among the Methodist missionaries. With a nine-year (later eight-year) course, divided into preparatory and college sections, this college aimed "to provide the youth of China with facilities for obtaining a thorough general education according to the standards which prevail in European and American Colleges."[152] As its founding president, Franklin Ohlinger, put it, "We do not propose to 'teach English' (as some of our opponents persist in saying) but to give a thorough general education which besides many other things embraces a knowledge of the English language. . . . We do not train men to be

Fig. 1.4. Pedagogy and curriculum diverged more from Chinese precedents at the higher levels of the Protestant educational system as it became more standardized from the 1890s on. This photograph shows a mathematics lesson in a Protestant girls' high school in Fuzhou, around 1900. Institute of Religion and Culture, Fujian Teachers' University.

cooks and butlers for the foreign merchants, but men who shall be leaders of thought, who shall carry the banner of Christianity and Western Science into every part of these Eighteen Provinces."[153] Tuition was high — the college was practically unique among mission schools in China in paying for itself (barring the salaries of the missionary teachers) — but preachers with fifteen years of service in any of the Protestant missions could have tuition waived for one son at a time to study in the college.[154]

As discussed earlier, a key factor in the founding of the Anglo-Chinese College was the establishment of the Foochow Annual Conference of the Methodist Episcopal Church, which gave the Chinese Methodist preachers the votes to override missionary opposition. As well as vigorously supporting the Anglo-Chinese College, the Chinese Methodist leaders pressed for the inclusion of English in the curriculum of the girls' boarding school that educated their daughters; the two missionary sisters who had run the school since 1859 were so opposed to this change that they resigned and left the field in 1883 rather than implement it.[155]

Documents in the Methodist mission archives reveal that almost twenty years after the founding of the Anglo-Chinese College, the question presented by its existence, namely, "whether it is a proper use of missionary money to employ teachers for educational purposes," remained a subject of controversy among mission administrators back home.[156] By that time, the issue was effectively moot, however; in response to Chinese aspirations, mission practice on the field had forged a fait accompli which policymakers at home had eventually to acknowledge.

The Methodist precedent and its success in attracting the sons of elite Chinese soon put pressure on the other missions. In 1891 the American Board mission established a similar school, which in 1898 became known as Foochow College (the Chinese name of the school was Rongcheng gezhi shuyuan, literally "Foochow Science Academy").[157] Slower to follow suit was the CMS mission, largely because the ever-opinionated J. R. Wolfe had always been strongly opposed to any educational work that might detract from the evangelistic effort of the church. In 1901, however, Wolfe changed his position, and the mission formally asked its home board for permission to open an "Anglo-Chinese School" in Fuzhou. Wolfe's account of the reasons for his change of stance provides another illustration of the ways the missions were ultimately forced to accommodate the wishes of their Chinese preachers and members. "I have come to the conviction," Wolfe wrote, "that it would not be wise on our part any longer to run counter to the wishes of our native Christians, or to ignore the evident trend of public opinion in favour of Western learning and towards acquiring a knowledge of the English language." Concerned that the "most promising young men" of the church had been entering the Anglo-Chinese schools of the other missions, Wolfe feared that "we shall not only lose most of our intelligent Christian young men but also lose influence especially among the higher classes all over the province" if the CMS failed to start such a school.[158] After some years' delay, the school was started as St. Mark's College in 1907, with ten students, and in 1912 it was renamed Trinity College after the famous college of Dublin University.[159]

Thus, over the thirty years from 1881 to 1911 the purpose of the mission schools, the content of the education offered in them, and the social standing of their clientele changed significantly (fig. 1.5). It is relatively easy to demonstrate that these changes resulted in upward mobility within particular Protestant families across the generations, but it is more difficult to evaluate the impact of the mission educational enterprise on the social mobility of Chinese Protestants as a whole. Ideally, to do this we would have full data on the Protestant schools as a proportion of all schools in a given area, on who enrolled in them, and on what happened to the students after they left the schools. Such data are not available before the late 1920s, and not even then in

Fig. 1.5. Graduating class of the Ponasang Women's College, run by the American Board mission, Fuzhou, 1901. Such schools aimed to attract an elite clientele, and like their counterparts in America and Britain, they taught etiquette and genteel arts in addition to their academic curriculum, as this picture reflects. All the graduates appear to have non-bound feet. Institute of Religion and Culture, Fujian Teachers' University.

most cases, but the few sources examined below, while far from complete, help to shed some light.

The Anglo-Chinese College enrolled many more students than it actually graduated from its eight-year course, some of whom went on to become nationally prominent — like Lin Sen, who became the titular head of state in China under the Nationalist Party (Guomindang) from 1931 to 1943. Lin was a member of the first class in 1881, but he left after a couple of years' English study to take up an appointment in the Imperial Maritime Customs.[160] In 1895 it was reported that the college had enrolled a total of 347 boys since 1881, and the student body then numbered 133.[161] Only nine had graduated by that time, however. Information about graduates alone, therefore, gives only a partial picture of the impact of the college, for those who did not graduate may still have been enabled by their education at the college to join the Customs, foreign companies, and the like, yet graduates are the only ones for whom systematic information is available.

A 1917 catalogue in Chinese for the Anglo-Chinese College lists the occupations at that time of 130 of its 157 graduates (14 had died, and for 13 no occupation is given). Fourteen were pursuing further studies (four in China, ten in America), so their occupations are also unclear. Of the remaining 116 graduates, a total of 46, or nearly 40 percent, worked in education, a little over half of them in Protestant schools, the remainder in government or unspecified schools. Forty (35 percent) were in some form of government service (aside from education); thirty of these were employed in the modern bureaucracies developed in the late Qing and early Republic under Western management, the Maritime Customs (eleven), the postal service (nine), and the salt administration (ten).[162] Nineteen were in business or commerce, a minority as compradors in the big foreign firms (Standard Oil, Jardine Matheson), or in the banking and mining sectors; most were apparently in business for themselves. Two graduates were working as the interpreters for the U.S. consuls in Fuzhou and Xiamen. Medicine accounted for six of the graduates (including two military physicians numbered under government service above), and another five were in church or YMCA work.

Locations are specified for 121 of the graduates. While many of them (forty-six, or 38 percent) had remained in Fuzhou, a larger number had been dispersed around China, ten in other parts of Fujian and forty-one beyond the province (including two in Hong Kong and one in Taiwan). Many of those working in other parts of China were in the Customs, postal, or salt services. Thirteen lived in Southeast Asia, mostly in Manila or the Straits Settlements, and eleven were in America (ten of them as students).[163]

This source gives only a synchronic snapshot, not a full picture of the career trajectories of these graduates. Some of those listed as educators in the Christian schools were also ordained clergymen. A good number of them were returnees from universities in America or Britain, but this is not mentioned. The proportion in business is strikingly small, and the proportion in government service very high. Overall, the best term to characterize this data is "professionalism"; the great majority of the graduates of the Anglo-Chinese College entered the growing professional elite, consisting of educators, Western-style medical doctors, civil servants, business managers, and church workers. This elite was to some extent an international one. One graduate, Xue Fenshi (Alfonso Sycip, 1903), was a leading member of the Chinese community in Manila; another, Yin Xuecun (Dr. S. C. Yin, 1898), studied in the United States, Canada, and Britain and became a prominent physician and community leader in Singapore.[164]

The transferability of locations and of government and private employment for some of these men is illustrated by the example of Xie Tianbao (Dr. Sia Tieng Bo), the most successful of the sons of the early Methodist preacher Xie Xi'en (Sia Sek Ong). Xie graduated from the Anglo-Chinese College in 1896 and was sent to the United States to attend university, where he earned degrees in medicine and dentistry. On graduating, he lived and worked for a few years in Singapore, then in Shanghai, before joining the new Board of Education established by the Qing in 1905. A few years later he was again practicing medicine in Shanghai, when Prince Su, minister of the interior, asked him in 1910 or 1911 to take charge of founding a new government medical university in Beijing. In 1917 he was serving as the Chinese consul in North Borneo.[165]

The Anglo-Chinese College had a very high standing in Fuzhou, and it attracted a large percentage of its students from wealthy non-Protestant families.[166] Perhaps reflecting this, the proportion of Anglo-Chinese College graduates to 1916 who moved into the career network formed by the Protestant churches, schools, and other institutions was relatively small, although it still stood at one-quarter of the total.[167] More were attracted to the new opportunities afforded by the expanding sphere of modern government bureaucracy. The case of Foochow College is a little different in that many more graduates went into the ministry or Protestant education, and of those not a few went to rural posts, whereas the Anglo-Chinese College graduates lived and worked almost exclusively in major cities. Like graduates of the Anglo-Chinese College, graduates of Foochow College had had an extensive education in English over an eight-year curriculum, and many of them were hired into government service, particularly the Customs, postal, and salt services.

In a Foochow College catalogue for 1915, the one hundred graduates to that time are listed (in English and Chinese), and employment data are given for eighty-three of them. Excluding two in further study, out of the remaining eighty-one names, those in church or YMCA work or Protestant education totaled forty-seven, or 58 percent (eighteen church workers, twenty-nine educators). Only five were teaching in non-Protestant schools. Eight (10 percent) were physicians, two of them connected to government hospitals. Government work accounted for 21 percent of the graduates (seventeen in all: two government physicians, six in the postal service, five in the salt administration, and four in the Customs). Three held other professional posts, and three were in the commercial sector. Locations are given for eighty-six of the graduates. Twenty-one (24 percent) worked in rural locations within Fujian, mostly as pastors or as teachers in the American Board schools in Shaowu, Changle, and Yongtai Counties. Another twenty-one were outside Fujian, but only four of those were overseas, three in Southeast Asia and one studying in America.[168]

The importance of the Protestant school system as a ladder of mobility between rural areas and Fuzhou (and from there to the world beyond) can be shown from the data in a gazetteer from Gutian County. Gutian is a mountainous and isolated county lying to the northwest of Fuzhou. Protestant work began there in the early 1860s, and by the turn of the century the county had one of the highest ratios of Protestant church members of any area in

Fujian.[169] Both the Methodists and the Anglicans worked in Gutian, and both had an extensive series of elementary schools, capped by boarding schools for girls and boys in the county seat, all founded between 1887 and 1893.[170] In 1923 the Methodists alone were operating a total of eighty-four schools in the county: forty-two girls' schools, with 43 teachers and 574 students, and forty-two boys' schools, with 53 teachers and 1,021 students.[171]

The gazetteer, published in 1942, lists all the men and women from Gutian who went on to higher education beyond the county, graduating from high schools (*gaozhong*), postsecondary professional programs, or universities in China and abroad. Overall, out of a total of 471 men who completed some level of education beyond that offered in Gutian (which ended at the *chuzhong* or junior middle school level), a minimum of 162, fully one-third of the total, went through the Protestant educational system.[172] The figures for women are even more striking, for they show that the Protestant schools remained practically the only channel for Gutian women to acquire a higher education right up until the early 1940s. Of the 162 women listed, at least 157 (97 percent) graduated from Protestant schools, including all seven of those who earned university degrees abroad and all thirty of the graduates of Chinese universities (twenty-eight of whom were alumnae of the Hwa Nan Women's College in Fuzhou, run by the Methodists).[173]

The impact of the Protestant churches on the life possibilities of Chinese women was enormous, as this example indicates. Unfortunately no more than a cursory discussion is possible here. As we have already seen, the conversion of men was often followed by a desire for the education of their wives and daughters. By the 1870s, Chinese Protestant men like Huang Naishang were writing against the practice of footbinding, and in the ensuing decades the churches worked to raise the age at which girls in Protestant families were married, from the customary fifteen or sixteen to eighteen or older.[174] Even more than for men, the Protestant churches offered a whole new set of public roles to women. From the beginning, the wives of the preachers played an important part in their husbands' ministries, associating with and explaining Christian beliefs to the women of the area, with whom their husbands could not with propriety have contact. For this reason it was considered very important for preachers' wives to have some education; in fact, in 1883 the CMS Church Council in Fuqing County voted to dock the salary of any catechist whose wife could not read the New Testament in their dialect within twelve months.[175] Sometimes preachers' wives ran schools for local women or girls in their homes, as Huang Naishang's wife did in the early 1870s. Some of them became noted public speakers; Xu Yangmei's wife, for example, took an active role in the annual women's conference of the Methodist church.[176] Others

Fig. 1.6. Xu Jinhong as a missionary doctor in Fuzhou, early 1900s. Carrying her bag is her younger sister Xu Shuhong, sometimes referred to in mission sources as "Little Dr. Hu," who was trained in medicine by her sister and who practiced medicine privately in Fuzhou into the 1950s. Methodist Collection, Drew University, Madison, New Jersey.

worked with women missionaries in running boarding schools for women or girls and gave those schools a stability and continuity that they would have lacked if managed by missionaries alone.[177] Widows, who had very limited social options in late imperial China, could play valuable roles as full-time deaconesses or Biblewomen, some of them being sent to new areas as pioneering evangelists, others working in the schools or women's hospitals.[178]

Some of the daughters of the first-generation Protestants had opportunities that would have been unimaginable in their mothers' youth. One of the most interesting cases is that of Xu Yangmei's daughter Xu Jinhong (Hu King Eng, 1865–1929), the first woman from Fuzhou (and the second Chinese woman from anywhere) to be sent to America to study (fig. 1.6).[179] With the approval of her parents and the backing of the Foochow Conference, Xu Jinhong went to the United States in 1884, knowing next to no English. She intended to earn a medical degree and return to serve the church as a physician.[180] After learning as much English as she could over her first summer in America, she enrolled in the preparatory course at Ohio Wesleyan University, and three years later she transferred to the Women's Medical College of Philadelphia. In 1895,

Fig. 1.7. Early Methodist preacher Xu Yangmei and family, around 1890. His wife is seated next to him. Four of his five children are shown: the oldest, Xu Zehan (at left, with his wife behind him), followed in his father's footsteps as a Methodist preacher; the two daughters shown, Xu Jinhong (standing in the center) and Xu Shuhong (at right) both became physicians; and the younger son, Xu Zepei (at right) became a teacher at the Anglo-Chinese College in Fuzhou. Xu Zehan had eight children, one of whom is shown here; four of them (two sons and two daughters) became physicians, and a third daughter became a prominent educator and high school principal in Fuzhou. Methodist Collection, Drew University, Madison, New Jersey.

after graduating, she returned to Fuzhou as the first Chinese missionary of the Woman's Foreign Missionary Society of the Methodist Episcopal Church and spent the next thirty years running a flourishing women's and children's hospital in Fuzhou.[181]

The Xu family provides a useful example with which to epitomize Protestant social mobility. As we saw earlier, when the father and sons came into contact with the missionaries in the 1850s, the family was apparently a respectable but not distinguished one in the southern suburbs of the city. In the first generation of converts, there were six brothers: three became preachers, and one a doctor, presumably trained by a missionary. In the next generation there were two preachers, one in other church work, four doctors (including Xu Jinhong and her sister), three teachers in Protestant schools (two of them men who graduated from and taught in the Anglo-Chinese College, the third a woman who had studied in America), and two naval officers (fig. 1.7).[182]

Subsequent generations have all had preachers, many high school and university educators (men and women), doctors (men and women), and (before 1949) naval officers in China, Taiwan, Singapore, North America, and Britain. Christianity became incorporated into the sense of family identity of the descendants of the first converts, as is evident in the preface to a Republican-era version of the family's genealogy, which begins: "Shangdi is the father-mother (*fumu*) of all creation, heaven and earth."[183]

2

Protestant, Professional, Progressive

Mission sources in English are unanimous in testifying to the dramatic zeal for social and political reform that swept through society in Fuzhou and the nearby counties in the years before the 1911 revolution. Missionaries recount with wonder the sudden shift in the public attitude toward opium smoking and the dramatic increase in the number of young men and women — too many to accommodate — willing, indeed eager, to submit themselves to the strict regimen, Christian indoctrination, and high fees of their schools in order to acquire Western learning. They report on public speeches by local notables denouncing footbinding, the worship of idols and ancestral tablets, gambling, and "other vices" (often a missionary euphemism for prostitution) and give rapt accounts of being asked to speak before the most prominent men of the city in large meetings of the reform societies, or of being invited to tour through the towns and villages of an inland county with a reform-minded county magistrate, giving speeches with him on reform topics.[1]

Missionaries also refer to their Chinese Protestant colleagues, church members, or students being involved in this reformist social activism. It is difficult to know how far to trust these accounts, however. They are often vague or general, and they usually omit Chinese names. Even with regard to the incidents that are discussed specifically enough to be corroborated, the missionaries were at best peripheral observers of Chinese society, and it is possible that they were seeing only part of what was taking place. Indeed, when one looks at the Chinese sources, it is clear that the missionaries were right about the zeal for reform and the interest in "Western learning" and about the involvement of Protestants in the reform movement, but they missed the importance to the movement of a new popular nationalism which was profoundly ambivalent toward the Western nations — admiring of their technological feats and their political and social institutions, but resentful of their encroachments on China's political and economic sovereignty. This ambivalence affected the missionaries' Chinese Protestant associates, students, and congregations to a greater degree than most of the missionaries realized.

As Mary Wright writes in her excellent introduction to the last decade of the Qing dynasty, the nationalism that developed in China at this time, which had no counterpart in earlier Chinese history, was characterized by a determination "not only to halt but to roll back" the incursions of the great powers (including Japan) and to build China into a "modern, centralized nation-state."[2] In Fuzhou in the early 1900s, national strength was pursued through social reform, and social reform was pursued through a plethora of new public associations. Some of these were established by government decree and led by the influential families of the city, such as the Educational Association, the local self-government associations, or the Fuzhou Chamber of Commerce. Others, like the student associations and the various reform societies, were independent of official sponsorship and drew together a variety of progressive-minded or revolutionary men, many of whom were members of the modern professional class, and a significant number of whom were active Protestants. The Protestants had a role in this political awakening — in the movement against opium, the anti-American boycott of 1905, the formation of new public associations from 1907, and the foundation of the Young Men's Christian Association (YMCA) in Fuzhou. The last brought together, more than any other body, Protestant, progressive, professional men in pursuit of nationalist aims. Over this decade, I argue, Protestants became an accepted part of the progressive elite by virtue of their representation within the urban professional sector, upon which the political dynamism of this period was largely based.[3]

Anti-Opium Activity

There were few issues of greater symbolic weight in the formation of modern Chinese nationalism than the opium trade, and that trade had particular resonance in Fuzhou, because Lin Zexu (1785–1850), the official whose efforts to suppress the trade at Canton in 1839 had precipitated the disastrous Opium War with Britain, was a native of the area. Protestant missionaries in

Fuzhou had from their first arrival decried the malignant physical, moral, and social effects of opium smoking and been involved in efforts to treat it. One of the many ironies of the missionaries' handling of the opium question is that within a few years of Lin's death, he was being invoked in missionary tracts on opium in the service of their Christian message.[4] Lin had hardly been a friend of the foreigners or of Christianity; indeed, shortly before he died, he had been instrumental in arousing strong local opposition in Fuzhou to the presence of British missionaries on rented premises within the walled city.[5]

The symbol of Lin Zexu as anti-opium hero was again invoked in 1906 (arguably, more appropriately so) when the Anti-Opium Society (Qudushe — literally, "Society to Eradicate Poison") was founded in Fuzhou. The chair of the society was Lin Bingzhang (Huiting), who, aside from being a high-ranking scholar-official in his own right, was a great-grandson of Lin Zexu.[6] Lin's heroic example was regularly cited in publications and activities of the society, and the city office of the society was located in a memorial shrine to him. Indeed, Lin Zexu's legacy even carried over into the society's medical practices, for the unfortunate addicts in the society's refuges were reportedly treated with a medicinal preparation devised by Lin over sixty years earlier.[7]

The Fujian Anti-Opium Society was formally established in June of 1906, several months prior to the imperial edict of September 20 announcing a campaign to eradicate opium cultivation nationwide over a ten-year period.[8] The founders were some of the most prominent scholar-officials from Fuzhou, many of them with high positions in the capital, and their stature enabled them to mobilize local support and secure the cooperation of the provincial officials. Chief among them was Chen Baochen, a Grand Secretary and Lin Bingzhang's father-in-law and patron. Chen had just moved back from Beijing to Fuzhou to head the Provincial Teacher's College, one of the new modern government schools established by order of the imperial court in 1905. He was also a leader of the Fuzhou Chamber of Commerce and chair of the provincial Education Association and was later appointed director of education for the province.[9]

Presumably the stature of its founders gave the society considerable leverage with the provincial authorities, for its constitution, which those authorities ratified, allowed it very wide powers of inspection and confiscation, in cooperation with the embryonic local police force. These powers were exercised vigorously. In early 1907 the opium dens were told to change their line of business by May 12 of that year or face forcible closure.[10] After that date, two inspection teams of four or five men each, drawn from a pool of thirty volunteers for each team, were on duty from 8 P.M. every night, one in the walled city and one in the Nantai business district, along the Min River, south of the city (map 2.1). These teams, with support from police or yamen runners (who were to be reported by the teams if they got out of hand), were charged with going to any establishment where the consumption of opium was reported and, if the report were true, to close it down and confiscate any opium or paraphernalia used in its consumption; no other property on the premises was to be damaged. Large public bonfires of the seized contraband, accompanied by parades and hortatory speeches on patriotism and the evils of opium use, were staged by the society several times a year from 1907 into the early years of the Republic (fig. 2.1).[11]

Those smoking the drug at home were not exempt either, for teams of three or more of these voluntary inspectors visited their homes and exhorted them to give up the habit, and the society's quarterly report, published from the fall of 1907, printed precise accounts of violations discovered, with the dates of unannounced inspections and the names and addresses of unreformed addicts and premises found clandestinely defying the ban. Addicts did have the option of entering one of four opium refuges (*jieyanju*) run by the society in Fuzhou, where they would be attended by qualified doctors and cured in two or three weeks in normal cases and in up to four weeks in cases of severe addiction, according to the society's published rules for the refuges. The report of fall 1907 claimed that a total of 2,465 addicts had been cured in this fashion in the four refuges.[12] The society also targeted the production side of the opium enterprise; members were appointed to inspect rural areas around Fuzhou and certify them free of poppy crops, and this inspection duty was taken up by branches in each county as the organization spread through the province.[13] In sum, it seems that one missionary observer who, with approval, likened the society to a vigilante organization was not far off the mark.[14]

These vigorous measures had, it is reported, a marked impact on Fuzhou society. One missionary testifies to an aspect of this impact that is not mentioned in the society's own sources, for she tells us that there was dreadful mortality at first, because many poor addicts who lived hand-to-mouth could not work without the drug and so died in the streets of a combination of withdrawal and starvation. This resulted in a modification of the society's policy to allow addicts to purchase a rationed amount of the drug for consumption at home, the ration to be decreased each year.[15] Nevertheless, the total prohibition on opium dens, where the drug was smoked on the premises, remained in force. The first anniversary of the society was marked by a parade of members and supporters, following an image of Lin Zexu, which proceeded from the Lin Zexu memorial shrine in the city, south through the business district, to the Customs office on the river, where the day culminated in a great bonfire of seized opium paraphernalia. Officials, foreign consuls, compradors,

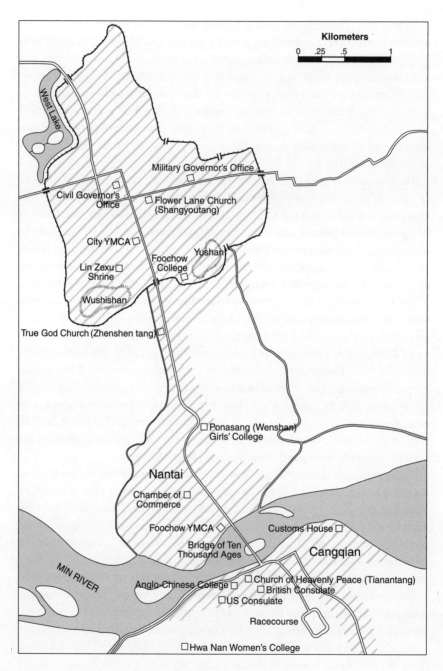

Map 2.2. Fuzhou, around 1915.

Fig. 2.1. Seventeenth parade and burning of opium paraphernalia by the Fujian Anti-Opium Society, probably 1912 or 1913. Judging from the quantities of confiscated materials reported, the pre-1911 parades and bonfires must have been on a larger scale. Methodist Collection, Drew University, Madison, New Jersey.

and missionaries were all invited to see the spectacle. A society publication records that the crowd was even larger than that at the founding of the society the year before, when over ten thousand had crowded into and around the Lin Zexu shrine, the largest crowd ever seen for any event in Fuzhou. This anniversary parade was held every year thereafter, and students of the Protestant schools joined in the festivities along with their compatriots in the government schools.[16]

The determination of the progressive elite to stamp out opium cultivation brought them into conflict with entrenched interests and with foreign powers, in particular with French, Japanese, and British firms and their consulates.[17] The dynamics of the opium trade and the diplomacy surrounding it were well understood by the society's elite leaders. In fact, their ultimate purpose was precisely to put the province in a position to pressure the British to end their importation of the drug into Fujian by stamping out the domestic cultivation of opium in the province. (Britain had made the suppression of domestic opium a precondition for cutting off the supply from British India.) Thus, once the society could certify that local poppy cultivation had been stamped out, it petitioned the provincial authorities to intercede with the British to end importation of the drug to Fujian ports—a request the British were unwilling to comply with, for their position was that opium cultivation in all parts of China must cease before Britain would stop imports to any part.[18]

Resentment toward British intractability on the opium question did not prevent the leaders of the Anti-Opium Society from being favorably disposed to Western learning and culture or from welcoming participation in the society by Chinese Protestants and even American and British missionaries. One English missionary states that Lin Bingzhang sent a message of greeting in his role as chair of the Anti-Opium Society, via the Bishop of Fujian, to the Pan-Anglican Conference held in London in 1908.[19] Several missionaries report being asked to address meetings of society branches in Fuzhou and in the county seats, and sometimes Chinese Protestants were asked to speak, notably on the occasion of the closure of the opium dens in 1907.[20]

The society's own publications also testify to a conjunction of the reformist zeal of the society's supporters and the long-held moral activism of the missionaries and Chinese Protestants. For example, in the winter of 1906, Lin Bingzhang gave the response to an address by a visiting representative of the British Society for the Suppression of the Opium Trade at a meeting in the principal Methodist church in Fuzhou, the one-thousand-seat Church of Heavenly Peace (Tianantang). Lin not only spoke about closing down opium dens, but also—no doubt to hearty applause from his Protestant audience—suggested applying the same measures to brothels.[21] In the spring of 1908 the same church was the site for a meeting of the society, with speeches by Lin and Chen Baochen, followed by the society's sixth public bonfire of opium paraphernalia, in which 467 pipes (*qiang*), 700-plus pipe bowls (*dou*), 1,000 lamps, 360 pipe trays, and enough opium paste and ash to load two carrying poles were burned. Many missionaries were present on this occasion, reported the society, taking photographs and joining in. "Well-intentioned foreigners (*waiguo you xin ren*) are overjoyed that our nation is prohibiting opium," the society's writer reflected.[22] A third example in the society's sources is provided by the "American missionary Ke," who inspected a sizable part of the Houguan County countryside for signs of poppy cultivation on behalf of the society, reporting on this subject to a society meeting in 1908 or 1909.[23]

One identifiable Chinese Protestant who was active in the Anti-Opium Society was a member of the Methodist Xu family, the doctor Xu Zeya (Wenzhi, Zi'an). Xu was the second son of the preacher Xu Bomei, and he was one of the two dozen or more Chinese men and women who received medical training in mission hospitals in Fuzhou in the late nineteenth century.[24] Most of these did not remain in mission employ but started their own medical practices, as Xu did some time before 1896. He had become a prominent and respected physician in the city by 1906, when he was elected as one of two heads of the medical work of the society, a position which implied some level of social parity for this preacher's son with the other officeholders of the society, among whom were members of the most influential families of the city.[25] Each of the four society opium refuges in Fuzhou also had a resident physician, and it is possible that the other anti-opium doctors listed in the society's reports were, like Xu, from the early cohort of missionary-trained practitioners of Western medicine in the city, but because the names of those trained by the missionaries are not known, this can only be speculation.[26]

Other known Protestants who were active in the Society include Chen Nengguang and the other Methodists active in the Qiaonan gongyishe, a reform society located in the Cangqian area, south of the Min River, to which the fourth branch office of the Anti-Opium Society was attached. This reform society and the Protestant role in it are discussed at length below.[27]

The publications of the Anti-Opium Society bear out the impression given in mission sources that church members were integrally involved in the upsurge of public action against opium that the society epitomized. Furthermore, they confirm that the progressive elite in Fuzhou was willing to make common cause with Chinese Protestants and Protestant missionaries in pursuit of shared goals. In addition to participating in the activities of the Anti-Opium Society, Chinese Protestants in the Fuzhou area continued their own activities against the opium trade. In 1911 a number of prominent Chinese church members of all three denominations in Fuzhou launched a signature campaign for a petition to the British crown requesting an end to the British trade in opium in China. This petition was sent out to all the churches in Fujian and parts of Jiangsu and Zhejiang Provinces; reportedly, 25,850 signatures were gathered from church members over a two-month period before it was passed on to the British consul in the fifth month of that year.[28]

The Anti-American Boycott and Mission School Students

According to an Anti-Opium Society report, one reason for the society's successful organization in 1906 was the public spirit aroused in Fuzhou during the boycott of American goods the year before.[29] The boycott movement spread from Shanghai to other port cities in the summer of 1905, in protest against the U.S. "exclusion laws," which prohibited Chinese "coolies" from entering the United States and led to long periods of detention and demeaning examinations for all Chinese, coolies or not, who sought to enter the United

States or its territories. As with the anti-opium movement, in which the aura of Lin Zexu and pride at being more "progressive" than other provinces had mixed with concern for "the nation," a curious combination of local pride and nationalism spurred the boycott movement in Fuzhou, for the boycott drive had been instigated by the Fujian guild in Shanghai, and its prime mover was a native of Fuzhou.[30] When the boycott was announced in May, this man had printed several thousand handbills and sent them for distribution by the Fuzhou Chamber of Commerce. On learning of this, the governor-general reached an accommodation with the chamber whereby it agreed not to hold public rallies to urge the boycott, and without the active support of the chamber of commerce the boycott did not take hold strongly in the northern part of Fujian. In December, however, the de facto leader of the Fuzhou elite, Chen Baochen, went to Shanghai and was greatly embarrassed by the reproaches of the boycott leaders there. On his return to Fuzhou he urged a renewal of the boycott, but by this time the movement was already on the wane around the country, and its renewal in Fuzhou was short-lived.[31]

The boycott itself was not strong in Fuzhou (in fact, there was little in the way of American trade at the port *to* boycott), but public resentment at the American exclusion laws ran deep in the city. As in the anti-opium movement, students were active in protesting the laws, and students of the major Protestant schools were involved along with those in the government schools. Although a radical pamphleteer of the period castigated the mission school students for lack of patriotism, saying that only one in ten among the men and fewer of the women were zealous nationalists, other contemporary sources reveal that the mission school students were not as devoid of patriotic spirit as that pamphlet alleged.[32] In this instance, the ties of these schools to the United States were actually a catalyst for protest, for anti-American feeling among the Anglo-Chinese College students was aroused by the case of some recent graduates who had been sent to America for further study. These men had been poorly treated by immigration inspectors when they arrived in the United States and had been held in detention for two to three months before their entry was approved, despite having valid student visas.[33]

In some ways, in fact, the students of the Anglo-Chinese College and Foochow College were ahead of their government school counterparts in protesting against the exclusion laws, for they held meetings on the subject before the government school students did, and even before the boycott was announced. They also joined with government school students in protest rallies in June 1905 and in the founding that summer of a "Fujian Public Association for the Protection of Laborers."[34]

In addition to rallies and boycotts, the mission school students made use of other strategies of protest that were available to them because of their relationship to the United States. Before news of the boycott had even reached Fuzhou, the U.S. consul at the port, Samuel Gracey, himself a devout Methodist and chair of the board of the Anglo-Chinese College, had given "two lengthy addresses" in the college chapel "at the request of the faculty, teachers, monitors, and students of the Anglo-Chinese College," and had accepted a petition signed by 350 Chinese teachers and students of the college outlining their objections to the exclusion laws.[35] Unlike some of the propaganda circulating in the city, this document showed an accurate and detailed understanding both of American history and of the policies governing the treatment of Chinese in the United States. Announcing themselves, on the one hand, grateful for the education and the Christian influence they had received from Americans, yet, on the other hand, duty-bound as subjects of the Chinese government to protest, the petitioners juxtaposed America's treatment of Chinese against America's self-image as a "Christian nation" and its self-proclaimed values of liberty and equal rights—equal rights which Americans had shed blood to extend to blacks and Cubans, yet now denied to Chinese. "In considering the races of the world, no matter how ignorant and how base the Chinese may seem to be, still they are not inferior to the negroes," the petition stated. "[The people of China] do not quite understand why your people in China [i.e., the missionaries] preach the doctrine of Love, while in America you treat Chinese worse than any other nation, nay, even the negroes! If you really love God you must prove your love to Him by first loving the brethren whom you can see on this earth," that is, the Chinese; only thus would the missionaries' words carry weight in China.[36]

It is significant that several other Protestant groups in China submitted petitions to the U.S. government over the exclusion issue in 1905, in contrast to the boycott movement as a whole, which relied on external protest strategies, like rallies, propaganda, and the boycott itself.[37] In the case of the Anglo-Chinese College petition, and probably Chinese Protestant petitions more generally, the exposure of the petitioners to the Protestant milieu gave them intellectual ammunition and a channel of access to the U.S. government. In fact, the medium was central to the message, for the very act of submitting a petition surely implied the appeal made explicit by the text: that the Chinese (at least, educated Christian Chinese) fell within the parameters of civilized humanity—in contrast, the petition implied, to "the negroes"—and should be treated accordingly.[38]

This petition is one of many instances through the years in which Fuzhou Protestants or mission-educated Chinese held up the standards of Christianity as a measure against which to criticize the actions of the self-proclaimed

Christian nations. In his two speeches to the students, Consul Gracey, finding himself in the unenviable position of having to defend a policy that he himself found distasteful (at least insofar as it affected the "better classes" of Chinese), urged the students to trust in the process of government-to-government negotiation of the issue. He also sought to justify the continued exclusion of "coolie labor" if the process of admitting the approved classes was improved and streamlined, and advanced the tit-for-tat argument that China had long excluded other nations or restricted their residence and activities in the empire.[39] It is clear from the petition, however, that the aspect of the American laws most irksome to the petitioners was the singling out of the Chinese as a race for discriminatory treatment not applied to immigrants from other nations, so it is doubtful that Gracey's remonstrations would have satisfied their objections.

In connection with the boycott movement, the sources indicate no tensions between Chinese Protestants and their American missionary associates in Fuzhou, although there were confrontations between missionaries and students threatening to boycott classes in the two major American mission schools, Foochow College and the Anglo-Chinese College. As noted earlier, the boycott was not pressed as strongly in Fuzhou as in other treaty ports. Also, American missionaries in China were not in general happy with the U.S. laws on Chinese immigration, or at least with the way they were implemented toward their students and associates, and this may have helped to defuse conflict within church institutions. However, the issue did bring a crisis for two of the most influential figures of the Fuzhou Methodist church, both working at that time in other cities more strongly affected by the boycott.

The first of these was the Methodist preacher and writer Huang Zhiji, generally regarded as the most intellectually accomplished Protestant preacher of any denomination in the Fuzhou area (fig. 2.2). In 1905 he was working with the missionaries Franklin Ohlinger and Young J. Allen on a Methodist magazine in Shanghai, but according to his biography, he fell out with the missionaries over the boycott issue and quit the magazine. He apparently published an article or articles critical of the U.S. exclusion laws, which aroused anger among missionaries in Shanghai; whatever their personal feelings about their country's actions, American missionaries did not want church writers to criticize the American government in print. Huang Zhiji's disaffection with the Methodist church, apparently dating from this incident, eventually resulted in him withdrawing from active involvement in it and becoming linked to the Chinese Independent Protestant Church in the early Republic.[40]

The other figure was Huang Naishang, who at time of the boycott was head writer for a daily paper in Xiamen (Amoy) in south Fujian. The Xiamen region

Fig. 2.2. The Reverend Huang Zhiji and family, early 1900s. Huang was widely considered the most intellectually gifted Fuzhou Protestant minister of his generation. He worked closely with Franklin Ohlinger and Young J. Allen in the publishing work of the Methodist church, but resigned in 1905 in connection with the Chinese protests against the American Exclusion Act. Special Collections, Yale Divinity School Library.

had close economic and kinship ties with the Chinese community in the Philippines, and the increasingly rigorous restrictions on movement between China and the Philippines since the U.S. annexation of the islands in 1898 had caused great resentment in Xiamen. Huang's newspaper, which had been critical of the U.S. exclusion laws well before the announcement of the boycott, became the principal vehicle for the boycott sentiment in Xiamen.[41] Tension between the paper and the U.S. consulate in Xiamen came to a head over the "flag incident" of July 1905, which became infamous in the patriotic press all over China. On the night of July 18, unknown vandals damaged the flag halyards of the consulate's flagpole and allegedly scattered excrement around the base of the pole. The consul, George Anderson, demanded that the Chinese authorities in the city give a public twenty-one-gun salute to the American flag to correct this "insult to the flag." The Chinese side pointed out, quite reasonably, that the flag itself was not on the pole at the time of the incident and therefore could not be said to have been insulted, and moreover that the flagpole was located in the foreign concession, where, according to treaty, the Chinese government had no jurisdiction and where the foreign Municipal Council was responsible for law and order. The justice of both these arguments was admitted by the consul's superiors in Beijing and Washington: "International law has not heretofore taken cognisance of insults to the halliards of a flag pole and to the grass plots around it," commented one ironic State Department reader.[42] In Xiamen, however, weeks of pressure from Anderson culminated in the local authorities giving way and firing the salute on August 6.

Huang Naishang's paper was very critical both of Consul Anderson's behavior and of the Xiamen authorities for complying with his demand for a salute. When the consul left the city a few weeks later, the paper accused him of being deranged and said that he had been removed by the U.S. government for his handling of the affair. (Even though this was not true, he was reprimanded both by the American minister in Beijing and by the State Department for his aggressive handling of the case.)[43] This provocative article outraged the foreign community in the port, and pressure from the U.S. consulate on local officials resulted in the paper being fined and forced to print an abject retraction. Nevertheless, the officials resisted the consul's demands that the paper be shut down entirely, and it continued to irritate the local foreign community over the succeeding months. Under foreign pressure it was ordered to discontinue publication late in 1905, but even then it was allowed to reappear a week later under a new title, under which it survived until the fall of 1906.[44]

In his autobiography Huang recorded that after the flag incident he and the American missionaries in Xiamen were no longer on cordial terms, and lamented: "Alas! Are we not all Christians, all seeking to bring blessing to China through preaching and through charitable and educational work? What have we to do with commerce? Yet, because they [the missionaries] were all Americans, all of one race [with the consuls and traders], they disregarded the forty years of service to Christianity of one known throughout China [i.e., himself] and worked for his downfall. This is certainly an unanticipated application of love for one's race and nation!"[45]

Thus, as with the opium question, Fuzhou Protestants were not inhibited by their links with American missionaries from taking a stand as Chinese nationalists when the United States or other powers took actions that they deemed detrimental to China. Like the petition by the students and teachers of Anglo-Chinese College, Hang's remarks show a readiness to apply the perspective of Christianity to criticize Christian nations. In fact, his words show the kind of fundamental difference in perception that could arise between missionaries and Chinese Protestants.

Protestants in the New Politics

The publication under Nationalist Party auspices in 1940 of the collection *Fujian xinhai guangfu shiliao* (Historical materials on the Xinhai revolution in Fujian) established the dominant interpretation of the events of the decade before the 1911 revolution in Fujian. This collection, sponsored by the Cultural Commission of the provincial Nationalist Party committee and nominally edited by the revolutionary veteran Zheng Zuyin, chair of the Fujian branch of the Revolutionary Alliance (Tongmenghui) prior to 1911, focused on certain progressive social bodies set up from 1902 and on the role of key revolutionary activists in the creation and running of those bodies. As with the "official" historiography of the 1911 revolution more generally, this collection in effect claimed a leading role for the revolutionaries in all the progressive initiatives of the decade and endowed those initiatives with the ultimate purpose of fomenting revolution under Revolutionary Alliance leadership in the province. This portrayal of the 1901–1911 decade in Fujian has been repeated with elaborations in more recent accounts on both sides of the Taiwan Strait.[46]

The surviving contemporary sources, however, indicate a much more fluid and multipolar situation in the years before the overthrow of the Qing dynasty, in which broadly "progressive" measures were undertaken or sponsored by a diversity of groups, including committed revolutionaries, local merchants, modern-educated moderate reformers, the cream of the local court-connected elite, and the provincial authorities. The mindset of progressive reform was not the sole property of the members of the Revolutionary Alliance, in other words, but was widely shared; indeed, its commonality serves to explain why the establishment of the Republic was so easily accepted in Fuzhou in the fall of 1911.

The first of the new political voluntary associations, or "reform societies," established in Fuzhou was the Yiwenshe (Society to Benefit the Hearer), set up in 1902.[47] The instigator was a naval student who had already written some tracts on the dangers facing the country and the province from the imperialist powers and who had, it is said, a "strong racial consciousness."[48] In the spring of that year he and some friends established the society on the premises of an old academy in the Cangqian area, some miles south of the city and close to the foreign consulates and residences. With a reading room and, from 1903, a school run by its members, the society was a prototype of the reform societies founded later. Evidence from a similar school indicates that revolutionaries used these private schools to funnel anti-Manchu reading matter to their students, including proscribed works on the massacres of Chinese by the Manchus during their conquest of China in the 1640s, texts of the anti-Manchu

Taiping regime, biographies of seventeenth-century Ming loyalists like Zheng Chenggong (Koxinga), and newly composed anti-Manchu tracts, such as Zou Rong's *Revolutionary Army* (1903). Outside speakers were invited to give lectures on such modern subjects as international relations, science, and Western political philosophy, and the school curriculum typically included physical training and military drill.[49]

Among the twelve founding members of the Yiwenshe was an identifiable Protestant, a Methodist layman named Chen Nengguang (Bingtai), an 1896 graduate of the Anglo-Chinese College.[50] Chen was one of the most prominent Protestants in the reform/revolutionary circles prior to 1911. He was the only son of a Methodist preacher, Chen Hengmei, who had served as Monitor of the Anglo-Chinese College before his death in 1892 at age forty-four.[51] After graduating, Chen Nengguang was hired as the first bilingual clerk in the newly established Imperial Postal Service in Fuzhou.[52] He resigned from the postal service in September 1907 and took up an appointment as the interpreter for the U.S. consulate in Fuzhou, where his political activism became something of an embarrassment for the consul.[53] He served on the board of directors of the YMCA in Fuzhou from its founding until 1914 or later, and church sources confirm that he was an active church member.[54]

At some point before 1911, Chen became a member of the Revolutionary Alliance, and he played a leading role in several of the reform societies in the Cangqian area of Fuzhou that became organizational centers for the Revolutionary Alliance. After the revolution he was made head of the Foreign Affairs Department of the new provincial government, a position for which his fluency in English and his connection with the U.S. consulate in Fuzhou must have equipped him well. In subsequent years he held high posts in the Customs, the Fujian government office to suppress opium cultivation, the province's salt administration, and the postal service.[55]

More encompassing than the Yiwenshe was the Qiaonan gongyishe (South-of-the-Bridge Public Welfare Society — hereafter the Qiaonan Society). This body, which was probably formed early in 1907, sought to broaden the activities of the Yiwenshe by appealing to "all patriotic scholars and merchants (*you zhi shishang*) south of the bridge [over the Min River]"that is, to those in the Cangqian suburb of the city (see map 2.1).[56] The Qiaonan Society sponsored public lectures, reading rooms, and, as mentioned earlier, a branch of the Anti-Opium Society. Later it published a newspaper and started a physical training association and a fire brigade (both of which became, in essence, revolutionary militia units in 1911), and in the fall of 1911 it became the mobilization headquarters of the revolution in Fujian.[57] Similar reform societies were established in other parts of the city and in some surrounding counties in imitation of the Qiaonan Society, most of them also called *gongyishe,* but it remained the "first among equals" of reform societies in the Fuzhou area.[58]

A published report of receipts and expenditures for this organization, covering the thirty-fourth year of Guangxu and the first year of Xuantong (roughly 1908 and 1909), survives in the Fujian Provincial Library. This document indicates that the body was truly a voluntary society, funded by small-scale donations from its members — quite different in this respect from the organizations sponsored by the government or by high-ranking scholar-officials, such as the new government schools or the Anti-Opium Society, which benefited from the time-honored Chinese elite tradition of public philanthropy. For example, in the first year covered by the report, the society took in a total of 368.7 (Chinese) dollars in regular contributions from a total of fifty-seven donors, some of them businesses but most of them individuals, the great majority of both giving between one and six dollars over the course of the year. Special donations, mostly from the same members and in similar amounts, brought in another 235 dollars. The entry for the following year makes it clear that the "regular contributions" were given on a monthly basis and were pledged in advance, suggesting a parallel to the pledge system that operated in the Protestant churches.

Outlays for the society in the same year included 67 dollars for the society's school, 14 dollars for reading material for the reading room, 30 dollars for lectures, 46 dollars for the annual commemorative meeting, 15 dollars to provide meals for the (otherwise uncompensated) officeholders, and money for various and sundry running expenses (stationery, printing costs, rent, and the like).

A separate accounting is given for the expenditures associated with the affiliated branch of the Anti-Opium Society and its opium refuge, which was massively expensive to run compared to the society's other activities. A total of 1,680 dollars was spent on the anti-opium activities in Guangxu 34 (1907–1908). The cost of medical care for the addicts accounted for almost one-third of this amount, for 378 dollars was spent on medicine and 160 dollars in order to retain the services of a doctor. The cost of the anti-opium program, however, was largely covered by subsidies from the Anti-Opium Society, amounting that year to 1,505 dollars.[59]

The only way to determine with any precision the extent of Protestant involvement in this and similar societies is to comb through the name lists of the churches and mission schools, on the one hand, and the reform societies, on the other. Aside from the inherent difficulties posed by the use of variant names (*zi* and *hao*) for the same individual, this task is hampered by the lack of sources: very few such lists have survived. We do not have congregational membership lists for the Fuzhou area churches from this (or any other) period, and in general, only ministers are identified by name in the church sources in Chinese that we do have. Even on this limited score there is more information for the Methodists than for either the Anglicans or the Congregationalists. By the same token, there are no extant name lists or indeed other documentary sources for the great majority of the reform societies that operated in and around Fuzhou in these years.

The fragmentary nature of the information makes it all the more striking that there are six identifiable Protestants and nine others with known Protestant ties among the eighty-seven members of the Qiaonan Society listed in the report of 1908–1909. One Protestant member was Chen Nengguang, the founding member of the Yiwenshe mentioned above. He was clearly quite wealthy, for he was among a handful of relatively large donors to the organization, giving a total of twenty dollars in 1908 (ten as a pledged contribution and ten as a special donation) and twenty-six dollars in 1909. Two others were prominent Methodist pastors, Yu Shuxin (Chuanzhen; U Seuk Sing), then serving as pastor of the large Church of Heavenly Peace, and Chen Wenchou (Ding Ung Tiu), dean of the Methodist seminary.[60] Yu, born in 1874, was from the inland county of Gutian, where he held *shengyuan* status; he joined the Methodist pastorate in 1901.[61] Appropriately, these two preachers were among the seven members of the society given particular responsibility for disseminating the society's agenda through the spoken word; they also served on the inspection teams of the Qiaonan branch of the Anti-Opium Society.[62] A fourth man, Li Qifan (Li Chi Van), who likewise served as one of the speakers for the society and on the opium inspection teams, was also one of the English secretaries of the association and head of a Protestant orphanage.[63] A fifth member, Chen Hongyi, was another Methodist preacher.[64] The sixth, Wang Ganhe (Uong Guang Huo), was a 1906 graduate of the Anglo-Chinese College then teaching at his alma mater; he later studied in America and became a prominent preacher in Fuzhou (fig. 2.3).[65] These men, living on their modest preachers' and teachers' salaries, gave between 1 and 3.6 dollars apiece to the society per year.[66]

A link to the Methodist church, though not necessarily personal religious adherence, can be shown for eight other men who are listed in this publication as members of or donors to the society or its affiliated branch of the Anti-Opium Society. Six of these were recent graduates of the Anglo-Chinese College. One was wealthy enough to donate twenty-six dollars in 1909; another had graduated just the previous year yet donated six dollars in 1908.[67] All six of these young men apparently worked in modern professional jobs, for some years later they were reported in a publication of the school to be em-

Fig. 2.3. The face of Protestant modernity: the Reverend Wang Ganhe, Anglo-Chinese College alumnus (1906) and pre-1911 reform activist, later a U.S. university graduate and prominent Methodist preacher in Fuzhou. Methodist Collection, Drew University, Madison, New Jersey.

ployed in salt administration, the Customs Service, mining, and education. Two other Qiaonan Society members from 1908–1909 are listed as teachers in the Anglo-Chinese College in 1917, making it probable that they were Protestants by then, although there is no evidence to determine whether or not they were in 1908–1909.[68]

The last name for whom a definite link to the Protestant church can be shown is that of the president of the Qiaonan Society, Zheng Jiming, who was a member of the Fuzhou City YMCA by early 1911.[69] Associate membership in the YMCA was open to non-Christians, so Zheng may not have been a church member himself, but the link does show that he was happy to be affiliated with a Protestant organization, just as the Qiaonan and other reform societies were happy to include Protestants among their members.

The Qiaonan Society was the most prominent and active of the reform societies in Fuzhou, and it played a crucial role in the 1911 revolution in the city. When Sun Yatsen visited Fujian in 1912, he contributed the calligraphy for a plaque acknowledging the society's importance in the revolution.[70] That at least fifteen of the eighty-seven members of the society in 1908–1909 were linked to the Protestant church indicates a significant level of involvement by Protestants — particularly given that Protestants in the city at this time numbered only around two thousand in a population of over half a million. Especially telling is the fact that three of the seven members designated to give speeches on behalf of the society were church workers, and a fourth (the president, Zheng Jiming) was a YMCA member, since their election to such an influential position must surely have implied a high degree of trust in their verbal abilities and progressive credentials on the part of fellow members.[71]

Significant Protestant involvement is also evident in another association for which we have relatively complete information. In 1908 members of the Qiaonan Society established a fire brigade to service the area of the city south of the Min River. Like the inspection teams of the Anti-Opium Society, this organization seems to have executed some quasi-police functions in addition to fighting fires. Soon after its establishment it became embroiled in a bitter dispute with the British consulate over its occupancy of certain temple premises adjacent to the consulate for which the British claimed to have a lease. Partly as a result of this dispute it became a gathering place for men of a radical or revolutionary bent; several of its members took part in the failed Huanghua-gang uprising in the spring of 1911, and its leader was one of the "seventy-two martyrs" killed in it.[72] According to a report of the brigade published in 1908, many of the men in the Qiaonan Society were active in it, including the Methodists Chen Nengguang (who served for a time as vice-president of the brigade), Chen Wenchou, Yu Shuxin, and the Anglo-Chinese College graduate Cheng Gongchen. Other identifiable Protestants listed are Xu Wenming (Hu Ung Ming), youngest son of Xu Bomei, who was Chinese superintendent of the Methodist Publishing House, and Dr. Lin Tao'an (Ling To Ang), a missionary-trained physician at the Tating Community Hospital in Cangqian who was a YMCA director and a leading layman in the Anglican church.[73] Also among the names is an early (1891) graduate of the Anglo-Chinese College and former interpreter for the U.S. consulate in Fuzhou, Lin Shufen, who was also active in the Anti-Opium Society and held the rank of prefect (presumably by purchase). After the 1911 revolution Lin became deputy head, under Chen Nengguang, of the provincial Foreign Affairs Department.[74]

What was the relationship of these Protestants to the revolutionaries in the reform societies? Although many discussions of the period classify political actors of the time as either constitutionalists or revolutionaries, the political situation in Fuzhou was actually more multipolar than that. This is hinted at by Liu Tong, one of the young revolutionaries in the Qiaonan Society, who in his oft-cited reminiscence makes a distinction between the constitutionalists, the "progressives" (*jinbu pai*), and the revolutionaries.[75] The available evidence, while not conclusive, indicates that most of the Protestants, with their nontraditional educational background and their acquaintance with American and European ways, belonged to the progressive camp rather than to the committed revolutionaries (with the notable exceptions of Huang Naishang and of Li Qifan, who had the boys in his orphanage making bombs for the revolutionary side on the eve of the battle with the Qing garrison in November 1911).[76] Chen Nengguang, for example, was a member of the Revolutionary Alliance, but his involvement seems to have been in what might be called a civilian context; he was not among the men making contact with the secret societies or the New Army soldiers and officers in the Fuzhou area.[77] Liu Tong confirms this impression, describing Chen as a "local notable with enthusiasm for public welfare."[78]

Moreover, although many post-1911 accounts place primary emphasis on the leadership of the revolutionaries and the secret revolutionary role of the Qiaonan Society and other reform societies, there is no reason to conclude from the sources of the time either that the visible social reform activities of these societies were somehow secondary to their revolutionary function or that all members of these societies knew about the revolutionary affiliation of some of their associates, given that Revolutionary Alliance members were sworn to secrecy.[79] Indeed, the common denominator among the progressive elite of the time was a commitment to restoring China to a position of strength in the international arena through social and political reforms, rather than a commitment to one particular means to that end (such as establishing a republic through revolution against the Manchu dynasty). Only this more general shared nationalist perception of the imperatives of the time can explain the cooperation of diverse social groups — revolutionaries, members of the "great houses" (*shijia*) of the city, men employed in modern commercial or service jobs, and Protestants — in reform causes. This is indicated also by P'engyuan Chang's classic study of the politics of the time, which concludes that there was an unusually high level of cooperation between revolutionaries and constitutionalists in Fujian. As Chang points out, many prominent posts in the postrevolution provincial government were held by former leaders of the Provincial Assembly, men with constitutionalist leanings.[80]

A related question is why the strongest reform societies were located in the Cangqian area, rather than across the river in the business district of Nantai or further north among the homes of the elite families within the walled city. No doubt one reason is that the distance from the provincial authorities, in an area to which the only land access from the city was via a single long bridge, was an advantage for those with revolutionary intentions. In addition, although there was no formal foreign concession in Fuzhou, the presence of all the foreign consulates and businesses in this area might have made it in some sense a de facto concession where the provincial authorities were hesitant to impose themselves forcefully.

A more important factor, however, was surely the prevalence in this area of members of the modern professional sector, who seem to have made up a significant proportion of the reform societies' membership. As noted above, in the Cangqian area were located the foreign consulates and firms, not to mention the foreigners-only Foochow Club and racecourse, plus the main institutions of the Methodist mission (schools, publishing house, and the Church of Heavenly Peace). In addition, the area housed the telegraph office, the main post office, the customhouse, the Hong Kong and Shanghai Bank, and many prominent Chinese-owned companies — all important employers for young professional men in the city. We have already noted that Chen Nengguang and the six Anglo-Chinese College graduates in the Qiaonan Society were employed in modern professional jobs. At least one other member of the society, who served as one of its English secretaries and who was also a secretary for the Minnan Fire Brigade, worked as a bilingual clerk for the postal service.[81] Several members of the Qiaonan Society and the fire brigade had worked as interpreters for the U.S. consulate.[82] As discussed in Chapter 1, the modern professional sector was a common field of employment for young men educated in the Protestant schools, and, as we shall see below, this sector provided the bulk of the membership of the YMCA in Fuzhou as well.

An interesting indication of the difference between the reform constituencies within the walled city and those across the river in the Cangqian area is provided by the list of members of the two inspection departments of the Anti-Opium Society in 1907. Because these teams were composed of volunteers who were each required to be on duty roughly one night per week, these men were presumably all highly committed to social reform. The thirty members of the inspection department within the city were all either holders of junior degrees in the classical examination system or graduates of the new schools in the city (most typically in the new discipline of *fazheng* — law and government — a favorite study of the men who would have aspired to government office through the examination system ten years before), or both.[83] By contrast, about half of the forty-two members of the inspection department in Cangqian are listed with no titles other than membership in a reform society (mainly the Shuobao she — Explain-the-News Society) or in the chamber of commerce. The remainder are listed with *shengyuan*, purchased, or educational titles, so the fact that some are not listed with a title probably indicates that they had no such titles, and this underlines the nontraditional nature of the progressive constituency in the Cangqian area.[84]

Much of the dynamism of the progressive cause in the final years of Qing rule in Fuzhou came from young men like these, employed in the emerging urban professional sector, which was concentrated in the Cangqian area of Fuzhou and in which Protestants were statistically far more numerous than in the general population. As an elite but nongentry political bloc, these men represented the emergence of citizenship in a modern China conceived as a nation, not a dynasty.[85]

The Protestant Social Reform Prototype: The YMCA

The organization in which the intersection between Protestant social progressivism, the activism of the reform societies, and the Fuzhou elite is most evident was the city branch of the Young Men's Christian Association (Jidujiao qingnian hui), which was established in 1907. Like the reform societies, the YMCA sought to change China through education and popular mobilization in the form of meetings, lectures, reading rooms, publications, and its own school. The YMCA shared not only methods but also moral outlook and membership with the reform societies. Many men prominent in the reform cause were YMCA members, and several members of the Provincial Assembly elected in 1909 were also active in the YMCA. It was founded in the Cangqian area of the city, where the strongest reform societies were located, and it deliberately targeted young men working in the commercial and service sectors, as well as students in the government and mission schools.

Whereas the YMCA movement had its origin among young white-collar working men in the industrializing cities of Great Britain and North America, only latterly developing a student wing, the YMCA began in China among the students of the mission colleges.[86] The first YMCA in Fuzhou, and in fact in all China, was established at the Anglo-Chinese College in 1885. According to the recollections of some of the first members, it was founded by four or five students in the college, with the encouragement of the college president, after they heard a talk by a visiting missionary entitled "The Work and Responsibilities of Youth." A student, Chen Mengren, was elected president of the small group. Its activities at first were confined to weekly prayer meetings, but after a couple of years the membership grew to a dozen or more students, and they began to go out in teams to preach in the neighborhood around the school each Saturday and Sunday afternoon.[87] Two attributes that are evident in this early history, Chinese leadership and Chinese initiative, came to characterize the Chinese YMCA, and distinguish it from the conventional mission societies, throughout its existence.

By 1902 there were sizable student YMCA branches at all the main mission colleges and seminaries in the city.[88] Reports of the activities of these groups make clear that for its first twenty years in Fuzhou, the YMCA remained exclusively a religious body working among students in the mission schools. The branches at each school typically had weekly prayer meetings, Bible classes, and occasional lectures or joint meetings with the branches at other schools. The organization of voluntary preaching bands made up of members was a common aspect of their activities.[89] The YMCA's overall aim in its student work was to develop students in the Protestant schools into earnest Christians with the qualities of character necessary for their future role as leaders in the church and the nation. As one foreign secretary put it in 1908, "China will become a great nation by becoming a Christian nation; she will become a Christian nation finally through the work of a Chinese Church led by educated ministers and laymen, and that educated leadership must come largely from the students in these Christian institutions" — those being the schools and colleges at which the YMCA was active.[90]

The student focus of the YMCA in Fuzhou changed in 1905 with the appointment of two Americans as full-time YMCA secretaries, with a mandate to start an association for the working men of the city.[91] A core group of two Chinese secretaries and four officeholders was formed; at least four of these men were graduates of the mission colleges and had most probably been involved in their college YMCA groups.[92] According to one of the foreign secretaries, the early policy was to concentrate on developing a solid leadership core for the organization before expanding it: "If we had yielded to the pressure from the young men," he wrote home, "we could have now a city Association with about two hundred members. We have rather discouraged numbers and worked for influential and representative leaders."[93] Early in 1907 a full board of directors of nine members, all Chinese, was created, and the Fuzhou City Young Men's Christian Association was formally established in a rented Western-style building in the Cangqian area. A second facility was opened within the walled city early in 1909, reportedly at the urging of a provincial official.[94] These first directors, who were all required by YMCA rules to be Protestant church members in good standing with their churches, included "the owner of a large silk and foreign goods store," two men in the postal service (including Chen Nengguang, whose role in the reform societies has been recounted above) and one in the Customs, two teachers in mission schools and one in the highest government college in the city (the Quan Min daxuetang, or Fujian Provincial College), one physician, and one pastor.[95] By the end of the first year, the city YMCA had 144 members, each paying an annual membership fee of six dollars, and the number had grown to 350 by April 1911.[96]

In the climate of enthusiasm for novelty and for forming voluntary associations that prevailed in this period there were probably many in Fuzhou who perceived the YMCA as simply another reform society, rather than as a distinctively Christian one. In 1908 there was a conflict over the use of the word "Christian" in the name of the organization, which prompted the resignation of about thirty members when the board of directors declined to change the name.[97] Significantly, however, this setback did not seriously retard the growth of the YMCA in the city nor impede its ability to attract non-Protestants to its program.

The aims and activities of the city YMCA were markedly different from those of the student groups in the mission schools. Whereas the student branches focused on religious activities designed to develop Christian character in Christian students, the city YMCA provided a wider range of activities and aimed to attract and provide services for non-Christians as well. This was accomplished by distinguishing between two kinds of membership: "active" membership, which was restricted to "members of orthodox Protestant churches," and "associate" membership, which was open to all "young men of good moral character." The Christian direction of each local association was ensured by restricting the rights to vote and hold office to "active members," but the YMCA was unique among Protestant organizations in China in deliberately recruiting and providing services for a mixed Christian and non-Christian membership.[98] In September 1910 there were 81 active and 223 associate members in the YMCA, and associate members continued to outnumber active members by a substantial margin through the early Republican period, both in Fuzhou and in other YMCAs in China.[99]

We may infer from these numbers that the YMCA program was based on values that were shared both by Protestants and by other progressive-minded men. A further indication of this is the very motto of the YMCA, *deyu, zhiyu, tiyu,* or "moral, intellectual, and physical education," represented by the three sides of its emblem, an inverted triangle. This echoed the language of China's developing nationalism. In some of their most widely read essays, nationalist writers like Yan Fu and Liang Qichao had employed a similar three-part phrasing, writing of the need to develop the people's virtue, the people's intellect, and the people's strength; and writings on educational reform around this time used the same formulation as the YMCA, *deyu, zhiyu, tiyu,* to encapsulate the goal of the new-style education.[100]

The activities of the city YMCA were remarkably similar to those of the Qiaonan Society and similar reform societies, with some distinctively Christian elements. Under "moral education" came religious activities like voluntary Bible studies for members, lectures on religious and moral themes, and a general stress on responsible citizenship. "Intellectual education" was pursued through weekly lectures, vocational and other courses offered in part-time night classes to attract working professional men, a reading room open to members in which, in the opening year, were stocked "forty-seven of the leading English and Chinese periodicals," and a seven-year high school (changed to five-year in 1910), which enrolled its first students in 1905 or 1906 and opened formally in 1908.[101] "Physical education" involved not simply team sports, gymnasium facilities, and tennis courts, but anything related to health promotion, including a series of ambitious mass education campaigns on public hygiene in Fuzhou in the early years of the Republic (fig. 2.4).[102]

Beyond its specific activities, the YMCA's appeal to men of non-Christian background and to the provincial officials and elite figures who patronized and supported its program was based on a consensus among the progressive elite, reform-minded officials, and Protestants concerning China's problems and China's needs in the early years of the twentieth century. China was facing a crisis, and the root of the crisis was widely perceived as a moral one. Thus, reformers like Lin Bingzhang of the Anti-Opium Society and the legislators of the Provincial Assembly could share with the YMCA the perception that opium and prostitution were destructive both to those who indulged in them and to the nation, and could view the YMCA as a constructive alternative for the young men of Fuzhou. Personal morality was construed as a matter of patriotism, and individual and national vigor — moral, intellectual, and physical — were intertwined.[103]

The way Protestants interpreted the needs of the nation and their role in meeting them can be seen in a surviving issue of the Fuzhou YMCA's magazine in 1910, the lead article of which discussed the question of the relation of morality to the nation.[104] The (unnamed) writer began with a densely argued section drawing on two core Confucian texts, the *Zuozhuan* (Zuo commentary) and the polemical essay *Yuandao* (An inquiry into the Way) by the Tang writer Han Yu, to show the interdependence of *dao* (the Way), *de* (virtue), *ren* (benevolence), and *yi* (righteousness) and to show that China's own tradition defined morality (*daode*) as a matter of the human heart.[105] The writer then criticized the emphasis of China's statesmen on political solutions to China's crisis, such as self-strengthening or the administrative changes after 1901 (*xinzheng*), and their lack of attention to the "foundation of governance" (*genbenshang zhi zhifa*), the people's morality (*minde*). History shows, he continued, that without education of the citizenry (or education in citizenship — *guomin jiaoyu*), the people will have no patriotic consciousness (*min wu aihu guojia sixiang*). The power to establish morality in people's hearts comes from religion, the writer claimed, and he ended with an appeal to citizens to embrace the Christian religion if they desired a moral and patriotic heart (literally, "a moral heart which is patriotic" — *aiguo zhi daode xin*).[106]

Fig. 2.4. Tennis court at the Fuzhou YMCA, early 1900s. Methodist Collection, Drew University, Madison, New Jersey.

This Christian writer's use of Han Yu's famous essay is significant, for Han had vigorously opposed both Buddhism and Taoism as corruptions of authentic Chinese tradition. As with much Christian apologetic writing in Chinese, Christianity in this essay was presented as incorporating and transcending the best elements of Chinese tradition, that is, Confucian ethical teaching as represented by the *Zuozhuan* and Han Yu. In this conception, Christianity was not an alien doctrine but rather the highest embodiment of the ethical ideals inherent in that pure core of Chinese tradition which Han Yu had sought to protect.

At the same time, however, the writer deployed these ancient texts to claim a role for Christianity in China on distinctly modern grounds, by linking religion with morality, morality with education, and all three with patriotism, and drawing arguments both from the past and from the contemporary world situation to place Christianity at the very core of national well-being through its claimed power to produce a moral citizenry.

A similar reasoning is evident, though less explicit, in some of the weekly lectures held by the YMCA that are summarized in the magazine. For example, in a wide-ranging talk late in 1910, the American Methodist bishop W. S. Lewis touched on the common ancestry of all humanity and their equality in the sight of God, the teachings of Christ and Confucius, the danger of the partition of China and the wrongness from a Christian perspective of the treatment of China by the great powers (excepting the United States), and China's need for a form of education stressing morality, which would lead to patriotism and national strength.[107]

A concern for China's survival as a nation also underlies the other lectures summarized in the magazine, even ones on apparently more prosaic topics. Lectures on technology and industry pointed to China's need to develop them; for example, a lecture by an American teacher of engineering in the Anglo-Chinese College on "the manufacture and uses of Portland cement" was more than merely factual, for it ended with an appeal to the industrialists of Fuzhou to take advantage of the lime deposits in the upland areas of the province and set up a cement factory, thus helping to revive the economy.[108] Lectures on current national and international affairs stirred patriotism by highlighting the threats facing China from within and without, be they the poor hygiene of its population, the drought in Anhui Province, the weakness of its navy, or Japan's aggressive intentions in Korea.[109]

In most of these lectures no explicit mention of religion was made, and the topics covered must have had a broad secular appeal. In 1910 an average of around 120 people per week attended the lectures, and an unknown additional number read the synopses of them in the Fuzhou YMCA magazine.[110] Some of the lectures, especially those comparing China with America or the Western powers, implicitly placed Protestant Christianity on the "winning side" in the international world. More to the point, the fact that the YMCA, an explicitly Christian organization, even held such lectures implied that Christianity, at least in its YMCA embodiment, was on the side of morality, enlightenment, and progress. Protestant Christianity was thereby aligned with the best elements of Western civilization, and speakers like Lewis—and Bishop Price, Anglican bishop of Fujian, who spoke on the opium question in the spring of 1911, introduced by Zheng Jiming of the Qiaonan Society—took pains to distance Christianity from the less attractive aspects of Western progress.[111]

The extent to which the YMCA in Fuzhou shared a common agenda with the progressive elite in the city can be seen in some of its public occasions. The opening of new and better YMCA premises in early 1908 was marked by a guest lecture by the Hanlin compiler Lin Bingzhang, the head of the Anti-Opium Society, on the work of the society. The new hall was bedecked with flags, and the assembled company of over two hundred men, young and old, sang a patriotic song before dispersing.[112]

The fourth anniversary of the establishment of the city YMCA, celebrated in the spring of 1911, shows more clearly the stature that the YMCA had attained in Fuzhou society over its brief existence. The anniversary was held only a few days after provincial officials from the Tartar general (*dujun*— commander of the military forces in the province, and the highest official in all Fujian aside from the governor-general) on down had come to the YMCA building to see a special presentation on electricity by the YMCA science lecturer, C. H. Robertson.[113] By this time, the board of the YMCA included three men prominent in the Provincial Assembly, including a vice-president of the body and its general secretary, as well as prominent members of the reform societies.[114]

At the anniversary, speeches congratulating the YMCA and praising its work were given by representatives of the government (*guanjie*), the gentry (*shenjie*), the commercial world (*shangjie*), and the reform societies (*shehui*). For the government, the Min County magistrate Xie spoke approvingly of the YMCA's emphasis on the "three educations" (moral, intellectual, and physical), and in particular its stress on morality. He expressed hope that the YMCA would grow and cause the coming generation of youth to develop a well-rounded moral character, for the good both of Fuzhou and of the nation.[115]

The first gentry speaker drew an extraordinary analogy between the three elements of the YMCA's motto and the six arts listed by Confucius as necessary for a scholar: rites and music, which the speaker likened to moral education; writing and arithmetic, which corresponded to intellectual education; and archery and chariot driving, which corresponded to physical education.[116] This speaker was not, as one might expect, an old scholar of the traditional stamp, but a young man not much over thirty, who had studied in England after graduating from the Beiyang Naval Academy and had worked in the Chinese embassies in London and Paris.[117] This speech reminds us that it was not only Protestants (like the YMCA writer discussed earlier) who were seeking to invest old texts with new meanings, or justify new ideas by clothing them in the language of old texts, in this period of rapid change.

The second gentry speaker was a Hanlin compiler and a leader in the movement for local self-government.[118] This man recounted a conversation between himself and the American consul in Xiamen concerning the opium question in which the consul had suggested that the best way to deal with the problem would be to get more men to join the YMCA so that they would no longer wish to take opium. The speaker urged his hearers to donate funds for the planned new YMCA building, predicting that the membership would soar from 350 to 3,500 if a modern facility were available.[119]

The commercial representative was a cofounder of the Anti-Opium Society and a member of the Provincial Assembly in addition to being prominent in the chamber of commerce, and he urged his colleagues in commerce to give generously for the new YMCA facility.[120] The reform society representative was Zheng Jiming, the head of the Qiaonan Society and a YMCA member.

By 1911, therefore, the YMCA in Fuzhou had established a place for itself in Fuzhou society and gained the respect of the pro-reform elements in official, gentry, and commercial circles. In a book on the YMCA in China, Shirley Garrett suggests that Chinese officials in the last years of the Qing dynasty saw the YMCA as a welcome alternative to the worrying radicalism of other student and youth associations. "The association provided an institution for young men that was not only nonpolitical but also based on a morality of which official China could approve," she writes.[121] While this is true in a sense, there was more both to the YMCA's appeal and to its politics. In Fuzhou, the YMCA was very definitely a Chinese organization, and its leaders were Chinese Protestants with stature and credibility beyond church circles. Its rhetoric was Chinese, too. Chinese classical texts were given a Christian interpretation and used to present new ideas, and the slogan of moral, intellectual, and physical education was both usefully malleable and strikingly memorable in Chinese. Furthermore, the organization was not only Chinese but Fujianese. Fundraising efforts appealed to local pride, local men were the directors and secretaries of the YMCA, and local notables and officials gave donations and other support.

Most important, however, the YMCA stood for a vigorous, masculine, *useful* style of Protestant Christianity, in contrast to the feminine imagery which had been dominant in Anglo-American Protestant piety through much of the nineteenth century (and shaped Chinese Protestant piety to some degree).[122] Physical vigor and useful knowledge were exalted in YMCA rhetoric along with moral purity, and these attributes had deep resonance in China among young men for whom the fearful prospect of national dismemberment and racial extinction seemed plausible, even imminent. After all, Yan Fu, whose translations of European scholarship (and particularly Thomas Huxley's exposition of Social Darwinism, *Evolution and Ethics*) had done so much to shape the thinking and apprehensions of this generation, was from Fuzhou.[123] This concern for the survival of race and nation is what gave urgency to the social reforms of the progressive elite in Fuzhou: their attempts to suppress opium and discourage footbinding, gambling, and prostitution and their encouragement of military drill and calisthenics in the new schools and in voluntary associations like the Physical Education Association attached to the Qiaonan Society. It also lay behind the concern with education itself, and with making education more widespread, more modern, and more practical. So when the Fuzhou YMCA magazine presented young Protestant professionals as modern equivalents of the classical "men of talent," it was both contrasting an implied image of the effete classical scholar with the social usefulness of the modern young mission-educated professional and claiming equal status for the latter with his contemporaries from the government schools and Japanese universities.[124] Young, modern, educated men, Protestants among them, would preserve the nation.

Politically also, despite the requirement in its constitution that the organization be "nonpolitical," the values of the YMCA—progress, purity, patriotism—made it attractive to men who were definitely political, and there was clearly a considerable overlap between the YMCA, the reform societies, and the Anti-Opium Society, as well as the Provincial Assembly.[125] Nevertheless, while it could not be aloof from politics, the YMCA in Fuzhou was not anarchist, radical, or committed to overthrowing the Qing dynasty (even though its chairman was a leading revolutionary), which was the sort of "politics" that most worried Qing officials.

In the end, the YMCA in Fuzhou was a Chinese incarnation of an optimistic, progressive Christianity, a Christianity that appeared right in tune with the temper of the times in China on the eve of the republican revolution of 1911 and would appear even more so in the years immediately thereafter. This was a period for Chinese Protestants when the changes in China could indeed seem almost to equate to the "progress of the Kingdom of Heaven" (*Tianguo zhi jinbu*), to borrow a phrase from one of the founding members of the Fuzhou YMCA.[126]

Protestants and the Progressive Elite

In the cases of the Anti-Opium Society, the anti-American boycott, the reform societies, and the YMCA, it is clear that Chinese Protestants were able to make common cause with the progressive elite in the Fuzhou area. On the one hand, Chinese Protestants saw in these movements an opportunity to join with non-Christians to work for social changes that Protestants had long cherished—and to strengthen the association between Protestant belief and modernity in the minds of those non-Christians. On the other hand, the acceptance of Chinese Protestant involvement by the progressive elite signifies a remarkable shift in elite attitudes toward Christianity and toward Chinese converts to it, at least in cosmopolitan centers like Fuzhou. The change was both in societal attitudes toward Protestants and in the way Protestants presented themselves and their religion to society. Even if we cannot say precisely whether their acceptance as part of the progressive elite was due to their religion, incidental to their religion, or in spite of their religion, we can certainly contend that it was inseparable from it. By this time the Protestants had been a highly visible presence in Fuzhou for over fifty years. Their buildings were local landmarks. Their schools were among the largest in the city (the Anglo-Chinese College remained *the* largest school in the province until at least 1907),[127] and their hospitals were likewise highly visible and respected. Protestant publications, among them the first periodicals and newspapers published in Fuzhou, which progressive Chinese were now emulating, and other works criticizing many of the cultural practices the progressive elite themselves now denounced, had circulated widely in the city for decades. In short, it was well known to the residents of the Fuzhou area that Protestants had long been trying to address many of the specific problems with which the progressives were now concerned, and this gave them credibility.

Moreover, the association of Chinese Protestants with the Western world had become more a positive asset than a stigma in the minds of their progressive compatriots. In this time of discussion of constitutions, parliaments, and national strength, educated Chinese Protestants were believed to have insights to share — why else would they be designated to speak on behalf of the reform societies, or invited to address the crowd at functions of the elite-led Anti-Opium Society? As one missionary put it in 1910, "Many of the influential men of Foochow have turned from a spirit of hatred and opposition to Christianity to a feeling of friendliness and sympathy, and some to a spirit of earnest inquiry after the truth. The active part which the church has taken in the reform movements . . . has won their approval and favor, and has helped to bring this class into closer touch with the church."[128]

Beyond the level of articulated moral and social ideas, it appears that on a less tangible plane there was an identification of things Western with modernity and strength, from which Chinese Protestants doubtless benefited. This can be seen in the imitation of Western architecture and purchase of Western-style furniture and decorations by the rich, or in the six-day week with Sunday off instituted in the modern schools in the city.[129] Similarly, the Shuobao she, a revolutionary-run propaganda society affiliated with the Qiaonan Society which made public presentations on social reform and political topics, followed a seven-day schedule, giving its presentations every Saturday afternoon.[130] It can also be seen in the enthusiasm of the Anti-Opium Society and the reform societies for publishing constitutions and electing their office-holders by ballot, or in the pervasive language of nationalism. In seeking to build China into a strong, modern nation, progressive Chinese drew freely on the models of the Western powers and Japan, and in that climate it was easy for Christianity to be accepted as part of the model.

Turning to the Protestants themselves, we can see that they were well equipped to take a place in these events. They had long experience with voluntary associations, the church itself being one. As we saw in the discussion of church government in Chapter 1, each of the Protestant denominations had a formal constitutional structure, with officers, constitutions, committees, regular meetings, and voting. Furthermore, the Protestants were naturally familiar with making and listening to speeches, whether in buildings or on busy streets, and with the production and distribution of printed matter for popular consumption. As we have also seen, and contrary to the common image of Chinese Christians as deracinated, the religious adherence of Chinese Protestants was not in conflict with a nationalism that was critical of the Western powers, but in fact gave them a supranational standpoint for that criticism that could actually add a dimension to the arguments of their secular compatriots. In sum, in this time of cosmopolitan borrowings, Chinese Protestant professionals in Fuzhou, with their cosmopolitan background and progressive social outlook, were perfectly situated to enter the mainstream of Chinese progressive nationalism.

3

"Welcoming a New China": Protestants in Late Qing Politics

The church's principal aim is to save human souls, while that of the Provincial Assembly is to free the citizenry from the cruel harm of despotism, but the effect of both is the salvation of the nation, one in the future and one in the present.

— *Chen Zhilin, Vice-President of the Fujian Provincial Assembly, 1909*

On November 17, 1909, a distinguished group of Fujian notables made their way south through the bustling streets of Fuzhou and its suburbs, crossed the long stone bridge over the Min River, and came at last to the rented premises of the Fuzhou city YMCA (fig. 3.1). These men, sixty out of the seventy-five members of the newly elected Fujian Provincial Assembly, had come to a reception at the joint invitation of the YMCA and the Foochow Annual Conference of the Methodist Episcopal Church, the meeting of which coincided with the inaugural session of the assembly.[1] On reaching the YMCA building around three in the afternoon, the guests were welcomed to the strains of a brass band (*junyue*), shown around the premises, and photographed, before being served refreshments inside the building.

Fig. 3.1. Sedan chairs and foot traffic crossing the Bridge of Ten Thousand Ages, Fuzhou, in the late Qing. Methodist Collection, Drew University, Madison, New Jersey.

Leaving the YMCA, the assembly members, again accompanied by a brass band, were conducted the short distance to the Church of Heavenly Peace, in which an audience of over one thousand people had already assembled, consisting of YMCA members, Methodist missionaries, preachers, laypeople, and male and female students from the Methodist schools nearby. As the honored guests entered the church, "Western music" (*xiyue,* presumably from the church organ or piano) took over from the brass band while the visitors were conducted to their seats. Words of welcome and a musical presentation followed, after which representatives of the assembly made speeches and representatives of the YMCA and the church responded.

Welcoming the guests on behalf of the church, the Reverend Yu Shuxin, one of the Methodist members of the Qiaonan Society, aptly expressed the excitement not only of Protestants but also of all progressive Chinese at the new era of participatory politics that the creation of the provincial assemblies heralded: "Our welcoming you here today can also be said to be welcoming a new Fujian, indeed a new China, and so we respectfully say, " 'Long live the Provincial Assembly, long live constitutional government, long live China!' " Following the speeches, the gathering proceeded (accompanied again by the brass

Fig. 3.2. YMCA and Methodist reception for the Fujian Provincial Assembly, November 17, 1909. Huang Naishang is at the center of the fourth row, below the mustached man in suit and tie; Lin Changmin, queueless and bearded, is sixth from the right in the second row. Special Collections, Yale Divinity School Library.

band) to the campus of the Anglo-Chinese College, adjacent to the church, for another photo opportunity on its spacious assembly ground, followed by more refreshments and a festive brass band sendoff as the reception adjourned (fig. 3.2).[2]

Protestants and the Provincial Assembly

To understand the symbolism and assess the significance of this reception, we must place the opening of the Provincial Assembly in its context and examine the role of Protestants within it. In the summer of 1908 the Qing court, under pressure to establish constitutional government, announced a program to create elected representative assemblies at the county and provincial levels, to meet first in 1909. The provincial assemblies, which were to have a deliberative rather than a true legislative function, were intended as a transitional step toward the creation of a national parliament in 1917. Representatives to the assemblies were to be chosen by electoral colleges, which were in turn to be elected by men over twenty-five who met certain narrow financial and educational conditions. It has been estimated that the electorate thus created amounted to around a million men, less than 1 percent of males over twenty-five and less than 0.4 percent of the total population.[3]

The general picture of the historical role of the provincial assemblies is well known. Once created, the assemblies did not long remain satisfied with their deliberative role and sought to hold the provincial governments accountable to them in many policy areas. As Min Tu-ki argues, the assemblies were dominated by young reform-minded men with a modern educational background: "The provincial assemblies had become the rallying places for the enlightened sector."[4] Leaders of the Fujian Provincial Assembly were prominent in the movement of late 1909 and 1910 petitioning the court to speed up the establishment of a national parliament, two of them serving as president and secretary of the conference of provincial representatives that drafted the initial petition in November 1909.[5] When a military revolt broke out in Wuchang on October 10, 1911, the assemblies in province after province took upon themselves the authority to declare their provinces independent of the Qing court and were thus instrumental in the overthrow of the dynasty and the establishment of the Republic of China.

Extant information on the formation and deliberations of the Fujian Provincial Assembly both confirms and adds detail to this general picture. The Fujian Provincial Library holds most of the published minutes of the 1909 session of the assembly and all of the 1910 minutes, plus a report of the preparatory office that registered voters for the assembly in 1908 and a list of the members of the assembly in 1909 and 1910. An examination of the issues debated by the assembly and of the role of the two Protestant assembly members in these debates shows the dominance of the rhetoric of nationalism and its connection to moral reform in this period and the way Protestants made common cause with the progressive elite.

The first point to note is that while the franchise for the election of 1909 was indeed very limited in its extent, it nevertheless extended well beyond the late imperial scholar-official elite. Indeed, its provisions appear to have recognized the changing nature of Chinese society, including the growth of a professional or service class in urban society. Specifically, men over twenty-five who were Fujian natives could vote if they met any one of five conditions: (1) having been involved in educational work or other public service (*qita gongyi shiwu*) in the province for a total of three years or more (not necessarily in an unbroken time span); (2) holding a graduation diploma from one of the new middle schools in China or the equivalent abroad; (3) holding the civil *gongsheng* degree or higher under the old classical examination system;[6] (4) having held substantive office at the seventh civil or fifth military grade or higher (and not been impeached and deprived of office); (5) having investments or capital of five thousand dollars or more in the province. Excluded from the franchise were Buddhist, Taoist, and other religious clergy (including Christian ministers) and anyone connected to opium use or prostitution.[7]

Clearly, some of these conditions were designed to allow politically active men in modern professional jobs — the sort of men who were active in the reform societies — to vote. The first condition in particular was quite elastic. Would three years' membership in the Qiaonan Society for Public Welfare (*gongyi*) have been accepted as "other public service" (*gongyi shiwu*)? Certainly many of the students returned from Japan would have qualified under condition 2, although mission school graduates, even of the eight-year secondary "colleges," probably would not have qualified on educational grounds, because mission schools had no status acknowledged by the Chinese government.[8] Even this, however, would have depended on the inclinations of the province's Provincial Assembly Preparatory Office, which interpreted the regulations and determined which individuals met the eligibility criteria.[9] The fifth condition might have been met by some of the wealthier compradors and commercial figures, as well as members of the more traditional scholar-official-landholding clans. Restrictive though it was, therefore, the franchise of 1909 extended the realm of legitimate political involvement beyond the old degree holders to the new social groups that were already claiming a political role for themselves through the voluntary societies discussed in Chapter 2.

The Fujian Provincial Assembly had seventy-two elected members, plus three appointed from the Banner garrison in Fuzhou. A published list of the representatives gives the names, county, age, rank, and address of each of the initial seventy-five members, and of six more who were elected subsequently to fill vacancies arising in the assembly.[10] From the data given on these eighty-one men, the most striking aspect of the provincial assembly was its youthfulness. Over half (forty-two men) of the representatives were aged forty-one or under (the youngest being thirty years old, the youngest eligible age for representatives as laid down in the regulations for the assemblies), and only 10 percent (eight men) were over the age of fifty-five. Three-quarters of the representatives were in their thirties and forties, including the president and the two vice-presidents of the body.

The other striking fact about the list is the near-total absence of really high-ranking men. While Frederic Wakeman states that the assemblies were "naturally dominated by the higher gentry," in the Fujian assembly there were only three *jinshi* degree holders, and two of these were among the four men elected by the assembly to represent Fujian in the newly created National Assembly, which was convened in October 1910.[11] Thus, by the 1910 session only one *jinshi* remained in the Fujian Provincial Assembly. The president, the two vice-presidents, and the most active members of the assembly were by and large holders of the *juren* degree, which was in theory a qualification for government office, but not often so in practice by the end of the Qing. *Juren* holders totaled twenty-five, or 31 percent, of the representatives. Below them were twenty men (25 percent) with various grades of *gongsheng* status (eleven regular and nine irregular), and twenty-eight (35 percent) with the lower-ranked *shengyuan* titles.[12] Finally, four representatives are listed only with honorary or purchased ranks, and one is listed as a graduate from an accelerated railway program in Japan. The composition of the Fujian assembly was thus broadly in line with that of the other provincial assemblies, although with more *juren* holders and fewer *jinshi* than average.[13]

In fact, the listing of the status of each representative according to the examination system abolished five years before was already something of an anachronism by 1910, when this list was published, and the credibility of many of the representatives must have rested on something other than their examination status. Certainly this would be true for the thirty-two men who are listed as holding *shengyuan* titles or no degree title, since *shengyuan* were not qualified either to vote or to be elected under the regulations governing the assemblies. These men, composing over 40 percent of the assembly members, clearly qualified for election on some other basis than their degree status.

Although biographical data are not available for all of them, some examples can be cited to show how misleading degree status alone can be. One of the youngest and in nominal terms lowest-ranking of the representatives, Lin Lucun, a thirty-one-year-old *shengyuan* from Anxi County, was actually a ten-year veteran of reformist politics, author (in association with Huang Naishang) of a noted memorial on reform of the Chinese language during the ill-fated reform movement of 1898, who had since worked in education in Guangdong and south Fujian and had traveled in Japan, Taiwan, Southeast Asia, Europe, and America. Presumably his formal qualification for election was his educational service. Lin was one of the most active members of the assembly.[14] Another *shengyuan*, Hong Hongru, was actually the head of the Xiamen Chamber of Commerce and presumably qualified under the property clause.[15] It is likely that a considerable proportion of the younger representatives had studied in Japan, as so many elite men of their generation had, and that the education in modern government which they had gained there rather than their degree title was their true qualification for office in the eyes of those who voted for them.[16]

For all these reasons, the question of whether the late Qing assemblies were dominated by "lower gentry" or "higher gentry," debated by some scholars, seems to me irrelevant as far as Fujian is concerned.[17] Predominant in the Fujian Assembly were young men in their thirties and early forties whose status came not from the old degree system but from new forms of educational and political qualification. In this sense, the Provincial Assembly must be regarded as a truly innovative institution, giving a foothold within the government structure for the new political dynamism that had been displayed in the organization of voluntary associations and political mobilization for reformist and nationalist goals in Fuzhou since 1902.[18]

The extent to which the Fujian Provincial Assembly was an outlet for entirely new political energies becomes very clear when the actual proposals debated and passed by the assembly are examined. A great number of these related to curbing the encroachments of the foreign powers on China and to strengthening and modernizing the administrative structure of the Chinese state (often in ways that would strengthen the hand of local progressive elites in the governing process).[19] The two goals of modernizing the state and curbing foreign encroachment were of course not separate but interrelated, and in many cases also intersected with the social reform aims that were characteristic of the progressive elite.

In the first session of the assembly, which met from October 14 to November 25, 1909, resolutions were passed on restructuring the education system, modernizing the police force, quelling the growing problems of banditry and piracy, and fostering industrial and commercial enterprises. Detailed measures on curbing foreign ownership of land in China and preventing interference by foreigners in lawsuits were debated and passed. Social reform topics such as opium, gambling, and footbinding were debated, and a resolution was passed requiring each county magistrate to organize a Natural Foot Society (*tianzu hui*) in conjunction with local gentry and to register a constitution for the society with the provincial government. This resolution shows a common tendency in the proposals debated by the assembly: having discovered the power of voluntary societies to effect social reform, the assembly members sought to make voluntary societies *in*voluntary — and thus to formalize, with modern tools such as written constitutions, the traditionally flexible relationship between magistrates and local elites, to the advantage of the latter.[20] Many proposals dealt with strengthening and broadening education in the province, and the relationship of education to nation-building was made explicit in the language of at least one measure which advocated setting up schools for women so that women would have patriotic spirit "as they do in England and America."[21]

Huang Naishang in the Provincial Assembly

To give a clearer view of the operation of the Provincial Assembly and the Protestant involvement in it, let us focus on the two known Protestant members, Huang Naishang and Chen Zhilin, both of whom played prominent roles in the body. Huang's career up to his passing the provincial examination for the *juren* degree in 1894 was recounted in the first chapter of this book. The following year he went to the capital to take the metropolitan examination and came into contact with the Cantonese reformer Kang Youwei and his circle, and he returned to the capital at the time of the Hundred Days reform movement in 1898. When the conservative backlash against Kang and the young reformers broke out, Huang left the capital to avoid being caught in the crackdown. Moving to Singapore in 1899, he spent time traveling through the British- and Dutch-ruled colonies of Southeast Asia, and in 1900 he signed a contract with Rajah Charles Brooke of Borneo to procure Chinese settlers for an area of Sarawak. In a time of agricultural difficulty at home the promise of fertile and abundant farming land was an attractive lure, and Huang was able to recruit hundreds of farming families within a few months, mostly from the Methodist churches in Huang's home county, Minqing, and neighboring Gutian and Yongfu Counties.[22] Also in 1900 he met Sun Yatsen in Singapore, and by the time he left Sarawak to take up residence again in China in late 1904 he was a committed revolutionary.[23]

Huang Naishang is a perfect illustration of the danger of imputing the class character or motivations of provincial assembly members on the basis of formal attributes such as age, degree rank, or place of residence, as so much of the literature has done.[24] Contrary to the assumption of some that most "constitutionalists" must have been conservative because they held "upper gentry" degrees and were in their forties or older, Huang, a sixty-year-old *juren,* was also the only member of the Revolutionary Alliance in the assembly until the election of Zheng Zuyin (the head of the Fujian branch of the Revolutionary Alliance, and a longtime associate of Huang) to fill a vacancy in early 1910.[25] He was also in all likelihood the one man with the most varied life experience and educational background in the assembly.

His credibility as a political thinker and an authority on reform topics was probably based mostly on his work in education in Fuzhou and Minqing, and even more on his work with magazines and newspapers in Fujian and Singapore. In 1896 he had founded the first newspaper in Fujian, *Fubao,* and his essays in that paper had touched on a wide variety of social and political topics, from concrete statecraft themes such as reform of the monetary system and the reasons for the decline of the Fujian tea trade to more abstract topics like how to nurture talent and how to apply Western learning.[26] His connection to the 1898 reformers was well known in Fujian, and his revolutionary leanings were also apparently widely rumored.[27] An American missionary described him rather colorfully as "the most eloquent man in the province, with a look and carriage that reminds one of [the British Liberal statesman] Gladstone."[28] His wide experience was recognized in his election by his fellow representatives to the standing committee of the assembly in 1909 and to other important review panels (subcommittees that handled much of the real legislative work of the assemblies) in 1909 and 1910.[29]

Huang Naishang was one of the representatives most active in proposing administrative reform measures, especially during the assembly's first session. As reflected in the minutes of the 1909 and 1910 sessions, Huang's proposals all hinged on state-building as the means to solve problems relating to social morality, rural hardships, and foreign intrusion. His proposals tended to be far-reaching and detailed — often too much so for his fellow assembly members. For example, in 1909, Huang proposed the abolition of Chinese government gunboats on inland waterways and their replacement with a modern water police force, to be trained in a new school for water police. This was intended to combat the problem of piracy on the rivers and coastal waterways of Fujian (the safety of river transport was, it should be remembered, crucial to the livelihood of producers and traders in his home county). The panel reviewing the proposal softened it considerably, recommending waiting for graduates from a new Police School already established rather than taking immediate steps to recruit and train a water police force. The amended version was attacked as too slow by supporters of the original measure.[30]

Early in the first session of the assembly, Huang also put forward a proposal to revive agriculture and forestry in Fujian that centered on dividing the province into four sectors, each with an agricultural school, and creating a new bureaucratic agency to foster farming and to police the use of forest resources. This proposal was in response to the drastic deforestation of the Fujian highlands due to the burgeoning interregional timber trade of the preceding decades, with which Huang was familiar from his extensive travels through the province. The reviewers of this proposal appear to have considered it unrealistic (as it probably was, given the overstretched finances of the provincial government), and suggested allocating these areas of responsibility to existing officials.[31] They also noted that the division of the province into four sectors ran counter to the conventional administrative system (by which Fujian was divided into nine prefectures and two departments).[32] A second review weakened the measure still further. Resorting to the expedient, evident in so many of the assembly's deliberations, of using elite-led public associations as a quasi bureaucracy, the amended version proposed that rural gentry and village elders in every county be required to form agricultural associations (*nonghui*), which would be responsible for giving lectures on forestry and agriculture and exhorting people to plant trees.[33]

The "unorthodox" idea of dividing the province into four administrative sectors and creating new specialist bureaucracies for specific objectives is evident in another proposal in which Huang Naishang was involved. In the 1910 session Huang and his Revolutionary Alliance associate and new assembly member, Zheng Zuyin, proposed a measure to stamp out opium cultivation in the province within certain time limits for each area. This very detailed proposal, with twenty-eight articles under nine subheadings, sought to create a government-financed bureaucracy directly accountable to the governor-general but with an institutionalized advisory role for reformist members of the local elite. With branches in every county, this bureaucracy was to be similar in intent to the existing Anti-Opium Society, but with a crucial difference: whereas each rural branch of the existing society was simply a local voluntary association, with loose ties to the central branch in Fuzhou but no official status, as a state organ the new body would have the capacity to enforce the opium prohibition.[34] The reviewers felt that the expense of the program was prohibitive, however, for it required the appointment of a head for an opium prohibition office in each of the more than sixty counties in Fujian, each to receive a salary of forty taels per month from the provincial government.[35] Ironically, the eventual outcome of the review process was in effect to subordinate the existing public anti-opium societies and their finances to the county magistrates, rather than to create a well-funded bureaucracy which could bypass or override what the reformers regarded as the corrupt and inefficient structure of local government. Zheng Zuyin, the co-drafter of the original proposal, spoke strongly against the amended version for this reason.[36]

Huang's non-elite background and his intimate knowledge of rural conditions in the upland counties along the Min River brought him into conflict with some of his fellow representatives in the 1910 session. One of the functions of the assembly was to receive petitions and appeals from citizens. For example, in 1909 a petition signed by over two hundred members of the elite in Xinghua Prefecture requested the assembly to take action against the activities of Standard Oil and certain German companies in the prefecture, and in 1910 forty petitioners from Luoyuan County complained of irregularities in the election of the county assembly.[37] Also in 1910 the assembly received a petition from (or on behalf of) tenant farmers in the four inland counties of Fuzhou Prefecture—Minqing, Gutian, Yongfu, and Houguan—complaining of the steep rents exacted by landowners in their counties. In accordance with normal procedure, the petition was submitted for review to a panel of assembly members, and the reviewers in turn submitted a report to the assembly. In this case the review panel found little merit in the petitioners' complaint. In the normal routine of the assembly, a vote would have been taken approving the findings of the reviewers, and there the matter would have ended. However, Huang Naishang objected strenuously to the review panel's report, pointing out that none of the reviewers was from the four counties in question (though all were from Fuzhou Prefecture, they were from the city itself or the more prosperous coastal counties; Huang, of course, was from Minqing).[38] Drawing on his own life experience and knowledge of the region, Huang presented a very different picture from that given by the reviewers:

> There may well be no equal anywhere to the suffering undergone by tenant farmers in these four counties. In all my travels through many provinces I have never seen the like of the ruthless maltreatment of tenants there. Landlords will take 70 or 80 per cent [of the harvest], leaving only 20 or 30 percent for the tenant. Those who are termed "upper peasants" have a yearly intake of no more than twenty or thirty piculs (*dan*).[39] Once the costs of seed grain, fertilizer, and the rental of work animals are subtracted from this sum, do you think that what remains will be enough to sustain the farmer's own life, not to mention support a wife and children? In my opinion the reviewers have no concept of these conditions . . . and so I oppose this report.[40]

Two of the reviewers responded to Huang's criticism. The first argued that Huang was exaggerating the hardships faced by tenants in these counties, and that in any case the proportion of the harvest claimed by the landlords was clearly spelled out in the contracts between landlords and tenants and accepted by the latter; therefore, tenants had no right to complain about it. The second said that 20 percent of the harvest was a perfectly adequate proportion of the harvest for tenants to receive, and that because tenants cheated the landlords by skimming off part of the harvest as it was gathered, they actually took in more than the contracted proportion.

Huang spoke again to refute these points. The first speaker's reasoning showed, he said, that he "does not understand that tenants rely on the land to live, and have no recourse against harsh treatment by their landlords." The second speaker simply reflected the widespread elite disdain for peasants, which was precisely the reason the petition had been submitted. Huang moved that, rather than accepting the report submitted by the reviewers, the assembly should refer the original petition back to the local self-government associations in the four counties for investigation and action, and his proposal was carried by the assembly.[41]

It would be possible to interpret this exchange in class terms, as bearing out the judgment of many scholars about the dominance in the provincial assemblies of conservative members of the traditional landed elite or the emerging bourgeoisie. It certainly appears that the five reviewers of the petition identified with landlords more than with tenants. One of them, Li Funan, was a prominent commercial figure in the city and a leader of the Fuzhou Chamber of Commerce, so he was probably wealthy and a landlord himself.[42] Huang Naishang, on the other hand, had firsthand experience of grinding poverty, both in his youth in rural Minqing and more recently in traversing precisely these four counties to recruit settlers for his Sarawak experiment.[43] His mention of the cost of supporting a wife and family also drew on his own experience, for Huang's father, the oldest of four brothers, had been the only one of his siblings who could afford to marry and raise children.[44] As a revolutionary. Huang was doubtless additionally influenced by the antipathy toward landlords and the commitment to equalization of landholdings that was part of the platform of the Revolutionary Alliance.[45]

However, there are aspects of this incident which tell against a simple interpretation of the Provincial Assembly as representing the class interests of the elite, whether "gentry" or "bourgeoisie." For one thing, Huang Naishang's intervention was sufficiently persuasive to his fellow representatives for his alternative motion to be carried, which surely means that a majority of representatives were at least prepared to entertain the possibility that something was seriously wrong with the customary state of social relations in the countryside, at least in these four counties. Second, whatever the chances of the local assemblies in each county being more sympathetic than the reviewers to the plight of tenants in their counties, that this petition could even be submitted to and considered by these new representative bodies is most significant. The creation of the local, provincial, and national assemblies provided for the first time a legal forum for the public consideration of citizens' grievances, one to which even the poorest peasants could have access. Where previously the only recourse for tenants aside from violent protest was to negotiate with their landlords, either directly or through local mediators such as lineages, they could now bypass these localized channels and bring their plight instead to the attention of the powerful in the provincial capital. Moreover, in doing so they could present the issue in a generalized form as a problem for rural society writ large in four counties, completely transcending the prevailing local and personal framework for addressing landlord-tenant relations. This must surely be seen as a significant change, and underlines the point that, looked at on their own terms, the provincial assemblies, for all their limitations, were a startling and far-reaching innovation in Chinese political life.

Chen Zhilin in the Provincial Assembly

The other Protestant member in the Fujian Provincial Assembly was one of its two vice-presidents, Chen Zhilin (Zhiting, born in 1878). Chen, who at age thirty in 1909 was one of the youngest members of the assembly, was a native of south Fujian, but he had been educated in Fuzhou at the Anglo-Chinese College, and his family seems to have been in business in Fuzhou. Chen earned *shengyuan* status in 1896, and in 1903 he both graduated from the Anglo-Chinese College and sat for and earned the *juren* degree in what turned out to be the final administration of the ancient examination in the province.[46] After graduation Chen spent some time in charge of a new government school in Anxi County in southern Fujian before traveling through British Malaya and the Dutch East Indies in 1904 and 1905. Returning to China, he again worked in education, and in 1909 he was elected to the Provincial Assembly. The assembly members in turn elected him as one of two vice-presidents of the body at the opening of its first session.[47]

It is not clear from the sketchy biographies available what qualities in Chen Zhilin impressed his fellow representatives enough for him to be elected to one of the three highest offices of the assembly. Being a *juren* was certainly one factor, since the president, the other vice-president, and many of the most active members held the *juren* degree. We can speculate that Chen was at least a passable orator, given that public speaking in Chinese and English was a regular component of the education given at the Anglo-Chinese College. Because many of the representatives had a background in educational reform, Chen's work as an educator in the new-style government schools no doubt added to his credibility. His experience abroad may have been important, also. Chen's travels in Southeast Asia probably meant he had developed contacts among the Chinese communities there; the circumstances of the Chinese in Southeast Asia became one focus of attention for the Provincial Assembly, as we shall see below. Japanese biographies indicate that Chen's family was a wealthy and influential one with extensive commercial interests in Fuzhou, apparently specializing in banking and salt.[48] The records of the Provincial Assembly indicate that Chen functioned as the assembly's expert on provincial finance, often interrogating the governor-general's representatives on financial matters; this impression is borne out by his becoming the head of the provincial Department of Finance (Caizheng bu, later Caizheng si) directly after the 1911 revolution and retaining the post for several years.

A biography of 1918 describes Chen Zhilin as a political moderate, but this probably refers more to the Republican political context than to his place on the spectrum in 1909.[49] In fact, Chen Zhilin was one of the most fiery and confrontational of the "young Turks" in the Fujian Provincial Assembly. In the stormy confrontations with the provincial government over the assembly's jurisdiction during the 1910 session, Chen Zhilin and his fellow vice-president, Liu Chongyou (who had become nationally prominent in the parliamentary petition movement the year before), were the most tenacious and blunt of the assembly members in their interrogation of the governor-general's representatives.[50] Moreover, as was the case with many of the ardent constitutionalists following the failure of the petition movement, Chen was at least in partial sympathy with the revolutionaries, though apparently not one himself.[51] For example, during the 1910 session Chen sponsored a resolution which in effect covered up for revolutionaries in Lianjiang County by asserting that the government, which had received accusations that a revolutionary association had been formed there, had mistaken the name of a commercial enterprise for the term *guangfu hui* (literally, "restoration society" — a reference to restoring Han rule to China).[52]

While we can only speculate on who voted for Chen Zhilin and why and on how his Christianity and his mission school background were perceived by his peers, we do know how Chen Zhilin himself related his election as Provincial Assembly member and vice-president to his Christianity. In his speech to the 1909 reception given for the assembly by the YMCA and the Methodist church, Chen referred to his education at the Anglo-Chinese College and his involvement in the YMCA and predicted that "as our nation comes to recognize the value of the church schools, the day will come when you gentlemen [of the church] will also be elected" to public office, as he had been. Describing the mission of the Protestant church as "reforming society, raising the morality of the people, and developing their knowledge," Chen drew a parallel between these goals and those of the Provincial Assembly.[53] To be sure, "the church's principal aim is to save human souls, while that of the Provincial Assembly is to free the citizenry from the cruel harm of despotism, but the effect of both is the salvation of the nation, one in the future and one in the present," he stated. Moreover, Chen declared the church to be the ultimate, though unrecognized, source of the political innovations in China:

> Without external stimulation our country would not now be on the verge of establishing constitutional government. The opening of China to foreign commerce gave access to the church, and the church thereupon [became] the midwife [literally, "grandmother"] of reform in our country (*woguo weixin zhi zumu*). For instance, the opening of modern schools, the founding of news [publishing] houses, and the establishment of constitutional government, although they may appear unrelated, are in fact all products of the church (*jiaohui zhi chanwu ye*). If some among the people [still] regard [Christianity]

as heterodox (*yiduan*), this is merely because its teachings do not accord with vulgar notions (*bu yu su tuo*). If the nation grants religious liberty to the people, the church will flourish even more in the future; if not, I fear the [nation's] future will still not be without obstacles. The present efforts of the church, the YMCA, and their schools will certainly bear good fruit in the future. Be sure not to underestimate yourselves: while the laws of the nation mold [outward] behavior (*fan renshen*), the laws of the church mold the heart (*fan renxin*). The two are like the right hand and the left hand, which must coordinate with each other to accomplish anything. Thus the church should diligently play its distinctive role, and the joy of religious liberty will surely be attained. Then, I am sure, the day will come when we who are guests at the church's reception today will become those who need no invitation, who are as close to the church as water mingling with milk, or as family members gathering together. This is my hope; let us exert ourselves together to attain it![54]

It is evident from this speech that Chen Zhilin situated the Provincial Assembly and his role as a Christian in it within a particular narrative of modern Chinese history, according to which external pressure had been the decisive catalyst in bringing about progress in China, progress in which the Christian (at least, Protestant) church had played a leading role. Barriers to this progress were due chiefly to the persistence of "vulgar notions" among the Chinese people, and to the lack of legal protection for religious liberty.[55] Now that constitutional government was within sight, the church could anticipate the dawn of an era of religious liberty and untrammeled progress in which the unique and indispensable role of the church in public life — cultivating a moral citizenry — could be fully exercised.

Evident in Chen's speech are significant echoes of American Protestant assumptions about the role of religion in the political order. The American revolution, in vesting sovereignty in "the people," implied that "the people" must remain virtuous in order to ensure the continued stability of the republic. As the Massachusetts constitution of 1780 put it, "The happiness of a people, and the good order and preservation of civil government, essentially depend upon piety, religion, and morality."[56] Religious leaders in the early years of the United States took advantage of this concern with virtue by equating Christian faith with the popular morality necessary for the survival of the republic — both by urging Christian adherence and by warning of the dire consequences of its absence.[57]

Given Chen Zhilin's statement that the opening up of China to international commerce marked the beginning of China's progress, one might expect Chen to be less nationalistically concerned than his contemporaries about foreign economic and political pressures on China. Nothing could be further from the truth. In the deliberations of the Fujian Provincial Assembly, we find Chen Zhilin (and Huang Naishang) taking the lead in efforts to curb the rights and powers of the foreign powers in China and in resolutions criticizing the colonial regimes of Southeast Asia and Taiwan for their treatment of the Chinese under their jurisdiction. Also, most interestingly for our purposes, Chen Zhilin even drafted and introduced a measure to limit the rights of those very Christian missions to which he attributed such beneficial results.

For example, in the 1909 session of the assembly, Chen Zhilin and Huang Naishang were both involved in a proposal to revise the treaty of 1903 by which the island of Gulangyu in the Xiamen harbor had been ceded to the control of its foreign residents.[58] Chen and Huang were also among the six sponsors of a resolution entitled "Proposals for Protecting Chinese Overseas," which was highly critical of the attitudes of foreign governments and people toward the Chinese and called for a team of four assembly members to be sent at government expense to review the conditions and laws under which Fujianese lived in Southeast Asia and Taiwan.[59] The provincial government declined to act on this proposal, asserting that the question of Fujianese abroad was outside the purview of the assembly.[60] In the 1910 session, therefore, when Chen Zhilin, along with the president (Gao Dengli) and the other vice-president (Liu Chongyou) of the assembly, sponsored a proposal in response to a petition concerning the mistreatment by the colonial authorities of Chinese in the Dutch East Indies, they did not propose that the Provincial Assembly itself act on the allegations, but that it petition the national Ministry of Foreign Affairs to investigate them.[61]

The discussions in the Fujian Provincial Assembly relating to the Chinese abroad seem to have been led by men who had themselves traveled in Southeast Asia and had thus had direct exposure to Western colonial administrations and their attitude toward the Chinese. Chen Zhilin and Huang Naishang were, of course, in this category, as was Lin Lucun, another sponsor of "Proposals for Protecting Chinese Overseas" in 1909. This suggests that travel in Southeast Asia may have been a radicalizing experience for Chinese of this generation, perhaps because seeing colonial rule firsthand made the European assumption of racial superiority more obvious than it was in the more ambiguous foreign presence in China itself. Certainly Huang Naishang became more radical during his years in Singapore and Sarawak, and we have already seen that Huang was not blind to the racial prejudice of foreigners in China, including missionaries. It is significant that the Fujianese communities in several locations abroad (specifically Rangoon, Jogjakarta, Surakarta, Kobe, Yokohama, and Nagasaki) were represented during the sessions of the Provincial Assembly by eighteen nonvoting representatives (*canyiyuan*).[62]

Given our interest in how Chen Zhilin's Christianity intersected with his political activism, another episode from the deliberations of the Fujian Provincial Assembly is in many respects the most intriguing. During the 1909 session of the assembly, Chen presented a "Proposal on Appropriate Measures [to Ensure] the Peaceful Coexistence of Christian Converts and the People" (*Tuochou minjiao xiang'an banfa tiyi an*), seconded by twenty-four other members, all "from areas where the people and the Christians are not at peace." Although the document opened with a perfunctory mention of the good intentions of Christian missions, in overall tenor it was highly critical of the behavior of missionaries and Chinese Christian clergy. The ongoing tensions between Christians and non-Christians in China, the document stated, were chiefly due to the "many wicked people" (*youmin*) who had joined the Protestant and Catholic churches and the many missionaries who were prepared to extend protection to such people.

Chen's proposal to remedy this situation contained two parts. The first clarified the status of foreign missionaries vis-à-vis Chinese officials, reiterating that missionaries had no formal status correlating to the various ranks of the Chinese bureaucracy.[63] The second and longer part of the proposal dealt with the issue of interference in litigation by missionaries and Chinese clergy. The proposal reviewed the history of Chinese government decrees prohibiting involvement by missionaries in any legal disputes other than religious persecution and forbidding partiality (toward Christians, due to pressure from missionaries or the fear of such pressure) in the administration of justice on the part of magistrates or their subordinates. It went on to note that despite these clear injunctions, magistrates were still unable to implement the law unhindered. The principal reason, the document stated, why missionaries continued to interpose themselves into lawsuits was that Chinese clergy misled them and incited them to it. However, Chinese clergy were commoners, and therefore legal cases involving them were within the power of the magistrate to adjudicate according to the law; any intervention by missionaries should be referred by the magistrate to the provincial authorities.

Chen Zhilin's proposal concluded with four specific measures, which are interesting not only for what they reveal about the extent of the problem, but also (in the case of the fourth measure) as another instance of the progressive elite seeking to use their newfound political activism to restructure the balance of power in local government for state-building ends. The four measures read as follows:

> 1. Private communications from missionaries are not to be regarded as formal documents and taken into account in resolving disputes unless they are

included in official consular documents transmitted through the [provincial] Yangwu ju [Foreign Affairs Bureau].

2. No portion of a public or private document should employ the term *jiaomin* [Christians].[64]

3. The commercial treaties only specify the right to rent public property and contain no clear language allowing for the purchase of private property [by foreigners]. Let the local officials be instructed to investigate the amount of public property owned by each church, according to the regulations of the Board [of Foreign Affairs] and compile the information into a statistical table to facilitate the resolution of legal disputes over public property.

4. In cases where Christian clergy, whether foreign or Chinese, intervene in legal cases among the people or disturb local order, the reform societies (*gongyi tuanti*) must bring [the situation] to the attention of the local magistrate, who should at once rigorously negotiate it on the basis of the treaties and not evade responsibility after a show of action.[65]

The reviewers proposed no change to the original wording of the first part regarding the status of missionaries. In the second part they kept the wording of the first, second, and fourth measures substantially the same while adding a request that the provincial government prepare a digest of the treaty rights of Christian missions and circulate it both to the officials in each locale and to the local self-government associations to use in preparing lectures on the subject, "lest the misunderstandings of ignorant people (*wuzhi xiaomin*) lead to disturbances."

It was on the thorny question of property, dealt with in the third of Chen's original four measures, that the reviewers made several revisions that strengthened the measure considerably. They specified that, according to instructions of the *Zongli yamen* dated Tongzhi 4 (1865), the purchase of land for churches by foreign missionaries was legal only if the wording of the deed of sale stated clearly that "the land sold is collective property to be used for a local church." If foreigners in the interior had bought property for private use, this was beyond the scope of the treaties and should still be forbidden. The reviewers reiterated the request that local authorities be instructed to investigate the property of each church and compile statistics on it, and they added a stipulation that property rented, as well as owned, by foreign missionaries should be registered in writing with the local government.

Last, the reviewers recommended an additional measure with rather far-reaching implications. They proposed that at the next population census, in addition to the ordinary population register (for tax purposes), Christians should be listed in a separate "Christian convert register," with one copy kept by the local self-government association and a duplicate one in the responsible yamen. Afterward, new converts should be entered into the register at the time they joined the church, "for convenience in investigation."⁶⁶

Presumably this last measure, rather than ending the sources of tension between Christians and non-Christians, which was the stated intention of Chen Zhilin's original proposal, would have institutionalized and perpetuated the distinction between Christians and "the people," to the detriment of the former. At any rate, when the amended proposal was debated clause by clause, Chen Zhilin moved that this clause was unnecessary and could be eliminated, and his motion passed. The amended proposal was passed without a second revision.⁶⁷

What can we conclude from these somewhat contradictory indications about Chen Zhilin's politics and his Christianity? Most basically, Chen's role in the Provincial Assembly underlines the general point that Chinese Protestants were capable of taking positions critical of foreign powers and of foreign missions in the name of nationalism. They could even advocate measures that were inimical to the interests of the missions, as with the property clauses in this proposal, which ran counter to the interpretation of the treaty rights of missions established in practice over the preceding decades. However, the contradiction between Chen's Christianity and his criticism of missionaries and Chinese pastors in the legislation examined above is to some extent more apparent than real. Protestant mission boards in the home countries had long recognized the problem of Chinese converting for financial gain or legal protection, and by this period their correspondence with missionaries in the field was peppered with exhortations to stay out of legal cases involving Chinese Christians. In part, this was a generational transition: entrenched older missionaries could be an obstacle to implementing a strict prohibition of interference in lawsuits, as we noted in Chapter 1 with regard to J. R. Wolfe of the CMS, who was convinced that his intervention or that of the Chinese clergy as "peace maker[s]" had "often prevented serious troubles" between converts and "their heathen neighbours."⁶⁸ American and British consuls in China were also increasingly critical of missionaries who created difficulties for them by interfering in legal cases, and refused to get involved except in clear cases of religious persecution.⁶⁹

As consuls and missionaries often found, however, the line between persecution and other causes of tension between Christians and non-Christians was a blurred one, and there were cases in which Chinese clergy claimed a status as de facto equivalents to the degree-holding literati, as was discussed in Chapter 1. This is presumably the background for the first section of Chen Zhilin's proposal, with its concern to clarify the rank of missionaries and Chinese clergy in relation to local officials: the proposal and the amended version repeatedly stated that "Chinese clergy are simply commoners." On the other hand, there had also been cases in Fujian in which Protestants had suffered abuse after no discernible provocation. From this point of view, Chen Zhilin's proposal is remarkable for its one-sidedness: responsibility for any and all tensions between Christians and non-Christians is laid at the feet of the former.

In view of this, it may be significant that Huang Naishang was not involved in this proposal, whether as a seconder or a reviewer, or even in the debate on it. As a youth of seventeen, back in 1866, Huang Naishang had become one of the first Protestant converts in his home district and had been ostracized and physically attacked as a result. He had served as a preacher himself for a time, and he retained a great respect for his mentors Nathan Sites and Xu Yang-mei.[70] In short, Huang Naishang, notwithstanding his progressive political views and his YMCA affiliation, knew firsthand the ambiguities and difficulties that faced Chinese Protestants and preachers in rural Fujian, and he had close ties of association and friendship with missionaries and Chinese preachers.

Chen Zhilin, by contrast, represented a more exclusively urban, progressive, YMCA style of Protestant Christianity. Because he graduated in January 1903, he had probably entered the Anglo-Chinese College around 1895, when the college was well established and beginning to attract enrollments from non-Christian commercial and degree-holding families in Fuzhou owing to the opportunities opened up by its bilingual education.[71] As stated earlier, Chen Zhilin was from a prominent business family, and it is reasonable to suppose that Chen's family was not Christian and that he converted sometime during his time at the Anglo-Chinese College. His primary religious affiliation seems to have been the YMCA, in which he served many years as a board member and as vice-president.

This background may explain why his proposal to the Provincial Assembly shows so little sympathy for the difficulties facing missionaries and Chinese preachers in rural Fujian. Chen's apparent disdain for semiliterate rural church members and clergy seems like a Protestant version of the more general elite suspicion of religious professionals in late imperial China, or of the disdain of urban modernizers in twentieth-century China for the "superstitions" of rural China.[72] Chen believed that Christianity would save the nation, but Christianity of a certain stamp: informed and informing, compatible with the best of Western scientific and political thought, and functioning to instill political and personal virtue. From this perspective, the messy complexity of disputes between Christians and non-Christians over scarce material and symbolic resources in the fractious society of the Fujian countryside would have seemed embarrassingly retrograde.

Progressive Politics and Elite Conversion: Lin Changmin

The convening of the provincial assemblies in the fall of 1909 provided an unprecedented platform for a new kind of political activism — petitioning the court in the name of "public opinion." In November 1909 representatives from sixteen of China's twenty-one provincial assemblies gathered in Shanghai to draft a petition urging the early convening of a national parliament. As mentioned above, the vice-president of the Fujian Provincial Assembly, Liu Chongyou, chaired this conference, and its secretary was Lin Changmin, general secretary of the Fujian assembly. As a result of this unprecedented meeting of elected representatives from most regions of the country, the petition was submitted to the throne on January 26, 1910. The court's response, released on the first day of the Chinese new year, rejected the petitioners' demands and censured them for their presumption in submitting the petition at all. Undeterred, the petitioners submitted a new petition pressing for the early establishment of a national parliament in the summer of 1910, with a claimed backing of 300,000 persons. The court rejected this petition also, and forbade the petitioners to raise the subject again. In October that year, however, the opening of the new National Assembly became the occasion for the presentation of a new petition, this time backed unanimously by the National Assembly, and by the governors and governors-general of several provinces, and with a claimed total of twenty-five million signatures. In response to this third petition, the court announced the curtailment of the probationary period, promising to convene a national parliament in 1913, instead of 1917 as originally planned.[73]

The petition movement of 1910 aroused public interest in fundamental political questions in a way never before seen or permitted in China. A British observer reported concerning the third petition that "this memorial and its probable reception by the Prince Regent, a question of purely internal politics, is the all-absorbing topic of conversation in all educated circles in the capital" — a statement that could have been echoed for Fuzhou. So much attention and so many hopes were fixed on the petition movement that the court's concession to the third petition, while it amounted to a partial victory for the petitioners, was immensely disappointing to the many who had hoped for a parliament to be convened immediately. In response, many of the provincial leaders of the constitutional movement became increasingly receptive to the idea of revolution.[74] In Fujian, Liu Chongyou and Lin Changmin approached the Qiaonan Society, in which revolutionaries were prominent, and suggested that the two groups cooperate in starting a newspaper with financial backing from members of the Provincial Assembly. This paper, staffed by Revolutionary Alliance members, was at times more radical in tone than its financial backers cared for. Nevertheless, it helps show the extent to which "constitutionalists" and "revolutionaries" were all united as nationalists and political progressives and could work together on that basis.[75]

As already mentioned, one of the key participants in these events, both in Fujian and nationally, was a young man named Lin Changmin, the general secretary (*shuji zhang*) of the Fujian Provincial Assembly. Lin's case gives us another instance of the intersection of Christianity with political life in Fuzhou. Lin (1876–1925), the son of a *jinshi* and Hanlin scholar, had been educated in English and Japanese before going to Japan, where he had graduated with honors in political economy from Waseda University in 1909. (Waseda University was founded by Okuma Shigenobu, the veteran leader of the "popular rights" movement of the 1880s in Japan, which had also used petitions and public mobilization to press for the establishment of a parliament and constitutional government. Okuma was an advocate of the British system of constitutional monarchy, a model rejected by the other leaders of Meiji Japan, and his liberal views were dominant at Waseda.)[76] In Japan, Lin had become a close associate of Liang Qichao, the exiled reformer of 1898, who was at that time the intellectual leader of the movement for constitutional government, and the two remained friends and political allies until Lin's death in 1925.[77] Returning to Fujian in 1909, Lin Changmin was appointed to the faculty of the new Provincial College of Law and Government (Fazheng xuetang) and also appointed general secretary of the assembly, upon the recommendation of fellow Waseda graduate Liu Chongyou, vice-president of the assembly.[78]

Lin Changmin's personality and his sophisticated knowledge of law and politics made him a natural leader. He was apparently highly idealistic, for he turned down a number of tempting offers of official appointment, reportedly because "they didn't offer the largest opportunity for unselfish service."[79] Like many Chinese students in Japan, he had cut off his queue and grown his hair (and a beard), and on his return to China he declined to adopt the queue again.[80] His political views were already evident during the reception described at the start of this chapter, which took place soon after the convening of the provincial assemblies in October 1909. At this event, in which Chen Zhilin and others spoke in exalted terms of the significance of the new era represented by the provincial assemblies, Lin Changmin struck a markedly more cautious note, stressing the difference between a true parliament and the provincial assemblies and projected National Assembly. Whereas the strong nation-states (*guojia shehui*) of the world all have national and local parliaments, Lin said, "our Provincial Assembly is no more than a special form of local self-government association. Small wonder, then, that we cannot stand up to other nations, despite our desire to do so!" Lin pointed out the absence of specific measures in the court's decree of the previous year announcing the intention to open a parliament in 1917, and, in a statement that foreshadows the petition movement's reliance on mobilizing public opinion, he stated that the implementation of that decree would depend on "the stage of development of the citizenry" (*guomin chengdu zhi gaoxia*).[81]

However, while Lin's political views were more realistic and tempered than those of Chen Zhilin, when he turned to the subject of the church, he made exactly the same connection as the Christian speakers had done between Christianity, morality, and citizenship. Adherence to the church results in a pure character, Lin stated, and "if the character is pure, then there is hope for constitutional government. This is not flattery on my part; it is a fact." In explaining how he envisaged the relationship between personal virtue and national life, Lin used a phrase drawn from a well-known passage in the ancient text *Zuozhuan* about a virtuous person's good name being remembered after death, but expanded it to apply to a whole society: "Now a society can avoid decay in the same way that an individual can have a life that does not decay (*bu xiu zhi shengming*): if I have a son, and my son has a son, and each prolongs virtue unbroken through the generations, continually perfecting it, is this not [the essence of] not decaying? Knowing this cannot fail to deepen our hope in the church."[82]

Given Lin Changmin's elite background and social prominence, it is small wonder that his baptism into the Methodist church early in 1910 created a stir in Fuzhou.[83] Lin had come into contact with Christianity through the work of the YMCA among Chinese students in Tokyo and had attended Bible classes there. One of the key influences in inducing him to consider Christianity had been a friendship formed with a man roughly his age, a YMCA secretary from his home city named Xu Shiguang (Hu Sie Guong); this Xu was a grandson of the Methodist preacher Xu Bomei and an 1898 graduate of the Anglo-Chinese College. On coming to Fuzhou in 1909, Lin made contact with the YMCA and sometimes had dinner at the home of its American secretary, even staying overnight on occasion. According to this man, Lin, "having the mind of a scholar and honestly wanting to know the real facts . . . began a scientific study of the Christian religion and a comparison of it with the other great religions systems [*sic*] now in China" and subsequently decided to be baptized. The night before his baptism he presented his "findings" in a lecture at the YMCA, which drew "the largest audience . . . we have had in the YMCA for two years."[84] Soon after his baptism, Lin joined the YMCA's board of directors and became its vice-president (under Huang Naishang, who served as president). After 1911, Lin was elected to the National Committee of the YMCA in China, and remained a member of that body until around 1920.

Over one thousand people attended the baptism service, and, according to a veteran missionary observer, it made a deep and generally favorable impression on the non-Christian elite of the city.[85] This may not be entirely true: Lin did arouse opposition from conservatives in the city who objected to his iconoclastic political and educational views, and in 1910 he was removed from the faculty of the government college where he taught. Ironically, after his dismissal from the college Lin, with Liu Chongyou and other allies in the Provincial Assembly, established a competing private College of Law and Government (Fazheng xuetang), an institution which lasted far longer than its government rival.[86] Lin's public conversion to Christianity may have been another reason for the opposition to him. Among the Fuzhou progressive elite, however, Lin remained popular and influential even after his conversion to Christianity, as was shown after the 1911 revolution when he was elected to represent Fujian in the National Assembly.

Protestant Involvement in the Revolution

From the evidence discussed in this and the previous chapter, it is clear that Chinese Protestants were deeply involved in the social and political life of Fuzhou in the years before the republican revolution of 1911. They played prominent roles in the movement against opium, in the voluntary associations for social reform, and in the Fujian Provincial Assembly. Nor were these men reticent about their religion. As one missionary put it concerning the Protestants in the Provincial Assembly: "They are open and avowed in their profession of Christianity and in their stand for righteousness."[87] Huang Naishang, for one, was forthright about his Christian identity; in the months before the revolution he started a fortnightly periodical containing current national and provincial news and essays on social and religious topics in which he serialized an account of his own religious experience and views.[88] Of course, as we have also seen, Chinese Protestants could take positions opposing the encroachments by foreign powers on China's economic and political sovereignty, including the special privileges accorded to foreign missions under the nineteenth-century treaties.

Given the role of Protestants in the social and political ferment leading up to the revolution of 1911, it comes as no surprise to learn that Fuzhou Protestants were prominently involved in it. Huang Naishang, who was something of an elder statesman in the underground revolutionary organization in Fujian and a personal friend of Sun Yatsen, had been instrumental in planning the 1907 uprising at Huanggang on the Fujian-Guangdong border and in inciting interest in republicanism and revolution in the Xiamen and Shantou regions as well as around Fuzhou.[89]

In addition to his roles in the Provincial Assembly and as an editor, Huang Naishang was attached to the faculty of the Anglo-Chinese College in 1910 and 1911 and also held appointments at the Methodist theological seminary and another Methodist high school close by. In this capacity he encouraged revolutionary sentiment among the mission school students. Student radicalism was by this time an important political force all over China, fueled by the rapid growth of the student population following the educational reforms of the previous decade.[90] As in the case of the anti-American boycott of 1905, students in mission schools were not unaffected by the climate of the times. Fuzhou society was electrified in the spring of 1911 by reports sent from the Shanghai Association of Fujian Students (in which revolutionaries predominated) that the powers had reached an agreement on the imminent partition of China under the terms of which Fujian Province would be taken over by Japan. In response to these reports the Fuzhou Chamber of Commerce established a militia, and more time was allocated to physical education classes in schools, a large component of which was military drill.[91] According to the Japanese consul in Fuzhou, students at the main mission schools, Foochow College and the Anglo-Chinese College, asked for permission to use real firearms in their physical education classes, but the requests were turned down by the missionary principals of the schools.[92] In fact, the missionaries' caution was essentially moot with respect to the latter school, since many of its students were already involved in military training with real firearms in the Physical Training Association set up by the Qiaonan Society, which met near the Anglo-Chinese College campus.[93]

One of the active revolutionaries among the Protestants was Li Qifan, head of the new interdenominational Protestant orphanage established in Cangqian in 1910 (fig. 3.3). His younger brother Li Rongfan worked with him in the orphanage and was one of the instructors in the Physical Training Association. Li Qifan, who was probably still in his twenties in 1911, had been raised and educated by a British woman missionary after his own father died. He had worked for a time as the interpreter for the U.S. consulate in Fuzhou before going to Shanghai for further study. In 1910 he returned to Fuzhou to become the superintendent of the orphanage and had two hundred orphaned boys under his charge. Li was involved in the Qiaonan Society and in the YMCA, and both he and his brother were members of the Revolutionary Alliance, which had its clandestine Fujian headquarters not far from the orphanage.[94]

Fig. 3.3. Protestant revolutionary and bomb maker Li Qifan with some of the orphans under his charge. Methodist Collection, Drew University, Madison, New Jersey.

In the weeks before the revolutionary battle for Fuzhou, the Li brothers were making hand-held bombs for the revolutionary side in the cellar of the orphanage building and allowing or encouraging some of the boys in their care to take part in this activity.[95] In doing this, they were relying on the status of the orphanage as an American institution, and thus under the treaty protection of the American consul, to protect their activities from discovery — but neither the missions nor the American government would have welcomed being implicated in Chinese domestic politics in such a manner, and when their activities came to light after the revolution, Li Qifan had to resign from the orphanage.[96] In addition, the Physical Training Association in which the younger Li was involved was training young men of the area in military drill. These young men, most of whom were students in the nearby mission schools, formed the nucleus of a student militia that took part in the battle for Fuzhou on November 9 and 10, 1911 — armed in part with the bombs made secretly in the orphanage.[97]

Contemporary reports provide different perspectives on the involvement of mission school students in the battle that overthrew the Qing garrison and ushered in the Republic in Fujian. Students of Foochow College, which was located at the foot of the hill on which the battle was fought, helped by serving as Red Cross workers, taking the wounded to the American Board hospital next to their campus, where they were tended by a consortium of missionary doctors.[98]

The students of the Methodist mission schools were more directly involved in the fighting, either in connection with the Physical Training Association or in a grenade corps organized at Huang Naishang's home (which also used the homemade bombs).[99] One of these young grenadiers, a student at the Anglo-Chinese College, went by mistake into the Banner garrison sector of the city, where he was captured, decapitated, mutilated, and thrown into a canal.[100] Missionary accounts focus on this young Christian's patriotic sacrifice and on the Christian tone of the official memorial service for him held a few weeks after the battle, at which Huang Naishang officiated.[101] American accounts also stress the general good order and minimal bloodshed in the revolution and the humane treatment of the Manchus by the new authorities after the battle. Even though the American consul witnessed the execution of some Manchu soldiers who had been "caught red-handed" starting fires in the foreign settlement, he reported that the executions were "humanely done."[102]

Some other foreign observers were far less impressed with the conduct of the revolution and the role of Protestants in it, however. The British consul in Fuzhou also watched some Manchus being executed (perhaps the same event as that observed by the U.S. consul). He reported that the execution was carried out by a "Chinese party . . . composed almost entirely of young students belonging to the American Presbyterian [*sic*] Mission." This mission "has been training large numbers of young revolutionaries" and was rumored to have been importing American rifles and bayonets surreptitiously, labeled as jam and other American goods. At any rate, he stated, "it was an American fluted bayonet that a Chinese youth of 20 in a new foreign uniform dug into the stomach of a captive Manchu soldier a few minutes after he had informed me, in excellent American, that he was 'one of Mr. Gowdy's Christians'!"[103]

There was no Presbyterian mission in Fuzhou, and from the reference to Gowdy, a Methodist and president of the Methodist Anglo-Chinese College, it is safe to conclude that the British consul intended the Methodist mission. Although he was certainly wrong in alleging that the Methodist mission itself (that is, the body of American Methodist missionary personnel in Fuzhou) was importing weapons and training revolutionaries, prominent Chinese members of the Methodist church were deeply involved in the revolution, as were students in the Methodist schools. With Chinese Methodists active in the Qiaonan Society and the Revolutionary Alliance and holding responsible posts in the Customs and the postal service, there may be some basis to the rumor that guns were being brought in under the name of the mission. The Methodist missionaries were in fact criticized by the other missions in Fuzhou for being too lax on the question of neutrality.[104]

The difference between the missions can be accounted for partly by the greater autonomy of the Chinese church in the Methodist system than in those of the other missions, and partly by generational turnover in the mission's American personnel. The Methodist mission was short-staffed throughout the first decade of the century, and the most senior male Methodist missionary in the city, John Gowdy, the president of the Anglo-Chinese College, had been in Fuzhou only since 1902 and may not have had the language skills or the contacts to know what was beneath the surface in the church or in the college.[105]

In addition to military preparation, the other aspect of student radical activity in the Anglo-Chinese College in 1910 and 1911 was antidynastic journalism, of which there is likewise no sign that Gowdy was aware. Students of the college founded a society called Jingxing she, or Awakening Society, in 1910, using the college as the contact address.[106] One of the founders of this society cut off his queue in 1910, becoming the first student in the college and reportedly in the whole city to do so.[107] The first magazine published by this society, *Jingxing bao,* was distributed through the Qiaonan Society, bookstores, companies, and medical establishments in Fuzhou, through various institutions (including one church) in the different counties and regions of Fujian, in Shanghai, Hankou, and Hong Kong, and in Paris and the United States through Fuzhou men studying there (one of them an alumnus of the Anglo-Chinese College).[108] Extant issues from 1910 show that this magazine carried articles on current events, foreign threats to Fujian, and citizenship and nationalism.[109]

The failure of the third petition for a national parliament late in 1910 was a watershed in the development of anti-Qing sentiment in Fuzhou, and for these student journalists in particular. In the spring of 1911 they started a new periodical, the tone of which was dramatically more anti-Qing, racialist, and pro-republican than *Jingxing bao.* This monthly periodical, *Minxin* (The hearts of the people), became so popular that the first four issues had to be reprinted within a few months of publication to meet the demand for back issues.[110] The magazine carried material on the Taiping Rebellion and the U.S. Constitution, and in its third issue it openly commemorated the "seventy-two martyrs" executed after the failed Huanghuagang uprising in Guangzhou in April 1911 and quoted Sun Yatsen's three principles of ethnic nationalism, sovereignty, and democracy (*minzu, minquan, minzhu*).[111]

From Dynasty to Republic

After the Wuchang uprising on October 10, 1911, the republican sentiment in Fujian became increasingly evident. Sun Daoren, commander of the New Army troops in Fuzhou, was approached and agreed to support the revolution. On November 7, 1911, the Provincial Assembly voted to declare the province independent of the Qing and in an effort to avoid bloodshed approached the governor-general, Song Shou, offering to continue the stipends of the Banner garrison if the Banner forces would surrender their weapons and ammunition and agree to submit to the new government. The governor-general wanted to accept the offer, but his military counterpart, the Tartar general Pushou, who had direct command over the Banner troops, refused to surrender.[112] In the subsequent battle, 280 Banner troops and 17 on the revolutionary side died, and the Tartar general was captured and executed. Song Shou committed suicide.[113]

The prominence of Protestants in the movement for change in the previous decade was evident in the aftermath of the revolution. On November 11 the victorious leaders of the revolutionary forces paraded the several miles into Fuzhou city to swear in the new military governor (the New Army commander, Sun Daoren) and declare the establishment of the Fujian Provincial Government of the Republic of China. Near the head of the parade, carrying the flag of the new Republic, was Huang Naishang.[114] When the parade reached its destination at the former governor-general's yamen, the ceremony, which included no fewer than four 21-gun salutes and three sets of three formal bows, was presided over by Li Qifan. In the new provincial government that took shape in the following days, active members of the Protestant church were appointed to head three out of the eight departments (*bu*, later *si*): Chen Zhilin of the Provincial Assembly took charge of the Department of Finance, Chen Nengguang of the Qiaonan Society became head of the Department of Foreign Affairs, and Huang Naishang was put in charge of the Department of Posts and Communications (fig. 3.4).[115]

Other Protestants were appointed to subordinate posts in the government. Lin Shufen, an 1891 graduate of the Anglo-Chinese College, member of the Minnan Fire Brigade, and onetime interpreter for the U.S. consulate in Fuzhou, became deputy head of the Foreign Affairs Department, with respon-

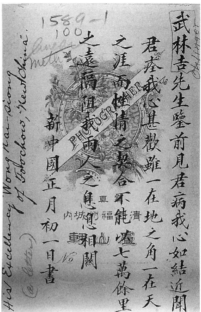

Fig. 3.4. Huang Naishang at the time of the 1911 revolution. Huang had "a look and carriage that reminds one of Gladstone," according to Fletcher Brockman of the YMCA. The reverse side of of the photograph reads: "To Mr. Ohlinger: I was troubled to see you ill earlier, and I rejoiced to hear recently that you have recovered. Even though we are now on opposite sides of the world, we are as close as breath to each other, and our mutual affection cannot be blocked by a mere distance of 7,000 *li*. First day of the first month of the New China" (January 1, 1912). Special Collections, Yale Divinity School Library.

sibility for the Xiamen region.[116] Li Qifan filled the third position in the department. Thus, the top three Foreign Affairs positions in Fujian were held by English speakers of a Protestant background, all three of whom had at one time been employed as interpreters for the U.S. consulate in Fuzhou. (The American tint in the new administration alarmed the British consul, who had already clashed with many of its members over the opium question and in the property dispute with the Minnan Fire Brigade. He especially detested Chen Nengguang, whom he regarded as "one of the worst scoundrels in the place. To transact business with him will be an unpleasant and difficult task, and . . . it is to say the least improbable that he will not show partiality to the American Missions and American interests.")[117] Li Qifan's brother Rongfan was also appointed to the new government, at the head of sections within the Finance

Fig. 3.5. Methodist reception for the new military governor and his cabinet, December 6, 1911. Governor Sun Daoren, in uniform, and Bishop James Bashford are in the center of the front row. Huang Naishang is fourth from the left in the front row. Methodist Collection, Drew University, Madison, New Jersey.

Department and the Police Department. Cheng Gongchen, one of the Anglo-Chinese College alumni in the Qiaonan Society, became a section head in the Department of Posts and Communications.[118]

Lin Changmin was initially suggested as head of the Foreign Affairs Department but was appointed instead as a Fujian delegate to the assembly of provincial representatives in Shanghai, which decided the form of the new national government, and he later served in the National Assembly in Nanjing.[119]

Four of these Protestant politicians — Huang Naishang, Lin Changmin, Chen Zhilin, and Chen Nengguang — were members of the board of directors of the Fuzhou YMCA, which led Fletcher Brockman, the national general secretary of the YMCA in China, to declare after visiting the city: "It is really a splendid Board of Directors. . . . One cannot fail to be in sympathy with a movement in which such men as these have replaced the old inefficient and corrupt officials. . . . There are no official robes, no peacock feathers, no elaborate etiquette, but true Jeffersonian simplicity."[120]

On December 6, 1911, less than a month after the revolution in Fujian, the Foochow Conference of the Methodist church convened in Fuzhou. The prestige of the Protestant church in the new order was aptly symbolized by a reception given by the conference for the military governor and his cabinet. "The most dramatic incident in this reception," reported Bishop Bashford, "was a request by the President of the Board of Posts and Communications [i.e., Huang Naishang] for prayers for the Cabinet and for General Sung [Sun Daoren, the military governor] and the promptness with which General Sung leaped to his feet and bowed his head the moment the request was made" (fig. 3.5).[121] The following week the governor returned the honor, inviting one hundred missionaries and Chinese church members to a reception in the city.[122]

Thus, with the establishment of the new republican political order, Protestants in Fujian suddenly found themselves enmeshed in the structures of power and taken seriously by the wielders of power. Protestants in the cabinet and governors (not to mention presidents) asking Christians to pray for them! The experience was a heady one. The realization of the Protestant hope of remaking China into a strong, Christian nation seemed for the first time within reach, and to Protestant eyes the new era held electrifying possibilities.

4

Protestants and the Symbols of Nationalism

I believe we shall see in the next five years a great advance in all Christian work. I can even believe that within ten years China will become a Christian nation. . . . There is no reason why we should be one whit behind our great example, the American Republic, and we do not intend to be. Our brains are not inferior, our ability is not less than theirs. We purpose to keep abreast of America, and I do not know but that we may even excel our twin Republic. They tell me the five broad bands of our national flag represent the five races in our Republic. I can believe they may yet stand for the five continents united in the Republic of the World. (Great applause.)
— *Huang Naishang, early 1912*

The spring of 1911 was a time of patriotic ferment in Fuzhou. Dissatisfaction with the Manchu dynasty had long been simmering, and revolutionary sentiment was gathering strength. Moreover, a rumor was sweeping through the city, in particular through its large student population, that the Japanese were on the verge of forcibly annexing Fujian Province following an agreement between the great powers to partition China.[1] On April 15, at the height of this time of anxiety, the American YMCA leader G. Sherwood Eddy gave a lecture at the Fuzhou YMCA on patriotism to a full crowd composed largely of students from the government schools in the city. Eddy was an accomplished orator, and his interpreter, the Fuzhou YMCA secretary Zhu Lide (Cio Lik Daik), was a practiced speaker in his own right. The lecture made such an impression on the listeners that the students of the Provincial College petitioned the college president to invite Eddy to speak at the college.[2] The unprecedented request was approved, to the great excitement of Eddy and the YMCA secretaries, and standing before the tablet of Confucius, he spoke for an hour to the students and faculty of the college, concluding with a presentation of "Christ as the only hope of China."[3]

The Fuzhou YMCA magazine carried a lengthy précis of Eddy's talk at the YMCA, which expresses an interesting vision of human history and the contemporary world situation. In essence, the talk was a moral prescription for building a strong nation, tinged with a striking synthesis of Protestant millennial optimism and nineteenth-century social progressivism, offering a vision of a world brotherhood of strong Christian nations as the providential destiny of the human race.

The magazine writer began by describing Eddy, who was on the first of what would become several visits to Fuzhou over the next three decades, as a "world-traveled American philosopher and world-renowned lecturer," in the middle of a world tour covering England, Germany, Russia, North and South America, India, Ceylon, China, Korea, and Japan — clearly a man eminently qualified to discuss a world question like patriotism.

Eddy's speech was suffused with the language of the progress of civilization, seen as a unidirectional evolutionary process of the human race. Human religion, politics, and art, even Western civilization itself, had originated in Asia, but Asia had fallen behind in the evolutionary process. Meanwhile, Europe had gone through stages in which feudal states were superseded by monarchies, and monarchies had been or were being superseded by constitutional governments. Now Asia was awakening, and Japan had already achieved parity with the Western nations.

The destination point of world history as Eddy presented it was the modern constitutional nation-state, made up of a citizenry conscious of liberty, equality, and fraternity (*ziyou, pingdeng, aiqun*). If a unified nation was the goal of civilization, however, there were impediments in China to its achievement, some of which Eddy identified. China's strong family and regional consciousness, for instance, was "an obstacle to the progress of civilization." America's strength was due to the true equality that its citizens enjoyed, and India's weakness was due to the strength of the caste system; China, by implication, fell in between these two polar examples.

In a letter describing these lectures, Eddy noted that his words concerning "the effects of sin upon their country" aroused a "deep sense of conviction" in the young men listening.[4] For world history was not only a tale of progress; it was also a cautionary tale showing the consequences of national sin. National progress, Eddy stated, required four elements: purity, loyalty, ethical ideals, and courage. Licentiousness in nations degraded the women and corrupted the youth: Rome and Babylon were destroyed because of it. A parallel between these negative examples and Chinese sexual morality was not made explicit in the magazine's account, but it was certainly intended. Soon after this, Eddy alluded to the threat of dismemberment (*guafen*) by the foreign powers which was of such concern to his audience and expressed his pious hope, as an American and thus ipso facto a friend of China, that "God has preserved China for over four thousand years; surely he will not permit anyone to carve China up now" — if, Eddy implied, the patriots listening could measure up to the requirements of loyalty, morality, and courage.

Modern history provided more positive examples than ancient history — for instance, American leaders like Washington or Lincoln, and the Italian nationalist Mazzini (a favorite icon for Chinese nationalists in this period), for whom love of country also implied love of all humanity. Eddy elaborated on the career of Garibaldi as a model of unselfish sacrifice, for Garibaldi had spent a dozen or more years in Latin America fighting for the independence of nations other than his own; only after that did he return to liberate and unite Italy. Speaking in 1911, before the first of the great conflagrations of the twentieth century, Eddy was much more sanguine than later figures might be about the compatibility of nationalism and internationalism; indeed, he insisted on the absolute necessity for the "progress of civilization" of both love for one's own nation and love for other nations. To emphasize the point he used himself as an example, claiming that he loved China and the Chinese as much as, or even more than, he loved his own country and people. Patriotism, in other words, would lead not to world conflict but to world brotherhood, because if everyone loved their nation, they would be prepared to sacrifice themselves for the good of others in the nation and by extension would be selfless with respect to other nations and peoples.

In sum, therefore, Eddy tapped into the anxiety of his audience about the future of their country, and he placed the question of national survival into a broad interpretive framework in which the judgment of God was embodied in the inexorable forces of civilizational decay and civilizational progress. Moreover, he distilled this potent mix into a call for individual action, which he expressed in closing in these words: "I hope each of you will summon your courage and work wholeheartedly for the welfare of your nation: this is my prayer as an American for you." The magazine printed this final exhortation in a larger, bold font and recorded that the listeners were moved: "At the end of the lecture, some were greatly excited, others were sighing, others stood dumbfounded, others bit their tongues in amazement."[5]

Fuzhou Protestants and Nationalism

By 1911, as we have seen, Chinese Protestants in Fuzhou had attained a prominence far out of proportion to their numbers and in startling contrast to their low social standing in earlier decades. Protestants held important positions in the reform societies, the Provincial Assembly, and most of all in the postrevolution government of the province. Some of the reasons for this change in status have already been discussed — the social mobility of Protestants and their high representation in the new professional career paths, for instance, and the way Chinese Protestants presented themselves as both Chinese and modern.

Ultimately, however, we cannot account for the new prominence of Chinese Protestants without situating it within the great sea change taking place in Chinese political culture between 1895 and 1920. Over this period politically aware Chinese came to understand themselves not as subjects of an empire, owing submission to the established authorities, but as constituent members — citizens — of a nation, to which they owed individual love, loyalty and, if necessary, readiness to sacrifice their lives. The language of *aiguo*, or patriotism (literally, "love for the nation") permeated public discourse in China after 1900. Conversely, as citizens, a growing number of Chinese claimed the right to a voice in national questions. It is not too much to say that politics itself as a public domain — public discussion of and participation in matters pertaining to local and national government — was created in China during this period, and with it the popular conception of China as a nation-state composed of citizens.

What was the substance, the stuff, of this new politics? On one level, it was an intellectual change, connected to material factors such as the spread of newspapers and periodicals, translations of Western social theory (often refracted through Japan), the new schools, and the growing numbers of Chinese traveling abroad.[6] It was also an organizational change, seen in the proliferation of new voluntary associations and political groups and of new practices like elections, public speeches, and mass petitions (following the court's crucial concession in principle to constitutional government).

When we look at the diffusion within local society of the new mode of thinking that we term nationalism, however, we must look beyond texts and organizations to relatively intangible factors, to what Ann Anagnost has called the "sometimes ephemeral ways in which the nation becomes an object of contemplative reflection."[7] In Fuzhou these included particular events which inscribed new meanings on old spaces, as with the Anti-Opium Society's mass parades and public burnings of opium pipes, and the dispute between the British consulate and the Minnan Fire Brigade over the occupancy of a previously neglected temple. More generally, however, they also included the adoption of new symbols by which patriotism, citizenship, and nationhood were ritually portrayed and thus embodied and given substance by and for the new citizens: since "the nation itself has no palpable existence outside the symbolism through which it is envisioned," symbols and rituals play a crucial role in making the nation "real" to its people.[8]

The starting point for any discussion of the phenomenon of nationalism is the recognition that the organization of the world into the political and territorial entities known as nation-states is neither inevitable nor primordial. Although human beings from ancient times have understood themselves in terms of communities based on common descent (the root of the English term "nation"), nations in the modern, political sense, far from being "as old as history," date only from the eighteenth century.[9] The essence of the modern understanding of a nation is summed up by E. J. Hobsbawm as "the equation nation = state = people," with nationalism being the assertion that a certain people (however defined) should be constituted as a sovereign nation-state. Even though the identity and bounds of a "people" have often appeared self-evident to human beings in history, there is no clear a priori criterion — whether language, geography, culture, history, religion, ethnicity, or some combination of these — by which all peoples or nations can be distinguished from others. Instead, the distinctions between nations depend on self-definitions, usually determined by privileging some criterion or criteria over others in defining membership, which is why the question of who belongs or does not belong to particular nations has been so bitterly contested in the modern world.[10]

The topic of nationalism has generated a large body of scholarly literature in recent years, literature that approaches the topic from a bewildering array of perspectives.[11] Broadly, this work has marked a shift from seeing nationalism as a more or less natural trait which lay latent within human populations until it was "awakened" in modern politics, to seeing it as a fundamentally new reshaping of identity (albeit from already existing elements). The most influential treatments of nationalism have drawn chiefly on the historical experience of Europe (Hobsbawm and others) or European colonies (Benedict Anderson), and in certain respects these treatments do not fit the Chinese case very well. For example, Prasenjit Duara has criticized the assumption in the work of Anderson and others that there is a radical disjuncture between the forms of community in premodern societies and the "imagined community" of the modern nation-state. For Duara, national/ethnic and cultural identities have existed in a porous and overlapping sense in China for millennia, and all forms of community are in some sense "imagined." On the other hand, Duara is in essential agreement with Hobsbawm and Anderson when he states that the "world *system* of nation-states," with the nation-state defined as "a political form with distinct territorial boundaries within which the sovereign state, 'representing' the nation-people, has steadily expanded its role and power," is a distinctive development of modern history.[12]

Others have approached the question of Chinese nationalism by viewing it as a prerequisite for modernization, or by attempting to define the difference between premodern Chinese "culturalism" and modern "nationalism."[13] There is a tendency in such discussions to reify nationalism into a definable attribute that is either present or absent; however, as Benjamin Schwartz has noted, nationalism is no more a *thing* than "culture" and "modernity" are.[14] While the specific application of Anderson's or Hobsbawm's terminology or ideas to China can be disputed, it is clear that an important shift was taking place in China in the first decades of the twentieth century, a shift in the way individual Chinese understood their relationship to the larger national/cultural community and the relationship of that community to the wider world; by the same token there was a shift in the way the wielders of power conceived their relationship to individuals. This becomes very evident if we turn our gaze away from definitions and back to the events in Fuzhou society and the ways these events were understood by those who participated in them.

"America, China's Pattern"

Benedict Anderson's most fundamental and convincing argument is that once the first nation-states had come into being in the late eighteenth century and had been defined in print, they became models or blueprints available for selective appropriation by aspiring nationalist movements in any part of the world. Anderson refers in particular to the influence of the United States as one such model, and he stresses the importance of bilingual elites in translating the models of successful national revolutions into new linguistic arenas.[15]

Chinese Protestants in Fuzhou were one such mediating group. While not all of them were bilingual, the politically prominent ones all were. More to the point, their education and religious milieu exposed Chinese Protestants to a view of the world as consisting of nation-states, and in particular exposed them to the United States as the paradigmatic republic. Thus, after 1911, Chinese Protestants in Fuzhou—like Huang Naishang and Huang Zhiji—spoke explicitly of America as the model for the new Chinese Republic.

As a young man, Huang Naishang had read the first detailed account of America in the Chinese language: Elijah Cole Bridgman's history of the United States. This work, published in Singapore in 1838, then reprinted in Hong Kong in 1844 and in a revised edition in Shanghai in 1861, had been influential in China, forming the basis for the descriptions of America given in the important world geographies written in the 1840s by Wei Yuan and Xu Jiyu.[16] In the 1890s Huang himself helped an American missionary in Fuzhou write a more up-to-date history of America, and in his preface to that work Huang commented on Bridgman's history of sixty years before and on the progress of America since that time. The preface was poignant, as it was written just a few weeks after the crushing of the Hundred Days reform movement of 1898, in which Huang had been a participant. In it Huang reprised Bridgman's depiction of America's republican system—rulers serving for a set term of only four years, the people having the power to elect their president, officials, and legislature—and attributed America's "preeminence in the world in wealth and power" to that system. In an oblique reference to his distress at the contrast between America's prosperity and China's gloomy outlook in the aftermath of the palace coup, Huang concluded the preface with the words: "Now that the book is completed, I cannot suppress my perturbed emotions, and so offer this as a preface."[17]

For Huang Naishang, therefore, the American political system was already an ideal in the 1890s, and one with which he was very familiar from his research and reading. George Washington was something of a hero for Huang, as he was also for Sun Yatsen. At the first meeting between Huang and Sun, in 1900, their conversation turned to Washington. It was Sun who raised the subject, calling Washington a "religious leader" who had liberated the thirteen colonies from England. Huang responded by likening Washington to the legendary Chinese sage emperors Yao and Shun, presumably alluding to Washington's reluctance to assume the presidency, as Shun demurred several times before finally accepting the throne, or to his relinquishing of it after two terms, as Yao had abdicated in favor of Shun.[18] On the eve of Sun Yatsen's inauguration as interim president of the Republic, Huang Naishang and Sun exchanged a series of telegrams in which Huang repeatedly referred to Sun as not merely *China's* Washington, but "the first Washington of the Orient."[19]

In Huang's speech quoted at the head of this chapter, given to a church audience in early 1912, he once more alluded to Washington. He likened republicanism to a tide, springing from the Christian religion, which had begun in Washington's time and spread throughout the world, now at last reaching China. Although he spoke of America as "our great example," his comments also contained a competitive edge, for Huang had had some conflicts with Americans in China, as we have seen. Huang spoke of China equaling or surpassing "our twin Republic," for "our brains are not inferior, our ability is not less than theirs." Nevertheless, his closing statement expressed the same global millennial optimism that we saw in Sherwood Eddy, for he expressed the hope that China would become a Christian nation within ten years and, further, that all the continents of the globe would soon be united in a World Republic.[20]

Huang Zhiji (Uong De Gi) had also gained familiarity with America through his translation work with missionaries. With the Methodist missionary Franklin Ohlinger he had translated a short booklet written by a Methodist Episcopal bishop in America, entitled "America, a World Power," which was published by the Methodist mission in 1907. This booklet attributed America's prosperity to the republican principles of liberty, equality, and fraternity (*tongbao* in this rendition), which, according to the author, were derived from Christianity and had spread from America to France and the rest of Europe. The booklet went on to outline the role of international law and diplomacy in defusing conflicts between nations, emphasizing America's leadership and Christian motivation in the development of peaceful international relations. It also credited America's Open Door foreign policy with preventing China from being carved up by the great powers.[21]

In December 1911, Huang Zhiji was elected to represent the Foochow Conference at the quadrennial General Conference of the Methodist Episcopal Church, to be held the following May in Minneapolis. Specifically, he was charged with seeking the support of the General Conference in urging the U.S. government to extend diplomatic recognition to the Republic of China.[22] Huang spent several months in the United States before and after the conference, studying local government on behalf of the Fujian government and speaking to churches on such subjects as "woman and progress in China," "the Republic of China and Christianity," and "America, China's pattern."[23]

At the General Conference, Huang Zhiji (interpreted by Franklin Ohlinger) was the first of four Chinese delegates—three of them from Fujian—to speak in favor of a motion supporting recognition of the Republic of China by the United States. The response of the assembled delegates to Huang's speech was extraordinary. Huang sketched the events leading to the establishment of a republican government in China and then said: "We of China are heartily thankful . . . for what God has wrought in China. A monarchy that stood five thousand years has been overthrown and a republic established almost without the shedding of a drop of blood. We cast about and determined which country in the world, which nation, should be our pattern and model in establishing a new form of government in China. You all know, without my telling you, that our preferences have for many years been for America."

At this point, Huang's speech was interrupted by one of the listening American delegates who, overcome by patriotic and religious enthusiasm, broke into "My Country, 'Tis of Thee," whereupon the whole assembly stood up and sang it. Huang then continued: "Our people in China are of one heart and mind. It is our fixed purpose to establish in Asia a second United States. We have formed this purpose in our minds, not simply for ourselves, . . . [but because] we have seen that of all the nations . . . none has benefitted the world more than America; and therefore we desire to imitate America in establishing a Republic of China."

After the next speech (by the Reverend Li Changshui [Li Diong Cui] of the Hinghwa Conference) the audience broke into the "Star-Spangled Banner," and after the final of the four speeches, from the woman doctor Li Meizhu (Li Bi Cu) of Fuzhou, the entire conference apparently exploded in patriotic excitement, all standing, cheering, and waving handkerchiefs. The resolution supporting recognition of the Republic of China was passed with ease, and on a motion from the floor the flag of the new Republic of China was hung over the platform with the American flag for the remaining days of the conference.[24]

For the primarily American delegates to this conference China's adoption of the American political model was a dramatic validation of the American Protestant version of internationalism that we saw in Eddy and in Huang Naishang, in which America was both the model nation and a vehicle of blessing under God to China and ultimately to the whole world. For Chinese Protestants like Huang Zhiji, nationalism, republicanism, international progress, and Christianity were likewise merged in a close-knit synthesis, and China's inclusion in the coming world fraternity of Christian republics was powerfully symbolized for both Americans and Chinese by the hanging of the Chinese flag with the American one. This was a highly idealized vision of the world, and one which became harder to sustain through the following years, as Chinese Protestants in Fuzhou and elsewhere became more aware of the undercurrent of paternalism in American Protestant internationalism and as the outbreak of war in Europe shook the vision of world brotherhood to its foundations. Still, in the charged atmosphere of 1911 and 1912, Fuzhou Protestants saw America as China's model, and American Protestants saw China's adoption of that model as evidence of God's work in China.

Protestants were not the only people in China who were intensely interested in the United States as a possible model for the nation. In Fuzhou radical journals carried articles on the American constitution; and Sherwood Eddy's lecture on patriotism, with its strongly American and Protestant perspective, was received with enthusiasm by young non-Christian patriots. After the 1911 revolution the national press often employed the term "China's George Washington," most often in reference to Sun Yatsen, as Huang Naishang did in the Fuzhou press.[25] American missionaries noted a great enthusiasm for things American in Fuzhou in the months following the revolution, seen in everything from the frequent references to Washington to the sudden popularity of Western-style clothing, Western hats in particular. They report being approached for advice on matters republican by young Chinese, who asked "if they are doing things like Americans."[26]

This was a period of cosmopolitan openness and an active quest for alternative political and social models among progressive Chinese in Fuzhou, and this openness is one reason that Chinese Protestants were able to assume a political prominence and social acceptance which they had not had before 1900. Chinese Protestants were perceived as cosmopolitan, as indeed they were, for their education included Western learning, some spoke and wrote English very well, and many had social contact with foreigners. In particular, Protestants were associated in their compatriots' minds with America; and the American revolution and republican government were influential political models for progressive Chinese in this period. It is not surprising that Protestants were regarded by Chinese nationalists as having a contribution to make.

Another point of intersection between Protestant and secular nationalist rhetoric in China was the connection drawn between morality and nation-building. In expressing the utility of Christianity in terms of the needs of nation-building, Chinese Protestants were drawing on a widely shared consensus that the crisis facing China was a moral crisis. In essence, patriotism was seen as a moral duty, and the transformation of people into citizens, without which China could not become a strong, prosperous, and modern nation, as a problem of moral education. This moral thrust is evident, for example, in Liang Qichao's influential essay of 1902 on national renewal, in which he equated renewal of the nation to renewal of the Chinese people and criticized the Chinese people for their lack of public morality and failure to take a personal interest in national affairs.[27] The famous translator Yan Fu, a Fuzhou native, held similar ideas about the importance of public morality to modern nations.[28]

In Fuzhou itself, the moral dimension of nationalism can be seen in the language of the founding manifesto of the Anti-Opium Society, drafted in 1906, which defined opium smokers as lacking in "national consciousness" (*guojia sixiang*). That is, their opium habit was not merely a habit harmful to themselves and their families, but a betrayal of the nation.[29] Also, numerous advertisements in the progressive press in Fuzhou enjoined "patriots" to buy their Western goods from Chinese companies rather than from foreign importers.[30] Whether in leisure habits or in commercial choices, therefore, "patriots" had the moral duty to filter their personal decisions through the prism of the needs of the nation.

This moral dimension of nationalism made nationalism and the Chinese Protestant self-understanding peculiarly compatible. As we saw in Chen Zhilin's speech at the church reception for the Fujian Provincial Assembly in Chapter 3, Chinese Protestants saw the moral elevation of the people as being at the core of the church's mission. Another Protestant speaker on that occasion spoke of "the heavenly calling" (*tianzhi*) of the YMCA to "create good citizens" (*zhizao liang guomin*) through moral, intellectual, and physical education.[31] In fact, the very motto of the YMCA in Chinese, *deyu, zhiyu, tiyu,* or moral, intellectual, and physical education, echoed the language of the developing nationalism: compare Liang Qichao's threefold reference in his seminal "Renovation of the People" ("Xinmin shuo") to the people's morality, the people's intellect, and the people's strength (*minde, minzhi, minli*), which in turn echoed Yan Fu's language in his influential 1895 essay "On Strength," apparently derived from the social theorist Herbert Spencer.[32] As we saw earlier, the YMCA's stress on moral education was frequently singled out for favorable comment by non-Christian Chinese, as it was at the fourth anniversary of the Fuzhou YMCA in early 1911.

In the early Republic, Chinese leaders of all religious persuasions remained intensely concerned with the need to raise the moral level of the people in order to forge a viable nation. Sun Yatsen clearly thought of citizenship as having a moral dimension, for he suggested in 1912 that opium smokers be barred from citizenship; in speaking to a Protestant audience in Beijing later that year, Sun spoke of the "indispensable" relationship between religion and politics, because of the power of religion to impart virtue.[33] Nor was it only Christians like Sun Yatsen who believed that there was a relationship between religion and nationhood. The attempts led by Kang Youwei and others in the 1910s to have Confucianism established as the state religion of the new republic, rather than being attempts by unreconstructed monarchists to turn back the clock, flowed from the same nation-building impulse that motivated other Chinese, including Protestants, but with the added and quite plausible assumption that a common religion was a necessary feature of modern nation-states.[34] The concern to find a way to construct a moral citizenry as the basis for a strong, unified state lay behind this effort, just as it lay behind Protestant nationalist rhetoric, and that of Liang Qichao, Yan Fu, and Sun Yatsen.

Symbolizing the Nation: Public Ceremonies

This concern to make China into a strong, modern, unified state also lay behind the innovations in political ritual of the late Qing and early Republican periods. Political rituals take place in all human political systems, in modern industrial societies as much as in more "primitive" settings, and they are of fundamental importance in making the abstract community tangible to individuals. As one political scientist has put it, "The state is invisible; it must be personified before it can be seen, symbolized before it can be loved, imagined before it can be conceived."[35] However, most scholarly work on ritual has been written by anthropologists studying preindustrial societies, and relatively little attention has been devoted to political rituals in modern societies.[36]

With respect to modern China, apart from a few pioneering efforts such as Levenson's fine article on Yuan Shikai's imperial pretensions, Western historians have only recently begun to study the role of political rituals and symbols.[37] Much of the literature that is beginning to take shape around this question has stressed the novelty and the Western or Japanese inspiration for the "validating rituals" of the new politics.[38] Some scholars have pointed to Christian missions as one route by which these new political practices entered China — such as Joseph Esherick and Jeffrey Wasserstrom, who identified missionary schools as one source for the "politics of public meetings, speeches, and demonstrations" that emerged before 1911.[39]

Why is this arena of rituals and symbols significant? First, the model of the nation-state which Chinese nationalists in this period sought to emulate was overwhelmingly Western, and it carried with it an extensive repertoire of rituals and symbols, ranging from the impressive to the banal, which were part and parcel of what it meant to be a nation.[40] To recognize this does not mean that Chinese nationalists played a purely passive or imitative role in adopting them; on the contrary, elements from this repertoire could be selected and put together in surprising and original ways.[41] Second, it is likely that the great majority of Chinese people learned about the new political order not through the writings of seminal thinkers, or even through the press, but through the symbolic presentations of it that they saw acted out in streets, halls, schools, and public spaces.[42] In Fuzhou, for example, the street parades connected with the opium suppression campaigns, the parade through the city to invest the new governor after the revolution, and the visit of Sun Yatsen in 1912 all drew large crowds of participants and onlookers — more, almost certainly, than would ever read a newspaper or travel to Japan.

In the Fuzhou area, the sources we have yield information on several instances of overlapping participation by Protestants and non-Protestant members of the local elite in ceremonies associated with modern nationalism. Protestants and non-Protestants participated together in ceremonies connected with the Fuzhou YMCA, such as the opening of its new building in early 1908, at which Lin Bingzhang of the Anti-Opium Society spoke, and its fourth anniversary in 1911, which was marked by speeches from representatives of the officials, gentry, commercial leaders, and reform societies. Non-Protestant political leaders joined with church members in singing and speeches at the reception for the new Provincial Assembly hosted by the YMCA and the Methodists in 1909 and at the reception given for the new provincial government by the Methodists in December of 1911. Protestants also played a role in the ceremonial inauguration of the new political order in Fuzhou after the 1911 revolution, carrying the flag of the new Republic and presiding over the investiture of the new military governor.

There were other instances of elite participation in Protestant ceremonial in the final years of the Qing. For instance, in January 1910 the governor-general, Tartar general, and other high officials were for the first time invited to attend commencement day at Foochow College. Not only did the officials accept the invitation; the governor-general even gave a short speech in which he referred to America as standing "at the head of the enlightened nations of the earth" and exhorted the students to have high ideals. The campus was decorated with flags, and the proceedings were punctuated by Western music and by the congregation rising to sing a Christian patriotic anthem.[43] In addition to the 1909 reception for the Provincial Assembly, the Methodist annual conference hosted members of the reform societies in 1908, and it hosted members of the reform societies and the Provincial Assembly together in 1910.[44]

These Protestant ceremonial events had certain elements in common. All of them included Western music (band or piano or organ), congregational singing, and speeches. Though not mentioned in every case, flags or banners were often used to mark the occasion. Most of these elements also appeared in the non-Protestant official ceremonies in Fuzhou during the early Republic, and were evident too in the inauguration of Sun Yatsen as president of the Republic on January 1, 1912.[45]

The government rituals of the Republic of China were significantly different from those of the Qing, both in general (despite Yuan Shikai's efforts to rehabilitate some aspects of the imperium) and in Fuzhou. In 1912 the national government abolished the elaborate rules of etiquette and the kowtow (ritual prostration) used in official ceremonies under the dynasty, replacing them with a straightforward bow from the waist, or three bows on the most solemn occasions.[46] In Fuzhou, foreigners remarked on the change in official dress and ritual under the early Republic and on the emergence of oratory as a political

skill. At the commencement for Foochow College in 1913, a missionary observer noted approvingly that the governor of the province led the procession
in a "tweed business suit," rather than in "the gorgeous silks and peacock
feathers of the old regime," and that he spoke audibly, clearly, and without
notes, in contrast to the former governor-general, who had read his speech
from a scroll "in such a soft voice that no one off the platform could hear what
was said."[47] As noted in the last chapter, Fletcher Brockman, general secretary
of the YMCA in China, visited Fuzhou just after the revolution and contrasted
(with some hyperbole) the "official robes, . . . peacock feathers, . . . [and]
elaborate etiquette" of the old regime with the "true Jeffersonian simplicity" of
the new.[48]

What models did the new leaders of the province have available to them in
Fuzhou from which to construct the ceremonial forms of the infant Republic?
We can assume that they had access to a diversity of sources. Some elements,
such as military uniforms and military brass bands, probably came via the
military reforms of the previous decade, for instance. There can be little doubt
that the mediation of Japan must have been significant in the transfusion of
Western nationalist ceremonial forms into Chinese usage, just as it was in the
translation of Western ideas into Chinese discourse. Many members of the
Provincial Assembly, the Revolutionary Alliance, and the new government
had spent time in Japan, and Japanese nationals had served as teachers and
drill instructors in the new schools established in the early 1900s in the city. It
is also probable that for many Chinese in Fuzhou the Protestant churches,
schools, and associations provided the most visible and accessible examples of
Western-style ritual in action, and thus that some of the new ritual forms came
from the Protestants. This is made more likely by the crossover in personnel
between the Protestants and the new government and by the high profile of the
YMCA in the city and the extensive non-Protestant involvement in it.

One example that suggests this kind of borrowing from the church comes in
a description of a rally of around five thousand students in Fuzhou in January
1912 celebrating the official establishment of the Republic of China. According to a missionary who attended the event, in addition to great numbers of the
five-bar Republican flags, they "had a pulpit and a baby organ there, though
neither was used."[49] The pulpit and the organ were, of course, elements of
church ceremonial, and their presence at this rally, unused, suggests that the
organizers had drawn on some acquaintance with church services in putting it
together. Their eagerness to do everything in proper American republican style
was shown by their asking the missionary observer whether patriotic meetings
in America were conducted along these lines.

My argument here is not that the Republican leaders in Fuzhou were making conscious comparisons and deliberately borrowing this element from Japanese ritual, that from Chinese ritual, and that from church ritual. Rather, they were looking to emulate a Western/modern/"civilized" way to conduct public affairs, one that they supposed to be basically unitary and to be the opposite of the outmoded practices of the dynasty, and they borrowed its presumed elements eclectically from the models most available to them. The assumption of a single way that "civilized nations" did things is evident in Sun Yatsen's rationale for insisting on the adoption of the Western calendar, which was a dramatic symbolic breach with China's imperial past: "We must learn from the West, and follow the civilized nations of the world," Sun stated.[50]

The result of this eclecticism was sometimes ceremonial overkill from the Western standpoint of the day: each element of the inauguration of the new governor was punctuated by a twenty-one-gun salute (four in all), for example (by contrast, Sun Yatsen's investiture as acting president of the Republic in Nanjing the next month was more modest, including only two such salutes).[51] As we have noted, a Protestant, Li Qifan, was master of ceremonies at that event and thus was probably responsible for putting together the proceedings. Before taking charge of the orphanage, Li had worked in the American consulate in Fuzhou, which may be where he developed his fondness for twenty-one gun salutes. It may also be where he picked up a knowledge of the ritual associated with national flags. The full ceremony, which came after the victorious revolutionaries paraded into the city (with Huang Naishang carrying the flag), took the following form:

    1. Twenty-one gun salute. Music.

    2. The military governor stood facing south. The representative of the Fujian Branch of the Revolutionary Alliance faced him, bowed three times with his hands clasped in front of his body, then read out the letter of appointment of the governor. After reading it, he bowed formally, stepped forward, and presented the document to the governor, who bowed in response, then accepted it.

    3. The governor stood facing south. The Revolutionary Alliance representative faced him and bowed three times, then stepped forward and presented the flag to him; the governor bowed in response, then accepted the flag, at which point music was played and a twenty-one gun salute was fired.

    4. The seal of office was presented to the governor in the same manner as the flag.

    5. The governor read out his oath of office, which was followed by another twenty-one gun salute and more music to conclude the ceremony.[52]

The ceremony was followed by cheers for the governor (*ganxie dudu*) and the nation (*Zhongguo wansui*).[53]

Such descriptions are sketchy, and ultimately the available materials permit us only to speculate on the sources for the rituals of the new Republic. Nevertheless, the fact that Protestants like Li Qifan and Huang Naishang were closely involved in them suggests that Protestants may have been seen by their contemporaries as having special expertise in the area of public ritual. One missionary noted what he saw as Protestant influence on official ritual in this period of change: "So closely are the men of the [revolutionary] movement in touch with the Church that the terminology of a political or memorial public meeting has often more the color of a Methodist class meeting than anything else. Everywhere the atmosphere is charged with Christian influence."[54]

Protestant Hymns and National Anthems

Two staples of modern nationalism are patriotic songs and anthems, and national flags. These symbols of nationhood and the rituals associated with them developed in the eighteenth century and gained importance through the nineteenth in Europe and the Americas, and were in turn appropriated by the emerging nation-states of the twentieth.[55] In some cases of popular origin, these and other symbols of nationhood were increasingly promoted and institutionalized by Western national governments in the decades before 1914. Hobsbawm ties this, convincingly, to the widening of the electoral franchise in Western nations, which created the problem of establishing and maintaining the loyalty of a population with an increasingly broad sense of participation in politics — a problem which faced Chinese governments from 1895 on.[56]

Despite a long tradition of ritual music, China had nothing resembling a national anthem until the final decades of the nineteenth century, when the increasing official intercourse with foreign nations made one necessary for state occasions.[57] The first such effort, based on Chinese court ceremonial music, was in use by 1884, but only in formal diplomatic settings.[58] It was not the court but the exiled reformist intellectuals Huang Zunxian and Liang Qichao who first saw the connection between corporate singing and the inculcation of nationalism, probably owing to their exposure to Japanese society; both began publishing patriotic songs for popular use in the early 1900s.[59] Indeed, it was the popularity of one of Liang's songs among students in the new schools after the educational reforms of 1904–1905 which prompted the court to make two further attempts to come up with an official national anthem in the final years of the dynasty. The first of these was set to the tune of the Japanese national anthem, and the second was composed on the very eve of the 1911 revolution using a tune adapted from court music by an imperial prince, with flowery lyrics by the translator Yan Fu.[60]

The political instability of the early Republic hampered efforts to determine a national anthem. Significantly, given the connections between anthems, citizenship, and education, the selection of a national anthem fell under the purview of the Ministry of Education, and competitions were held to solicit entries. In a striking parallel to the clothing of modern innovations in the garb of antiquity discussed by Hobsbawm for Europe, the anthem eventually chosen used a text from the ancient *Shangshu* (Book of history), a short stanza of verse attributed to the legendary sage emperor Shun, set to a modern tune.[61] Sun Yatsen and his Nationalist Party in Guangdong explicitly rejected it in 1924, and during the Northern Expedition it was informally supplanted by a revolutionary ditty set to the French tune "Frère Jacques," then officially replaced by the Nationalist Party anthem in the 1930s.[62]

In Fuzhou, the earliest evidence of the corporate singing of songs with patriotic content outside Protestant circles dates from 1907, when an unspecified patriotic song was sung in the streets by students celebrating the closing of the opium dens.[63] Anti-Manchu songs in Fuzhou dialect set to well-known folk tunes were current at the time of the 1911 revolution, distributed in hastily printed wood-block booklets, and in 1912 Sun Yatsen's visit to Fuzhou was marked by the appearance of a laudatory narrative in song set to a regional opera tune.[64] However, these latter examples seem to have been vehicles for revolutionary propaganda, to be sung by a soloist, rather than collective expressions of patriotism, since they are quite long and in content consist of a mixture of narrative and exhortation.

Given the absence of collective singing of patriotic songs in China, it must have been a striking experience for the members of the Provincial Assembly when, at the reception given for them by the YMCA and the Methodists in 1909, in the company of over a thousand Chinese Protestants in the stately surroundings of one of the largest Western-style buildings in the city (the Church of Heavenly Peace), everyone stood and sang together "the Chinese Christian National Hymn to the tune of America."[65] This hymn was one of several patriotic hymns in Chinese set to the tune of "My country, 'tis of thee, sweet land of liberty, of thee I sing" — a tune better known through most of the world, despite its American appropriation, as that of the British national anthem.

The British national anthem is the world's oldest national anthem (its first recorded performance took place in 1745), and its tune was appropriated very quickly for patriotic songs and even official national anthems in a host of countries in Europe and beyond.[66] In fact, the American author of "My Country, 'Tis of Thee" came across the tune in a German songbook in the 1830s and was apparently unaware at the time of its British origin.[67] In Britain itself the anthem gathered importance through the nineteenth century as state ritual grew in elaboration and pomp, and by 1893 its lyrics had been translated in whole or part into "fifty of the most important languages spoken in the Queen's Empire."[68]

In Fuzhou, the first patriotic hymn to this tune in Chinese appeared as early as 1871, in a hymnbook published by the American Board mission. In sentiment this hymn bore more resemblance to "My Country, 'Tis of Thee" than to "God Save the Queen," since its lyrics celebrated the glories of China's history, civilization, and natural endowments, only in the final verse entreating God to protect the rulers and people and prevent disasters.[69] Later hymnbooks added versions more reminiscent of "God Save the Queen" in their lyrics while retaining (with some revisions) the earlier, more "national" text also. Thus, the 1891 revised edition of the American Board hymnbook contained two hymns to this tune, one of each type, and the Fuzhou Methodist hymnbook of 1892 (which Huang Naishang edited) contained two different hymns on the "God Save the Emperor" theme, plus a variation on the other version.[70] After 1911 the "God Save the Emperor" variants naturally disappeared, but the first version persisted in Fuzhou hymnbooks with remarkably little change from the text of 1871.[71] It was probably this hymn in its Methodist rendition that the members of the Provincial Assembly sang at the Protestant reception in 1909.

The Fuzhou churches seem to have been exceptional in including hymns on patriotic themes in their hymnbooks so early. Up to the early 1900s, the only national-type hymns in most Protestant hymnbooks in China were hymns calling for the salvation of China, with English titles like "O Save My Country, Lord" or "O Pity China, Lord."[72] As far as I can determine, it was not until the first decade of the twentieth century that Chinese patriotic hymns of the celebratory variety became common in Protestant hymnbooks in China — and they were also set to the tune of "God Save the King." For instance, the 1907 revision of the influential Mandarin hymnal of Henry Blodgett and Chauncey Goodrich included for the first time a hymn to this tune entitled (in English) "National Hymn," with the opening line "Wo ai Zhonghua meidi" (China, thy land I love), and this version became well known around the country.[73] (A descendant of this hymn is retained in the present-day Protestant hymnal in China, albeit with alternative words, written by the noted author Xu Dishan while he was at Yenching University in the 1920s, and a Chinese-style tune.)[74] The YMCA used a different version, known in English as "China Renowned We Sing," with the opening line "Zhonghua wenming dabang" (China, great, cultured land), but it too did not appear in the association's hymnals until 1909.[75]

Were these patriotic hymns actually used in the Fuzhou churches, and if so, on what occasions? Generally speaking, hymns were important in the Fuzhou churches. One missionary wrote that many hymns were well loved by Chinese Protestants; also, being easy to memorize, they were useful vehicles for the instruction of converts of limited literacy.[76] While several hymns were sung at every worship service in the churches, and hymns were used during special services and meetings as well, there is little to indicate the relative popularity of different hymns. However, the evidence available indicates that the patriotic hymns were used on formal occasions, such as during the graduation ceremonies of the mission schools, or when representatives of the government attended church events. That is to say, they were used on those occasions when a patriotic hymn would have been appropriate at the equivalent event in the United States or Britain. Thus, the 1897 commencement ceremony of Foochow College (American Board) opened with the whole assembly singing Hymn 172, "God Save the Emperor."[77] The same hymn opened the college's commencement in 1901 and again in 1910, when the provincial officials were in attendance.[78] A Methodist variant of this hymn — probably the "national" rather than the monarchical version — was sung to close the reception given for the Provincial Assembly by the YMCA and the Methodists in 1909 and during the similar reception for the new Republican government in December 1911. Some version of the hymn was sung at a large public meeting celebrating the U.S. recognition of the Republic of China in May 1913 as well.[79] As in the missionaries' home countries, all in attendance at these events stood while these songs were sung.

There is little direct evidence to clarify the frequency with which these patriotic hymns were sung, but a spirit of patriotism and concern for "the nation" was clearly part of the Protestant milieu in Fuzhou, and particularly of Protestant education. This is shown in general by the involvement of Chinese Protestants in patriotic causes in the final decade of the dynasty and by the use of the national flag in the schools. It is also shown by the titles of the speeches and essays presented by the graduating students of Foochow College, as recorded in the extant commencement programs, which were all on topics of national interest, such as "The Ravages of Opium" and "China Needs to Strengthen Itself" in 1897; "Educational Reform," "The Recovery of China," and "How May China Be Strengthened?" in 1901; and "The Relationship Between Civilized Religion and Democratic Government (*qunzhi*) in Contemporary China" in 1910.[80]

The English class song of the 1901 graduating class, which was performed by the college choir during that year's commencement, also shows the close link in Protestant education between patriotism, religion, and Western learning. It began:

Young men in Christ the Lord,
We bear the truth, our sword,
    Great is the prize.
From every enemy
We would our country free;
This shall our watchword be,
    China, arise!

Bid learning's host advance,
Battle with ignorance,
    Boasting and lies [etc.].[81]

Whatever its literary merits, this class song — probably, given the meter, set to the familiar tune of "God Save the King" — expressed the essence of Chinese Protestant patriotism: China would "rise" through the efforts of educated Christian men to "free" her from "ignorance" and "boasting" (the latter term probably refers to the self-sufficiency of Chinese classical learning, whose proponents saw no need for the Western knowledge that these young men had acquired).[82]

The Protestant patriotic hymns are significant because the act of corporate singing of a national anthem is a proclamation of one's identification with an abstraction termed "the nation," and it implies a very different relationship between the individual and the state than that prescribed in late imperial Chinese political culture.[83] This is true for the hymns of the "God Save the Emperor" variety, which made the emperor's health and religious status a matter of personal concern to the singer — what business did a Chinese commoner have concerning himself or herself with the well-being of the Son of Heaven, let alone beseeching an alien deity on the sovereign's behalf?[84] It is even more true of the "national" version, the words of which personified "China" as a nation attached to a certain history and territory, and connected the individual organically to that nation: China was "my native land" (*wo benguo Zhonghua*). The lyric in the Methodist version probably sung at the 1909 reception ran as follows:

China, my native land,
Rich in treasures of old,
    I sing aloud;
Land of my ancestors,
Where Confucius and Mencius once walked,
Since ancient Yao and Shun
    Never without true hearts (*chang you liangmin*)!

Land of our birth, and of
Men of wisdom and learning
    I love this name!

Clear mountains, sparkling waters,
Glories of wood and plain
Make the heart leap with joy
   In happy praise!

Everlasting God,
Watch over our people, forsake them not;
   I praise thy name!
Ever protect our rulers,
Save all the land from harm,
Grant grace to all generations to come,
   Forever preserve the people of China (*yongbao Huamin*)![85]

This hymn conveyed no "pity China, Lord" sentiment, but a strong pride in Chinese history, civilization, and natural endowments. As we have seen in other contexts, this hymn appropriated the ethical Confucian stream of Chinese high culture for Christianity (Yao, Shun, Confucius, Mencius, "men of wisdom and learning"). The authorship is unknown, but the standard missionary language about "the heathen" is noticeably absent, and the hymn even declares that China had had good people (*liangmin*) in every generation.[86]

At the reception given by the Methodist annual conference for the new government shortly after the revolution, which was attended by the new military governor and the leading men of his cabinet, including its Protestant members, a version of this hymn, suitably modified for the occasion, was sung. The first verse was little changed from the version above, and changes to the third were minor also, though interesting — for example, in the sixth line "descendants of the Yellow Emperor" (*Huangyi*) was substituted for the more generic "generations to come" (*houyi*) of the original. This reflected the racial nativism that was part of the revolutionary movement, and even shaped its calendar. Chinese radical magazines in Japan had since 1903 been numbering years from the supposed date of accession to the throne of the legendary Yellow Emperor.[87] This dating was adopted by the Fujianese revolutionaries in Shanghai, and the revolutionary government in Fujian used it in its official documents in the first weeks of its existence (before the official adoption of the Western calendar on January 1, 1912).[88]

It was in the second verse of the hymn that the significant changes were made. This verse was modified to read:

Land of our hearths and homes
Long under Manchu dominion
   Now at last reclaimed!

Reclaimed, these mountains and waters,
These glorious woods and plains,
These features that make our hearts leap
    In joyous thanksgiving![89]

As is evident from these various examples of patriotic hymns used by Fuzhou Protestants, which are equivalent in form, if not in official status, to national anthems, the national anthem was an element of the international repertoire of nationalism which was adopted by Chinese Protestants long before it became part of the practice of Chinese nationalists in general, and was modeled by Protestants to their compatriots in some instances. With their simple, well-known tunes, these hymns could become vehicles for alternative, even competing, versions of nationalism and could be modified for different settings and new circumstances. While we cannot prove that this practice by Chinese Protestants had a direct influence on non-Protestants, it is certainly possible that non-Protestant nationalists found the experience of proclaiming their love for the nation in collective song a moving one worthy of emulation. Beyond that, we can safely say that the use of these hymns is one of several respects in which Protestants appeared to their compatriots to be up-to-date, modern, cosmopolitan — which is why they could take the place they did in the politics of the day. We can also take these hymns as indicating that Chinese Protestants were predisposed toward understanding China as a nation and themselves as citizens in it, which helps to explain why they played the roles they did in Fuzhou between 1895 and 1920. Lastly, these patriotic hymns furnish another example of the way contact with Western missionaries served to foster the nationalism of Chinese Protestants, not (as is often supposed) to subvert it.

Protestants and National Flags

A national flag is probably the most basic symbol of nationhood in the modern world. Easy to manufacture and display, national flags have become, like national anthems, one of the defining marks of the nation-state. In the United States the flag acquired particular significance over the late nineteenth century, and allegiance to it was pledged on a daily basis by students in schools across the country from the 1880s on.[90] The American flag remained important to at least some American missionaries in Fuzhou. It was prominently displayed during the annual July Fourth celebrations at the missionaries' summer retreat at Guling (Kuling), in the mountains east of the city. It was flown above the U.S. consulate in Fuzhou, on the ridge south of the Min River, and at

least one Fuzhou missionary (Franklin Ohlinger, whose first language, ironically, was German) flew a U.S. flag at his residence in China between 1896
and 1908.[91]

The U.S. flag was also sometimes displayed at church events for Chinese, as
it was at the annual rally of the Young Person's Society of Christian Endeavor
in Fuzhou in 1895.[92] This seems to have been the exception rather than the
rule, however; I have not found any photographic or documentary evidence
for Albert Feuerwerker's assertion that "even the tiniest chapel flew a [foreign]
national flag."[93]

Chinese Protestants could absorb the symbolic importance of the U.S. flag to
Americans by negative example. Huang Naishang may have done so during
the "flag incident" in Xiamen in 1905 (recounted in Chapter 2), when the U.S.
consul's concern to redress the "national insult" of vandalism to the consulate's
flagpole (unadorned by any flag at the time, as it happened) reached obsessive
levels — as Huang's paper bluntly pointed out. More important, however, just
as with the patriotic hymns, was the use in churches and mission schools of the
Chinese national flag in ways analogous to the uses of the national flag in
America and Britain, both before and, more particularly, after 1911.

The development of the Chinese national flag during the late Qing period
illustrates the process by which European conventions of nationhood spread
to other parts of the world. The flag was originally devised in the early 1860s
as an ensign for the ships of the foreign mercenary army employed by the
dynasty to help put down the Taiping rebels. Later, in 1872, the core element
of this ensign — an imperial dragon on a triangular gold background — was
made the official state flag. In 1890 the flag was changed to a rectangle to bring
it into conformity with European usage.[94] The genesis and design of the imperial dragon flag appear to indicate that it was originally intended to represent the sovereign rather than the nation. By the early 1900s, however, it was
being used in public contexts in Fuzhou to represent the nation, as in the
frequent parades of the Anti-Opium Society from 1906, which were headed
not only by the image of Lin Zexu, as mentioned in Chapter 2, but also by the
Qing flag.[95]

In the early Republic the matter of the national flag came to carry a great
deal of symbolic importance.[96] In Fuzhou, the flag used for the new Republic
directly after the 1911 revolution consisted of eighteen stars, representing the
eighteen provinces of China proper, arranged in two concentric circles on a red
field and connected by an outline of a single nine-point star. The origin of this
design is obscure, but it was apparently devised at the headquarters of the
Revolutionary Alliance, and it was used in Fujian in tandem with the five-bar
flag in late 1911 and early 1912, before Yuan Shikai's accession to the presi-

dency.[97] In Fuzhou, the very making of this revolutionary flag was charged with the symbolism of revolutionary purity and sacrifice, for it was sewn together by the young widows of some martyred Fuzhou revolutionaries just in time for the battle for the city. When the revolutionary forces paraded into the city to inaugurate the new government, it was this flag that headed the procession, carried by the veteran Protestant revolutionary Huang Naishang, and during the inauguration of the new provincial government, it was to this flag that the governor and other officeholders bowed to signal their loyalty to the Republic.[98]

This flag, with its federalist implications and its apparently American inspiration in the use of stars to represent the component political units of the nation, did not remain the flag of the Republic of China, although it was made the ensign of the army. Instead, the Republican National Assembly adopted a flag with five horizontal bars representing the constituent *races* in the nation, despite opposition by Sun Yatsen to the change.[99] In an important speech in 1919, Sun called this "ill-omened" five-color flag "the cause of all the Republic's misfortunes," both because of its racial imagery, which he interpreted as meaning the persistence of racial divisions rather than amalgamation into one nation on the (successful, in his view) American melting-pot model, and because of its origin as a Qing military ensign.[100]

Between 1900 and 1920, then, the national flag became an important symbol in China, and controversy over its design became a focus for the competing ideologies of different claimants to national power. In the Protestant milieu in Fuzhou, the Chinese national flag was evidently used in two main contexts, in connection with marching and drill in the mission schools and on ceremonial or festive occasions, beginning in both cases before the 1911 revolution.

The main evidence regarding the use of the flag in connection with drill in the mission schools comes from extant photographs in the missionary archives. Taken together, these images show that military-style drill exercises had become an integral part of Protestant mission education in the Fuzhou area by the last years of the Qing, and that the Chinese national flag was closely associated with these exercises. One of the earliest instances is also one of the most striking: it shows a class of pre-teenage boys in an elementary school of the American Board mission with their two (Chinese) teachers and their drillmaster (in uniform); the boys are posed in rows, holding what appear to be real firearms, with the dragon emblem from the Qing flag displayed on the wall behind them (fig. 4.1).[101]

During the early Republic the use of the national flag in connection with drill and exercise became pervasive in mission schools. Children as young as kindergarten age, girls as well as boys, were taught to line up behind the

Fig. 4.1. American Board mission day school class with drill instructors and rifles, showing Qing flags in the background, early 1900s. Special Collections, Yale Divinity School Library.

national flag bearing arms and were even taught to strike combat postures with model rifles, as figures 4.2 and 4.3 show vividly.[102] As already noted, the connection between nationalism and martiality was a close one in early twentieth-century China, due to the threatening international conditions in which that nationalism was forged. In Fuzhou the martial spirit was as pervasive in the mission schools as in the government schools, as was shown shortly after the revolution when large numbers of students from the Protestant schools — women as well as men, to the horror of their missionary teachers — joined a student volunteer army which went to Shanghai to take part in the anticipated military campaign against Qing forces in north China.[103]

Hobsbawm and others have pointed out the important role played by the national education systems that developed over the nineteenth century in Europe and America in inculcating a popular consciousness of nationalism and citizenship — often using national flags or anthems.[104] In China under the Nationalist Party from 1927, official nationalism pervaded the school system (state and private), with compulsory rituals such as bowing to Sun Yatsen's picture and reciting his final testament, obligatory classes in the Three Principles of the People and citizenship, and celebrations of patriotic holidays. The

Fig. 4.2. Methodist kindergarten class in Fuzhou drilling with model rifles, around 1915. Methodist Collection, Drew University, Madison, New Jersey.

use of flags in the context of drill in the mission schools in the Fuzhou area in the late Qing and early Republic anticipates these later developments (fig. 4.4). Perhaps missionary educators were reproducing in their schools the models that they knew from their own schooling, or perhaps the mission schools were simply adopting these practices as they came into vogue in the fast-growing new government schools in the city. Either way, we find Protestants among the earliest to make use of symbols and methods that later became central to official Chinese nationalism, to inculcate in their students in the cities and towns of Fujian the concept that China was a nation of which they were constituent members and to which they owed loyalty and love.

This use of flags in connection with drill also highlights the connection between patriotism, moral character, and physical fitness. In mainstream American and British cultures in this period patriotism had a quite natural and taken-for-granted connection to religion, which in turn was connected to "character."[105] This was expressed in many ways, from the flag rituals and prayers devised by Lord Baden-Powell for the Boy Scouts (an organization introduced into Fuzhou in connection with the YMCA in the 1910s) to the clichéd linking of "God and country" in mottoes and slogans. In Fuzhou during the early Republic, Protestant institutions adopted Western modes of

Fig. 4.3. Methodist kindergarten class marching with drum, Republic of China flags, and model rifles, 1910s. Methodist Collection, Drew University, Madison, New Jersey.

affirming patriotism in religious contexts, using the Chinese flag — for example, in daily flag-raising ceremonies at YMCA camps, with the boys saluting.[106]

Protestant organizations for youth, such as the Christian Endeavor societies and the Daily Vacation Bible Schools (in which Christian youth volunteered to teach children during their summer vacations), both of which were active in Fuzhou, placed a strong emphasis on patriotism during the early Republican period. Extant Christian Endeavor literature from the 1910s specifically transposed the July Fourth topics of the American originals from which the literature was prepared to the Chinese national day, October 10; the thrust of the patriotic topics was that the Christian gospel was China's greatest need and its propagation the highest expression of one's patriotism.[107]

A teacher's manual for the Daily Vacation Bible Schools dating from 1921 gives detailed guidelines on incorporating education in patriotism into the daily lessons. A flag parade was to be held punctually at 10:50 each morning, at which pupils were to recite in unison a pledge of allegiance to the flag and sing a patriotic song (the texts and music for several such songs were provided — one of them eulogizing the flag itself). The teacher was to follow this ceremony with a short patriotic message on one of a list of suggested topics,

Fig. 4.4. Boys of the Christian Herald Industrial Mission drilling for the provincial governor, Li Houji, at the award ceremony for Emily Hartwell, 1918. The picture illustrates both the importance of military drill in Protestant education and the Protestant use of the flags of the nations (here Chinese, American, and others) as a decorative motif on ceremonial occasions. Special Collections, Yale Divinity School Library.

some tied directly to Christianity, others drawn directly from Chinese nationalist myth/history, beginning with "the founding of the nation by the Yellow Emperor." Not surprisingly, the pledge of allegiance to the flag of the Chinese republic corresponded rather closely to the pledge of allegiance familiar to American schoolchildren of the day; its first line can be rendered in English as "I pledge allegiance to this flag, and to the Republic for which it stands . . ."[108]

The Chinese national flag was also used in Fuzhou church circles on ceremonial or festive occasions. One interesting example occurred in the Anglo-Chinese College in the final years of the Qing (between 1908 and 1911). The student YMCA organized a meeting at the start of one spring semester to welcome new students, and the Qing national flag was displayed on the stage. Elizabeth Gowdy, the wife of the president, suggested that the American flag be displayed along with the Chinese one, but the president of the student YMCA argued with her that since the meeting had no bearing on international relations, it would not be appropriate to display the American flag.

For Mrs. Gowdy, presumably, hanging both flags would represent friendly cooperation and equality between Americans and Chinese, which American missionaries saw as the ideal for their Christian institutions. At the Methodist

General Conference in 1912, the hanging of the Chinese flag with the American had precisely this connotation. Similarly, in Sherwood Eddy's large-scale evangelistic campaign in Fuzhou in 1913, the climactic moment came when he and his Chinese interpreter clasped hands, then pulled their hands apart, in the process unfolding between them the flags of the United States and the Republic of China, joined together. The audience was electrified, according to William Hung's account of this event.[109]

The young Chinese Protestant student who clashed with Mrs. Gowdy had, he tells us, already been radicalized by stories of the American mistreatment of Chinese laborers and by the U.S. annexation of the Philippines, both of which convinced him that America was not essentially different from the other great powers. For him, presumably, the symbolism of displaying the American flag along with the Chinese one was different: a representation of American encroachment on China, not of American benevolent partnership with China.[110]

During the early Republic, we find instances of the use of the national flag at the dedication of a new building for the theological school in Xinghua (Hinghwa) Prefecture in April 1914, when two Chinese national flags were hung diagonally across the door of the building, and at the annual Sunday School Rally in Fuzhou in the spring of 1914, when a large Republican flag was flown on the stage.[111]

YMCA leaders, Chinese and Western, regarded love for the nation and enthusiasm for their association as complementary virtues, and this is reflected in the use of the national flag at YMCA functions. One photograph, for example, shows the tables for the annual membership campaign banquet decorated with miniature Chinese national flags and white flags bearing the names of the recruiting teams.[112] During these membership campaigns, key YMCA members were organized into teams, each led by someone of high social standing, and the teams competed with each other to see which could bring in the most new members and the most in financial contributions over a set period. In the June 1915 campaign, there were five teams of twenty-five men, named for the five colors of the Chinese flag.[113]

Another way national flags were used in Protestant contexts in Fuzhou, again on ceremonial occasions, was to string rows of flags across a hall or a stage, the flags being miniatures of the different national flags of the world. The YMCA hall was so decorated for its first annual banquet, in January 1908, and the rows of flags became a staple of YMCA ceremonial decoration in Fuzhou.[114] This use of flags can be seen in a photograph of the stage taken during the province-wide evangelistic campaign of 1914, which shows the flags of the nations hanging above the front of the stage (see fig. 5.8).[115] The content of the preaching on this occasion appears to have echoed the international imagery of the flags, for the chart by the preacher on the stage is a graph showing the exponential growth of adherents to Christianity in the world from the sixteenth to the nineteenth centuries.

What was the message conveyed by this use of the flags of the world's nations to decorate halls and podiums for formal occasions? It is important to remember that this period was the watershed of Protestant missionary internationalism, and the quintessence of Protestant internationalism was the YMCA.[116] True, the International Committee had its headquarters in New York, many of the prominent leaders of the movement were American, and most of the foreign YMCA secretaries in China were American. But the guiding figure of the YMCA, John R. Mott, often termed a "missionary statesman," was the key organizer of the International Missionary Conference in Edinburgh in 1910, and he continued throughout his long career to play a leading role in international and interdenominational Christian movements, including the YMCA and the World Student Christian Fellowship (based in Geneva). In China, YMCA literature fostered an international awareness from the outset—for example, in the *Cycle of Prayer* published in Chinese and English editions in 1896, which listed different nations or regions of the world to be prayed for on each day of the month.[117] We saw the international utopianism in Sherwood Eddy's vision of the world at the start of this chapter. Similarly, American YMCA secretaries in Fuzhou thought of themselves as participants in "Christ's world program," intended to bring about the "brotherhood" of nations. As one of them put it in 1915,

> We all must think in terms of a world religion and must be prepared to make sacrifices to carry out Christ's world program. At this time when the foundation[s] of society are being shaken by venom and bitter hate of this awful War it seems imperative that some world organization with virile leaders should sound the call to brotherhood [and] [s]hould go one step further and definately [*sic*] plan and work to bring about the conditions that make brotherhood possible. What interdenominational and international organization of the church is better prepared to do this than the Young Men's Christian Association! What leader in our movement is better qualified than Dr. Mott to undertake this task![118]

In hindsight it is evident that the "internationalism" that Mott and the YMCA represented bore a heavy American or "Anglo-Saxon" tint, as well as a distinctly masculine one.[119] At the Edinburgh missionary conference, the unprecedented "international" mission convention which Mott organized in 1910, over 1,000 of the 1,200 delegates were North American or British; only 170 were from European countries, and only 17 were from the non-Western world.[120] Nevertheless, in their own minds YMCA workers in China represented a modern, Christian world civilization, one in which there was no inherent contradiction between nationalism and internationalism; in fact, the one implied the other, as in Eddy's speech in Fuzhou in 1911. The use of world flags as decoration for evangelistic or ceremonial events reflected the assumption of both Protestants and non-Protestant nationalists of the normative nature of the world system of nation-states in which they wanted China to take a place — it being the plurality of nation-states which has made nationalism so important in the modern world.[121] These flags represented a world made up of political-territorial entities known as nations, each equal in status, just as their flags were equal in dimensions and placement. It is significant that the same decorative use of world national flags graced an early attempt to assert China's credentials as a modern nation, the international exposition in Nanjing in 1910.[122]

Queues

The simplest and yet most unmistakable symbol for Chinese men that they adhered to the new Republic was the shedding of the queue, the wearing of which had been required of all adult males since the Manchu conquest of China in 1644. While the evidence for songs and flags comes mostly from the urban setting of Fuzhou, in the shedding of the queue we see an indication of the instrumental role of the Protestant churches in diffusing the symbols of the new Republic into the towns and villages of rural China.

Before 1911 the Chinese without queues were mainly men who had been educated abroad and not resumed the queue on returning to China. Lin Changmin, the Japanese-educated general secretary of the Fujian Provincial Assembly who converted to Christianity in 1910, was one such man. Chinese Protestants who had returned from America also seem not to have resumed the queue, and some of these were active beyond Fuzhou. One such man was Y. C. Koh of Xinghua Prefecture, a 1905 graduate of Ohio Wesleyan University who returned after his graduation to teach mathematics in the Methodist high school in his home city. Koh taught his classes dressed in Western clothing and did not shave his forehead or wear a queue (fig. 4.5).[123]

In the Anglo-Chinese College in Fuzhou, the first student to remove his queue was the president of the student YMCA, who cut off his queue in late 1910. His example was followed the next March by four other students, at least one of whom was a Christian. These men, all of whom were associated with the Revolutionary Alliance, were allegedly the first students in the whole city to cut off their queues, and they had a photograph of themselves taken to

Fig. 4.5. Y. C. Koh, 1905 graduate of Ohio Wesleyan University, teaching in the Methodist boys' high school in Xinghua in the last years of the Qing. He has no queue and wears Western clothing; his students wear Chinese clothes. Methodist Collection, Drew University, Madison, New Jersey.

commemorate the occasion.[124] Both the power and the ambiguity of this symbolic act is shown by the conversion account of Chen Wenyuan, a student from a non-Christian scholarly family who later became a bishop in the Methodist church in China and dean of the School of Religion at Yenching University. He was drawn to the queueless YMCA president, and they became roommates, although Chen was vigorously opposed to Christianity. One time at a street meeting with this student, an onlooker "began to berate my friend for not wearing his hair long," saying it proved that Christianity was a foreign religion. Chen spoke up in defense of his friend, arguing that "the queue was itself foreign and had been imposed on the Chinese by the Manchus. . . . Then I went on, almost without being aware of it, to defend Christianity." This experience made him realize how close to accepting Christianity he had become without realizing it, and soon afterward he decided to become a Christian. Instrumental in his conversion, therefore, was the association between Christianity, modernity, and racial nationalism symbolized by his queueless Christian classmate.[125]

From the spring of 1911 many more students in Fuzhou removed their queues, and within a few months after the revolution most men in the city had shed their queues. In the lesser cities and in the countryside people were slower

Fig. 4.6. A Chinese Methodist preacher as a visible symbol of the new order in the early Republic: he has a queueless hairstyle, eyeglasses, accordion, and posters; the village men wear coiled queues. Methodist Collection, Drew University, Madison, New Jersey.

to take this step. Scattered references indicate that Protestant preachers were the first to do away with their queues in some of these areas (fig. 4.6). In Xinghua city, two Methodist preachers were among the first in the city to cut off their queues.[126] One American Board preacher in a village on the coast refrained from removing his until he overheard some men discussing the question and saying that since the preacher had not cut off his queue, it was better to wait. The preacher thereupon went to the barber, and once the people saw that he had removed his queue they did likewise.[127]

The clearest evidence that Protestants, and particularly the Methodists, were closely identified by rural people as well as the Fuzhou elite with the new Republic is provided by the Xinghua rebellion of 1912 and 1913, which centered in part on the wearing or nonwearing of the queue. This rebellion arose against the new Republic in opposition both to taxes and to attempts by the new government to suppress opium cultivation in the area, which had recommenced during the confusion after the 1911 revolution. The Methodist churches throughout the prefecture were active in reporting on the opium situation and in pressing the local authorities to stamp out the poppy, and in January 1913 some Methodist missionaries took the step of publishing an account of the opium crop planted in Xinghua in the national press.[128]

According to missionary reports, the rebel forces in Xinghua captured men without queues and investigated them for links to either the government or the church. They blamed the church for the 1911 revolution, for the campaign against opium, and for the sending of troops against them.[129] The rebels identified Protestants, particularly Methodists, as enemies because of their close ties to the new Republic, and those ties were symbolized by their lack of the queue.[130]

The severing of the queue was a symbol of the new Republic, and even more than that, it was a symbol of the nation-building aspirations of those who wanted China to become a strong nation-state in the world system of nation-states. As we saw with regard to the Provincial Assembly, Chinese Protestants were among those people, and the Xinghua rebels were entirely correct to perceive a coercive aspect to the efforts of the new Republic to extend the authority of the state. In cutting their queues, Chinese Protestants aligned themselves with this vision of the nation. "Our preachers are looked to as the exponents of patriotism and the new life," reported one Methodist missionary soon after the revolution.[131] Outside cosmopolitan centers like Fuzhou, queueless Chinese Protestants may have provided the most visible sign for many of their compatriots of the new Republic and the new model of nationhood on which it was based.

Conclusion

The underlying question of this chapter has been how Chinese people in the Fuzhou area came to understand themselves as citizens of a nation and what the role of Protestants was in that process. We have focused on the ways Protestants drew on concepts that other nationalists shared, and applied symbolic and ritual expressions of nationhood that developed importance in China through the Republican period, in ceremonies, proto-national anthems, and national flags. I have suggested that owing in part to their familiarity with these concepts and symbols, Chinese Protestants were predisposed to understand themselves as citizens of a Chinese nation. For Protestants, national wealth and power, republicanism, and Christianity went together, and in the birth of the Republic of China they anticipated the swift realization of national prosperity and the Christianization of China.

I have also suggested that Protestants provided the most accessible models of some of the ceremonial and symbolic forms of nationalism to Chinese society on the local level; that is, the Protestant churches were one of the routes by which the international political rituals associated with nationalism made their way into Chinese practice. Some of the ways that Western ceremonial practices could be transferred from Protestant settings into a public arena can be seen on a ceremonial occasion which took place shortly after the revolution in Fuzhou.

This event, the memorial service for the two Protestant students executed by Manchu troops during the battle, was a public, not a church, event, yet a number of the nationalistic features seen in Protestant ceremonies are evident in it. The ceremony was held on December 2, about three weeks after the battle, in a temporary structure of bamboo built for the occasion, and it was decorated "with the flags of every nation," as well as "hundreds" of scrolls eulogizing the two martyrs. In the center were placed pictures of the two, surrounded by wreaths of flowers. The number of people in attendance is variously estimated at between three thousand and five thousand. The program was presided over by Huang Naishang and consisted of music and speeches, culminating in different constituencies coming forward to pay their respects by bowing to the pictures of the two martyrs. Leaders of the revolutionary government and friends of the dead students spoke, and according to the missionaries who attended, several speakers paid tribute to the Protestant schools or spoke of the relevance of Christianity to the new Republic. For the first time at a public meeting in Fuzhou (outside the churches), the speakers included women, two of whom were Protestants, one a returned student from America. Missionaries in attendance remarked on the "absolute absence of all heathen rites" and noted that the memorial song composed for the occasion was "sung to the tune of one of our most familiar gospel hymns."[132]

Some elements of this ceremony were clearly Chinese: the scrolls, the object representing the dead, and the act of honoring the pictures. Others elements were Western in inspiration: using the flags of the nations, singing congregationally and borrowing a Western tune, using pictures instead of tablets, bowing rather than kowtowing, having women speak in public. All of these had parallels in long-standing Protestant practices in Fuzhou. In fact, a public ceremony of this size with its program of speeches, music, and ritual elements had more in common with church events (such as the annual conferences of the Methodist church dating back to 1877, in which Huang Naishang had often been involved) than with any Chinese festivals or large gatherings.

It is tempting to dismiss issues like this — the use of flags, patriotic hymns, ceremonial forms — as trivial, or as nothing more than evidence of the aping of foreign ways by Chinese Protestants — that is, to see these Protestants as merely "Imitation Foreign Devils," to quote Lu Xun's fictional character Ah Q. The point, however, is precisely that the spread of modern nationalism has been a process of selective emulation, not only with respect to China or the former colonial world, but even within Europe and America. The British national anthem spawned a host of derivatives around the world, as did the French flag.[133] Trivial though national flags and national anthems may appear in themselves, by the early twentieth century they were becoming a defining mark of every nation-state or would-be nation-state in the world.

This brings us back to Benedict Anderson's most fundamental and convincing argument: once the first nation-states had come into being and were defined in print, they became models or blueprints available for selective appropriation by aspiring nationalist movements in any part of the world.[134] Or, to refer back to my formulation at the beginning of this discussion, there existed a repertoire of symbols and rituals associated with modern, even (as Sun Yatsen put it) "civilized" nation-states, from which the Chinese borrowed elements in order to gain acceptance as one of those nation-states. And in Fuzhou, some elements of that repertoire became familiar to Chinese people through their use by the Chinese Protestant community.

5

Kingdom Come?
The Protestant Heyday in Fuzhou, 1912–1922

Wei fuwu ye, fei yi yi ren (To serve, not to be served)
— *Motto on cornerstone of new YMCA building in Fuzhou, laid by the provincial governor in 1914*

The people here are not worried about their souls, but a surprisingly large number of them are ready to work and sacrifice on a program that looks practical to them for the remaking of their country, beginning with the local community, and if the Christian program of establishing the Kingdom of God on Earth is in line with that and can furnish power to do the job, they are interested.
— *Thomas C. McConnell, YMCA secretary, 1920*

Fuzhou Protestants in the early twentieth century presented Christianity as an ingredient of nation-building through its presumed power to inculcate a spirit of public morality and public service. In presenting it thus they drew on and appealed to a deep strain of moralism in Chinese nationalist rhetoric in this period, a moralism which, in fact, remained a staple of Chinese nationalism right through the twentieth century, seen in such diverse examples as Chiang Kaishek's New Life Movement, Mao Zedong's "Serve the People," and the image of self-sacrifice employed by the hunger strikers in Tiananmen Square in 1989.[1] One of the key terms that linked Protestant and non-Protestant versions of nationalism in Fuzhou was *gongyi*, "public welfare" or "public good." Protestants presented themselves as working for the "public good," just as the *gongyishe*, or reform societies, of pre-1911 Fuzhou did, and this Protestant self-definition was an important factor in their acceptance by other members of the Fuzhou political world.

The public nature of the Protestant role in Fuzhou society can be seen in the new Protestant structures that sprang up in the city after 1900, and particularly in the first few years of the Republic. The new building for the American Board hospital inside the south gate of the city opened in 1912, towering over the low roofs of the city residences.[2] Four years later the same mission opened a new two-thousand-seat brick church next to Foochow College; it boasted the first pipe organ in Fuzhou, the strains of which could be heard all through the southeast quadrant of the city.[3] The Methodists opened a large new church in the heart of the walled city in 1915, and the CMS, belatedly emulating their American brethren, opened new schools for men and women offering English instruction in the early 1900s.[4] In the 1910s the three missions combined resources with those working in south Fujian to found the Fukien Christian University, one of only two universities in the province in the Republican period (the other being Amoy [Xiamen] University, founded in the 1920s).[5] The Methodist college for women, Hwa Nan, received its first students in 1908 and moved into a magnificent new Sino-Western-style building in 1914 (fig. 5.1).[6]

In the county seats and country towns, too, physical signs of the Protestant presence multiplied during the early years of the Republic. Some examples will suffice to illustrate the general trend. In 1915, Bishop James Bashford dedicated a new Methodist church in a village south of Fuzhou, built of brick and seating three hundred people. The members of the church bought the land and contributed five hundred Chinese dollars, which the mission matched with a grant of eight hundred U.S. dollars to erect the building (fig. 5.2).[7] In Yongfu (Yongtai) County, a new building for the church in the county seat was opened in 1915, and a new chapel in another market town in 1921.[8] In Gutian County, a wave of new church construction beginning in 1910 saw eleven new churches built over the next fifteen years; by comparison, sixteen had been built in the forty years since mission work began there in 1870.[9]

Fig. 5.1. The pinnacle of Protestant architecture in Fuzhou: the imposing Hwa Nan Women's College, completed in 1914. Methodist Collection, Drew University, Madison, New Jersey.

The early Republican period was, then, a time of expansion in membership and facilities for the Protestant churches in the Fuzhou area. It was also a time when Protestant Christianity enjoyed a largely favorable public image and when Protestant moral positions seemed to many Chinese to provide possible answers to the needs of the nation. In short, the early Republican period was the heyday of Protestant influence in the Fuzhou area.

The YMCA and Public Life in Fuzhou

As we have seen, the YMCA was unusual among Protestant institutions in encouraging the participation of men who were not Christians. Its membership in Fuzhou grew swiftly after its establishment in 1907, reaching a total of 350 by the spring of 1911, the majority of whom were not church members. Its twelve-member board included the most influential lay members of the Chinese Protestant churches in the city, among them the three Protestants who became department heads in the provincial government after the revolution — Huang Naishang, Chen Zhilin, and Chen Nengguang — and Lin Changmin, already "looked upon as one of the most promising younger statesmen" in the land, who became prominent in national politics in the early Republic.[10] Several other key figures in the new government were among the non-Protestant members of the YMCA, including Gao Dengli and Liu Chongyou, former president and vice-president of the Provincial Assembly, now respectively head and deputy head of the Department of Civil Affairs (Minzheng bu), and Zheng Lie, head of the Judicial Department.[11]

Fig. 5.2. Protestant modernity in the Chinese countryside: the opening ceremony for a new rural church near Fuzhou, 1915. Bishop Bashford is visible in the middle of the crowd to the right of the church door. The church, seating three hundred people, was built by the villagers with the aid of a matching grant from the mission. Methodist Collection, Drew University, Madison, New Jersey.

The membership of the Fuzhou city YMCA dropped to 200 in 1912, but in the ensuing years it grew swiftly, approaching 2,400 in the early 1920s, as table 5.1 shows.

Membership is only one measure of growth; similar growth is evident in the annual figures for attendance at YMCA lectures, circulation of the Fuzhou YMCA magazine, *Fuzhou qingnian hui bao* (more than 1,000 by mid-1913), use of the YMCA building, budget, enrollment in the YMCA school, and the number of people involved in public service under YMCA leadership, culminating in the participation of 2,700 volunteers in a one-week health and sanitation education campaign in Fuzhou in the summer of 1920.[12]

It is when we look at the identity of the members that the degree of elite support for the YMCA in Fuzhou in the first years of the Republic becomes clear. In extant issues from 1913 and 1914, the Fuzhou YMCA magazine published the names of members, listed according to the level of their membership: ordinary members, who paid $5.50 per year; sustaining members, $24 per year (later $30); and extra-sustaining members, $100 per year. Notably, it

Table 5.1. Membership of the Fuzhou City YMCA, 1908–1929

Year	Total	Active Members	Associate Members
1907	60	—	—
1908	144	—	—
1909	260	—	—
1910	304	81	223
1911	347	54	293
1912	200	—	—
1913	845	—	—
1914	1,114	332	782
1915	1,607	412	1,195
1916	1,835	424	1,411
1917	1,616	—	—
1918	1,427	—	—
1919	1,721	—	—
1920	2,038	—	—
1921	2,369	—	—
—	—	—	—
1924	1,875	—	—
1925	1,569	—	—
—	—	—	—
1929	1,641	198	1,443

Sources: YMCA Archives, Annual Reports of L. E. McLachlin, 1909, 1910, 1913, 1914, 1915, 1916, 1917; E. H. Munson, 1917, 1920, 1925; A. Q. Adamson, 1911; E. H. Munson Report on Seventh Annual Membership Campaign, July 15, 1919, Box 30–100; *Qingnian hui wushi zhou nian,* p. 139; *Fuzhou qingnian hui bao* 3:3 (Xuantong 3/4/29), pp. 5–6; YMCAs of China, *Year Nineteen Sixteen,* statistical insert; *Annual Report of the YMCAs of China* (1920), p. 10; *Annual Report of the YMCAs of China* (1921), p. 21; *1930 Special Study Report of the Young Men's Christian Associations,* statistical appendix.

is this distinction rather than the potentially divisive religious-based distinction between "active" and "associate" members which was emphasized in the Chinese publications of the Fuzhou YMCA. The extra-sustaining category was created in 1913, and three of the first four men to sign up in that category the first year were the military governor, the civil governor, and the military chief of staff of the province.[13] By 1916 there were 31 of these extra-sustaining members—one of them a Buddhist monk—and 256 sustaining members, more than in any other YMCA in China.[14]

Among the identifiable YMCA members in these published lists are prominent scholars and educators (including the principal of the provincial middle school, Wang Xiu); Fujian delegates to the National Assembly (including the famous revolutionary and pioneer of vernacular journalism, Lin Baishui); veteran revolutionaries (including Zheng Zuyin, the pre-1911 head of the Fujian branch of the Revolutionary Alliance); leading bankers and industrialists (including several members of the "Electric Light Liu" family, which owned and operated the city's only electrical plant); and, naturally, a good number of Protestant pastors, postal and Customs employees, physicians, and mission school graduates.[15] Many of these men had been educated in Japan, others in America or Europe. These lists (the longest of which includes over nine hundred names) show that the YMCA had made inroads by 1913–1914 into all sectors of urban professional society in the city: government and bureaucracy, commerce and industry, education, and medicine.

An important factor in the YMCA's expansion in the early Republic, especially up to 1916, was undoubtedly the official patronage the association enjoyed in those years. As noted in Chapter 2 this began prior to 1911, when officials and leading citizens began to give public recognition to the YMCA by attending events or accepting invitations to speak at YMCA functions. After the revolution, the leading officials of the province continued to give public recognition and support to the YMCA. This was especially marked during the tenure of Xu Shiying as civil governor of Fujian, from 1914 to 1916. Xu laid the cornerstone for the new YMCA building in 1914, and he presented a scroll and a plaque in his own calligraphy for the building's dedication in March 1916 (the plaque, reading *dao yi zhi men*, "the door to morality," hung thereafter over the entrance of the building; figs. 5.3 and 5.4). Xu was not alone in honoring the opening of the new building: over the six days of festivities marking the event, congratulatory messages were also received from the national president and would-be emperor Yuan Shikai (written on a scroll of imperial yellow) and from the former premier Tang Shaoyi, and scrolls were presented by "the leading societies, guilds, and individuals of the city."[16]

The regular missions as well as the YMCA were beneficiaries of this new favorable attitude of officials in Fuzhou. An early instance took place in 1905, when the old American Board missionary Charles Hartwell, who had lived in Fuzhou since 1853, died. The governor-general honored Hartwell's half-century of service in the city by sending three officials to represent him at the funeral (one of them the future revolutionary and post-1911 governor Sun

Fig. 5.3. Provincial Governor Xu Shiying laying the foundation stone for the Fuzhou YMCA, 1914. Special Collections, Yale Divinity School Library.

Daoren) and ordering the streets cleared, as for an official, while the funeral procession passed out of the city.[17]

By 1910, the provincial officials were not only attending the graduation ceremonies of the major mission colleges but even making occasional social calls on missionaries. This kind of official patronage continued in the early Republic, especially in regard to the philanthropic endeavors of the missions. In 1915, Governor Xu Shiying presented an honorific plaque to the CMS School for the Blind, and his military counterpart, Li Houji, wrote a highly laudatory preface of endorsement for a fundraising brochure for the school. Li Houji also presented a plaque to Emily Hartwell, the founder of the orphanage of which Li Qifan (the Protestant revolutionary and bomb maker) had been superintendent in 1910 and 1911, when her work for the orphans of Fuzhou was honored by the national and provincial governments in 1918.[18]

The broad elite support for the YMCA is very evident in the involvement of prominent men in the annual membership campaigns, during which association members were mobilized to recruit new members for the coming year and collect their membership dues. These campaigns were organized as competitions to see which team could bring in the most in pledges and contributions.[19] Each team had a prominent man at its head. In the 1915 campaign, four of the teams were headed respectively by the governor (Xu Shiying again), two influential bankers, and the vice-chair of the chamber of commerce. The fifth and

Fig. 5.4. Fuzhou YMCA entrance, showing the plaque in his own calligraphy donated by Governor Xu Shiying at the building's dedication in March 1916. Special Collections, Yale Divinity School Library.

winning team was led by Liu Hongshou, the provincial salt commissioner, who had recently converted to Christianity and been baptized. Presumably, their subordinates would have been under a certain degree of pressure to join the YMCA; and indeed, "it is due to [Liu's] influence that practically all the men working in the Salt Department of the city and province have become members of the Association," noted YMCA secretary Ned Munson, with unconscious irony.[20]

The team captains in 1917 included the new governor and the new salt commissioner, both of whom had only recently arrived in the province but had been in contact with the YMCA in their previous posts; the president of the Provincial Assembly; the manager of the city's branch of the Bank of China; and the chair of the chamber of commerce. In 1919 they included Admiral Sa Zhenbing, a Fuzhou native who had played a crucial role in the 1911 revolution and later served as both Minister of the Navy in the national government and governor of Fujian in the mid-1920s; Guo Youpei, an elderly scholar who was head of the Confucian Society in Fuzhou yet was also a strong supporter of the YMCA over several years; and Chen Jishi, a son of the eminent Qing official Chen Baochen.[21]

The YMCA Land Campaign, Spring 1911

Support for the YMCA brought these benefactors the rewards of recognition in print, the social prestige of being identified as community leaders, and, for the winning teams, prizes and acclaim. In seeking to enlist the interest and aid of prestigious men, the YMCA seems to have harnessed Chinese concepts of prestige and patterns of elite philanthropy, in which visibility and publicity were central and giving was proportional to and a mark of one's social position. This can be seen in the major land campaign which the YMCA undertook in the spring of 1911, a campaign that raised pledges of $48,000 in two months, many times more than had ever been given to a Christian organization in Fuzhou up to that time. The largest contribution, $10,000, was made by one of the city's wealthiest men, a timber merchant named Lin (Ling Diong Hok in the Fuzhou dialect romanization), and his elderly father, Lin Rushan (Ling Oi Seng). In a passage that reveals a great deal about how Chinese modes of philanthropy as a public expression of status played into the campaign, one of the secretaries reports: "The progress of the whole campaign 'hung fire' upon the action of Mr. Ling and his father. The two other rich families who finally gave $5,000.00 each, waited for Ling Diong Hok to sign up and establish a scale. The same was true of all the merchants' and bankers' guilds. It was only a few days before the Campaign closed that the actual signatures were secured. The other families and guilds then speedily dropped into line signing up for sums large or small in proportion as their wealth is to that of Mr. Ling."[22]

The Lin family's contribution was recognized in 1918 by the placement of a bronze bust of father and son in the lobby of the building that they had made possible. The bust, commissioned by the board of directors and made by an American artist, was unveiled by the military governor, Li Houji, in the presence of the older Lin (the son having died) and several hundred distinguished guests, and was said to be the first bronze statue in China.[23] As with the Protestant use of flags and anthems, this incident furnishes one of many examples in which a Chinese impulse — here, to give public acknowledgment to philanthropy — took a new, Western-influenced form in a Protestant context, a form which anticipates the whole genre of public statuary that was to develop in China over the ensuing decades.

The final pledge list included $10,000 from this Lin family, $5,000 each from two other families and the provincial officials as a body, large pledges from the Fujian native-place associations in Shanghai, Singapore, and Nan-jing, $1,000 dollars each from the silk, lumber, cloth, and Jiangxi guilds in Fuzhou, $400 from the Ningbo guild, $150 from the doctors' guild, and another $4,280 from individual Chinese donors. In addition, the small for-eign missionary and business community in Fuzhou pledged over $10,000 of the total.[24]

Why were wealthy non-Christian Chinese willing to give at all toward a new building for a Christian institution like the YMCA? To answer this we must look at the campaign in more detail. The campaign came about because YMCA supporters in America had offered to provide $45,000 for a building for the Fuzhou YMCA, which had hitherto used rented premises, if its board of directors could raise a matching amount locally with which to purchase a suitable building site. In line with the YMCA emphasis on developing local leadership and initiative, the offer, which reached Fuzhou on March 15, 1911, was a conditional one: the board had to raise the necessary amount in reliable pledges by June 10 that year; otherwise the money would be offered to some other city in China.[25]

The first inclination of the Fuzhou directors was to judge the task impossi-ble, but they did not want Fuzhou to be shown up by some other city if they refused the challenge, so they agreed to undertake it. Local pride was inter-twined with nationalism in the publicity surrounding the campaign, which centered on the prospect of a building that would benefit the nation and the city for decades, even "centuries" to come. A lead article in the YMCA maga-zine related how the YMCAs in Tianjin, Shanghai, Guangzhou, and Hong Kong had all met similar challenges and erected buildings, and asked rhetori-cally if it were possible that "people of other provinces know the value of philanthropy, but in Fuzhou we are too hesitant, and content to watch a chance for doing good slip by." Educated readers would have recognized the last phrase, *"jian yi bu wei,"* as a quotation from Confucius (*Analects* 2:23), and they would have known its ending also, for Confucius in this passage describes a person who would see an opportunity to do good and fail to do it as *"wu yong ye,"* "devoid of courage." The following sentence in the YMCA magazine, printed in boldface using a larger font than for the rest of the text, hammered home the point: "The success or failure of this building campaign will directly affect Fuzhou's reputation and our own good names" in China and abroad.[26]

The man found to chair the campaign was Xu Zeya (1860–1937), a doctor active in the Anti-Opium Society. As we saw Chapter 2, Xu was a son of the Methodist preacher Xu Bomei who, like many other children of the first generation preachers, had been trained in Western medicine by a medical missionary. After spending some years in mission service, Xu had set himself up in private medical practice in the commercial suburbs of Fuzhou some time before 1896. He reportedly gained a reputation in Fuzhou for a treatment for measles which combined Chinese and Western medicines, and by this time he had become a wealthy and respected figure in the city.[27]

As his role in the Anti-Opium Society indicates, Xu had access to the highest levels of Fuzhou society, and he used this access to the full in enlisting elite support for the YMCA land campaign. First, after some weeks of quiet cultivation of contacts, he hosted a banquet at the YMCA building for a select group of fifty or sixty leading citizens and convinced the president of the chamber of commerce to join him in issuing the invitations. After the banquet, described by a foreign participant as "bountiful" and "conforming in every detail to strict Chinese etiquette," the visiting YMCA evangelist Sherwood Eddy addressed the gathering. He explained the work of the YMCA and the opportunity being offered to Fuzhou and asked them whether, as leading citizens of the city, they would accept responsibility for the success of the fundraising appeal. After a lengthy discussion they agreed unanimously to back the project and help solicit pledges among their friends, and so the public appeal started with the support of influential non-Christian men.[28]

Another key factor in generating donations was a visit by the colorful C. H. Robertson, the entrepreneurial science lecturer for the YMCA. Robertson (whose exploits formed the basis for the fictional protagonist David Treadup in John Hersey's wonderful historical novel of the American missionary experience in China) had come to China early in the decade and worked in the Tianjin YMCA, where he had developed some demonstration lectures on science which were found to be so successful in capturing the interest of Chinese audiences that he was asked to begin a Lecture Department for the whole country, attached to the YMCA National Committee in Shanghai.[29] He visited Fuzhou in early April 1911, on his way back from the United States with a load of new scientific equipment, and he came again in early May to help generate support for the land campaign.

Robertson was an imposing figure with an infectious enthusiasm for science, Christianity, and China, and his presentations made a great impression on some of those who later made large pledges to the building fund. The Lin father and son attended a special demonstration of electricity, the gyroscope, a monorail car, and a wireless telegraph, and the older Lin was reportedly in "high ecstasy" when Robertson took an X-ray of the bones in his hand. They sent Dr. Xu word of their $10,000 pledge a few days later. The Tartar general was described as "immensely pleased—and a little excited over his happy escape"—following Robertson's demonstration of a boomerang, which returned in a perfect arc and shattered against a tree right next to him.[30] Soon after this the provincial officials gave the YMCA and its building campaign an invaluable public endorsement by pledging $5,000.[31]

The one very large gift from the Lin family created pressure on those of similar means to give to the campaign. One report states: "With the securing of this pledge it will now become possible to bring pressure to bear on other wealthy Chinese here." Equally significantly, it created an incentive for other people to give in order to demonstrate that they *were* of similar means to the Lins; the same report tells of a rich man who had been overlooked, who asked Dr. Xu "why he had not been called upon and given the opportunity to accept the honor of making a large contribution to the campaign fund?"[32]

One further aspect of the campaign that deserves mention is the use of publicity for it. The fortnightly Chinese-language magazine of the Fuzhou YMCA carried extensive commentary on the campaign, appealing to local pride and stressing the public welfare (*gongyi*) nature of the association. It listed endorsements of the work of the YMCA from contemporary world leaders, among them the American presidents Theodore Roosevelt and William Howard Taft, Edward VII of England, the former French president Emile Loubet, Germany's Wilhelm II, the Meiji emperor, the Japanese statesman Ito Hirobumi, and the prominent Qing statesman Duan Fang. One interesting passage prefigures a familiar technique in fundraising appeals today, breaking down the target amount into more manageable components: with only a couple of weeks left in the campaign, the magazine pointed out that the substantial amount still needed could be attained with five pledges of $5,000, plus five at $1,000, five more at $500, and five at $100.[33]

The message that the success of the campaign was a matter of public concern was visibly signaled by another novel form of publicity, the erection of a huge clock face showing the progress in funds pledged, the twelve points marked in gradations of $4,000, passing the target total of $45,000. Official permission was requested and granted for this unprecedented advertising device, which was suspended across the entrance to the only bridge over the Min River, in the heart of the city's commercial district. As figure 5.5 shows, it would have been well-nigh impossible for anyone crossing that busy thoroughfare to overlook it. The YMCA magazine made the meaning of the clock explicit: "This fundraising has bearing on the public good (*gongyi*) and the external reputation of the people of Fuzhou, and you must know that only money has the power to advance the hands of the clock."[34]

The YMCA land campaign was successful in securing pledges of $48,000 within a few weeks, surpassing the target of $45,000. The 1911 revolution and the ensuing political and commercial disruption delayed collection of

Fig. 5.5. YMCA advertising: the fundraising clock over the Bridge of Ten Thousand Ages, 1911. The clock is labeled "Fuzhou YMCA Benevolent Fund Progress Display" along top and bottom; the vertical writing on the sides announces the goal, $45,000, and the deadline, the fifth day of the fifth lunar month. The clock face shows the pledged total, in increments of $4,000; this photo was clearly taken at either the beginning or the end of the campaign. In the center of the clock face is the YMCA symbol, the inverted triangle, with the corresponding motto, *deyu, zhiyu, tiyu,* "moral, intellectual, and physical education." Photo courtesy of the Kautz Family YMCA Archives, St. Paul, Minnesota.

some of the pledges, and difficulties with the plans drawn up by the architect in America delayed the building further, but when it did open early in 1916, it was a state-of-the-art facility, centrally located right on the Min River a short walk from the north end of the Bridge of Ten Thousand Ages (fig. 5.6; and see map 2.1). At four stories high it was the tallest building in the city, excepting the pagodas, and the only building to have flush toilets, showers, and hot and

Fig. 5.6. The Fuzhou YMCA, the most modern building in the city when it was opened in 1916. Special Collections, Yale Divinity School Library.

cold running water throughout — supplied by its own pumping plant and electrical generator. In addition to office and meeting space, it housed an indoor swimming pool, game rooms, a restaurant serving Western food, a dormitory, a barber shop, and the YMCA secondary school with its more than two hundred students.[35] The gymnasium doubled as an auditorium until the originally planned separate auditorium was added in the early 1920s.

Public welfare, publicity, and public reputation were what mobilized private donors in Fuzhou to give funds for the construction of a new kind of public space in the city, the YMCA building, with its facilities for leisure pursuits and public meetings and its ideology of public service. If the early twentieth century was a time of unprecedented expansion in politics as a public domain in Fuzhou, the fundraising for the new YMCA building points to the importance of physical space in the parallel restructuring of public life in the city. YMCA leaders saw the YMCA as a physical space offering the only "wholesome" leisure alternative to the brothels, gambling houses, and theaters, which increased in number and visibility through the 1910s — sometimes in direct relation to the physical changes in the city, as when a long block of brothels sprang up along the new paved road from the south gate to the river. "The city seems to have gone amusement mad," wrote one YMCA secretary in 1917, referring chiefly to this new visibility of prostitution. His conclusion: "The Association must spring into the breach and create a wholesome social atmosphere, permeated with Christian influence, for Foochow young men."[36]

Organizationally, as we have seen, there was a close parallel between the YMCA and the voluntary associations, or "reform societies," that mushroomed in Fuzhou in the early years of the twentieth century.[37] After the 1911 revolution these associations seem to have atrophied, however. The Qiaonan Society, which was so active leading up to the 1911 revolution, disbanded in 1912, and the functions of the Anti-Opium Society were assumed by the Opium Prohibition Bureau of the new government. A guide to the city published in 1917 listed none of the pre-1911 reform societies under *shetuan,* "associations." Of the eleven associations which it did list, most were based on particular professions, such as educators, policemen, doctors, and businessmen, or particular interests, such as the Confucian Study Society or the Society to Protect Domestic Manufacturing. The YMCA was the only one on the list that aimed to provide a broad range of activities for a diverse group of members.[38] The unique place of the YMCA in the associational life of the city is reflected in the comment of a leading local lawyer in 1919 that "the Association is the only live reform society in Foochow. None of the others can get their members to their buildings so frequently nor enlist them in so much service."[39]

The YMCA was also notably different from the older types of public association in the city: the commercial guilds and native-place societies.[40] These served more limited constituencies and were vulnerable, as were all associations in early Republican Fuzhou, to fluctuating political and commercial conditions (even the powerful chamber of commerce was forced to close down temporarily in the spring of 1917, during the political upheavals which followed the death of Yuan Shikai the year before).[41]

The "regular routine work" in the new YMCA building included "gym classes and swimming pool; movie shows and student theatres, socials, billiards, pool, ping-pong and chess; reading room and weekly educational lectures; the restaurant; the weekly religious meeting and Bible classes; night school with its seventy students and day school with its 250." In addition, the restaurant and the auditorium were made available for dinners or meetings of other associations. The YMCA ran a second facility within the walled city, less grand since it was a remodeled Chinese dwelling rather than a new building, but still spacious enough to offer "basket, volley, and hand ball courts, . . . an auditorium seating 1,000, a big game room, a parlor, a reading room, two offices, three committee places, four rooms for dormitories, a place for physical work, kitchens, servants' quarters, and a beautiful Chinese garden."[42]

That these buildings could provide the setting for novel forms of informal public contact between men of diverse ranks, ages, and backgrounds is indicated by the example of Admiral Sa Zhenbing (1859–1951). Sa, one of the most famous Fujianese of the Republican period, lived in Fuzhou in 1918–

1919, between national appointments. Although neither a Christian nor, at close on sixty, a young man, he became an enthusiastic member of the YMCA in these years; his friendship with Huang Naishang, who had once been his teacher and whose younger brother had been a navy man, was apparently instrumental in getting him involved. Besides serving as a team leader in the membership campaign in 1919, he headed the Fuzhou YMCA delegation to the Eighth National YMCA Convention in Tianjin in 1920.[43] According to the American secretary of the YMCA branch within the walled city, the admiral was "a most frequent visitor" to the YMCA building in 1918–1919. He "gets nervous if fussed over too much, but will be occupied for hours if left alone to play billiards and pool with whoever happens to come in to make up a game."[44]

The success of the 1911 building fund campaign was thus attributable in part to a particular combination of Chinese social mores and Western novelty. The work of contacting people and securing their support was undertaken by Chinese Protestants of standing, like the physician Xu Zeya: "To [Dr. Xu] is due the credit for the entree into the three wealthiest families of the city," the YMCA general secretary reported.[45] Huang Naishang, president of the YMCA at the time, also played a role. The appeal drew upon Chinese notions of prestige, both personal and provincial, and Chinese modes of philanthropy, involving public recognition and the rhetoric of public welfare. The image of the YMCA as on the cutting edge of modernity was underlined by Robertson's vivid scientific demonstrations and by the repeated reminder of the generosity of Americans in making the matching funds for a building available.

Ultimately, however, the campaign was successful because the YMCA managed to position itself in the public domain, not as an organization for one particular clientele — whether Christians or youth, though it was for men, not women — or, in theory at least, for one socioeconomic group, but for the benefit of the whole city, indeed the whole nation. The donors included men of all ages, as figure 5.7 illustrates.[46]

The pattern evident in the campaign, and indeed in the support for the YMCA in Fuzhou through the first decade of the Republic, is not so much of a "public sphere" in the sense used by Jürgen Habermas of an arena for dissent as of an interlocking domain of acknowledged public service supported by officials and eminent citizens alike.[47] More than anything, elite support for the Fuzhou YMCA from about 1910 to 1922 is reminiscent of what has been called the informal Protestant establishment in America, where the legal separation of church and state did not prevent broad cultural agreement and interlocking ties of patronage and support between political and financial power centers and mainline churches.[48] The flourishing of the YMCA in America was

Fig. 5.7. Support for the YMCA was not restricted to the young: this elderly man was one of the principal donors to the building campaign for the city branch of the YMCA in the 1910s. Special Collections, Yale Divinity School Library.

based upon such ties: its leaders had the ear of politicians and presidents, and in fact the offer of building funds to YMCAs in China had come about because then President Taft had convened a conference at the White House of the wealthiest men in the country and pressed them to give generously for the uplift of mankind through the expansion of YMCA facilities worldwide.[49] The Fuzhou YMCA sought to forge a similarly beneficial link to men of wealth and influence in the city, and during the 1910s it did so with a degree of success that was nothing short of astonishing given the very different social setting.[50]

The Eddy Campaigns of 1913 and 1914

The public interest in Protestant Christianity in early Republican Fuzhou was dramatically evidenced during the evangelistic visits of Sherwood Eddy to the city in 1913 and 1914. In March 1913, Eddy came to Fuzhou at the end of a three-month preaching tour of thirteen Chinese cities with John R. Mott, and the results in Fuzhou greatly surpassed those in any of the other locations. As on his previous visit to Fuzhou in 1911, Eddy was accompanied by the YMCA science lecturer C. H. Robertson, whose role in these meetings was described in a YMCA publication as "breaking down prejudice . . . and showing the students of China that there is no contradiction between true science and true religion."[51]

The largest auditorium within the walled city—the Zhejiang Guild Hall, which could seat over two thousand people—was secured at a nominal rent for the meetings, and the response was so positive that for the six days of meetings Eddy had to give each lecture twice, to a packed hall each time, while Robertson lectured to the overflow crowd waiting for admission in the court-yard outside. On the first day, Eddy records, "We spoke . . . on 'The Crisis in China.' Our point of contact with the audience was their new national flag. . . . When they were aroused to burning interest and concern for their country we spoke of the moral and religious needs of the Republic."[52] Eddy and Robert-son both gave separate lectures for women in the same building, which were also well attended. Between the two of them they spoke to 30,000 people over the six days, and over 1,500 men and women signed cards promising to study the Bible and investigate the claims of Christianity.[53] Of these, 562 were en-rolled in Bible classes over the next few months, and by the end of the year 159 had been baptized and joined the churches, and another 166 had been received as probationers.[54]

Elite interest in Eddy's message is evident in the fact that the principals of the thirteen government schools in the city canceled afternoon classes for the week and postponed their examinations to allow their students to attend the meet-ings. As with the leading citizens during the land campaign two years earlier, these men had been cultivated in advance at a special banquet, and as a result, they issued a formal invitation to Eddy and Robertson to visit Fuzhou. They also held a banquet for the visitors at which they discussed "plans for helping the students in their moral characters."[55] "Never have I received such support from professors in any Christian country," Eddy noted after leaving the city.[56] Similarly telling was the fact that the new Republican Provincial Assembly invited Eddy and Robertson to come and address the assembly, adjourning for an afternoon to hear them. The man acting as interpreter for Eddy during the meetings, the YMCA secretary Zhu Lide (who had interpreted for Eddy dur-ing his 1911 visit), was himself a member of the assembly, and all ninety-six members of the body were present to hear Eddy and Robertson speak.[57]

Sherwood Eddy described the 1913 campaign in Fuzhou as "the most mem-orable week in our lives," and it was a galvanizing experience for the churches in Fuzhou as well. Out of the enthusiasm generated by this campaign came an ambitious scheme for a province-wide evangelistic campaign for the fall of the next year to cover fourteen of the principal cities of the province.[58] Nothing so extensive had ever been attempted in China before. The plan for the 1914 campaign, which was to be a united effort of all six Protestant missions in north and south Fujian as well as the YMCA, was that Eddy and Robertson would hold the meetings in Fuzhou and Xiamen, and five other pairs of speakers (like Eddy and Robertson, one evangelistic and one scientific speaker) would hold meetings along the same model in the lesser cities, each pair spending four or five days in each of two or three cities. The evangelistic speakers in these five teams were all Chinese, some from Fujian and some brought in for the occasion; the science speakers were all Westerners.[59] The churches in each city would coordinate the local effort and make contact afterward with those who signaled an interest in Christianity during the meetings. The YMCA would provide the overall coordination and training for the members of the local teams.

A full year's preparation went into this effort, and consequently a higher proportion of those pledging to study Christianity were actually contacted and enrolled in Bible studies than in 1913. In the eleven cities covered in north Fujian, total attendance ran to 87,000 people, and 6,006 signed inquirers' cards, of whom 2,400 were attending Bible classes within three months of the meetings. In Fuzhou itself, the crowd for the first lecture of the campaign was 8,900, but as the hall (again the Zhejiang Guild Hall) could accommodate only 2,400 people at a time, the same lecture had to be delivered four times in succession over eleven hours to accommodate all who wished to hear it.[60]

In many of the secondary cities visited, the crowds that gathered for these meetings were larger than had ever before been witnessed there. For example, in the inland city of Jianyang, where 700 people, the county magistrate among them, assembled to hear David Yui (Yu Rizhang) give an evangelistic address, the missionary remarked that "large public meetings are unknown to Kienyang [Jianyang] — the only large meetings known being theatres which are not conducted on 'quiet lines.'" In these cities, attendance at each of the several meetings per day ranged from 500 to over 1,000; in Minqing the daytime meetings drew from 650 to 900 people, and those at night, 500, while in neighboring Gutian the morning and evening meetings for men had over 1,000 in attendance on average, and the meetings for women, held each afternoon of the campaign, drew around 800 listeners on average.[61]

While elite support was evident during the 1913 campaign, in 1914 that support took the form of an actual public endorsement of the meetings by the provincial government and by the magistrates and leading citizens of the other cities. Well before the campaign, Governor Xu Shiying had joined with the Fuzhou Chamber of Commerce, the head of the provincial Department of Education, and the principals of the government schools in Fuzhou in sending a telegram officially inviting Eddy and Robertson to the province. As in 1913, the government schools in Fuzhou were recessed for the afternoon during the week of the meetings, and the school principals encouraged their students to attend. The governor also issued proclamations urging the people of Fuzhou to attend the meetings and instructed the magistrates of the other cities where meetings were to be held to do the same. The governor chaired the first lecture, and he, the educational leaders, and the chamber of commerce each feted the visitors at banquets during their week in Fuzhou.[62] The flags of the United States and the Republic of China "provided the decorative motif" for the menu at the banquet hosted by the governor.[63]

In the secondary cities the officials and leading citizens were equally receptive, in no small measure because of the influence of the Fuzhou YMCA. After touring the province with a Chinese pastor in preparation for the fall campaign, the YMCA secretary, E. H. Munson, reported: "In each center which we visited we found that either the local magistrate or the president of the chamber of commerce or representative to the Provincial Assembly were members of our Foochow Association. In every instance we secured the hearty support and cooperation of the local officials, gentry, and heads of the government schools."[64]

Elite support was equally evident in the cities during the meetings themselves. In several of them (Yongfu, Yanping, Jianyang, Shaowu) the meetings were opened or attended by the local magistrate. In Yongfu interest was so great that two more meetings were held after the speakers had left, and enrollment in Bible studies was urged by one of the leading non-Christian educators. In Shaowu and Fuqing the magistrates were among the hundreds of people who signed inquirers' cards, and in Yanping the Taotai, the magistrate, the head of the local Anti-Opium Society, and several other leading citizens signed cards. Some of these cities had been intensely resistant to missionary work in the late nineteenth century, notably Jianning, where riots and church burnings had repeatedly forced all missionaries from the city, most recently in 1899, just fifteen years earlier; on this occasion, by contrast, 548 men in Jianning signed cards, including "practically all the leading men in the City."[65]

Reports on campaigns like this published by the sponsoring organization naturally tend to emphasize success, and their claims must be treated with care. In this case, however, even allowing for a certain degree of exaggeration, it is clear that the level of response to the meetings took the missionaries who reported on it by surprise, and the support for the meetings by local and provincial officials struck them as significant. Why was there such a level of official and elite support for these meetings? To answer this question, we must look more closely at the content of Eddy's presentation of Christianity.

The essence of his presentation was that Christianity was the basis for progress and national strength. Eddy expressed his core message this way to the Provincial Assembly in 1913: "[China's] greatest need was character and . . . Christ produced the highest character."⁶⁶ In 1914 he urged the governor and leading officials of Fujian to "give their hearts to him who could make them and China strong."⁶⁷ The five Chinese evangelists who visited the secondary cities in 1914 shared with Eddy the idea that in Christianity lay the secret of Western progress and national strength; one of them, C. T. Wang, described the hundreds who signed cards in Xinghua as "signifying their desire to study the Book which furnished and is still furnishing the dynamic of growth and progress to the West."⁶⁸

The officials who patronized these meetings also seem to have considered Christianity a potential source of moral resources for strengthening the nation. The head of the provincial Department of Education is quoted as saying at a banquet for Eddy and Robertson in 1914 that "Confucianism alone cannot save China. We need the moral dynamic and principle of progress which Christianity can give." This man, incidentally, had placed his own son not in one of the government schools under his charge but in the mission-run Foochow College.⁶⁹ Similarly, a provincial legislator from Jianning gave his support to the planned campaign, saying, "The most pressing need of our city is the moral uplift of our young men," and the Yanping Taotai stated, "The great weakness in our nation is that we have so few real leaders who can . . . lectur[e] on morality and religion. . . . We need someone to teach us how to live moral lives."⁷⁰

A typescript précis of Eddy's talk entitled "The Hope of China" shows more clearly how he presented Christianity to Chinese audiences. This was the third and climactic address on his China tours in 1913 and 1914, at the close of which he called for decisions to sign inquirers' cards. In the talk Eddy dealt first with the meaning of Christianity for individuals, but his emphasis was on the impact of Christianity on societies and nations, Christianity as "a *mighty dynamic for national* life," in Eddy's underlined phrase. Socially, Eddy claimed that Christianity worked against famine, poverty, and ignorance, and it worked against sickness by motivating Christians like Pasteur and Florence Nightingale to devote themselves to medical service. Christianity had resulted in the abolition of slavery in the Roman Empire and ("finally"—passing in silence over the very recent history of slavery and its religious rationalization in his own country) in every Christian country.

Most of all, however, in the "progress or evolution" of religion "from lower to higher forms," Christianity was proving itself "the fittest" and was "fast becoming universal." Eddy used various charts and statistics to imbue this

Fig. 5.8. The Reverend Wang Ganhe preaching to an audience in Minqing County during the province-wide evangelistic campaign of 1914. The graph on the stage beside Wang, entitled "The Growth in Numbers of Christian Believers," shows a steep increase in the number of Christians in the world since 1800. Minqing native Huang Naishang is seated immediately to the right of the white backdrop at the rear of the stage. Barely visible hanging from the ceiling above the stage are several strings of flags of the nations of the world. Methodist Collection, Drew University, Madison, New Jersey.

claim with an aura of scientific validity, such as the graph showing the exponential growth in numbers of adherents of Christianity over recent centuries, visible on the stage in the photograph of the rally in Minqing (fig. 5.8).

Eddy's overall line of reasoning is evident in the following passage:

> Once the world was governed by polytheistic races. There is now no polytheistic self-governing nation in the world, while 95% of the world's area is governed by Christian nations. Once the world was ruled by national religions. Today 50 countries have become Christian, and only two countries with a national religion are left. . . . Buddhism was once a powerful religion. Today there is no self-governing Buddhist country in the world. Mohammedanism was once powerful in many nations. Today it has lost control of Europe. It does not have political control of any country in Africa. It has lost influence over all educated races. One religion only is becoming universal,

appealing equally to East and West, rich and poor, wise and ignorant. Truth in the end must prevail. The fittest must survive. Christianity uplifts a nation. Will China discover this in time?[71]

In other words, the conquest and colonization of the world by Western nations demonstrated the evolutionary superiority of Christianity over tribal polytheism and "national religions" and over the other potential contenders for the title of "universal" religion, Buddhism and Islam. The argument is breathtakingly self-serving from today's perspective. To be fair to Eddy, however, he was probably not advocating world domination so much as attempting to turn to the service of Christianity what he saw as a fait accompli. As Hutchison argues in his influential study of American Protestant mission thought, American missionary thinkers in this period tended to see themselves as "chaplains and tamers of Western expansion," regarding imperialism as a regrettable but inexorable force which they were called upon to elevate and spiritualize.[72]

It is important to note also that Eddy's argument is almost entirely utilitarian. There is little reference to Christian doctrine in the speech, let alone explanation of it; indeed, there is little reference to God or to Jesus Christ. Instead, Eddy presents "Christianity" in the abstract as a force in national life and world history and as a tool in nation-building. As we have seen, nation-building was the great imperative for patriotic Chinese in the early twentieth century, and Chinese Protestants in Fuzhou tended to clothe their religion in the language of nation-building. Significantly, the five Chinese evangelists in the 1914 campaign apparently used variants of Eddy's three speeches, with similar charts and other props (see fig. 5.8). And in China in the early years of the Republic, any possible means to national wealth and power could gain a hearing, as the response to the campaigns in 1913 and 1914 shows.

Elite Conversion and Its Limits, 1910–1922

Given the association of republicanism and progress with Christianity, broad elite support for the YMCA, and the prominence of individual Protestants in Fuzhou society after 1911, it is small wonder that both Chinese Protestants and American missionaries in Fuzhou anticipated a great influx of Chinese into the Christian church. As L. E. McLachlin put it in the afterglow of the 1914 campaign: "The tide Christward is rapidly rising. A mighty mass movement like that in England during Wesley's time is beginning here. The Chinese Church promises a great advance."[73]

In hindsight, of course, the Eddy campaigns of 1913 and 1914 were not the beginning of a "tide Christward," nor did China become a Christian nation in the ten years after the creation of the Republic, as Huang Naishang had hoped. Nevertheless, there were conversions to Christianity during the early Republic, and for the first time since the early decades of the Jesuit mission in Fujian in the seventeenth century, Christian converts came from the highest levels of elite society in the Fuzhou area — not just from among the wealthy, but from the *shijia* or eminent scholar-official households of the city.[74] A look at some of these converts — all of whom were involved in the YMCA — helps to clarify the appeal of Christianity and the limits of that appeal in this time of rapid social change.

The first such convert in Fuzhou was Lin Changmin (1876–1925), who was discussed in connection with the late Qing Provincial Assembly in Chapter 3. Lin was the son of a late nineteenth-century official and Hanlin scholar, and he became interested in Christianity through contact with the YMCA while he was a student at Waseda University in Japan between 1903 and 1909. In 1910, while serving as first secretary of the Fujian Provincial Assembly, Lin decided to convert publicly to Protestant Christianity and was baptized. The YMCA secretary who knew him best among the missionaries said that he reached this decision after "a scientific study of the Christian religion and a comparison of it with the other great religions."[75] Soon after his baptism, Lin was elected to the board of directors of the Fuzhou YMCA, and in 1911 he was elected to the National Committee of the YMCA in China, on which he served until 1920.[76]

That is where evidence of Lin Changmin's Christian involvement ends, however. After 1911 he no longer lived in Fuzhou, but was instead active in national politics in Nanjing and Beijing. He was a close friend and associate of Liang Qichao, forming the Progressive Party with him, and his daughter Lin Huiyin (Lin Whei-yin) later married Liang Qichao's son Liang Sicheng. In 1920–1921 he lived in London in connection with the Chinese League of Nations Association, where his daughter (still unmarried) became the object of affection of the romantic poet Xu Zhimo, and Lin developed an interest in the socialist writings of Sidney and Beatrice Webb.[77]

In 1913, a visiting pastor from Beijing told the American Board pastors in Fuzhou that Lin Changmin was known in Beijing to be a Christian (as were five or six other members of the National Assembly) but did not attend church regularly.[78] Around the same time, he took a concubine, which would, if known, have excluded him from membership in any Protestant church. In the biographies of him, which deal for the most part with Lin's political career after 1911, no mention is made of Christianity or of his YMCA affiliation.[79] In sum, it appears that Lin Changmin's interest in Christianity while he lived in Fuzhou from 1909 to 1911 was not lasting, and that Christianity to Lin was probably just one of the sequence of ideologies he adopted in his quest for a solution to the problems facing China, rather than a central element of his political identity, as it was for Huang Naishang.[80]

The most important Protestant convert in the early years after the 1911 revolution was the salt commissioner of the province, Liu Hongshou, who was persuaded to become a Christian during Sherwood Eddy's time in the city in November 1914. As salt commissioner, Liu was responsible for one of the main sources of revenue for the provincial government, and he was the chief architect of the restructuring of the old Qing gabelle system into a bureaucratic monopoly under the provincial government. Liu had a reputation for honesty in public life, a reputation that was strengthened when he was found to be substantially in debt after his untimely death in April 1916 (since it showed that he had not used his position to enrich himself from the public purse).[81]

Liu was married to a sister of Chen Baochen, the leading Fujianese scholar-official of the early twentieth century, and he was closely associated with Chen's son-in-law Lin Bingzhang, of the pre-1911 Anti-Opium Society — although Liu was still smoking opium after the 1911 revolution, according to one source.[82] After Eddy addressed the provincial officials at the banquet in his honor in 1914, Liu asked for a personal interview with him, and as a result of that conversation he decided to declare himself a Christian. Despite some criticism from other members of the Fuzhou elite, Liu went on to be baptized in May the next year, and was soon thereafter elected to the board of directors of the Fuzhou YMCA and became its president.[83] According to the YMCA secretaries' reports, Liu was the most able president the Fuzhou YMCA had ever had, very keen in serving the association and eager to see other members of the "official and gentry classes" join the church. However, he had served in the position only half a year when "this great man laid aside his earthly tasks to take up life more abundant in the immediate presence of his Heavenly Father," as a YMCA secretary put it.[84]

Liu Hongshou's time as a public Protestant in Fuzhou was short, but he did indeed influence some other members of the "official and gentry classes" to convert to Christianity, in particular some members of the Wang lineage of Fuzhou. This wealthy and influential lineage produced many scholars and officials in the Qing dynasty, among them two of the major Fujianese officials of the nineteenth century, Wang Qingyun (1797–1862), who earned the *jinshi* degree in 1829 and had a long and successful career as a Hanlin compiler and an official in Beijing and in the provinces, and his grandson Wang Renkan (1849–1893), the *zhuangyuan,* or top-ranking graduate, in the palace examination of 1877. As the only *zhuangyuan* from Fuzhou in the late nineteenth century, Wang Renkan achieved instant fame in the province, fame which reflected on his relatives and descendants, even though his subsequent official postings were at middle rank (he fell afoul of the Empress Dowager and the powerful Li Hongzhang) and he died quite young.[85]

Wang Renkan had eleven sons, seven of whom survived to maturity. The ninth son, Wang Xiaozong (Yangong, born in 1889), was educated in the Fujian Military Preparatory School and then in a military academy in Japan, and, like Lin Bingzhang, was married to a daughter of Chen Baochen (whose wife was herself a sister of Wang Renkan and thus Wang Xiaozong's aunt). Wang Xiaozong served in the Chinese diplomatic corps in the 1920s, holding vice-consular positions in Italy, Vancouver, San Francisco, and Korea.[86] In 1934 he returned to Fuzhou as head of the Fujian Provincial Library, which position he held until 1940.[87]

In the mid-1910s, Wang Xiaozong was a senior official in the Salt Commission of the Fujian government, where he was "a very intimate friend" of Liu Hongshou.[88] Liu Hongshou's conversion to Christianity influenced Wang, and sometime in 1915 he also decided to declare himself a Christian.[89] Soon afterward he was elected to the YMCA's board of directors, and according to the YMCA secretary Ned Munson, he had "a very deep religious experience and . . . an intense prayer life."[90] The Methodist church and the YMCA both urged him to enter full-time Christian work, and in 1917 he left his government position to work for the YMCA at less than one-half his former salary. In speaking to people about Christianity, Wang used to draw a spiritual analogy from his illustrious family background, quoting his mother's injunction to him to "remember whose son you are and endeavor to be like your father," and using it to "remind men that they are sons of the Heavenly Father."[91]

In 1919, Wang Xiaozong became the YMCA secretary in charge of membership development in Fuzhou, but he seems to have remained in the position for just a few months before going into the diplomatic service. Later sources shed no light on his subsequent Christian involvement. His name does not appear in the reports of the YMCA secretaries in Fuzhou after 1921, when Ned Munson lamented the "withdrawal into the Chinese Diplomatic Service" some time before of this "most outstanding Christian leader." His daughter graduated in 1936 from Hwa Nan College, and worked for the YWCA in Nanjing for a time, but this does not necessarily mean that her father remained Christian.[92]

Whatever Wang's religious position in later life, in his time as a public Protestant in Fuzhou he influenced two other members of this important family to convert to Christianity. One was his younger brother Wang Xiaoxiang (Yanyun, 1891–1992), the tenth son of Wang Renkan. Wang Xiaoxiang had graduated from a medical college in Japan, where he had been involved with the Revolutionary Alliance, and he had a long career in military medicine and public health administration in Fujian, elsewhere in China, and, after 1949, in Taiwan.[93]

From 1912 until the early 1920s, Wang Xiaoxiang was working in Fuzhou as head of the Fujian Police Hospital, and he established a reputation as "one of the rising young doctors of the city," according to a YMCA secretary. He had been "won to Christ by his older brother who left a high official position to enter Christian service."[94] In 1920 he served on the board of management for the walled city branch of the YMCA, and he was on one of the teams for the YMCA membership campaign that year. His wife Lin Jianyan (born in 1892) was on the board of directors of the Fuzhou YWCA in 1920, and both Wang and his wife were involved in organizing a large-scale educational exposition at the grand new Methodist "institutional church" in the heart of the walled city in 1922.[95]

This "institutional church," which opened in 1915 and was the first such facility in China, was in essence the church equivalent of a YMCA, aiming to be "a strong Christian force in the heart of the big city, an influence touching the educational, political and religious life of the entire provincial capital."[96] Like the Fuzhou YMCA (the secretaries of which were not at first pleased with the competition), it provided a range of social and educational as well as religious services to the people of the city, including movie showings, a reading room, public classes in civics, hygiene, and literacy, social clubs, free tea for rickshaw pullers, and a museum. The museum was the site for the educational exposition, which was organized by the church with government sponsorship and aimed to showcase the achievements of the Protestant schools of the city along with those of the government and private schools.[97]

Like other high-status converts, Wang Xiaoxiang and his wife, Lin Jianyan, quickly took on public roles in the Protestant churches and in Protestant associations like the YMCA and YWCA following their conversion in the 1910s. However, the sources give no indication of whether they remained active in the church after leaving Fuzhou in the mid-1920s. Wang Xiaoxiang was one of the cohort of men whose families were left on the mainland when the Nationalist government retreated to Taiwan in 1949, and he married and had three more children in his sixties in Taiwan (in addition to four surviving children in China). In the 1993 revision of the Wang clan genealogy, which probably reflects the knowledge of his Taiwan family, Wang Xiaoxiang is described as a devout Buddhist who saw his medical practice within a Buddhist framework of relieving suffering (*jiuren jishi*). He remained a patriot throughout his life; at the age of eighty he had himself photographed in the same pose as that in a picture of him as a revolutionary youth in Japan and wrote a patriotic verse on the picture. Wang Xiaoxiang's Christian period may have ended well before he arrived in Taiwan, for the same account mentions that Wang's wife Lin and a concubine named Chen were both already deceased when he came to Taiwan.[98]

For Wang Xiaoxiang, as for Lin Changmin, then, Protestant Christianity seems to have been one staging post in the century spanned by his long life, a life that began and ended with the ideal of patriotism through service, beginning with his medical studies and revolutionary activism in Japan, framed in the early 1920s in the terms of YMCA Christianity, and finally finding expression through Buddhism.

The third member of the Wang lineage to convert to Protestant Christianity in the early Republican period was a cousin of these two brothers, Wang Xiaoquan (Zhenxian, Fuchu; 1882–1967).[99] Wang Xiaoquan was an outstanding scholar who went three times to Japan, studying education at Meiji University before 1909 and political economy at Waseda University in the early 1910s. His later career reflected both these fields of expertise, for he held high posts at different times in both the Department of Education and the Department of Finance of the Fujian Provincial Government and wrote books and essays on law and fiscal administration as well as on education. For most of his life he worked not in government but as an educator, teaching Chinese studies at Fukien Christian University, at Amoy University, and, from 1925 until his retirement in 1951, at Hwa Nan College, of which his niece Wang Shijing was president from 1928.[100]

Wang Xiaoquan converted to Protestant Christianity in 1916 or 1917 through the influence of Wang Xiaozong and became "one of the strongest and most earnest personal workers that we have," in the words of one YMCA secretary. By 1917 he had become one of the directors of the Fuzhou YMCA, a capacity in which he continued to serve into the 1930s.[101] In 1920, Wang was employed as a section head in the provincial Department of Education, and he was reported to be "a man of fine Christian spirit and of such ability that for practically all local matters he is the acting Educational Commissioner."[102] He was made chair of a new board of management formed that year to oversee the work of the YMCA branch within the walled city, and in 1922, no doubt because of his seniority in educational circles, Wang chaired the advisory board for the church-sponsored educational exposition in which his cousin Wang Xiaoxiang and his cousin's wife were also involved.[103]

As with Wang Xiaoxiang, the recollections of those who knew him later in life give a different, and somewhat fuller, picture of Wang Xiaoquan's religious life than the YMCA reports do. Wang's first wife, by an arranged marriage, died at age twenty-nine in 1914, while Wang was studying in Japan. On his return he married again, to a woman named He Xiuying (1901–1931), nineteen years his junior. Their first child was born in 1918, when He was seventeen and Wang thirty-six, and seven more followed over the next eleven years before He Xiuying's brief life ended. Wang Xiaoquan seems to have been devoted to her, for he wrote two moving laments for her which appear in the clan's 1935 genealogy, and he determined not to remarry after her death.[104]

After their mother's death, chief responsibility for raising the eight young children fell to Wang Xiaoquan's sister, who had been married at age sixteen and widowed at seventeen. According to Wang's eldest daughter, born in 1918, her aunt was an ardent Christian, but the daughter was less clear about her father's belief. He was much older than his children and did not confide in them about such matters. The family went to church sometimes during her childhood, but not regularly. The two daughters who went to Taiwan after 1949 remained Christians, but not the other six siblings, who stayed in China. The two youngest, and perhaps others, joined the Chinese Communist Party in the late 1940s.[105]

Others who worked with Wang Xiaoquan in the 1930s and 1940s recall him as a Christian, but not as fervent in his belief as his nieces Wang Shijing (president of Hwa Nan College from 1928) and Wang Shixiu (wife of Chen Zhimei, the president of the Anglo-Chinese College from 1927). Since he and his family lived in the walled city rather than in the Cangqian area, where the main churches and educational institutions of the Methodist church were located, he remained on the periphery of the life of the church, at least from the perspective of those who lived and worked in that area.[106]

Conclusion

It is notoriously difficult to deduce from indirect evidence anything about the meaning of religious belief to individuals, and that certainly applies to the elite Protestant converts of 1910–1920 discussed here: Lin Changmin, Liu Hongshou, Wang Xiaozong, Wang Xiaoxiang, and Wang Xiaoquan. Nevertheless, we know that they all made their decisions to profess Christianity in the intellectual milieu of the YMCA in early Republican Fuzhou, a milieu in which Christianity was routinely presented as a means toward the goal of national renewal through the creation of a moral citizenry. There are indications that this is what these men cared most about — for example, in Lin Changmin's later political career and in extant articles by Wang Xiaoquan on education, which show his sense of the connections between education, morality, civil government, and national survival.[107] Moreover, in the case of three of them (Lin Changmin, Wang Xiaoxiang, and Wang Xiaoquan), there are indications that their Christian involvement lessened after the early 1920s, when the link between Christianity and national renewal became less apparent to Chinese and even to Protestants themselves.

However, that men of this status in Fuzhou society converted at all underlines the influence and the respectability of Protestant churches and the YMCA in Fuzhou in the early twentieth century. Protestants, many of them in the new professions, became active and accepted participants in the new forms of political life that developed in the city in the first decade of the century and in the postrevolutionary government. From its founding in 1907 until 1922, and particularly between 1911 and 1916, the YMCA in Fuzhou enjoyed extraordinary levels of elite and government patronage and support. Finally, not only did members of elite society in Fuzhou support the YMCA, some of them actually converted publicly to Protestant Christianity between 1910 and 1922. Underlying all of these developments was the deep concern of politically aware Chinese in the early twentieth century with the question of how to make China a strong nation, a question which they were predisposed to see in moral terms.

6

Why China Did Not Become
a Christian Republic

Obliterate all church institutions!
— *Fujian Student Federation, 1925*

For a very long period, U.S. imperialism laid greater stress than other imperialist countries on activities in the sphere of spiritual aggression, extending from religious to "philanthropic" and cultural undertakings.
— *Mao Zedong, 1949*

Many phases of the work of the church in China I should have written about thirty or more years ago with much confidence. I cannot write this confidently now.
— *W. L. Beard, American Board missionary in Fuzhou, 1933*

A palpable, if somewhat anxious, optimism is evident in the reports and writings of Protestants in Fuzhou, both missionaries and Chinese, during the first few years of the Republic. By and large Chinese Protestants, like the missionaries, interpreted the political changes since the beginning of the century and the current unprecedented levels of interest in Christianity among their compatriots as confirmation of the impending "ultimate triumph of Christianity in this land" — if only the Protestants could rise to the challenge presented by the opportunities of the day.[1] The change must have seemed especially dramatic to veterans like the old pastor Ye Yingguan (Iek Ing Guang, 1840–1923), last surviving member of the original seven Methodist preachers ordained in 1869, who had seen Methodism in China grow from nothing to around forty thousand communicant members in a few decades. Recalling an age when the attention paid to Protestant pastors by the elite was of a far less welcome kind, he was well able to believe in the heady years of the early twentieth century that "Christianity will ultimately conquer China."[2] Such optimism was no doubt reinforced by the books on Christian history published in Chinese by the Fuzhou churches, which furnished narratives of mass Christianization, such as the "conquest of paganism" by Christianity in the Roman Empire and the Wesleyan revival in eighteenth-century England, as well as the New Testament itself.[3] It was fostered also by their knowledge of modern world history, in which they read the story of the parallel progress through the nineteenth century of constitutional government, political liberty, scientific knowledge and enlightenment, and Christian religion, all embodied supremely in the United States of America, the altruistic Christian republic.[4]

Protestants in the Fuzhou area were able to anticipate the future with such hope because the period from 1900 to 1920 was characterized by a flexibility and openness in China unparalleled in modern times. The setbacks of the last years of Qing rule, beginning with the defeat of China by Japan in 1895, opened up deep questions about the viability of the late imperial political and cultural system, and indeed about the nature and future of Chinese civilization and the Chinese people. In such a time, the course charted by Protestants toward a modern, Christian, republican Chinese nation held considerable appeal, as we have seen. For that short period, Protestants and their religion seemed to a significant number of people to offer possible solutions to the many problems that prevented China from being a strong and united nation.

In hindsight, far from being the beginning of a "tide Christward," the early years of the Republic turned out to be the high-water mark of Protestant influence and Protestant optimism in the Fuzhou area. Ultimately, the Protestant vision of a Christian China was never realized, and its passing marked the eclipse of the politically involved, progressive style of Protestantism of the previous decades. The reasons for its decline were international and national as well as local and in the final analysis are connected to the failure of constitutionalism, liberal politics, and civil society in Republican China.

Some of the weaknesses that underlay the Protestant political vision of a

Christian China were already becoming evident at its peak in the 1910s. For one thing, that vision implied a stable constitutional and electoral political order, but this most basic foundation of the Republic never materialized. Moreover, the model to which the Protestants looked, America, had never in reality lived up to the ideal of the Christian republic, as Chinese Protestants had known full well in 1905 and were to rediscover in the 1910s. Also, the churches never really had the resources, in finances or personnel, to effect the wholesale reshaping of Chinese society — despite the creativity, idealism, and dedication of individual Protestants and the impressive amount which they did accomplish. By the 1920s the social and intellectual context in which the Protestant political vision had flourished had changed dramatically. Socially, the novelty of Protestant social service initiatives like those of the YMCA had worn off in the Fuzhou area, and other public bodies began to use Protestant methods to compete with the Protestants for public support. More important, however, was the political emergence in the 1920s of a new generation with a new conceptualization of nationalism, a nationalism that discredited the Protestant vision of China's future and called into question the very possibility of Chinese Protestants being true nationalists.

Protestants and Politics in the 1910s

The first difficulty which undermined Protestant influence and optimism even at its peak was one that bedeviled the new Republic as a whole: the unsettled political conditions, and particularly the weakness of civil and parliamentary politics compared to military power. In achieving their objective of overthrowing the Manchu dynasty, the revolutionaries of 1911 made common cause with social forces whose commitment to the new republican order was, to say the least, questionable, including secret societies, officers and troops in the Qing armies, and, most important, the Qing general Yuan Shikai, who agreed to induce the abdication of the emperor in return for the presidency of the Republic. As president, Yuan turned out to be an authoritarian and devious ruler. Relying on the loyalty of his Beiyang Army to maintain his power and hold the country together, he dissolved the national parliament and its provincial and local counterparts and eventually tried to proclaim himself emperor of a new dynasty. Under Yuan's rule, military men became important power brokers in the provinces, and after he died in 1916 de facto power devolved into the hands of regional and local warlords.[5]

In Fujian, one of the recurring features of provincial politics through the Republican era was the control of military power by a succession of non-Fujianese cliques, with a consequent alienation of locally based civilian elites from politics.[6] The first instance of this was the split between Hunanese and Fujianese within the revolutionary ranks, which became evident soon after the 1911 revolution, to the detriment of the Protestants within the provincial government, all of whom were from civilian backgrounds. An essential ingredient in the success of the revolution in Fujian had been the participation of the New Army detachment in Fuzhou, which was composed largely of Hunanese troops brought into the province by Zuo Zongtang in the 1860s. One Hunanese officer in that army, Peng Shousong, had been instrumental in securing the agreement of his commander, Sun Daoren, to support the revolution. After the revolution, with Sun installed as military governor, Peng assumed a dominant position in the province and soon showed himself to be unscrupulous and violent. When an official who had criticized the heavy non-Fujianese presence in the new government was murdered in April 1912, Peng Shousong was widely believed to be responsible, although most did not venture to say so in public. However, a radical young Protestant journalist (a student in the Anglo-Chinese College and a nephew of Huang Zhiji, then in America as the Fuzhou delegate to the Methodist General Conference) published a newspaper article impugning Peng. Huang Naishang, who was an old friend of his family, tried to mediate between Peng and the young man and personally guaranteed his safety if he would accompany him into the city to make peace with Peng. It is not clear from the accounts whether Huang was simply naive about Peng (with whom he had worked closely to bring about the revolution a scant six months earlier) or whether he believed that his own stature would be sufficient to deter Peng from harming the young man; either way he miscalculated badly. He conducted the young journalist into the city on May 7, where Peng received him graciously, shook his hand, and assured him of his safety. On his way out of the city after this meeting, however, the bodyguard supplied by Huang was overpowered, and the young man was dragged from his sedan chair and murdered.[7]

Huang used all his influence in pressing a charge against Peng in the court, but the court, under intimidation and lacking firm evidence, exonerated him. Soon afterward, pressure from Beijing and a hefty payoff from the Fuzhou Chamber of Commerce succeeded in dislodging Peng and the Hunanese troops from Fujian, and after his removal the provincial court did find Peng guilty of both murders. By that time, however, Huang Naishang had taken the time-honored Chinese course of the upright man caught in bad times, resigning his government position (along with the presidency of the YMCA) and retiring to his home county.[8] Huang Naishang's political trials did not end there, either, for early in 1914 the revolutionary veteran, now in his mid-sixties, was sentenced to life imprisonment as part of Yuan Shikai's suppression of the revolutionary party, on a trumped-up charge that Huang had violated the ban on opium cultivation. The charge was so ludicrously at odds with his character and convictions that there was an intense outcry in China and among the Chinese in the Straits Settlements, which forced his release after a few months.[9]

Another local Protestant, Chen Nengguang, retained his position at the head of Fujian's Department of Foreign Affairs for less than a year after the Republic was established. He did not leave government service entirely, however, but served for a time as superintendent of the Customs in Fujian and as head of the province's Opium Suppression Bureau, before moving to Shanghai, where he became deputy director of the division of the postal service dealing with remittances and money orders.[10] He remained on the board of the Fuzhou YMCA only until 1914 or 1915, presumably until his move to Shanghai.

Li Qifan's career in the Fujian government — also the Department of Foreign Affairs — was similarly brief, and in 1914 he too moved to Shanghai, joining the staff of the Shanghai YMCA.[11]

Of the initial Protestant members of the postrevolution provincial cabinet, only Chen Zhilin remained in office beyond the first year of the Republic, serving (except for a brief stint as the Xiamen Taotai in 1913) as head of the Department of Finance until the middle of 1914. In 1917 he returned briefly to politics as a Fujian representative to the short-lived national Senate in Beijing, but after that he left political life entirely and devoted his energy to the promotion of industry and commerce in Fuzhou and Xiamen.[12] He remained on the board of the Fuzhou YMCA until at least 1924 and served on the YMCA National Committee in the 1920s.[13]

In addition to holding office in government as individuals, Protestants in Fuzhou attempted to effect social change through legislative measures and public mobilization, but here again the unsettled conditions of the early Republic were not always conducive to their efforts. For example, the senior Chinese YMCA secretary, Zhu Lide, who was a member of the Provincial Assembly elected in 1913 and recalled in 1917, was attempting to get antiprostitution legislation passed when the assembly was once more disbanded in the summer of that year.[14]

From 1920 the YMCA became increasingly active in voicing opposition to and coordinating mass campaigns against opium, gambling, prostitution, and official corruption, but this brought it into conflict with the administration of the warlord governor, Li Houji.[15] In contrast to many of the civil officials and local notables, Li Houji, a Jiangsu native and protégé of Yuan Shikai who held military power in Fujian from 1914 until 1922, had only given token support to the YMCA and had discouraged his staff from joining it or being identified with its activities.[16] The YMCA membership in Fuzhou (and throughout China in the early Republic) tended to be strongly republican in political sentiment and socially active, so the YMCA was a natural focus of Li's suspicion. Yuan Shikai's attempt to proclaim himself emperor in 1915 reportedly "outraged the sense of justice" of the members of the Fuzhou YMCA, and relations between the YMCA and Li Houji reached their nadir the following year when Li put a military guard on the YMCA building for part of the year, had the building searched periodically, and had those entering or leaving monitored.[17]

The ousting of Li Houji from the province at the end of 1922 did not improve things for the YMCA, however, for a succession of increasingly unstable and venal warlord regimes competed for control of the province through the mid-1920s.[18] In 1923 a YMCA secretary lamented that "no man of means dares to make any contribution to any cause however good, for if it became known to the military men they would squeeze some more out of him for the support of their own projects, and he would have no possible protection nor redress."[19]

Both the idealism and the vulnerability of Protestant attempts to effect social change in the unstable conditions of the early Republic are summed up in the brief career of Zhou Daojian (Donald Ciu Do Gieng, 1891–1921). Zhou was from a poor peasant family in a village of Gutian County, in inland Fujian. His parents were Methodist converts, and his mother had been placed in charge of a day school for girls in the village after her own education in the Methodist school for women in Gutian. Zhou acquired his basic literacy in his mother's school, then entered the Methodist boarding school in the county seat at the age of twelve. Later he was sent with church support to Fuzhou, where he graduated from the Anglo-Chinese College in 1911. Following a short time at the Methodist seminary in the city, Zhou was sent to the United States in 1913, where in the space of seven years he earned a B.S. at Wesleyan University, an M.A. at Columbia, a B.Div. at Drew Theological Seminary, and a Doctor of Pedagogy degree at New York University. Rejecting both lucrative job offers and modernist theology, he returned to China late in 1920 and was appointed to oversee the Methodist church's social and educational programs in Gutian, the first returned U.S. graduate appointed by the church to a country station.

Zhou Daojian threw himself into this task with extraordinary energy and creativity, using all the tools and methods with which his U.S. training had equipped him. Within a few months of his appointment he had conducted a survey of the social, educational, industrial, and religious situation in the city and had started, on a shoestring, a public reading room, a boys' club, preaching bands, a training course in modern pedagogy for the teachers in the mission schools (in which he included instruction in conducting flag drill), and weekly lectures on "hygiene, church history and Christian doctrine."[20] He opened three Bible classes and a literacy class at night in different parts of the city and hoped to open many more night schools, reasoning that only at night could "the truth of Jesus, the Christian ideal, and knowledge" be inculcated "into the minds of the poor folks who work all day long without leisure or rest, and can have time only in the evening — who constitute the overwhelming majority of the citizens in town."[21] Nor did he neglect the days, for he often preached on street corners, with two flags — the Chinese national flag and a Christian cross on a white field — as his background.

Zhou was fond of summing up his philosophy of life as "to work as a horse and to live like a hermit," but he ate poorly, slept little, and worked at a pace that could not be sustained.[22] With his health breaking down after a frenetic six months, Zhou was finally prevailed upon to come down to Fuzhou for a week's rest in August 1921. However, by mischance the launch he took down the Min River was shot at by river pirates trying to hold it up and rob it, and Zhou was hit by one of the bullets and killed instantly.[23]

Anti-Imperialism and the Discrediting of Protestant Patriotism

As we have seen, Chinese Protestants both admired and critiqued the Western nations from which their missionary associates came. In particular, representations of the United States as a strong and free republic founded on Christian citizenship captured the imagination of Chinese Protestants seeking models for their nation around the time of the 1911 revolution. As discussed in Chapter 4, in 1912 leading Fuzhou Protestants like Huang Naishang and Huang Zhiji spoke in glowing terms of America as "China's pattern" and "our great example"; in the first flush of building a "new China," their reservations about America were outweighed by their optimism and by the possibility that the United States would give early recognition and strong support to the new Republic. This sanguine outlook was naturally aided by the nature of the Americans with whom they had the closest contact: "missionary statesmen" like Sherwood Eddy, John Mott, and James Bashford, the Methodist delegates who responded so enthusiastically to Huang Zhiji's speech in 1912, and the missionaries they knew in China were among the most idealistic, broad-minded, and internationalist of their generation.[24]

Among Fuzhou Protestants and the Chinese population more generally, those positive images coexisted in tension with less complimentary ones: awareness of American racial discrimination against Chinese immigrants, for instance, and skepticism about the supposedly benevolent nature of American foreign policy.[25] The Protestant involvement in the 1905 protests against America's racist immigration laws was discussed in Chapter 2. On the second score, in 1907 Huang Naishang told an audience of mission school students in the Church of Heavenly Peace that America's annexation of the Philippines proved that it was in essence no different from the other great powers.[26]

The reservations of Chinese Protestants about America resurfaced very quickly after 1911, particularly in the experience of the YMCA secretary and principal of the YMCA school, Zhu Lide. Zhu, who proclaimed the glories of Christian America to Fuzhou audiences as the interpreter for Sherwood Eddy in 1911, 1913, and 1914, was sent abroad in the summer and fall of 1913 to gain experience of YMCA work in the United States. Zhu was incensed by the treatment he received from the immigration officials at San Francisco, and even more at the interrogation he observed of a young Chinese woman who came in on the same boat, who was asked "questions which, while very hard for a Chinese woman to answer, were of no consequence concerning either the immigration laws or the quarantine rules." He relayed this experience along with what he had been told of conditions on the infamous Angel Island in an eloquent and impassioned letter to Fletcher Brockman, the general secretary of the YMCA in China, who in turn passed it on to John R. Mott, suggesting that he take up the matter in Washington.[27]

Zhu seems to have enjoyed his time in America and to have made a good impression in Scranton, Pennsylvania, where he spent most of his time.[28] In a lecture at the YMCA soon after his return to Fuzhou in late November, he spoke with admiration of the public institutions of American city life: parks and playgrounds, libraries and museums (in which he even saw porcelain from Fuzhou displayed), and charitable enterprises. However, Zhu prefaced his favorable comments by telling his listeners of the way Chinese were despised by foreigners, citing his experiences and observations at the U.S. and Canadian borders, and this aspect of Zhu's time overseas was featured in the Fuzhou YMCA magazine on at least three occasions. In line with the moralistic nationalism of the YMCA, Zhu asserted that this American prejudice was ultimately made possible by the lack of self-confidence of the Chinese themselves.[29]

The nagging doubts of politically aware Chinese about America were transformed into wholesale disillusionment by the American betrayal of China's interests at the Paris Peace Conference following World War I. Despite his opposition to imperialist diplomacy and his stated commitment to the "self-determination of peoples," President Woodrow Wilson acceded to Japanese demands that Japan retain control over the former German concession in Shandong Province. When the news reached China on May 4, 1919, a protest movement arose against Japan, against the warlords and weak government that had failed to defend China's interests, and more generally against the aggression and hypocrisy of the Western powers and the United States.

The May Fourth Movement, as this protest movement came to be called, has often been regarded as the beginning of modern nationalism in China. It is more accurate to say that the May Fourth Movement broadened the social reach of nationalism and caused it to develop in new ideological directions. The nationalism that developed in the wake of May Fourth was more radical and more iconoclastic toward Chinese traditions than the nationalism of the previous generation. It was also significantly more skeptical of the intentions of Western nations, because it drew for the first time on a systematic analysis of imperialism, the chief source for which was Lenin's work on the subject. The phrase used to translate "imperialism" in Chinese, *diguo zhuyi,* had come into the language through Japanese as early as 1895, but it did not enter into general usage in Chinese until the 1920s, when Lenin's writings began to be translated.[30] For nationalist Chinese of the May Fourth generation, the concept provided a powerful explanatory framework for the sufferings of China at the hands of the Western powers and Japan and a clear justification for anti-imperialist and nationalist revolution; by the mid-1920s nationalism and resistance to imperialism had become so closely linked as to be nearly inseparable in Chinese discourse.

The grafting of this new terminology onto Chinese nationalism had important implications for the social role of Christianity in China. As we have seen, the earlier generation of nationalists, including Protestants, had been intensely critical at times of Western incursions on Chinese sovereignty. The Fujian Provincial Assembly attempted to legislate against Western mining and oil concessions in the province, Zhu Lide attacked American racism, and, as head of the provincial Department of Foreign Affairs, Chen Nengguang was decidedly assertive against the British in particular. However, they attacked specific countries or specific actions; when general critiques of foreign aggression were voiced, the term used by these Protestants and their non-Protestant contemporaries was *lieqiang,* "the powers." It was clearly quite consistent in this intellectual framework to attack particular Western impositions on China without tarring missionary institutions in China with the same brush. Indeed, given that patriotic Chinese saw Western countries as models as well as aggressors, the Western associations of Protestant individuals and institutions could be seen as assets, as we have discussed.

The terminology of imperialism, by contrast, created instant guilt by association for all Western-linked people and institutions in China. As the quotation from Mao Zedong at the head of this chapter indicates, viewing imperialism in Leninist terms as an inexorable outgrowth of the material conditions of industrial capitalism implied that all Western endeavors in China, however altruistic, noble, or service-oriented they might seem, had a hidden agenda of aggression against the Chinese people. While there had been previous critiques of missions in China from many perspectives, from the early 1920s missions and missionaries came increasingly to be seen as forms of "cultural imperialism," having as their object the goal of subjugating the Chinese to Western ideological domination in order to solidify Western economic and political control.[31] As an analytical tool, "cultural imperialism" is frustratingly imprecise, and the relationship between the modern missionary movement and imperialist expansion is more complex than the phrase tends to convey.[32] Regardless of its deficiencies as a concept, however, "cultural imperialism" has had an enduring currency as a pithy summation of the missionary effort in China and other parts of the world.

The implications of the new theory for the social acceptance of Christianity in China were not long in appearing. The convening in Beijing of a world conference of the World's Student Christian Federation in April 1922 was the catalyst for an Anti-Christian Movement, which quickly spread through student circles across the nation, declaring both that religion and science were incompatible and that Christianity was a means by which imperialists oppressed weaker nations. This was followed in 1924–1925 by the Recovery of Educational Sovereignty Movement (*shouhui jiaoyu quan yundong*), which advocated bringing all church schools under government control, arguing that church schools "denationalized" Chinese students—although, as we have seen, that had hardly been the case in the Fuzhou area to that time. Then, during the Northern Expedition of 1926–1927, when the joint forces of the reorganized Nationalist Party and the Chinese Communist Party pressed northward from Guangdong to try to reunite the country, outbreaks of violence against Christians and Christian institutions accompanied the armies in many parts of the country.[33]

In Fuzhou, this new strain of nationalism engendered a new attitude toward the Protestant institutions that had enjoyed such widespread favor up to 1922. The change was very clear with respect to the YMCA. In 1920 and 1921 the YMCA in Fuzhou was the leading public association in the city (fig. 6.1). It was very active in enlisting Protestants of all denominations and non-Christian Chinese in social causes, providing the social leadership and the physical premises for the North Fukien Anti-Opium Association, the Moral Welfare Association, and the Health and Sanitation Association, all of which included both Christians and non-Christians.[34] In 1920, prompted by a devastating cholera outbreak that had claimed over 20,000 lives in the city the previous summer, the YMCA organized a massive effort in health education,

Fig. 6.1. Staff of the Fuzhou YMCA in 1920, near the peak of the organization's popularity. Zhu Lide is at the center of the front row. Institute of Religion and Culture, Fujian Teachers' University.

involving over 2,700 volunteers in an intensive one-week campaign. Using parades, street theater, and models of giant flies and coffins, the campaign activists literally carried the hygiene message over 90 percent of the streets of the entire city, reaching a total audience of approximately 320,000 people.[35] The patriotic student movement in the city supported this campaign, showing that nationalist opinion had not yet turned against Christian institutions.[36] In fact, students in the YMCA school were active in the student movement, and the YMCA school was at the center of what became an international diplomatic incident in November 1919, when some of its students were badly beaten on the street by Japanese subjects (following a student-led boycott of Japanese-owned businesses in the city in which YMCA members had been heavily involved).[37]

By 1923, however, the tone in the city and in the YMCA school had changed. When the YMCA unthinkingly scheduled a play for its members on National Humiliation Day (May 9, the anniversary of Yuan Shikai's acceptance in 1915 of Japan's infamous Twenty-One Demands for special rights in China), fifty students from the YMCA school disrupted the event, breaking furniture and directly defying their principal, Zhu Lide, when he attempted to restore order. Subsequently, during the summer recess the faculty sent out letters to forty-two students asking them not to return for the next school year. This action ignited "a barrage of letters to faculty and students threaten[ing] the life of anyone who would dare to return to school in the fall." The threats, it turned out, had some substance, for shortly before the school reopened in September, Zhu Lide was stabbed in the back in broad daylight on a main street close to the YMCA building.[38]

The wound was not life-threatening, and Zhu recovered within a few weeks and resumed control of the school at the end of the semester. However, the incident is a telling indication of the gulf that had opened between the preceding generation of nationalists and those of the 1920s. Zhu Lide was one of the most prominent exemplars in Fuzhou of the Protestant model of moralistic nation-building of the early twentieth century. Ironically, he belonged to the first wave of student patriots in Fuzhou, having graduated from Foochow College around the time of the anti-American boycott of 1905. He had won respect in the city for his capabilities as a YMCA secretary, an educator, a translator and public speaker, and, after 1911, a legislator in the Provincial Assembly. He had criticized American discrimination against Chinese immigrants in the 1910s. But by 1923 his patriotic credentials did not necessarily carry weight with student nationalists.

Although the Fuzhou YMCA was run and financed by its local Chinese members (excepting the salaries of the foreign secretaries, which were paid by the International Committee), it was still a Christian organization with ties to America, and that made it suspect in the climate of anti-imperialist nationalism in the 1920s. On the other hand, its nation-building goals — social service, education, morality — were shared by the new crop of patriots, and some groups even adopted YMCA methods to compete against it. In 1923 the YMCA began planning and publicizing a mass education campaign for the spring of 1924 and sought support, as in their past campaigns, from officials, educators, and commercial leaders as well as Christians. However, they found themselves facing a competing movement announced by student leaders allied to the Nationalist Party (then still based in Guangdong), who threatened to block any effort not conducted through their headquarters. "This group . . . is most anxious to prevent any such popular movement being started or carried through to success under Christian leadership, and [is] gunning for the YMCA as it is probably the centre around which any such union effort of the

Christians would organize," reported one secretary.[39] Similarly, in 1925 two new private schools founded during the recovery-of-educational-sovereignty ferment attempted to conduct financial campaigns using the YMCA's methods and deliberately timed to compete with the annual membership campaign of the YMCA. They threatened harm to anyone working for the YMCA campaign, preventing the YMCA from publicizing the names of team members in the customary manner.[40]

Political radicals were not the only ones who adopted Protestant methods to compete with Protestant institutions from the 1920s. Buddhist and Confucian activities in the city were also taking novel, Protestant-influenced forms, as the following quotation shows:

> Confucianists and Buddists [*sic*] are both holding preaching services. Recently a group of Buddist scholars held a series of meetings in the temple at the White Pagoda, and for days they drew large crowds of sympathetic listeners of middle and higher class people. There has been recently established in the city a reading room and a distributing centre for Buddist literature. I know a number of young government school teachers, lawyers and the like who are deeply interested in a study of Buddism. They have also been meeting at the YMCA to study Christianity. The Confucian temple which in former years I remember as seeing open only twice a year for the Confucian worship—a matter for the officials and not for the populace—is now frequently opened for public exposition of the classics. In an adjoining building they have a kindergarten too. In a number of places old Chinese scholars are giving lectures in which they discuss the teachings of Buddha, Confucius and Jesus and point out their similarities, and say that Jesus has often been misinterpreted by the Christian Church. There seems to be a real searching for a moral and religious foundation for the new day, and a new emphasis on the moral basis of society, to combat the materialistic emphasis which has been in the ascendancy.[41]

These competing efforts all used such Protestant strategies as public lectures, revival meetings, reading rooms, educational work; they all aimed at the same social constituency as the YMCA; and they all even raised the basic issue which underlay everything the YMCA did, "the moral basis of society," but pointed to different answers.[42] Buddhists in Fuzhou later drew further on Protestant precedents, founding a hospital in the city and a secondary school near Foochow College, both in 1948—the former sponsored by Admiral Sa Zhenbing, whose friendship with Huang Naishang and support for the YMCA in the 1910s and 1920s was noted in Chapter 5.[43]

Simply as a public space for leisure activities the YMCA faced more competition in the 1920s as electricity, motorized transport, and new notions of urban planning made their mark upon the physical space of the city. At the same time as the new nationalist discourse cut the YMCA off from much of the public support it had enjoyed up to 1922, new public cinemas and public parks created new leisure options for young men, and the new buses running from the city center south to Cangqian on the newly widened Bridge of Ten Thousand Ages brought more activities within range for those willing to seek them (fig. 6.2). In the 1930s the Nationalist Party's youth organization, the Sanqingtuan (Three-Principles-of-the-People Youth Corps), provided an alternative in the schools and in society to the boys' clubs, Boy Scouts, and youth activities of the YMCA. As Fuzhou society became more complex, the novelty of the YMCA as a site for public life in the city became less marked.

The educational institutions of the three missions were under great pressure during the same period, and particularly after the May Thirtieth Incident in 1925, when British police shot unarmed Chinese demonstrators in Shanghai. The Fujian Student Federation, in which Chinese Communist Party activists had become prominent, organized students under slogans such as "Pass the death sentence on national-character-robbing church education" and "Obliterate all church institutions."[44] The first issue of the Federation's magazine *Juejiao* (Sever relations), dated August 1925, called for a boycott of all British and Japanese goods and services and carried an article accusing America of being the "craftiest" of the imperialist powers, pretending peace but actually practicing cultural imperialism through hospitals, schools, the YMCA, churches, and the like.[45]

In the midst of these unsettling developments, to the south in neighboring Guangdong, Sun Yatsen, himself a Protestant, was taking the steps which would turn the political movement he led away from liberal politics, representation, and pluralism to revolution, mobilization, and the single party-state. As John Fitzgerald's rich study of the Nationalist revolution has shown, that transition was signaled in part by symbolic changes: Sun's rejection of the five-bar flag and the corresponding national anthem was explicitly connected to the rejection of liberalism in favor of a single, united revolutionary party with a firm grasp on state power.[46]

In the fall of 1926 the movement thus created launched the Northern Expedition to overthrow the twin evils of warlordism and imperialism and unite China under the leadership of the revolutionary party. Sun had died, but the alliance that he had helped forge between the Nationalists and the Communists persisted, and in many areas the Northern Expedition was accompanied by outbreaks of violence against "imperialist" institutions, including missionary schools, hospitals, and churches.

Fig. 6.2. Foot, rickshaw, and motor traffic on the widened Bridge of Ten Thousand Ages, 1920s. Division of Special Collections and University Archives, University of Oregon Library System.

The Nationalist revolution of 1926–1927 brought the coup de grâce for the era of popular receptivity to the Protestant political vision in Fuzhou. The Nationalist army took Fuzhou in early December 1926, and for a time, as radical and moderate factions within the Nationalist forces jockeyed for control of the new government, there were no adverse effects on the churches.[47] Then, on January 18, 1927, Nationalist soldiers and some elements of the local population (missionary sources claim the soldiers had little popular support) ransacked several major Protestant institutions inside the walled city. Ironically, the brunt of the violence was borne by the institutions most independent of foreign missionaries and most symbolic of the social service efforts of Chinese Protestants. The Methodist institutional church, site of the church-sponsored educational exposition in 1922, was vandalized, its furniture, piano, and the personal belongings of the (Chinese) pastor and staff all smashed or taken.[48] The city branch of the Fuzhou YMCA was looted; equipment worth approximately nine thousand dollars was lost (the total YMCA budget for 1926 had been just over fifty thousand dollars).[49] Already facing an accumulated debt from the unrest of the previous few years, the YMCA board of directors was forced to take drastic measures: the budget for 1927 was halved from its 1926 level, and almost half of the staff released; the walled city YMCA branch was closed and the building leased out for three years; and YMCA service work to the wider community was "almost entirely eliminated."[50]

The agitation in the missionary schools came to a head later that spring — before Chiang Kaishek's coup against the Communists in April 1927 — when a coalition of radical teachers and students in the main church schools and Fukien Christian University attempted to take over their institutions and turn them over to the new Nationalist provincial government. In the course of the unrest, arson attacks destroyed buildings in Foochow College and Fukien Christian University, Chinese teachers in the church schools were threatened and assaulted, and the Chinese principal of an Anglican school, the Reverend Lin Buji, was capped and paraded through the streets, then denounced at a mass meeting, in a manner that was to become all too familiar in China after 1949.[51] Many of the schools closed for a semester, some for a full year.[52]

The most poignant loss of all was the destruction of the Methodists' Woolston Memorial Hospital in the city, which had been operated for almost thirty years under the control of the Chinese missionary doctor Xu Jinhong (Hu King Eng, 1866?–1929). As was recounted in Chapter 1, Xu, daughter of the Methodist preacher Xu Yangmei, was the second Chinese woman, and the first from Fujian, to study in the United States. She went to America in 1884, earned a medical degree, and then returned to Fuzhou, in 1895, as a missionary of the Women's Foreign Missionary Society of the Methodist Episcopal Church, which placed her in charge of a hospital for women and children inside the walled city in 1899. In her years in this position, she had devoted herself to serving the people of the city and to teaching young women medical students, the first of whom, her sister, became her assistant. Her practice included both the elite and the poor (who were treated for free, subsidized by the fees paid by the rich); the hospital quickly became busy and prosperous, and remained so until it closed.[53]

According to an account by one of her close friends, Xu's hospital became a target for the revolutionaries when she refused to confirm their charge that babies in a nearby Catholic orphanage had died from maltreatment, insisting on the contrary that the Spanish nuns in charge cared for the children conscientiously.[54] Whatever the cause, on January 18 soldiers of the Nationalist army came and destroyed everything in the hospital and in Xu's adjacent residence — furniture, medical equipment and supplies, personal belongings. Almost every windowpane was broken. Her granddaughter, who was five or six at the time, recalls that the mob was made up of soldiers, not local people, and Xu and her family had to stand and watch as their facilities and personal property were demolished. The destruction of her life's work by her own people was a great shock to Xu. She took her family (sister, adopted daughter, the daughter's husband, and the wife and children of her invalid adopted son) and went to stay with relatives in Singapore, but she never recovered her strength, and she died there in 1929 at the age of sixty-five. The hospital never reopened.[55]

The Protestant Moment in Modern China

The turn toward revolution and the rejection of the Sino-Western synthesis of citizenship and social service represented by Protestant figures like Zhu Lide and Dr. Xu Jinhong had implications far beyond the Protestant community in the Fuzhou area. It was one reflection of a more general shift: the foreclosing of many of the possible paths for China that had laced the fluid decades since 1900 and the molding of the national future into the disciplined channels of the revolutionary party-state. That change would be decisive for China itself, as well as for Protestant Christianity within China, for the rest of the century.

In investigating the place of Protestants within Fuzhou society from 1900 to the 1920s, we have found our course of inquiry intersecting repeatedly with the development and denouement of nationalism and progressive politics. Chinese Protestants in the Fuzhou area were centrally involved in the new politics that developed after 1900, a politics expressed in the growth of new voluntary associations in response to a visceral anxiety about China's place in the world and in line with a progressive, modernizing agenda. This new politics drew eclectically on Chinese and foreign sources and centered on a vision of making China a strong, modern nation-state through renewal of the Chinese people by education, citizenship, and social reform. Protestants sought to stake a place for their version of the Christian religion in this emerging reality by stressing its value in building a moral citizenry. Protestant organizations and individuals became important and respected components of the developing public life of the city and region, reaching the peak of their influence in the first decade of the Republic. Their success in gaining the interest and recognition of their peers was an exhilarating experience and led some Chinese Protestants to expect that the Christianization of China would soon become a reality; in this they were to be sorely disappointed.

The crisis year of 1927 was an ending of sorts, but it is important to be clear about what came to an end. Protestant Christianity in China did not go into permanent decline after the 1920s. There were twice as many Protestants in China in 1949 as in 1927, and there were at least ten times as many at the end of the 1990s as there were in 1949. However, the upheavals of 1927 marked the end of the era of widespread public receptivity to the Protestant political vision in Fuzhou, and with it ended the Protestant optimism about building China into a Christian nation through activism in the political realm. Official endorsements of Protestant services to society continued under the Nationalists, and the Protestant schools (having made the transition to Chinese leadership) and hospitals remained important in the life of the city and province.[56] By the 1930s, the Fuzhou YMCA had restored its damaged public profile, in part by making the most of the Protestant affiliation of the late "Father of the Nation," Sun Yatsen, publishing his picture along with quotations from him endorsing the YMCA at the front of its annual reports.[57] Still, after 1927 the patriotism of Chinese Protestants and their place in national and local life were never unchallenged, and while Protestants applied themselves to local efforts to improve social conditions in China, particularly in rural reconstruction projects, Christianity never again had a credible claim to be *the* solution to China's problems in a political sense.[58]

Nor did Protestants make such claims after the 1920s. Within the Protestant churches, the demise of the Protestant synthesis of nation-building and progressive Christianity brought a renewed emphasis on individual piety, seen both in revivalism within the mission-planted churches and in the emergence of new indigenous Christian sects which eschewed political and social involvement altogether in favor of personal spiritual experience. One of the most important of these, the Local Assembly or "Little Flock" movement, actually began in Fuzhou, and its example well illustrates the changes in Chinese Protestantism following the 1920s. Its founder, Watchman Nee (Ni Tuosheng, 1903–1972), was a third-generation Fuzhou Protestant, grandson of the first American Board pastor in Fuzhou and son of a Customs official who served on the board of the Fuzhou YMCA in the 1910s and 1920s. Nee rejected outright the mission and YMCA-style Christianity of his father and grandfather; his movement was anti-mission, anti-clerical, anti-institutional, explicitly non-political, and theologically conservative, refusing to acknowledge or work with the denominational churches.[59] Many aspects of the history of Protestantism in China up to the present have their roots in the developments of the 1920s and 1930s, such as the stress on individual piety and the tensions between the mission-planted churches and the indigenous sects. That story is a fascinating one, but one that falls outside the scope of this book.[60]

What does this local history have to tell us about the broader trajectory of change in China from about 1900 to the 1920s? First, these decades were an exceptionally open time in China, one that calls for new modes of analysis. Much of the historiography on this period, centering as it does on particular milestone events (the 1911 revolution, the May Fourth Movement) and discussing them in terms of set analytical dichotomies (gentry/bourgeoisie, constitutionalist/revolutionary), obscures the fundamental freshness of the new social and political realities taking shape. In Fuzhou, the dynamism of the time was connected, I have argued, to the emergence of the urban professional sector, which was neither gentry nor bourgeois in any strict sense and in which Protestants were relatively numerous.

Moreover, this was the period when nationalism as ideology and practice first became widespread and politically important in China. The disintegration of imperial authority was far more than a political change; it raised fundamental questions about culture, identity, and social organization for Chinese who lived through it. In trying to negotiate a new basis for the Chinese state and nation, Chinese nationalists in the early twentieth century drew on multiple currents: indigenous and foreign, ritual and practical, local and national, civilian and military, reformist and revolutionary. "Becoming national" was by definition a synthetic and open-ended project; consequently, it was one from which Chinese Protestants were not necessarily excluded and which in the Fuzhou area they did much to shape.

Having said that, let me draw an important distinction between what I am claiming here and the many works written in the early twentieth century that traced all positive change in China back to the benevolent activism and example of Westerners, missionaries and others.[61] My intention has been to demonstrate that Chinese Protestants, for better or worse, were integral to Chinese society and to the shaping of Chinese modernity as it emerged in the Fuzhou area, not to assert that they were exclusively responsible for it or that their impact was always "positive" in the teleological unfolding of some destined national state.

Even this limited conclusion may be unwelcome to those who, reacting to the admitted Eurocentrism of much social theory, have sought to assert a wholly distinctive Chinese trajectory to modernity, those who remain convinced that Christianity was only and unalterably a "foreign religion" to Chinese, or those who are affronted by the assertion of an imitative dimension to nationalism.[62] Certainly we cannot ascribe all change in modern China to the Western impact, but equally we cannot divorce what was happening in China entirely from Western pressures and Western models.

In my view, even juxtaposing "Chinese" and "Western" as two distinct and mutually exclusive structural formations in this period is misleading; instead we need to see "Chinese" and "Western" elements as constantly overlapping and interpenetrating and to recognize that culture is endlessly dynamic, malleable, and individual (the same could be said of "local" and "national," "modern" and "traditional," "state" and "society," and a host of similar binaries).[63]

Here, the case in point is Christian conversion itself, which for too long has been viewed as an abandoning of one culture and identity ("Chinese") to take on an alien one. It was nothing of the sort for the Fuzhou Protestants examined here. By the same token, to regard the adoption and adaptation of nationalism as a process of westernization is far too simple. The act of translation is necessarily transformative, and like Christianity, modernity and nationalism were translated into China—incorporating as well as replacing existing social and cultural patterns—and transformed in the process.[64]

One theoretical model which has been used to analyze this transitional period in China is that of the growth of "civil society," which has been defined as "the realm of organized social life that is voluntary, self-generating, (largely) self-supporting, [and] autonomous from the state."[65] The term derives from the work of the German social thinker Jürgen Habermas, who traced the development of modern politics based on the notions of popular sovereignty, representation, and citizenship to the emergence of civil society and a public sphere in early modern western Europe.[66] In Chinese studies the term "civil society" has been applied to three distinct periods. It was used to conceptualize the changes taking place in Chinese cities over the eighteenth and nineteenth centuries, then applied to urban social life in the early decades of the twentieth century, and, after 1989, extensively employed to analyze the forces in post-Mao China that had generated the democracy movement.[67]

The application of the term to China has been vigorously criticized on a number of grounds. Critics have pointed out the element of wishful thinking in its use—"civil society" as an analytical framework has appeal because it stands for a kind of open, free, and politically constructive organizational life that many would like to see take root in Chinese society.[68] As the critics have pointed out, Habermas's conception of civil society implies a conceptual and practical autonomy from state power that has never been more than sporadically and imperfectly realized in China (and is probably overly idealized by Habermas for Europe as well).[69]

Nevertheless, others have continued to argue for the usefulness of the civil society concept for analyzing social change in China, provided that it is recognized for what it is: a conceptual tool rather than an empirical reality. Of the three periods in question, the one in which changes in China came closest to meeting the description of civil society in the Habermasian sense is clearly the second, the early decades of the twentieth century, when the cultural hegemony and political monopoly maintained more or less successfully by the imperial state for so long had broken down and before the modern party-state had begun to impose its disciplinary presence on social organization. In this context we are not discussing the relatively slow evolution of merchant guilds toward greater autonomy and public activism in the late imperial period, nor the gradual loosening of the bonds of "state corporatism" in post-Mao China, but the swift and dramatic appearance of new forms of political association and the transformation of existing ones in the absence of effective state power. The application of the term "civil society" to these developments is less problematic than its use for the other periods, as even those critical of the term seem to concede.[70]

In my view, the concept of civil society provides a useful lever for interpreting the changes in Fuzhou society from 1900 into the 1920s. As we have seen, among the new associations which multiplied after 1902 were many that were quite determinedly autonomous from official patronage; they were made up of voluntary members, supported by voluntary contributions from those members, and devoted to local action to promote what they termed *gongyi,* "public welfare."[71] In their organizational features, their public activism, and their critical politics, these associations, for the few years in which they were active, represented a growth of both civil society and a public sphere in Habermas's sense. In some respects, although called into being by the Qing state, the Provincial Assembly of 1909–1911 can also be seen as an outgrowth of civil society in that it explicitly represented non-state and local interests, it cooperated with the "reform societies," and it attempted to hold the provincial government accountable to it.

If civil society is defined in part by autonomy from the state, then the YMCA and the churches had a distinct advantage in asserting that autonomy, because the treaty provision of extraterritoriality provided them a degree of independence from the Chinese government which purely Chinese public associations did not enjoy. Moreover, in organizational terms they showed attributes typically identified with civil society: they were locally based, autonomous, and, like the reform societies, explicitly concerned with public welfare and social life. They were also potentially critical of the state, as we have seen, and very much concerned with fostering public spirit, patriotism, and an ethic of social service as moral attributes of the Christian citizen and building blocks of the new China.

In this light, we can regard the developments in Fuzhou in these decades as the birth and articulation of a vision of a Chinese modernity based in and growing organically from local civil society. For the progressive elite in Fuzhou, that modernity would be built upon the educated individual citizen, patriotic and internationalist, working for the public good, locally engaged and nationally aware. Nationalism was essential to the vision, but it was a locally grounded, participatory nationalism sprouting from the late imperial local elites and nourished by new elements like the urban professionals, whose growing significance had so much to do with the incorporation of the Protestant minority into elite circles. As John Fincher argued long ago, provincial loyalties were not barriers to but a basis for nationalism in this period, and Bin Wong reminds us that Sun Yatsen himself originally expected nationalism in China to be built by extension from kin and locale.[72]

In Fuzhou the assertion of local pride combined easily and often with the nationalism of these new social forces, as in the invocation of Lin Zexu by the Anti-Opium Society, or in the fundraising for the new YMCA building. Though based in local civil society, that nationalism was also cosmopolitan, perhaps schizophrenically so in resisting Western incursions while also identifying Western ways with the "modern" and the "civilized" and seeking to incorporate them into Chinese life, locally and nationally.

Seen in these terms, the developments that we have traced in Fuzhou were intimately connected to what Philip Kuhn has identified as the core issue behind the notion of civil society: constitutional development, or the development of "conventions about the proper ordering of public affairs," conventions which would define the limits of state power and the rights and duties of citizens.[73] Prasenjit Duara has argued that "the potential for civil society to play a major role in the emergence of Chinese modernity certainly existed" as the twentieth century opened, and his words are borne out in the Fuzhou setting.[74] Especially in the years around 1911, the Fuzhou Protestants and their associates were immensely optimistic about the possibility of ending "despotism" and establishing a "new China" based upon constitutional order and a citizenry morally awakened to patriotism.

Whatever the disagreements about the existence of civil society in China in the first decades of the twentieth century, there is near-universal agreement that the growth of coercive state power from the 1920s meant that any civil society was short-lived. Duara, for instance, goes on to attribute the collapse of civil society to both practical and rhetorical developments: practically, the intrusive and extractive zeal of the warlord, Nationalist, and Communist regimes undermined autonomous social organizational capacity, to their own detriment; rhetorically, the embracing by civilian nationalists of a statist, centralizing vision of nationalism displaced and marginalized alternative visions of China's future rooted in local and civil autonomy.[75]

Of course, "civil society" is not the only term available to analyze these changes. John Fitzgerald does not use it in *Awakening China,* his wide-ranging study of the development of the Nationalist revolution. He speaks instead of the displacement of liberal politics based on representation and pluralism by the revolutionary party-state acting in the name of the united people. As he notes, however, the Nationalist party-state was determined to regulate all existing social organizations and incorporate them into the revolutionary program, as were the Communists after them.[76]

Nor does Myron Cohen use the term "civil society" in his important essay on Chinese nationalism and identity in the twentieth century. Cohen instead juxtaposes the gradual development of nationalism in most societies — which he characterizes as drawing on a mix of traditional and new sources — to the elitist nationalism divorced from and antagonistic to Chinese traditions and popular culture which took hold in China after 1919. The result, Cohen argues, was to deprive Chinese people of the rich cultural resources which held late imperial Chinese civilization together, substituting in their place "the culture of the barracks," a militarized, shrill, and authoritarian state nationalism with no cultural depth or substance.[77]

The transition which both these scholars are discussing in their different terms is the hardening of a hegemonic "national" culture beginning in the 1920s, which in its commitment to national unity delegitimized and attacked many elements of local identity and cultural diversity: popular religion, dialects, local customs, and alternative imaginings of the nation. Again, we can see this transition being played out in the Fuzhou Protestant setting. The locally grounded, civilian vision of Chinese modernity that I have sketched here existed in uneasy tension with another vision for most of the post-1900 period: a more manipulative, statist, militarized nationalism built not on the participation of the citizen but on the mobilization of the people. The line between these visions was thin at times; they overlapped considerably in the 1911 revolution, for instance. But that they were distinct is evident, as in the split between military/non-Fujianese and civilian/Fujianese authorities in the province in the early Republic, and later in the alienation of local politicians from the provincial government.

In this context, the popularity of the YMCA in the early Republic may represent in part an assertion of the locally based civil-society vision of China's national future against the military and nonlocal dominance of the province under Li Houji. The Nationalist victory in the Northern Expedition marked the triumph of the latter vision over the former; it is aptly summed up by the contrast between the parades against opium in the late Qing and early Republic — sponsored by local leaders, incorporating Protestants, inspired simultaneously by the image of Lin Zexu and the national flag — and the parading in 1927 of the Protestant school principal Lin Buji, whose efforts in Christian education made him a suspect figure in the new nation.

In a sense, then, we see in this unlikely social setting, Fuzhou Protestants and their associates in the Fuzhou area, the potential for building a new China out of a synthetic nationalism that drew in part on traditional sources and developed organically from local initiative. The Fuzhou Protestants thought they knew what would "save China." They envisioned a strong and confident China, regenerated through Christianity, built upon an uplifted citizenry educated to the moral duty of patriotism, taking its place confidently in a world community of nation-states progressing toward a bright global future.

Such a vision can be criticized on many grounds. Its proponents unconsciously accepted as normative the world order of nation-states defined by Western hegemony, and glossed naively over the harsh realities of violence and exploitation in international affairs. (Much the same could be said of their missionary counterparts, who tended to overestimate the social influence of Protestant institutions and ideals in the Western world and were shocked by the carnage of the First World War.) Also, the vision was clearly elitist and selective in its appropriation of Chinese traditions, rejecting popular religion almost as wholeheartedly as the nationalist intellectuals whom Myron Cohen decries, and significantly reinventing elements of the Confucian legacy to reconcile them to Christianity and the priorities of a modern society.

Protestant progressives were not alone among Chinese of their own and later generations in doing this, however, and their vision of a Protestant Chinese modernity certainly represented a less radical rupture with the world of late imperial China than the revolutionary modernity that actually emerged after the 1920s. On the positive side, for all its flaws, theirs was a positive and vigorous imagining of a better China and a better world: inventive in melding Chinese and foreign elements and integrationist in connecting rural to urban society and clan and region to nation without subordinating everything to the center. What emerged instead to dominate the history of China in the twentieth century was the militant, mobilizing, censoring party-state that cornered the market on envisioning and creating "new Chinas." A century on, the issues that nurtured the Protestant vision — defining a workable framework for individual citizenship and social service, for social diversity and voluntary association, for international harmony and the place of China in the world — remain salient, and the answers are no more clear now than they were then.

Notes

Introduction

1. *Qishi nianlai zhi Minqing Meiyimei hui*, p. 3.

2. This passage exemplifies the "Western impact, Chinese response" reading of China's modern history, discussed by Paul Cohen in *Discovering History in China*, pp. 9–16.

3. Studies of missions include Latourette's magisterial *History of Christian Missions*; Fairbank, *Missionary Enterprise*; Hunter, *Gospel of Gentility*. Studies of elite rejection of Christianity in three different centuries are Gernet, *China and the Christian Impact*; P. Cohen, *China and Christianity*; Lutz, *Chinese Politics and Christian Missions*.

4. See, e.g., Peel, "For Who Hath Despised the Day of Small Things?"; Harper, "Ironies of Indigenization"; Larson, "Capacities and Modes of Thinking." Works focusing on Chinese Christians rather than missionaries include Kwok, *Chinese Women and Christianity*; T'ien, *Peaks of Faith*; Standaert, *Confucian and Christian*; and Bays, *Christianity in China*.

5. E.g., Hunter, *Gospel of Gentility*, esp. chap. 6.

6. P. Cohen, "Littoral and Hinterland."

7. Tseng, "Chinese Protestant Nationalism," p. 31 and passim.

1. Protestant Christianity in the Chinese Context

1. White is associated with death and mourning in Chinese culture. To the villagers the missionary in his pith helmet may have resembled the demon-spirit Si you fen, "Death-has-gradations," who was always pictured dressed in white and wearing a conical white hat; see Spence, *God's Chinese Son*, p. 41.

2. *Qishi nianlai zhi Minqing Meiyimei hui*, p. 17. Xue Cheng'en was the Rev. Nathan Sites, a Methodist missionary in Fuzhou since 1861; his 1866 journey to Minqing is fancifully sketched in Sites, *Nathan Sites*, pp. 48–50.

3. [Huang Naishang], "Zongjiao guan," p. 7.

4. [Huang Naishang], "Zongjiao guan," p. 7; *Qishi nianlai zhi Minqing Meiyimei hui*, pp. 17, 53; Huang Naishang, *Fucheng qishi zixu*, p. 181. Citations of Huang's autobiography refer to the text as reprinted in Liu Zizheng, *Huang Naishang yu Xin Fuzhou*, which is far more accessible than the original (1925) edition.

5. Latourette, *History of Christian Missions*, pp. 70–71, 108–110, 122–124; Zürcher, "Jesuit Mission in Fukien."

6. Differences between the Congregationalists and the Methodists are discussed in Hatch, *Democratization of American Christianity*, esp. pp. 81–93; Finke and Stark, "How the Upstart Sects Won America," pp. 27–44.

7. Carlson, *Foochow Missionaries*, pp. 66–68.

8. Carlson, *Foochow Missionaries*, esp. chap. 6.

9. Metzger, *Escape from Predicament*; Brokaw, *Ledgers of Merit and Demerit*; Ko, "Thinking About Copulating."

10. [Huang Naishang], "Zongjiao guan," pp. 7a–b. The quotation is from the *Analects* XI:12.

11. Cf. Duara, "Knowledge and Power."

12. Cf. Paul Cohen, "Christian Missions and Their Impact," pp. 543–544. The refer-

ence is to Matthew 5:17, where Christ states that he has come not to abolish the Law but to fulfill it. Protestant respect for the Confucian tradition is evidenced by the annotated translations of the Four Books into the Fuzhou dialect by the Methodist preacher Xu Zezhou (Hu Caik Ciu). His edition of the *Mencius* is extant in FPL: *Mengzi (Fuzhou tuhua zhujie)*. According to the back cover, the book was sold through the Methodist churches as well as through bookstores.

13. E.g., Huang Naishang, "Pigui pian shang"; Huang Naishang, "Pigui pian xia." On elite attitudes see Overmyer, "Attitudes Toward Popular Religion"; de Groot, *Sectarianism and Religious Persecution*, pp. 96–118, 137–148; Yang, *Religion in Chinese Society*, chap. 8.

14. Ai'an xiansheng [Huang Zhiji], *Jiandaoji*; Huang Zhiji, *Ye Mo henglun*; "Essay on Mihcius by Uong De Gi," in Ohlinger Papers, YDS RG 23-11-204; *Fuzhou Meiyimei nianhui shi*, pp. 91–93. For a parallel use of Mozi by a prominent non-Protestant thinker, see Schneider, *Ku Chieh-kang*.

15. Popular religion and the struggle for sagehood were not wholly unrelated, however; see Overmyer, "Dualism and Conflict," tracing the theme of struggle against evil forces running through Confucian thought, Buddhism, liturgical Taoism, and popular religion.

16. Seminal works on Chinese popular religion include Yang, *Religion in Chinese Society*; and Wolf, "Gods, Ghosts, and Ancestors." Doolittle, *Social Life of the Chinese*, gives valuable information on religious practice in and around Fuzhou in the mid-nineteenth century, esp. in vol. 1, chaps. 5–11; vol. 2, chaps. 1–4.

17. The building and its opening are described in detail in Maclay, *Life Among the Chinese*, pp. 194–200. A large stele recounting the history of the church was erected outside it in 1910 and is now preserved on the grounds of the Fuzhou Municipal Library.

18. Xu Yangmei, *Xu Mushi xinxiaolu*, translated with embellishments as [Xu Yangmei], *Way of Faith*.

19. Maclay, *Life Among the Chinese*, pp. 215–216, 313–319; *Fuzhou Meiyimei nianhui shi*, pp. 69–73; *Minutes of the Foochow Conference* (1898), pp. 81–83. Dates for Xu Bomei were supplied from the family genealogy by his great-grandson, the Rev. Xu Lebin; interview with Xu Lebin, Fuzhou, Feb. 20, 1994. The 1869 ordination is described in many mission sources; see, e.g., Wiley, *China and Japan*, pp. 205–238.

20. Xu Yangmei, *Xu Mushi xinxiaolu*, pp. 2b–3a; cf. [Xu Yangmei], *Way of Faith*, pp. 15–16.

21. Xu Yangmei, *Xu Mushi xinxiaolu*, pp. 1, 5–8; cf. [Xu Yangmei], *Way of Faith*, pp. 7–8, 26–39. Xu's father is described by missionaries as a minor military official connected to the county yamen. Xu describes him as head of the night watchmen for the Nantai sector of the city. He was apparently well-off and respected in the local community; during the rebellions of the early 1850s he had been put in charge of a local militia brigade (*tuanlian*), for which service he was later awarded an honorary title of the fifth rank. On the roles and status of subcounty officials, see Ch'u, *Local Government*, pp. 56–73.

22. Xu Yangmei, *Xu Mushi xinxiaolu*, pp. 44–46; cf. [Xu Yangmei], *Way of Faith*, pp. 136–142. The English text diverges from the Chinese here, saying that the two men took him "by the hands."

23. [Xie], *Sia Sek Ong and the Self-Support Movement,* pp. 3–4, 9–10; the Chinese original of this text is apparently not extant. On Xie's life see also *Fuzhou Meiyimei nianhui shi,* pp. 73–75; funeral invitation in Ohlinger Papers, YDS RG 23–14–243. For a similar dynamic behind Protestant conversion among the Hakka in Guangdong, see Lutz and Lutz, *Hakka Chinese,* p. 122.

24. [Xie], *Sia Sek Ong and the Self-Support Movement,* pp. 7, 8–9.

25. Pakenham-Walsh, *Some Typical Christians,* p. 2.

26. Date in *Fuzhou Meiyimei nianhui shi,* p. 178.

27. For this practice, cf. Yang, *Religion in Chinese Society,* p. 92. The absence of official involvement in the account indicates that the god concerned was probably a local *tudi* or a rain deity rather than the city god *(chenghuang)*. Plural gods are also possible as a reading of the Chinese text.

28. For mediums in Chinese popular religion, see Jordan, *Gods, Ghosts, and Ancestors.*

29. Xu Bomei, untitled 100-page MS in Chinese, original preserved by Xu Lebin, now lost; copy obtained from Professor Xu Rulei of Nanjing Theological Seminary.

30. See, e.g., Matthew 13:10–17.

31. [Xu Yangmei], *Way of Faith,* pp. 178–181, 217–218; Xu Yangmei, *Xu Mushi xinxiaolu,* pp. 37–38, 61–62.

32. [Xu Yangmei], *Way of Faith,* pp. 197–200; Xu Yangmei, *Xu Mushi xinxiaolu,* pp. 55–56. For Lin Zhenzhen, see *Fuzhou Meiyimei nianhui shi,* pp. 77–78; Baldwin, *Ling Ching Ting.*

33. Peel, "For Who Hath Despised the Day of Small Things?" p. 595. Peel argues that for Protestant missionaries, and even more for African converts, the Bible "was their supreme paradigmatic history, through which they recognised new situations and even their own actions."

34. Lamin Sanneh argues that the impulse to translate lay at the core of Christian mission; see Sanneh, *Translating the Message,* esp. pp. 4–8.

35. On the whole, the Methodists were more frank than the CMS and the American Board in reporting supernatural experiences of their Chinese converts, perhaps because of the strong supernatural emphasis in early American Methodism; see Butler, *Awash in a Sea of Faith,* pp. 238–241.

36. See, e.g., Methodist Archives, Miss. I/1, 1259–6–2:06, R. S. Maclay, "A Remarkable Experience," dated Foochow, Apr. 26, 1871, recounting a vision of Christ experienced by a young Christian in an inland town.

37. This man's name was Wei Jinzhong, in mission sources Ngoi Cheng-Tung, baptized in 1868. For his experiences see Xu Yangmei, *Xu Mushi xinxiaolu,* pp. 39–40; [Xu Yangmei], *Way of Faith,* pp. 184–187; Stock, *For Christ in Fuh-Kien,* pp. 103–104.

38. CMS, C CH/O 85/32, Robert W. Stewart Annual Letter, 1880, on Biblewomen. For another exorcism story from the early twentieth century, see "Fox Devil Stories," one-page typescript in University of Oregon Special Collections, Skinner Papers, Ax 209 Box 1.

39. "Jiao linguo you dao hu?" As discussed below, this is a quotation from *Mencius,* and I have rendered it here according to its meaning in that context. It is also possible that in this story it is meant to be taken rather differently, as asking whether they obtained the true way in their visit to the neighboring region.

40. *Qishi nianlai zhi Minqing Meiyimei hui,* p. 41.

41. Following D. C. Lau's translation, *Mencius,* vol. 1, pp. 27–30; cf. Dobson, *Mencius,* pp. 14–15; Legge, *Mencius,* pp. 155–157.

42. Spence, *God's Chinese Son,* esp. pp. 34–46.

43. For an overview of Chinese mythology, see Maspero, *Taoism and Chinese Religion,* book 2.

44. Interview with the Rev. Xu Lebin, Fuzhou, Apr. 21, 1994.

45. Duara, "Knowledge and Power."

46. Huang Naishang, *Qishi zixu,* p. 181.

47. *Qishi nianlai zhi Minqing Meiyimei hui,* pp. 72 (Huang Bichang), 63 (Huang Bihong/Yongquan), 17, 69; Huang Naishang, *Qishi zixu,* p. 181.

48. Huang pays tribute to his former teacher in his preface to Xu Yangmei, *Xu Mushi xinxiaolu.*

49. Huang Naishang, *Qishi zixu,* pp. 181–182.

50. Xu Yangmei, *Xu Mushi xinxiaolu,* p. 34; [Xu Yangmei], *Way of Faith,* pp. 124–129.

51. *Qishi nianlai zhi Minqing Meiyimei hui,* p. 18. The diffusion of the Protestant church through Minqing County could be traced in exact detail from this source.

52. Huang Naishang himself, and Huang Fuju and Huang Bihong, who became "local preachers" in the Methodist terminology; for biographies see *Qishi nianlai zhi Minqing Meiyimei hui,* pp. 63–64. Very similar patterns are traced by Lutz and Lutz in *Hakka Chinese,* pp. 246–248; see also Wiest, "Lineage and Patterns of Conversion," on the role of kinship in Catholic conversion in this period.

53. Carlson, *Foochow Missionaries,* p. 99.

54. On New England clergy's suspicion of revivalism, see, e.g., Miller, *Life of the Mind in America,* chap. 1.

55. Goertz, "Development of the Chinese Indigenous Church," pp. 179–191, 210–211; cf. chart after p. 124. Two men were ordained in 1876, the next not until 1890.

56. Chinese works by American Board missionaries in Fuzhou are listed in Goertz, "Development of the Chinese Indigenous Church," pp. 298–303. On the hospitals see Carlson, *Foochow Missionaries,* pp. 87–89.

57. Burns, *Memoir of the Rev. Wm. C. Burns,* pp. 315–318.

58. Charles Hartwell, "How Far Should Self-Government Be Allowed in the Native Churches at the Present Time," undated MS (probably early 1900s), Hartwell Papers, YDS RG 8-92-3.

59. Dates of the visits of the Bishop of Victoria to Fuzhou are given in Stock, *For Christ in Fuh-Kien,* pp. 179–181.

60. CMS, *Register of Missionaries and Native Clergy,* pp. 317, 331–332, 336–337. The pace of ordinations increased later, with twenty-one men being ordained between 1887 and 1904; ibid., pp. 346, 348, 352, 479, 481, 486, 490–493.

61. Carlson, *Foochow Missionaries,* pp. 95, 99; *Annual Report of the Church Missionary Society* 83 (1881–1882), p. 171.

62. CMS, G1 CH1/O 1886/9, Wolfe to Fenn, Dec. 13, 1885.

63. CMS, G1 C CH/O 1884/51, Bishop Burdon to Fenn, Jan. 10, 1884. Problems with the Chinese clergy came to a head during the meeting of the mission in 1886, and the

bishop laid down tighter guidelines for their ordination and employment; see CMS, G1 CH1/O 1887/4, "Minutes of the Fuh Kien Sub Conference of the Church Missionary Society, Nov. 1886."

64. The history of the mission and its problems are reviewed in CMS, G1 CH1/O 1886/109, Banister to Fenn, Aug. 16, 1886. Banister compared the lack of clear organization of his own mission unfavorably with the clearly defined structure of the Methodist church.

65. Xu Yangmei, *Xu Mushi xinxiaolu,* p. 53; cf. [Xu Yangmei], *Way of Faith,* p. 160; Carlson, *Foochow Missionaries,* pp. 97, 100–106, 111–113. The problem and Wolfe's role in it were recognized by other CMS missionaries in Fuzhou as early as 1870, but neither they as his juniors nor the mission board in far-off London could effectively curb Wolfe's impulsiveness; see CMS, C CH/O 28 Cribb/7, Cribb to Fenn, Mar. 14, 1870, in which Cribb reports that "nearly all" of the difficulties reported (by Wolfe) as persecution were "over some pecuniary or personal matter."

66. This affair is discussed in detail in Carlson, *Foochow Missionaries,* chap. 8.

67. The courses are detailed in *Minutes of the Foochow Conference* (1901), pp. 89–92; (1906), pp. 96–103; (1928), pp. 92–98.

68. The dates, place, and officers of each session of the conference are listed in *Fuzhou Meiyimei nianhui shi,* pp. 227–231, and in the English minutes for each year, e.g., *Minutes of the Foochow Conference* (1938), pp. 434–436.

69. The terminology used reflected this willingness, for becoming a member of the conference was referred to as "entering the travelling connection"; see, e.g., *Minutes of the Foochow Conference* (1947), p. 206.

70. Two installments of the first translation are in the Bodleian Library, Oxford University: *Meihui liwen* ([1869]), consisting of *juan* 1–4; and *Meihui liwen* (1872), consisting of *juan* 6. The 1892 translation, *Meiyimei hui ganglie,* is in the Institute of Religion, Fujian Teachers' University. For Huang Naishang's role in both translations see *Fuzhou Meiyimei nianhui shi,* p. 210.

71. Lacy, *Hundred Years of Chinese Methodism,* p. 57.

72. The Chinese minutes for 1868 and 1874 are in the Bodleian Library, Oxford University: *Zhonghua Meiyimei jiaohui nianlu; Meiyimei hui nianhui dan.*

73. This bishop, Kingsley, died on his return journey from China, and the Fuzhou church published a biography of him in Chinese, *Jin Jiandu zhilue,* a copy of which is in the British Library. Methodist bishops did not have charge of particular areas but instead exercised spiritual oversight collectively over the whole church, through visiting different areas and presiding over their annual conferences. In China this role was played by bishops visiting from America until 1904, when James Whitford Bashford was appointed the first resident Methodist bishop in China.

74. Lacy, *Hundred Years of Chinese Methodism,* pp. 79–81.

75. See *Minutes of the Foochow Conference* (1901), pp. 91–92.

76. For a more detailed study of this school, see Dunch, "Mission Schools and Modernity."

77. This fascinating episode is explored in Robert, "Methodist Struggle over Higher Education."

78. See Bishop Burdon's comments on Plumb's case: CMS G1 CH/O 1883/142, Burdon to Wigram, May 9, 1883.

79. E. H. Smith, "The Devolution Process in the Foochow Congregational Church," three-page MS in Smith Family Papers, YDS RG 5–8–5. Printed agendas in Chinese for the annual meetings of 1896 and 1908 can be found in the papers of G. H. Hubbard, MS 965, Manuscripts and Archives, Yale University Library.

80. Goertz, "Development of the Chinese Indigenous Church," pp. 312–317.

81. The terminology used in Chinese for the body would have added to the impression of overall authority. It was called the *sheng zonghui,* "Provincial General Council," and the "Chairman" was termed the *zongli,* the term now used to translate "premier / prime minister." The character *zong* connotes a central authority with broad oversight responsibilities, and the whole structure was a quasi-constitutional one, with elected delegates (*tuoshi*), a schedule, an agenda, and minutes kept. The Chinese minutes of this council's meetings from 1883 until 1909 are preserved in a large manuscript volume in the Institute of Religion, Fujian Teachers' University.

82. There is a great deal of correspondence concerning this complex dispute in the CMS archives. As always, Wolfe was more in sympathy with the Chinese perspective than were the bishop, the other missionaries, or the mission board. For his views see CMS G1 CH4/O 1901/58, Wolfe to Baring Gould, Jan. 17, 1901; cf. CMS G1 CH4/O 1901/7, Bishop [Hoare] of Victoria to Baring Gould, Dec. 5, 1900; CMS G1 CH4/O 1901/8, Lloyd to Baring Gould, Nov. 22, 1900.

83. CMS G1 CH4/L1/62, CMS Secretaries to Lloyd, Feb. 1, 1901.

84. *Minutes of the Foochow Conference* (1947), pp. 206–216.

85. The Methodists had an advantage in having their own publishing house in Fuzhou; its publications are listed in *Fuzhou Meiyimei nianhui shi,* pp. 208–210. Three early tracts by Fuzhou Methodist preachers are preserved in the Bodleian Libary, Oxford University: Lianfeng jushi [Xie Xi'en], *Yesu shi shei lun;* Xie Xi'en, *Jiuling shiyao;* Xu Bomei, *Xinde tonglun.* Many essays by Chinese church members were printed in the church periodical published from 1874 on, initially under the title *Xunshan shizhe* and after 1876 as *Minsheng huibao.*

86. Cf. Goertz, "Development of the Chinese Indigenous Church," pp. 210–211.

87. In China and Taiwan, much effort has gone into compiling and publishing documents related to these cases, many of which are preserved in the *jiaoan* archives of the Qing *Zongli yamen.* A classic analysis is P. Cohen, *China and Christianity;* see also Lin Wenhui, *Qingji Fujian jiaoan zhi yanjiu.*

88. Examples of the first perspective are too many to cite; though moderated since 1980 or so, it remains the dominant paradigm in mainland Chinese scholarship on the *jiaoan.* For the second outlook see, inter alia, Hevia, "Leaving a Brand on China."

89. Cf. Sweeten, "Catholic Converts in Jiangxi Province"; Litzinger, "Rural Religion and Village Organization."

90. See, e.g., Bernhardt, *Rents, Taxes, and Peasant Resistance,* p. 5 and passim; Reed, "Money and Justice," p. 377.

91. Rawski, *Agricultural Change,* pp. 73 ff; Ownby, *Brotherhoods and Secret Societies;* Eastman, *Family, Fields, and Ancestors,* esp. chaps. 1, 4, and 10.

92. Freedman, *Lineage Organization;* and Freedman, *Chinese Lineage and Society.*

93. Lamley, "*Hsieh-tou,*" esp. pp. 3–16.

94. For recent exceptions, see Bays, *Christianity in China;* Lutz and Lutz, *Hakka Chinese,* esp. chap. 12.

95. Pomeranz, "Ritual Imitation," p. 4.

96. See, e.g., Carlson, *Foochow Missionaries,* pp. 106–107; Esherick, *Origins of the Boxer Uprising,* p. 200.

97. E.g., Naquin, *Millenarian Rebellion;* Overmyer, "Alternatives"; Macauley, "Civil Reprobate," esp. chap. 6; Reed, "Money and Justice"; Huang, *Civil Justice.*

98. Xu Yangmei, *Xu Mushi xinxiaolu,* pp. 34, 37; cf. [Xu Yangmei], *Way of Faith,* pp. 126–127, 175–176.

99. Xu Yangmei, *Xu Mushi xinxiaolu,* pp. 34, 56–59; cf. [Xu Yangmei], *Way of Faith,* pp. 125, 202–212.

100. Fuqing's lawless image is echoed in other mission sources, and persists today also; the county is a principal point of origin for illegal emigrants smuggled from China into the United States and other countries.

101. Xu Yangmei, *Xu Mushi xinxiaolu,* pp. 67–68; cf. [Xu Yangmei], *Way of Faith,* pp. 233–240.

102. Ch'u, *Local Government,* p. 173.

103. Rev. Martin, cited in CMS G1 CH4/O 1903/144, Rev. Iek Duang Me to CMS, London, May 8, 1903.

104. CMS G1 CH4/L1/178, Baring Gould to Wolfe, Oct. 24, 1902.

105. CMS G1 CH4/O 1903/29, Minutes of Executive Committee of Fukien Provincial Church Council, Nov. 12, 1902; G1 CH4/O 1902/56, Wolfe to Baring Gould, Dec. 30, 1901.

106. Chen and Yang Taotais to Consul Playfair, Oct. 16, 1900, transmitting a communication from Feng, District Magistrate of Fuqing; translated and signed by Playfair; encl. in CMS G1 CH4/O 1902/56, Wolfe to Baring Gould, Dec. 30, 1901.

107. See Reed, "Money and Justice," pp. 371–373; Huang, *Civil Justice.*

108. CMS G1 CH4/O 1903/32, Martin to Baring Gould, Dec. 2, 1902.

109. CMS G1 CH4/O 1902/56, Wolfe to Baring Gould, Dec. 30, 1901; for the connotations of the term "shepherd," see CMS G1 CH4/O 1903/144, Rev. Iek Duang Me to CMS, London, May 8, 1903.

110. CMS G1 CH1/O 1888/173, Wolfe to Fenn, Oct. 5, 1888.

111. CMS G1 CH/O 1884/51, Bishop Burdon to Fenn, Jan. 10, 1884.

112. CMS G1 CH/O 1884/165, Wolfe to Fenn, June 20, 1884.

113. CMS G1 CH1/O 1891/53, J. S. Collins, "Memorandum on the History of the Lo Nguong City Congregation from 1882–1890," Jan. 5, 1891.

114. CMS G1 CH1/O 1886/16, Wolfe to Fenn, Jan. 7, 1886.

115. Specifically, single catechists earned $4–6 per month depending on experience, married catechists $5–8, ordained deacons $12, and priests $15; CMS G1 CH1/O 1897/261, Wolfe to Baring Gould, Sept. 20, 1897. The conversion rate of around 0.66 taels to the Mexican dollar for the 1890s is from Rawski, *Education and Popular Literacy,* pp. 27, 206 n. 17, citing Liang-lin Hsiao, *China's Foreign Trade Statistics, 1864–1949* (Cambridge: Harvard University Press, 1974), p. 191 table 9a.

116. Rawski, *Education and Popular Literacy,* pp. 99, 103–104.

117. USDS, *Despatches from Foochow,* S. L. Gracey to Department of State, Aug. 15, 1903, #137, encl.; cf. CMS C CH/O 28/7, Cribb to Fenn, Mar. 14, 1870; on the clothing and sumptuary privileges of degree holders, see Ch'u, *Law and Society,* pp. 135–154.

118. CMS G1 CH4/O 1906/36, Martin to Baring Gould, Dec. 8, 1905; CMS G1 CH4/O 1906/47, "Minutes of the Executive Committee of the Provincial Council," Nov. 17, 1905; cf. CMS G1 CH4/O 1906/19, Wolfe memorandum on this case, Dec. 2, 1905. The title simply meant that the individual was a delegate to the Provincial Council of the Anglican Church, but in this case it was apparently phrased in Chinese on his card in such a way as to imply a connection to the political power of Great Britain.

119. See, e.g., Nind, *Mary Clarke Nind*, p. 90; *Church Missionary Intelligencer and Record* 28, n.s., vol. 2 (1877), pp. 210–211; CMS, *Mr. Wigram's Tour*, p. 207.

120. Esherick, *Origins of the Boxer Uprising*, pp. 214–215; see also pp. 74–95, 184–205.

121. Reed, "Money and Justice," pp. 367–373; Ch'u, *Local Government*, p. 187.

122. Duara, *Culture, Power, and the State*, pp. 55–56.

123. John Martin of the CMS heard this from both the Rev. Yek Siu Mi (Ye Shoumei), who approved, and the doctor Ling Do Ang (Lin Tao'an), who did not; CMS G1 CH4/O 1903/32, Martin to Baring Gould, Dec. 2, 1902.

124. *Meihui nianlu* (1868), p. 6. The geography text was entitled *Dili tu;* it may have been the world map with explanatory text produced in Fuzhou by the Methodist missionary Erastus Wentworth in 1857, listed in Wylie, *Memorials of Protestant Missionaries,* p. 236. On the impact of world maps on Chinese individuals, cf. Tang, *Global Space*, pp. 1–2; Fitzgerald, *Awakening China*, pp. 127–128.

125. *Meihui nianlu* (1868), pp. 8b, 9b, 11, 12, 15b.

126. Jan. 17, 1864; see [Xu Yangmei], *Way of Faith*, pp. 106–114; Carlson, *Foochow Missionaries,* p. 133.

127. Huang Naishang, *Qishi zixu*, p. 182; he describes his illness as "coughing blood disease."

128. In some respects Huang Naishang is a Fuzhou analogue to the earlier missionary literary assistant turned pioneer journalist Wang Tao (1828–1897), except that Wang's Christian commitment was never entirely clear, whereas Huang's was throughout his life; see P. Cohen, *Between Tradition and Modernity.*

129. The translations included books of the Bible, catechisms, the *Discipline,* biographies of Wesley and Tyndale, and a work on astronomy. His last cooperative project was a history of the United States, on which he worked with the Myron C. Wilcox in 1895. Huang's own editorial efforts included the Chinese minutes of the Foochow Conference for 1872–1874 and 1876 and successive editions of the Methodist hymnbook. See Huang Naishang, *Qishi zixu*, pp. 182–184; cf. *Fuzhou Meiyimei nianhui shi,* pp. 208–210; Zhan, *Huang Naishang zhuan*, pp. 16–17, 212–215.

130. Issue 5 (Mar. 8, 1875) is preserved in the Ohlinger Papers, YDS RG 23–13. McIntosh, *Mission Press,* pp. 40–46, gives a useful annotated list of the publications of the Fuzhou Methodist Publishing House.

131. Huang Naishang, *Qishi zixu*, pp. 182–184. Neither of these works is known to be extant.

132. Huang Naishang, *Qishi zixu*, pp. 183, 185; the total number is from the *juren* list for 1894, in Chen Yan, *Fujian tongzhi,* "Xuanju zhi," *juan* 14, pp. 19b–20b. This total was apparently somewhat higher than the usual *juren* quota for Fujian; see Chang, *Chinese Gentry,* pp. 124–125.

133. Zhan, *Huang Naishang zhuan,* pp. 20–21, 24–27. Huang Naishang was the eldest of four boys and one girl. The fourth brother, Naimu (born in 1870, over twenty years after Huang Naishang), also had opportunities for advancement through his brother, but was a disappointment to him; Huang says he "did not amount to anything" (*wusuo chengming*); Huang Naishang, *Qishi zixu,* p. 211.

134. Huang Naishang, *Qishi zixu,* pp. 182, 185, 211.

135. Song, *One Hundred Years' History,* pp. 236–237. For biographies of Lin and Wu, see their entries in Boorman and Howard, *Biographical Dictionary.*

136. Huang Naishang, *Qishi zixu,* pp. 185, 186. Specifically, a *bagong,* a high grade of *gongsheng.*

137. *Minhou yishi gonghui nianjian* 3 (1937), p. 42. Huang had another five sons and two daughters by his second wife, whom he married in 1895.

138. Cf. the mobility of Hakka Protestants across generations; Lutz and Lutz, *Hakka Chinese,* p. 142.

139. Ho, *Ladder of Success,* pp. 54–67; Elman, "Political, Social, and Cultural Reproduction," pp. 17–18.

140. Ho, *Ladder of Success,* pp. 249–251, 254.

141. On village schools, see Rawski, *Education and Popular Literacy,* esp. chap. 4.

142. Elman, "Political, Social, and Cultural Reproduction," p. 17 and passim.

143. Carlson, *Foochow Missionaries,* pp. 50–53, 85–87; Ford, *Methodist Episcopal Education,* pp. 32–48.

144. Maclay, *Life Among the Chinese,* pp. 222–225, 287–309; Xu Yangmei, *Xu mushi xinxiaolu,* p. 20b; cf. [Xu Yangmei], *Way of Faith,* p. 80; *Fuzhou Meiyimei nianhui shi,* p. 131.

145. The Li clan of the neighboring village of Guifeng was also converted at this time, and individuals from that generation and later ones became prominent preachers, doctors, and educators in Fuzhou and beyond. According to a descendant, in the early twentieth century every remaining member of the clan came down to Fuzhou for schooling and moved out from there, so that at the time of land reform in the early 1950s no members of the original Li surname were left in Guifeng. Interview with Li Shuren, Fuzhou, Apr. 21, 1994.

146. Hook, *"Save Some,"* pp. 32–33.

147. On the Protestant primers, see Rawski, "Elementary Education." For sample elementary curricula from the Methodist schools, see Ford, *Methodist Episcopal Education,* pp. 76, 82–83

148. This progression was spelled out systematically by R. W. Stewart but was probably never as clear-cut in practice; see *History of the Dublin University Fuh-Kien Mission,* pp. 8, 31.

149. After the early 1920s the missions gradually ceased to operate elementary schools, but the intermediate and higher schools remained important right until 1949; cf. Dunch, "Mission Schools and Modernity."

150. Ford, *Methodist Episcopal Education,* p. 170.

151. There are many petitions from the churches in the mission archives requesting the provision of doctors and schools for their areas; see, e.g., CMS G1 CH1/O 1893/182, Petition of 1893 from Gutian/Pingnan District Council of the Anglican church; CMS G1

CH1/O 1898/185, Petition from "the Christians of Xianyou County," 1898; Methodist Archives, Miss. I/1, 1259–5–3:12 (Miscellaneous), Petition from Xinghua church leaders, Apr. 6, 1907.

152. *Constitution of the Anglo-Chinese College* (1887), in Methodist Archives, Acc. 79–16, 1459–4–2:09.

153. Ohlinger to Fowler, Aug. 9, 1881, quoted in Robert, "Methodist Struggle over Higher Education."

154. See Lacey Sites, *Educational Institutions,* pp. 4–5; Methodist Archives, Miss. I/1, 1259–6–2:43, George B. Smyth to Rev. A. J. Palmer, D.D., Mar. 27, 1899; cf. Dunch, "Mission Schools and Modernity."

155. Robert, "Methodist Struggle over Higher Education."

156. Methodist Archives, Acc. 1973–044, Letter Books of the Methodist Episcopal Mission Society, Book 125 (series 233: China 1890–1902), 1261–6–1:10, Palmer to George B. Smyth of Anglo-Chinese College, Apr. 22, 1898.

157. Korson, "Congregational Missionaries in Foochow," pp. 59–61. The initial Methodist reaction to this "competition" was not favorable; Methodist Archives, Miss. I/1, 1259–6–2:43, Smyth to McCabe, Aug. 28, 1891.

158. CMS G1 CH4/O 1902/33, Wolfe to Baring Gould, Nov. 30, 1901.

159. Gwynn, *"T.C.D." in China,* pp. 50–51. The school was run by the Dublin University Fukien Mission, consisting of graduates of Dublin University; the mission operated as a distinct agency under the aegis of the CMS.

160. Boorman and Howard, *Biographical Dictionary,* pp. 379–382.

161. Fryer, *Educational Directory for China* 1 (1895), p. 40.

162. On these three services, see Feuerwerker, *Foreign Establishment,* chap. 4. The remaining ten government employees were road and rail administrators (three), diplomats (one), legislators (two), provincial government bureaucrats (one, in the Finance Department), and military men (three, two of them physicians with the army or navy).

163. *Heling Yinghua shuyuan zhangcheng* (1917), pp. 16–19.

164. On Xue/Sycip, see the biography of his brother Hsueh Min-lao (Albino Sycip, who also studied at Anglo-Chinese College but is not listed as a graduate) in Boorman and Howard, *Biographical Dictionary;* I am indebted to Professor Edgar Wickberg of the University of British Columbia for alerting me to the importance of the Sycip brothers in the Chinese community in Manila in the 1920s and 1930s. On Yin, see Song, *One Hundred Years' History,* pp. 422–423.

165. Song, *One Hundred Years' History,* p. 359; Lacey Sites, *Educational Institutions,* p. 6; Lo, *Correspondence of G. E. Morrison,* vol. 1, p. 559; *Heling Yinghua shuyuan zhangcheng,* p. 16.

166. Lacey Sites, *Educational Institutions,* p. 4.

167. Twenty-nine out of 116, including 24 in education, and 5 in the church or the YMCA.

168. *Catalogue of Foochow College, College Year Feb. 1915–Jan. 1916,* pp. 18–22.

169. A rare gazetteer from 1906 gives the population of Gutian as 119,463 persons in 23,654 households, among whom were 2,700 Anglicans and 2,300 Methodists (plus 3,400 Catholics), making Protestants about 4 percent of the population in 1906; *Gutian xian xiangtu zhilue* (no *juan* numbers or pagination; hand copy in Fujian Teachers'

University Library). These figures accord roughly with church statistics, and the overall population estimate is roughly in line with more reliable Republican-period figures: in 1913, a census of dubious reliability put the Gutian population near 240,000, but a better survey in 1928 found 140,851 persons in 25,595 households; see *Minguo Fujian gexian shi (qu) hukou tongji ziliao,* p. 74.

170. The Anglican schools were founded in 1887 (girls) and 1893 (boys), and the Methodist in 1892 (boys) and 1893 (girls); see *Gutian Jidujiao zhi,* pp. 33–36.

171. Ford, *Methodist Episcopal Education,* pp. 203–204, citing a report by Ida Belle Lewis to the China Central Conference of the church in 1923.

172. The breakdown is as follows: 5 of the 35 who had studied overseas had graduated from Protestant institutions, as had 24 of 49 graduates of Chinese universities and 133 of 169 high school graduates. The remainder consists of 28 military or police graduates, 80 normal or technical school graduates, 69 law and government (*fazheng*) graduates, and 41 vocational school (*shiye*) graduates; none of these are listed as having attended Protestant schools. However, many of them could have received their early schooling in the church schools in Gutian without its being reflected in this list, for in general only the latest school attended is specified.

173. The remaining 125 are 5 graduates of vocational or normal courses and 120 high school graduates, 40 from Anglican schools in Fuzhou and 80 from Methodist ones (the Hwa Nan College Middle School); *Gutian xianzhi* (1942), *juan* 15 (*xuanju zhi*), pp. 79b–96.

174. E.g., the delegates to the Anglican Provincial Council in 1888 decided formally that Christian girls should not be married if they were under eighteen years of age, and that the girls should be consulted and not married against their will; CMS G1 CH1/O 1889/6, Martin to Wigram, Dec. 5, 1888, and 1889/14, Wolfe to Fenn, Dec. 12, 1888.

175. CMS G1 CH/O 1884/82, "Hok Chiang Church Council. Minutes of Meetings," meeting of Sept. 25, 1883.

176. Burton, *Notable Women,* p. 19; cf. *Fuzhou Meiyimei nianhui shi,* pp. 110–111.

177. This comes through very clearly in the autobiography of Persis Li, matron of the CMS girls' school in Gutian from 1887 to 1928; [Persis Li], *The Seeker.*

178. See, e.g., the biographies in Codrington, *Hot-Hearted; Fuzhou Meiyimei nianhui shi,* pp. 111–112; for widows in late imperial China, see Mann, "Widows."

179. There has been some confusion in secondary work in English concerning Xu Jinhong's Chinese name. Kwok Pui-lan gives one version in *Chinese Women and Christianity,* p. 222, and Weili Ye gives another in " 'Nu *Liuxuesheng,*' " p. 318. For the correct name, see glossary.

180. On the role of the conference in sending her, see Robert, "Methodist Struggle over Higher Education."

181. Burton, *Notable Women,* pp. 15–70. The Methodist Episcopal WFMS was unusual in making Chinese women official missionaries of the society; in all there were five women from Fuzhou who were sent back there as WFMS missionaries after studying in America, all between 1895 and 1905; see *Minutes of the Foochow Conference* (1947), pp. 284–286.

182. One of these, Xu Jixiang, rose to become head of the Military Justice division of the Ministry of the Navy in the early Republic. In 1940 he came out of retirement to join the Navy Ministry under the collaborationist government of Wang Jingwei; see Xu You-

chun, *Minguo renwu da cidian,* p. 844. For the biography of another family member, naval doctor Xu Shifang, see ibid., p. 833.

183. In addition to church sources cited earlier in this chapter, this information is compiled from interviews with family members the Rev. Xu Lebin (Fuzhou, Feb. 20, 1994), Ms. Xu Daofeng (Feb. 17, 1994), Mr. Xu Shihui (Fuzhou, Mar. 1, 1994), Mr. Xu Tianfu (Shanghai, May 14, 1994), and the Rev. Xu Daowu (Shanghai, May 14, 1994); correspondence with Dr. Katharine H. K. Hsu (Xu Hanguang) of Houston, Texas; and genealogical materials on the family compiled by Dr. Hsu and printed for private distribution in 1995 (*Gaoyang Xu shi zupu*).

2. Protestant, Professional, Progressive

1. For some examples see *Minutes of the Foochow Conference* (1898), pp. 42–43, 55; ibid. (1902), p. 40; ibid. (1906), p. 79; ibid. (1908), pp. 63, 93, 99; ibid. (1909), pp. 14, 33.

2. Wright, "Introduction," pp. 3–4.

3. The term "progressive elite" is employed to avoid the problematic term "gentry" (except where it is used specifically to translate the Chinese term *shen* as one component of the local elite), the misleading dichotomy between "constitutionalists" and "revolutionaries," and even Esherick's more useful "urban reformist elite" (*Reform and Revolution,* esp. pp. 99–105). Esherick juxtaposes the "urban reformist elite" to the revolutionaries, whereas my reading of the situation in Fuzhou is that there was a coalition of people of reformist and revolutionary leanings behind a broadly progressive agenda. Reformers and revolutionaries were neither static groups nor opposing camps. This is argued in more detail later in this chapter, and in connection with the Provincial Assembly in Chapter 3.

4. See, e.g., *Quanjie yapian lun,* published in Fuzhou in 1853, in HY.

5. Carlson, *Foochow Missionaries,* chap. 2.

6. Lin Bingzhang earned the *jinshi* degree in 1895 and was appointed to the Hanlin Academy soon after that. A colorful if rather anecdotal account of Lin's life is Wu Jiaqiong, "Lin Bingzhang."

7. Wu, "Lin Bingzhang," p. 100; *Fan nietai lilin qudu zongshe kai huiyi an,* p. 2; Wu Jiayu and Lin Jiazhen, "Fujian jinyan yundong," pp. 16–17. The latter incorrectly dates the founding of the society to 1905.

8. For the edict see Lodwick, *Crusaders Against Opium,* pp. 117–122. For a much more detailed study of opium suppression in Fujian, see Madancy, "Ambitious Interlude."

9. Wu, "Lin Bingzhang," p. 98; *Fujian jiaoyu zonghui yilan,* p. 7; *Fujian qudu zongshe jibao* 1 (Fall, Guangxu 33 [1907]), *lishi* p. 1. On Chen Baochen see Xu Youchun, *Minguo renwu da cidian,* p. 1075.

10. Wu and Lin, "Fujian jinyan yundong," pp. 15–16.

11. Cf. Lodwick, *Crusaders Against Opium,* p. 126.

12. *Fujian qudu zongshe jibao* 1 (Fall, Guangxu 33 [1907]), *zhangcheng* pp. 5–8. For lists of violators see ibid., 1–4 (1907–1908), passim.

13. See, e.g., *Fan nietai lilin qudu zongshe kai huiyi an,* pp. 6a–b; for the founding and activities of the Gutian branch of the society, see *Gutian xianzhi* (1942), *juan* 38, "Jinyan xiaoshi" (Brief history of opium prohibition).

14. Rev. Llewelyn Lloyd in *C.M.S. Gazette* (1907), p. 214.

15. Faithfull-Davies, *Banyan City*, p. 17; on opium addiction and the poor, see Spence, *Chinese Roundabout*, p. 230.

16. Wu and Lin, "Fujian jinyan yundong," p. 17; *Fujian qudu zongshe jibao* (Fall, Guangxu 33 [1907]), *lishi* pp. 1a–b; Faithfull-Davies, *Banyan City*, pp. 17–19.

17. See Wu and Lin, "Fujian jinyan yundong," pp. 16–17; Chen Yan, *Fujian tongzhi*, "Waijiao zhi," p. 20b.

18. The petition was signed by several hundred community leaders, all members of the newly formed county and local assemblies in Min and Houguan Counties, and published as *Lieming kenqing Min-Zhe zongdu;* cf. Wu and Lin, "Fujian jinyan yundong," p. 17. For the British position see Wright, "Introduction," pp. 14–15; Lodwick, *Crusaders Against Opium,* chap. 5.

19. Faithfull-Davies, *Banyan City,* pp. 23, 19.

20. See, e.g., *C.M.S. Gazette* (1907), pp. 214, 244, 341, 372; (1908), pp. 186–187, 243.

21. *Fujian qudu zongshe jibao* 1 (Fall, Guangxu 33 [1907]), *lishi* p. 1b; on the Society for the Suppression of the Opium Trade, see Lodwick, *Crusaders Against Opium,* pp. 55–65.

22. *Fujian qudu zongshe jibao* 3 (Spring, Guangxu 34 [1908]), *zazhi* pp. 9b–10; *C.M.S. Gazette* (1908), p. 243. A careful reading shows that the two accounts describe the same event, although the church location is not mentioned in the former; cf. also *Fuzhou Meiyimei nianhui lu* (1908), *juan* 2, p. 2.

23. *Fan nietai lilin qudu zongshe kai huiyi an,* p. 6b. This Ke was probably Dr. Hardman Kinnear, the medical missionary in charge of the American Board hospital in the city, whose Chinese surname was Ke.

24. Spence, *Chinese Roundabout,* pp. 216–217, citing *China Medical Missionary Journal* 12 (1898).

25. *Fujian qudu zongshe jibao* 1 (Fall, Guangxu 33 [1907]), *zhangcheng* pp. 3b, 4b. Detail on Xu's life is from an interview with his grandson Xu Lebin and his nephew Xu Shihui, Fuzhou, Apr. 22, 1994; and Xu Hanguang, comp., *Gaoyang Xu shi zupu.*

26. The modernist bent of the society makes it unlikely that these were practitioners of Chinese medicine, but by this time it is possible that graduates of Japanese medical schools were also practicing in the city.

27. *Fujian qudu zongshe jibao* 1 (Fall, Guangxu 33 [1907]), *zhangcheng* p. 7; for more on Chen's role see Madancy, "Ambitious Interlude."

28. The petition text is printed in *Zuohai gongdao bao* 1:8 (Xuantong 3/6/15 [1911]), pp. 3–5.

29. *Fujian qudu zongshe jibao* 1 (Fall, Guangxu 33 [1907]), *lishi* p. 1.

30. Zeng Shaoqing. On the role of regional loyalties in generating nationalism in China in this period, see Fincher, "Political Provincialism"; Goodman, "Locality as Microcosm of the Nation?"

31. USDS, *Despatches from Foochow,* 12/23/1905, Gracey to Department #181.

32. *Minjing* (Fujian, be warned!), pp. 38–39. *Minjing* is an anonymous printed tract of around seventy pages, dating probably from 1904 or 1905, which focuses on the threat of Western and particularly Japanese imperialism and on the economic, military, and ideological degeneracy of the province.

33. USDS, *Despatches from Foochow,* 6/3/05, Gracey to Legation, #284, enclosed in 6/7/05, Gracey to Department, #164, p. 2.

34. *Xinwen bao* (News) of 5/15, reprinted in *Meiguo huagong jinyue jishi erbian,* part 2, p. 15b, in FPA *Ziliao* Collection, 2-8-18; *Minbao* (Fujian daily), Guangxu 32/5/15, enclosed in USDS, *Despatches from Foochow,* 6/21/05, Gracey to Department, #167.

35. USDS, *Despatches from Foochow,* 6/3/05, Gracey to Legation, #284, enclosed in 6/7/05, Gracey to Department, #164.

36. The text of the petition, dated June 2, 1905, is enclosed in USDS, *Despatches from U.S. Ministers,* 7/26/05, Rockhill to Department, #38. It seems likely that the petition was drafted and submitted in English, because of the language, because there are original signatures of two representative signatories on the English text, and because the accompanying despatch makes no mention of its having been translated.

37. Chinese church leaders in Xiamen petitioned the U.S. legation in Beijing through the Xiamen consul after a "stormy" meeting on July 19 and received a reply through the consul on August 24; see USDS, *Despatches from Amoy,* 7/25/05, Anderson to Department, #39; 8/28/05, Lupton to Department, #47. A petition from students and teachers of the Canton Christian College (later Lingnan University) is enclosed with the Anglo-Chinese College petition in USDS, *Despatches from U.S. Ministers,* 7/26/05, Rockhill to Department, #38. Note also the 1911 petition of Fujian Protestants to the British crown over the opium question, discussed above.

38. White American views of race and civilization around this time are insightfully discussed in Bederman's *Manliness and Civilization,* esp. pp. 31–41. For a nineteenth-century Protestant view of the racial hierarchy of evolution/civilization as the students of the Anglo-Chinese College might have encountered it, see the discussion of animal and human skull shapes in Williamson, *Gewu tanyuan, juan* 2, pp. 16b–17; this book was used in Protestant education in Fuzhou.

39. Gracey's "humiliation" at the way America's laws on Chinese immigration were being implemented is expressed in USDS, *Despatches from Foochow,* 8/5/05, Gracey to Department, #168.

40. Biography in *Fuzhou Meiyimei nianhui shi,* pp. 91–93; on the Chinese Independent Protestant Church see Bays, "Growth of Independent Christianity," pp. 310–311.

41. See *Fujian riri xinwen* (Fujian daily news), Guangxu 31/4/21, reprinted in A Ying, *Fan Mei huagong jinyue wenxueji,* pp. 604–606. No original copies of this newspaper are known to be extant.

42. USDS, *Despatches from Foochow,* 8/5/05, Gracey to Department, #168, handwritten note on the despatch; cf. USDS, *Despatches from U.S. Ministers,* 8/15/05, Rockhill to Department, #58.

43. See USDS, *Despatches from Amoy,* 8/26/05, Lupton to Legation, enclosed in 8/28/05, Lupton to Department, #47; 9/14/05, Lupton to Department, #54.

44. It was renamed *Fujian ribao* (Fujian daily). For this episode see Zhan, *Huang Naishang zhuan,* pp. 127–136.

45. Huang, *Qishi zixu,* p. 197; cf. *Fuzhou Meiyimei nianhui shi,* pp. 112–115.

46. Zheng Lansun, *Fujian xinhai guangfu shiliao,* chaps. 2–4. For later accounts see *Zhonghua minguo kaiguo wushi nian wenxian,* series 1, vol. 12, pp. 68–90, which simply reprints much of the text of chap. 2 of Zheng's volume; Pan Shouzheng, "Xinhai

geming zai Fuzhou," pp. 1–33; Fan Qilong, " 'Shiyi/jiu' qiyi-xinhai geming zai Fujian," pp. 128–146.

47. The term "reform societies" is used in missionary sources of the time as the collective designation for the host of new voluntary associations formed to foster progressive social causes around this time. Chinese discussions generally refer to them collectively simply as *shetuan*, "associations." While terming them "reform societies" tends to prejudge the question of whether they were "revolutionary" in intent, I have employed it as the least unwieldy and most descriptively accurate of the English labels available.

48. Zheng, *Fujian xinhai guangfu shiliao*, p. 3. This man, Zheng Quan (Zhongjin), later worked with Huang Naishang on the *Fujian Daily News* in Xiamen, discussed above, and was inducted by Huang into the Revolutionary Alliance during this time; see Zhan, *Huang Naishang zhuan*, p. 136.

49. Pu Hanzi, "Sanbo geming zhongzi de Qingmo Houguan liangdeng xiaoxuetang," pp. 58–62.

50. Zheng, *Fujian xinhai guangfu shiliao*, p. 3. Chen Nengguang's date of graduation is given in *Heling Yinghua shuyuan zhangcheng*, p. 16.

51. The father's biography in *Fuzhou Meiyimei nianhui shi*, pp. 90–91, gives a good deal of information on the son (and grandchildren) also.

52. Fukien Post Office, "Native Staff Record: Clerks and Inland Agents from 1897 to 1908," first entry, in FPA 56-1-1. Bilingual clerk was the highest grade of appointment open to Chinese.

53. *Fuzhou Meiyimei nianhui shi*, p. 90. On his political activities while employed by the consulate, see National Archives, USDS 3823/109, Gracey to Department #318, Aug. 14, 1909, and encl.; USDS 3823/114, Gracey to Department #321, Aug. 27, 1909, and encl. I am indebted to Dr. Joyce Madancy for sharing these documents with me.

54. See, e.g., *China Mission Year Book* (1910), p. 147.

55. Zheng, *Fujian xinhai guangfu shiliao*, pp. 116–120, 143; *Fuzhou Meiyimei nianhui shi*, p. 90; Madancy, "Ambitious Interlude."

56. Zheng, *Fujian xinhai guangfu shiliao*, p. 5. In dating the founding of the society to 1907 I am following Fan, " 'Shiyi/jiu' qiyi-xinhai geming zai Fujian," pp. 134–135. Some sources give 1908 as the date, apparently based on Liu Tong's "Xinhai Fujian guangfu huiyi," p. 455. The society's second annual financial report covers the year Guangxu 34 (February 1908 to January 1909), so Liu Tong's date of late 1908 is definitely wrong.

57. Zheng, *Fujian xinhai guangfu shiliao*, p. 5; *Zhonghua minguo kaiguo wushi nian wenxian*, 1:12, p. 85. The newspaper was the *Jianyanbao*.

58. The other *gongyishe* are listed in Zhang Pengyuan, *Lixianpai yu xinhai geming*, p. 164.

59. *Qiaonan gongyishe zhengxinlu* 2–3 (Guangxu 34 and Xuantong 1 [1908, 1909]), pp. 1–3, 3b–4b.

60. *Fuzhou Meiyimei nianhui shi*, pp. 85–86; *Gutian Jidujiao zhi*, pp. 68–69; *Baoling fuyin shuyuan*, p. 2.

61. For Yu, see *Tianantang bashi zhou jinian kan, zhuanlue* p. 42; *Minutes of the Foochow Conference* (1947), p. 245; *Gutian xianzhi* (1942), *juan* 15, p. 79b.

62. *Qiaonan zhengxinlu*, pp. 9, 10.

63. *Qiaonan zhengxinlu*, pp. 9–10; *Zuohai gongdao bao* 1:8 (1911), p. 4; Hartwell,

"Story of the Christian Herald Industrial Homes"; Zou Tianhuan, "Fujian gua'er yuan huiyi."

64. *Qiaonan zhengxinlu*, p. 3; *Fuzhou Meiyimei nianhui shi*, p. 234; *Fuzhou Meiyimei nianhui lu* (1908), *juan* 2, p. 2.

65. Biography in *Fuzhou Meiyimei nianhui shi*, p. 105.

66. In 1913, a few years after this, Methodist ordained preachers earned between $7 and $10.50 per month, with additional allowances of $3 if they were married and $1.25 or $1.50 per child. By contrast, graduates of the mission colleges appointed to the postal service as bilingual clerks on probation in 1906 and 1907 began at a monthly salary of 25 Haikuan taels (around $37) and could expect to be earning 35 or 40 taels after their second year of service. See *Minutes of the Foochow Conference* (1913), p. 43; Fukien Post Office, "Native Staff Record," FPA 56-1-1.

67. The six were Wu Guanluan, Chen Shixing, and Lin Hanguang, all 1902 graduates; Lu Guantai and Wang Qiuding, 1907; and Cheng Gongchen, 1908.

68. Liu Huiru (Youwen) and Liu Meicun (Xieyuan). The information in this paragraph comes from comparing the list of graduates and teachers in *Heling Yinghua shuyuan zhangcheng*, pp. 2b, 16–17, with the names in *Qiaonan zhengxinlu*.

69. *Fuzhou qingnian hui bao* 3:2 (Xuantong 3/4/10 [1911]), p. 9.

70. *Zhonghua minguo kaiguo wushi nian wenxian*, series 1, vol. 12, pp. 70, 85.

71. Another Methodist preacher, Xu Zehan (Hu Caik Hang), son of Xu Yangmei, served as a speaker (*yanshuo yuan*) for the *Chating gongyishe*, one of the many reform societies on which no detail is available; *Fuzhou Meiyimei nianhui lu* (1908), *juan* 2, p. 2.

72. *Fuzhou Ying lingshi*; Li Jinqiang, "Qingji Fuzhou geming yundong," p. 113; Lin Denghao, "Liu Yuandong lieshi xiaozhuan."

73. *Minnan jiuhuohui di yici baogao shu* (Guangxu 34 [1908]), pp. 1–2; cf. *Minutes of the Foochow Conference* (1912), p. 85; *Fuzhou Ying lingshi*, p. 1; *Fuzhou qingnian hui bao* 2:3 (Xuantong 2/12 [1911]), inside front cover.

74. *Minnan jiuhuohui di yici baogao shu*, p. 2; *Fuzhou Ying lingshi*, p. 1; *Heling yinghua shuyuan zhangcheng*, p. 16; *Fujian qudu zongshe jibao* 1 (Fall, Guangxu 33 [1907]), *zhangcheng* p. 7; cf. Zheng, *Fujian xinhai guangfu shiliao*, p. 144. Unfortunately I have found no information on Lin's religious affiliation or how he attained the title of prefect.

75. Liu, "Xinhai Fujian guangfu huiyi," p. 454.

76. Li's revolutionary activities will be discussed further in Chapter 3; see Zou, "Fujian gua'er yuan huiyi," p. 181; Wang Tiefan, "Fujian Tongmenghui zai Cangshan," pp. 16–18.

77. Cf. Zheng, *Fujian xinhai guangfu shiliao*, chap. 2, for these activities and those involved in them.

78. "Rexin gongyi fu you xiangwang renshi"; Liu, "Xinhai Fujian guangfu huiyi," p. 455.

79. The revolutionary ties of reform society members became more widely known after the Huanghuagang uprising; as we have noted, the leader of the Minnan Fire Brigade was among the several Fuzhou revolutionaries killed in it; Lin Denghao, "Liu Yuandong lieshi xiaozhuan."

80. Zhang Pengyuan [P'eng-yuan Chang], *Lixianpai yu xinhai geming*, pp. 164–166.

81. Zheng Zhonglin, born in 1880 and appointed to the postal service in 1904; see Fukien Post Office, "Native Staff Record," name 13, in FPA 56–1–1. Zheng's educational background is not recorded: he may well have acquired his English at a mission school. For his role in the reform societies, see *Qiaonan zhengxinlu* pp. 1, 9b; *Minnan jiuhuohui baogao shu* 2 (1910), p. 1b.

82. Chen, Lin Shufen, and Li Qifan, all mentioned earlier; a fourth is Lin Fucun, a Qiaonan Society member, who was the interpreter in 1905; see *Meiguo huagong jinyue jishi erbian,* part 2, p. 15b.

83. For the *fazheng* schools and their graduates, see Thompson, "Political Impact of Students."

84. *Fujian qudu zongshe jibao* 1 (Fall, Guangxu 33 [1907]), *zhangcheng* pp. 8b–11.

85. Cf. Zarrow, "Introduction"; Tsin, "Imagining 'Society.'"

86. Garrett, *Social Reformers,* chap. 2, recounts the early history of the YMCA and its entry into China.

87. *Zhonghua Jidujiao qingnian hui wushi zhou nian,* pp. 147, 170–173; cf. Garrett, *Social Reformers,* pp. 25–26. Garrett's mention of forty-five founding members holding daily prayer meetings is based on a misreading of this source.

88. *Qingnian hui bao* 5:1 (April 1902), pp. 8a–b, gives figures of 80 YMCA members and 40 associate members out of a total of 240 students at the Anglo-Chinese College, 58 members and 15 associate members out of 150 students in Foochow College, and groups connected with the American Board seminary (37 members), the Anglican boarding school (26 members), and the Anglican theological college (35 members).

89. *Qingnian hui bao* 5:1 (April 1902), pp. 4–5, 8a–b; 5:4 (October 1902), p. 12b; 5:6 (December 1902), p. 12b; 6:1 (February 1902), pp. 7b–8b; 6:3 (April 1903), pp. 12a–b; *Qingnian* 8:8 (December 1905), pp. 5–6.

90. [YMCA], *Work of the YMCAs of China and Korea During 1908,* p. 15.

91. The rapid expansion of the YMCA in China between 1900 and 1914 is well summarized in Latourette, *History of Christian Missions,* pp. 584–593.

92. The names are given in *Zhonghua Jidujiao qingnian hui wushi zhou nian,* p. 139. Of the six, Zhu Lide and Liu Shufan were graduates of Foochow College; *Catalogue of Foochow College, College Year February 1915–January 1916,* pp. 18–22, in the Beard Papers, YDS RG 8 Box 255–28. Chen Nengguang and Chen Minwang were graduates of the Anglo-Chinese College and represented the college YMCA at an early YMCA national gathering—consisting mostly of missionary educators—in Shanghai, either in 1888 or 1892; *Zhonghua Jidujiao qingnian hui wushi zhou nian,* pp. 147, 172.

93. L. E. McLachlin, quoted in *Foreign Mail Annual* (1906), p. 37.

94. *Zhonghua Jidujiao qingnian hui wushi zhou nian,* p. 139; *Fuzhou qingnian hui bao* 3:3 (Xuantong 3/4/29), pp. 5–6; *Foreign Mail Annual* (1908), p. 37.

95. *Foreign Mail Annual* (1907), p. 37; cf. *Qingnian* 10:10 (January 1908), p. 2.

96. *Qingnian* 11:3 (April 1908), p. 88; *Fuzhou qingnian hui bao* 3:3 (Xuantong 3/4/29), p. 13; [YMCA], *Record of the Seventh Annual Conference, 1909,* p. 28.

97. *Zhonghua Jidujiao qingnian hui wushi zhou nian,* p. 139.

98. Cf. "Model Constitution for a City Association," in [YMCA], *Record of the Seventh Annual Conference, 1909,* pp. 57–59.

99. Report of L. E. McLachlin, in *1909–1910 Annual Reports,* p. 116, YMCA Ar-

chives. Figures for YMCA membership in Fuzhou from 1907 to 1929 are given in Chapter 5.

100. Yan Fu, "Yuan qiang," p. 51; Liang Qichao; "Xinmin shuo," p. 212; cf. Schwartz, *In Search of Wealth and Power*, pp. 59–60; de Bary, *Sources of Chinese Tradition*, pp. 755–759. For writings on educational reform, see McElroy, "Transforming China Through Education."

101. *Foreign Mail Annual* (1907), p. 37; *Sili Fuzhou qingnian hui zhongxue ershiwu zhou, xiaoshi* p. 1; *Qingnian* 11:6 (September 1908), p. 168.

102. For the way the YMCA's "physical education" came to encompass "health promotion" in the Chinese context, see [YMCA], *Record of the Seventh Annual Conference, 1909*, p. 14. The YMCA's activities in the early Republican period will be discussed in Chapter 5.

103. For instance, the constitution of the Anti-Opium Society defined opium smokers as "lacking in national consciousness" (*guojia sixiang*) — see *Fujian qudu zongshe jibao* 12 (1909–1914), *zazhi* p. 1.

104. The magazine began publication in 1909 and continued into the 1920s (first as *Fuzhou qingnian hui bao,* then, from 1918, as *Fuzhou qingnian*). This discussion is based on three extant issues from 1910 and 1911 in FPL, which also holds an incomplete series from 1913 on.

105. For the latter text in translation see Chan, *Source Book in Chinese Philosophy,* p. 454.

106. *Fuzhou qingnian hui bao* 2:3 (Xuantong 2/12/25), pp. 1–2.

107. *Fuzhou qingnian hui bao* 2:3 (Xuantong 2/12/25), pp. 9–11.

108. *Fuzhou qingnian hui bao* 3:2 (Xuantong 3/4/10), pp. 7–9; cf. ibid., pp. 11–12; 2:3 (Xuantong 2/12/25), pp. 13–15.

109. See *Fuzhou qingnian hui bao* (Xuantong 2/12/25), pp. 12–13, 18, 15–16, 7–8.

110. The estimate of 120 people is derived by dividing by 50 the total attendance for 1910 — 6,080, given in *Foreign Mail Annual* (1910–1911), p. 37.

111. *Fuzhou qingnian hui bao* 3:2 (Xuantong 3/4/10), pp. 9–11. Like many British church leaders by this time, Price was critical of his country's policies on opium; see his article on the issue in *Church Missionary Record*, 62 (1911), pp. 274–282.

112. *Qingnian* 11:6 (September 1908), p. 168.

113. *Fuzhou qingnian hui bao* 3:3 (Xuantong 3/4/29), pp. 11–12; cf. [YMCA], *Among Young Men in the Middle Kingdom,* p. 18.

114. The YMCA board members are listed on the inside front cover of *Fuzhou qingnian hui bao*. Huang Naishang, Chen Zhilin, Lin Changmin, Chen Nengguang, and Lin Tao'an are the individuals referred to here.

115. *Fuzhou qingnian hui bao* 3:3 (Xuantong 3/4/29), p. 12.

116. *Fuzhou qingnian hui bao* 3:3 (Xuantong 3/4/29), pp. 12–13.

117. Yan Qu (Boyu); see Xu Youchun, *Minguo renwu da cidian,* p. 1662.

118. Chen Peikun (Yunshan); see Xu Youchun, *Minguo renwu da cidian,* p. 1045.

119. *Fuzhou qingnian hui bao* 3:3 (Xuantong 3/4/29), p. 13.

120. Li Funan (Yuzhai); see *Shangye zazhi* 2 (1910), p. 2; *Fujian ziyiju . . . yiyuan yilan biao,* p. 1; *Fujian qudu zongshe jibao* 1 (1907), *lishi* p. 1.

121. Garrett, *Social Reformers,* pp. 83–84.

122. On feminine imagery in American Protestantism see Douglas, *Feminization of American Culture;* Mathews, *Religion in the Old South,* esp. chap. 3; for feminine symbolism in Chinese Protestantism, see Kwok, *Chinese Women and Christianity,* chap. 2.

123. On Yan's work and importance, see Schwartz, *In Search of Wealth and Power,* esp. pp. 98–112.

124. *Fuzhou qingnian hui bao* 3:2 (Xuantong 3/4/10), p. 6.

125. See, e.g., *Foreign Mail Annual* (1910–1911), p. 36.

126. Chen Minwang, in *Qingnian* 9:8 (November 1906), p. 2. For the parallel optimism in American Protestantism around this time, see Hutchison, *Modernist Impulse in American Protestantism.*

127. *Minjing* pp. 35–40; Arnold, "Educational Activity in Foochow"; see also Dunch, "Mission Schools and Modernity."

128. Rev. W. A. Main, in *Minutes of the Foochow Conference* (1910), p. 33.

129. Arnold, "Educational Activity in Foochow," pp. 211–212.

130. *Fuzhou shuobao she zhangcheng,* pp. 3b–4.

3. *"Welcoming a New China": Protestants in Late Qing Politics*

Epigraph: *Fuzhou Meiyimei nianhui lu* 33 (1909), *juan shang* p. 7.

1. The thirty-third session of the Foochow annual conference of the Methodist Episcopal Church met in Fuzhou from Nov. 17–24, 1909; the Provincial Assembly met for about six weeks from Oct. 14, 1909.

2. *Fuzhou Meiyimei nianhui lu* 33 (1909), *juan shang* pp. 6–7. It is noteworthy that Yu did not include the dynasty in his litany of "long lives"; similarly, a foreign observer of the opening of the Fujian Provincial Assembly noted that the banners read not "Long Live the Emperor," but "Long Live China"; Fincher, *Chinese Democracy,* p. 198.

3. Fincher, "Political Provincialism," p. 210.

4. Min, "Late-Ch'ing Provincial Assembly," pp. 164–165.

5. Liu Chongyou, vice-president of the Fujian Provincial Assembly, and Lin Changmin, its general secretary; Fincher, *Chinese Democracy,* pp. 148–149.

6. There is some confusion in the literature about this condition. The Chinese text of the relevant article reads "you ju gongshengyuan yishang zhi chushenzhe." In this context, *gongshengyuan* should mean not "*gongsheng* and *shengyuan*," but just *gongsheng,* and so it is taken by Fincher ("Political Provincialism," p. 146; *Chinese Democracy,* p. 109), by Chang ("Constitutionalists," p. 147), and by Buck (*Urban Change,* pp. 64–65). However, Esherick includes *shengyuan* in the electorate (*Reform and Revolution,* p. 94), as does Min Tu-ki ("Late-Ch'ing Provincial Assembly," p. 160), and, following Min, Thompson (*China's Local Councils,* p. 139). Since these regulations (with the higher age minimum of thirty) also applied to candidates for election, the difference is crucial for assessing the nature of the assemblies, as many members of the Fujian assembly held degrees lower than *gongsheng;* see the discussion below.

7. *Fujian ziyiju chouban chu.*

8. Missionaries in Fuzhou complained to the U.S. consul that even nonclergy mission school graduates were being denied the franchise under the provision excluding clergy; Fincher, *Chinese Democracy,* p. 133.

9. The composition, work, and findings of this body are detailed in *Fujian ziyiju chouban chu*, in FPL.

10. *Fujian ziyiju . . . yiyuan yilan biao*. Four vacancies were created by those elected from Fujian to the National Assembly; illness and death produced three other vacancies, only two of which had been filled by the 1910 session, when this document was apparently published.

11. Wakeman, *Fall of Imperial China*, p. 236. Wakeman is surely mistaken in stating that nationally, 18 percent of the assemblymen held the *jinshi* degree. In the Fujian assembly, one member is listed as a *jinshi* (Kang Yong), and two others as Hanlin scholars, who presumably also held the *jinshi* degree (Yang Tinglun and Zheng Xiguang); see *Fujian ziyiju . . . yiyuan yilan biao*, pp. 1a–b, 3.

12. In sorting out the relative ranking of these titles, I have followed Ho, *Ladder of Success*, pp. 27–34, and Chang, *Chinese Gentry*, pp. 8–20. The precise numbers for each title (in descending order of rank) in the three categories of regular *gongsheng*, irregular *gongsheng*, and *shengyuan* are as follows: *you gongsheng*, 2; *bagong*, 5; *fugong*, 1; and *sui gongsheng*, 3 (11 regular *gongsheng*); *lin gongsheng*, 2; *zeng gongsheng*, 2; and *fu gongsheng*, 5 (9 irregular *gongsheng*); *you linsheng*, 8; *linsheng*, 8; *zengsheng*, 1; *you fusheng*, 1; *fusheng*, 10 (28 *shengyuan*).

13. Using newly accessible sources for fifteen of the twenty-one assemblies, Chang P'eng-yuan finds that, overall, 4.35 percent of assemblymen held *jinshi* degrees, 21.27 percent were *juren*, 28.73 percent were *gongsheng*, 34.78 percent were *shengyuan*, and 10.87 percent held no classical degree; Chang, "Background of Constitutionalists," p. 67. As with his earlier work on the subject, Chang uses data on the degrees held by assembly members to advance a general argument concerning the social conservatism of the "constitutionalists" in late Qing China; the problems with this kind of argument will become more evident as we look at the actual beliefs and actions of the so-called upper gentry in the Fujian Provincial Assembly.

14. Biography in Tahara, *Shinmatsu minsho jimmeiroku*, p. 244. On the language reform memorial see Zhan, *Huang Naishang zhuan*, pp. 47–51.

15. Tahara, *Shinmatsu minsho jimmeiroku*, p. 302.

16. It is not clear how many of the representatives were educated in Japan. Liu Chongyou and Zheng Zuyin were; so also were Lin Changmin and the other four members of the secretariat of the assembly, aged between twenty-eight and thirty-five, who were graduates of schools of politics and law or normal schools in Japan; *Fujian ziyiju . . . yiyuan yilan biao*, p. 17. Fincher mentions the predominance of Japan-educated men in the Sichuan assembly; *Chinese Democracy*, pp. 140, 153 n. 73.

17. Wakeman, *Fall of Imperial China*, p. 236; cf. Min, "Late-Ch'ing Provincial Assembly," p. 259 n. 132, disputing the stress of Wright and Fincher on the importance of lower gentry in the assemblies.

18. Cf. Rankin, *Elite Activism*, p. 259. It may be that the Fujian assembly was more lively than most; Fincher notes that in some provinces only a handful of representatives were active in debating resolutions, while "in Fujian as many as 30 out of 72 could be called activists"; Fincher, *Chinese Democracy*, p. 140.

19. Cf. Wright, "Introduction," pp. 3–4, 21; her comment that "discussion of many local issues inevitably led to national issues concerned with resistance to imperialism" applies very well to the Fujian assembly.

20. *Fujian ziyiju diyi jie yi'an zhaiyao.*

21. *[Diyici] Fujian ziyiju yishi suji lu* 13 (Xuantong 1/10/1 [Nov. 13, 1909]), pp. 6–7b. For the topics debated by the provincial assemblies in general, see Fincher, *Chinese Democracy,* pp. 134–138.

22. Liu Zizheng, *Huang Naishang yu xin Fuzhou;* Chew, *Chinese Pioneers.* The settlement, at Sibu in Sarawak, became known as "New Fuzhou"; it is still predominantly Fuzhou-dialect-speaking and Christian.

23. Zhan, *Huang Naishang zhuan.*

24. Cf. Esherick, *Reform and Revolution,* pp. 99–105.

25. Chang, "Background of Constitutionalists," esp. pp. 68, 72. On Huang and Zheng as the only revolutionaries in the assembly, see Zhan, *Huang Naishang,* p. 153 n. 1. Lee, "Revolution in Treaty Ports," p. 87, states that three other members were also revolutionaries: Yu Zhongying, Huang Jixing, and Lu Chuhuang.

26. The titles of the extant issues of *Fubao* are listed in Zhan, *Huang Naishang zhuan,* appendix 3 (pp. 227–229). Huang's most recent educational effort had been founding the Minqing County Educational Association in 1908 and setting up thirty-four new-style elementary schools through the county in 1909; ibid., pp. 151–152.

27. The U.S. consul in Xiamen relayed this rumor during the controversy involving Huang's paper in 1905; USDS, *Despatches from Amoy, China, 1844–1906,* 9/14/05 Lupton to Department, #54. Also, in his autobiography Huang recounts that while he was still in Singapore the Chinese consul there notified the Min-Zhe governor-general of his revolutionary ties; Huang received a warning to tone down his activities, conveyed through Chen Baochen; Huang Naishang, *Qishi zixu,* pp. 15b–16b.

28. YMCA Archives, Box 23/52, Fletcher S. Brockman to Willard Lyon, Dec. 4, 1911.

29. *Fujian ziyiju . . . yiyuan yilan biao,* pp. 7, 10, 11b, 12b. On the standing committees, which continued the work of the assemblies between the plenary sessions, see Fincher, *Chinese Democracy,* p. 140.

30. *[Diyici] Fujian ziyiju yishi suji lu* 9 (Xuantong 1/9/22 [Nov. 4, 1909]), pp. 1b–2b.

31. Huang was not alone in the tendency to propose ambitious and expensive reform measures. Esherick cites a contemporary comment on the Hubei assembly that the proposals of members were often "complicated and regardless of financial resources available"; *Reform and Revolution,* p. 105.

32. *[Diyici] Fujian ziyiju yishi suji lu* 9, pp. 3b–4b. After 1911 the prefectures were abolished and Fujian was indeed divided into four administrative areas along these lines; *Minguo Fujian sheng xingzheng qu hua,* p. 1.

33. *[Diyici] Fujian ziyiju yishi suji lu* 10 (Xuantong 1/9/24 [Nov. 6, 1909]), pp. 8b–11.

34. *[Dierci] Fujian ziyiju yishi suji lu* 12 (Xuantong 2/9/29 [Oct. 31, 1910]), pp. 12b ff.

35. *[Dierci] Fujian ziyiju yishi suji lu* 21 (Xuantong 2/10/17 [Nov. 18, 1910]), pp. 9b–11.

36. *[Dierci] Fujian ziyiju yishi suji lu* 23 (Xuantong 2/10/19 [Nov. 20, 1910]), pp. 16b–24. A specialist opium suppression bureaucracy in four sectors was in fact created by the new provincial government after the 1911 revolution, probably drawing on elements in this proposal; cf. Madancy, "Ambitious Interlude."

37. *[Diyici] Fujian ziyiju yishi suji lu* 18 (Xuantong 1/10/11 [Nov. 23, 1909]), pp. 6b–11; *[Disanci] Fujian ziyiju yishi suji lu* 7 (Xuantong 2/11/6 [Dec. 7, 1910]), pp. 25–27; cf. USDS, *Records,* 893.00 1518/357, Arnold to Secretary of State, Jan. 10, 1910.

38. The five reviewers were Wu Tingcheng (Guangchen), sixty, a *juren* from Lianjiang County; Li Zhongye (Cihou), forty-six, a *juren* from Fuqing County; Huang Zhongfeng (Zhizhai), fifty-four, a *fusheng* from Fuzhou's commercial suburbs; Li Funan (Yuzhai), sixty-nine, a brevet magistrate from Fuzhou; and You Zhaoyuan (Shaoquan), thirty-one, a *fusheng* from Luoyuan County.

39. The picul was a measure of weight, normally equal to 100 catties (*jin*), or about 110 pounds; however, Eastman notes that a picul of rice in late imperial Fuzhou equaled 180 catties; *Family, Fields, and Ancestors,* p. 107.

40. *[Disanci] Fujian ziyiju yishi suji lu* 10 (Xuantong 2/11/11 [Dec. 12, 1910]), pp. 5b–7.

41. Ibid.

42. *Shangye zazhi* 2 (1910), p. 2; Li was also a founder of the Anti-Opium Society and was the speaker representing the commercial sector at the fourth anniversary of the Fuzhou YMCA discussed in Chapter 2.

43. Huang's home area in rural Minqing remained poor and isolated in the 1920s and 1930s, when Ruth Hemenway served as doctor in the Methodist hospital there; for fascinating detail on life in the area, see Drake, *Ruth V. Hemenway.*

44. Zhan, *Huang Naishang zhuan,* pp. 198–200, concludes that the family's poverty prevented the three uncles from marrying. Huang later arranged for the continuation of their lines by allocating some of his sons and brothers as adopted heirs of his uncles, an arrangement common in such situations in Chinese society.

45. For the position of the Revolutionary Alliance on land reform, see de Bary, *Sources of Chinese Tradition,* pp. 766–767.

46. *Heling yinghua shuyuan zhangcheng,* p. 16b; Chen Yan, *Fujian tongzhi* (1938), *xuanju zhi, juan* 14, p. 33b.

47. For biographies of Chen, see Xu Youchun, *Minguo renwu da cidian,* p. 1009; Tahara, *Shinmatsu minsho jimmeiroku,* pp. 383–384; Gaimusho johobu, *Kaitei gendai Shina jimmeikan,* p. 199.

48. Tahara, *Shinmatsu minsho jimmeiroku,* p. 383. Gaimusho johobu, *Kaitei gendai Shina jimmeikan,* p. 199, substitutes opium for salt; however, since Chen himself was an active opponent of the opium trade, leading both official and church efforts at opium suppression after 1911, and since he later worked in the fields of banking and salt administration, the salt reading of his background is probably preferable to the opium one.

49. Tahara, *Shinmatsu minsho jimmeiroku,* pp. 383–384.

50. E.g., *[Dierci] Fujian ziyiju yishi suji lu* 4 (Xuantong 2/9/8 [Oct. 10, 1910]), pp. 4 ff.; *[Dierci] Fujian ziyiju yishi suji lu* 8 (Xuantong 2/9/17 [Oct. 19, 1910]), pp. 4–5; *[Dierci] Fujian ziyiju yishi suji lu* 12 (Xuantong 2/9/29 [Oct. 31, 1910]), p. 9.

51. Lee, "Revolution in Treaty Ports," p. 180, argues that the failure of the petition drive in November 1910 pushed constitutionalists in Fujian more toward cooperation with the revolutionaries.

52. *[Dierci] Fujian ziyiju yishi suji lu* 11 (Xuantong 2/9/24 [Oct. 26, 1910]), pp. 3b–5b. In the spring of the following year the whole standing committee of the Provincial Assembly (of which Chen was a member) intervened to prevent the governor-general from disbanding all the reform societies in Fuzhou after the capture of many Fuzhou revolutionaries in the Guangzhou Uprising exposed the extent of revolutionary activity within the societies; on this affair see Zheng, *Fujian xinhai guangfu shiliao,* pp. 34–40.

53. "Gailiang shehui, zengjin guomin daode, kaitong guomin zhishi." The term used here for "people," *guomin,* connotes citizens of a nation.

54. *Fuzhou Meiyimei nianhui lu* 33 (1909), *juan shang,* p. 7.

55. On Christian efforts to secure a constitutional guarantee of religious liberty in the early Republican period, see Keller, "Nationalism and Chinese Christians," pp. 34–37.

56. Quoted in Butler, *Awash in a Sea of Faith,* p. 214.

57. Butler, *Awash in a Sea of Faith,* pp. 212–224; cf. Bloch, "Religion and Ideological Change," pp. 55–57.

58. *[Diyici] Fujian ziyiju yishi suji lu* 15 (Xuantong 1/10/6 [Nov. 18, 1909]), pp. 7b–19; cf. USDS, *Records,*893.00 1518/357, Amoy Consul to Secretary of State, Jan. 10, 1910.

59. *[Diyici] Fujian ziyiju yishi suji lu* 15, pp. 29–32b.

60. *[Dierci] Fujian ziyiju yishi suji lu* 18 (Xuantong 2/10/13 [Nov. 14, 1910]), pp. 22b–23.

61. *[Disanci] Fujian ziyiju yishi suji lu* 10 (Xuantong 2/11/11 [Dec. 12, 1910]), pp. 12–13b.

62. *Fujian ziyiju . . . yiyuan yilan biao,* pp. 16–17. Fincher notes that elections for the provincial assemblies were held in some overseas Chinese communities, but there was no explicit provision for overseas Chinese representation in the regulations governing the assemblies; see Fincher, *Chinese Democracy,* p. 137.

63. *[Diyici] Fujian ziyiju yishi suji lu* 12 (Xuantong 1/9/29 [Nov. 11, 1909]), pp. 16b–17a. The measure noted that a *Zongli yamen* decree of 1899 had in fact instructed local officials to receive bishops and archbishops with certain marks of official rank, but this decree had been rescinded.

64. The intent of this clause appears to have been to prevent Christians from being identified as *jiaomin* in official correspondence, which might have led officials to treat them with favoritism to avoid trouble.

65. *[Diyici] Fujian ziyiju yishi suji lu* 12 (Xuantong 1/9/29 [Nov. 11, 1909]), p. 17.

66. *[Diyici] Fujian ziyiju yishi suji lu* 18 (Xuantong 1/10/11 [Nov. 23, 1909]), p. 6; and *[Diyici] Fujian ziyiju yishi suji lu* 20 (Xuantong 1/10/13 [Nov. 25, 1909]), pp. 16b–18a.

67. *[Diyici] Fujian ziyiju yishi suji lu* 20 (Xuantong 1/10/13 [Nov. 25, 1909]), pp. 16b–18a.

68. Wolfe to Baring Gould, Dec. 30, 1901, CMS Archives G1 CH4/O 1902/56. On generational conflict in the American Board mission, see Korson, "Congregational Missionaries in Foochow," pp. 89 ff.; Edward H. Smith, "The Devolution Process in the Foochow Congregational Church," three-page MS in the Smith Family Papers, YDS RG 5-8-5.

69. Consuls sympathetic to the church, as was Samuel Gracey, U.S. consul in Foochow in the 1890s and early 1900s, could interpret their own "non-intervention" rather flexibly; see Gracey's report on an incident in Minqing in 1903 that turned out not to be "religious persecution," in which Gracey nevertheless asked/required the local magistrate to issue a placard forbidding molestation of the Christians. USDS, *Despatches from Foochow,* Gracey to Department of State, Aug. 15, 1903, and encl.

70. See Zhan, *Huang Naishang zhuan,* pp. 14–15; also Huang Naishang's preface to Xu Yangmei, *Xu mushi xinxiaolu;* and his glowing eulogy of Nathan Sites, Huang Jiumei, "Xue Mushi zhuanlue."

71. Fryer, *Educational Directory for China* 1 (1895), p. 40.

72. Qing law contained a number of clauses reflecting this suspicion, and the 1908 regulations for the provincial assemblies themselves excluded religious clergy of all sects from the franchise; on the hostility of modernizing elites to "superstition" in the twentieth century, see Duara, "Knowledge and Power"; Cohen, "Being Chinese."

73. Chang, "Constitutionalists," pp. 160–173; Fincher, *Chinese Democracy,* pp. 148–149.

74. Cf. Chang, "Constitutionalists," pp. 168–183; Judge, *Print and Politics,* pp. 186–197.

75. See Liu Tong, "Ji *Jianyan bao,"* pp. 46–52; cf. Lee, "Revolution in Treaty Ports," pp. 179–181.

76. Hane, *Modern Japan: A Historical Survey,* pp. 120–130, 154–157. There are striking parallels between the ideology and tactics of the popular rights movement in Japan and the parliamentary petition movement in China in 1909 and 1910, in which Chinese educated in Japan—many of them at Waseda—played a prominent role, parallels which lead one to wonder whether the Japanese example provided a template for political action for Chinese constitutionalists, and whether the liberal milieu of Waseda University was important in transmitting this template.

77. For Lin's relationship with Liang see Fairbank, *Liang and Lin;* Nathan, *Peking Politics.*

78. Boorman and Howard, *Biographical Dictionary,* pp. 368–372; *Who's Who in China* (1920), pp. 112–113.

79. YMCA Archives, Box 22/43, L. E. McLachlin to John R. Mott, Mar. 31, 1910.

80. F. Ohlinger, "Some Chinese Republicans," *Christian Advocate,* Oct. 3, 1912, clipping in "Ideal" scrapbook, Ohlinger Papers, YDS RG 23.

81. *Fuzhou Meiyimei nianhui lu* 33 (1909), *juan shang* (part 1), pp. 7b–8a.

82. *Fuzhou Meiyimei nianhui lu* 33 (1909), *juan shang* (part 1), pp. 7b–8a. The *Zuozhuan* is an early commentary on the *Spring and Autumn Annals,* and one of the core texts of the Chinese classical canon; see Watson, *Early Chinese Literature,* pp. 40–66.

83. Lin's conversion features prominently in church reports for the year: see, e.g., *Foreign Mail Annual,* 1910–1911, p. 36; Ohlinger, "Some Chinese Republicans," in "Ideal" scrapbook, Ohlinger Papers, YDS RG 23.

84. YMCA Archives, Box 22/43, L. E. McLachlin to John R. Mott, Mar. 31, 1910.

85. Ohlinger, "Some Chinese Republicans," in "Ideal" scrapbook, Ohlinger Papers, YDS RG 23.

86. Zhou Bangdao, *Jindai jiaoyu xianjin zhuanlue,* pp. 347–348.

87. *Minutes of the Foochow Conference* (1910), p. 33.

88. Huang Naishang, "Zongjiao guan." An incomplete run of the periodical, *Zuohai gongdao bao* (Fuzhou Christian journal), from mid-1911 to early 1912, is preserved in the Institute of Religion, Fujian Teachers' University, and there are also some issues in FPL.

89. Zhan, *Huang Naishang zhuan,* pp. 116–155; Liu Zizheng, *Huang Naishang yu Xin Fuzhou,* pp. 194–204; Lee, "Revolution in Treaty Ports," pp. 127 ff., 178–179; Yen, *Overseas Chinese and the 1911 Revolution;* Leung, "Religion and Revolution," pp. 74–78; Li Jinqiang, "Qingji Fuzhou geming yundong," pp. 94–96.

90. Cf. Esherick, *Reform and Revolution,* pp. 40–58; Borthwick, "Students and Revolutionary Culture."

91. Ono, "A Deliberate Rumor." On "physical education" being military drill, see Arnold, "Educational Activity in Foochow," pp. 196, 211–212, 217–218.

92. Ono, "A Deliberate Rumor," p. 34. The denial of a similar request (on the grounds of neutrality) soon after the revolution by the principal of Foochow College led to a mass walkout of the students and considerable bad publicity for the American Board mission; see ABCFM Archives, ABC 16–3–5, Hardman Kinnear to Enoch Bell, Jan. 6, 1912; Korson, "Congregational Missionaries in Foochow," pp. 78–80.

93. Zheng, *Fujian xinhai guangfu shiliao,* pp. 27–28.

94. *Qiaonan . . . zhengxin lu,* pp. 9–10; *Zuohai gongdao bao* 1:8 (1911) p. 4; Hartwell, "Story of the Christian Herald Industrial Homes"; Zou, "Fujian gua'er yuan huiyi."

95. Zou, "Fujian gua'er yuan," p. 181; Wang Tiefan, "Fujian Tongmenghui zai Cangshan."

96. Hartwell Papers, YDS RG 8–92, has correspondence between Li and Hartwell concerning his resignation.

97. Zou, "Fujian gua'er yuan," p. 181; Wang, "Fujian Tongmenghui zai Cangshan," pp. 17–18. Storage of the unused bombs proved a problem after the battle; Wang reports they were finally all dumped into the Min River.

98. See *Foochow Messenger* (January 1912), pp. 11–13.

99. Zheng, *Fujian xinhai guangfu shiliao,* p. 48; Huang, *Qishi zixu,* p. 200.

100. Zheng, *Fujian xinhai guangfu shiliao,* p. 53.

101. Cf. Sites, *Nathan Sites,* pp. 205–206; YMCA Archives, Box 23/52, Brockman to Lyon, Dec. 4, 1911.

102. USDS, *Records,* 893.00/883, Thompson to Secretary of State, Nov. 15, 1911.

103. PRO FO 228/1800/35, Nov. 20, 1911.

104. Korson, "Congregational Missionaries in Foochow," pp. 86–87; YMCA Archives, Box 2, A. Q. Adamson Quarterly Report, July–September 1911; CMS Archives G1 CH4/o 1911/253, Dr. B. van Someren Taylor to Dr. Baring-Gould, Nov. 17, 1911; USDS, *Records,* 893.00/1005, Thompson to Secretary of State, Dec. 20, 1911.

105. Some sense of the difficulties Gowdy faced in managing the Anglo-Chinese College can be gathered from his report of a student strike in 1906; Methodist Archives, Miss. I/1, 1259–6–1:11, Gowdy to Dr. Carroll, May 18, 1906; another missionary cited Gowdy's strict personality and the lack of old and experienced missionaries on the faculty as causes of the unrest in the college; Methodist Archives, Miss. I/1, 1259–5–3:25, W. S. Bissonnette to Dr. Carroll, June 23, 1906.

106. On the society and its aims, see Zheng, *Fujian xinhai guangfu shiliao,* p. 29.

107. Qi Xuan; see Pan Zuchang, "Xinhai geming Tengshan renwu yiwen," p. 46.

108. See list of distribution points on the back cover of *Jingxing bao* 5 (Xuantong 2/9/15 [Oct. 17, 1910]).

109. Based on an examination of issues 4 and 5 in the FPL.

110. On this publication see Ding Shouhe, *Xinhai geming shiqi qikan jieshao,* vol. 3, pp. 667–681.

111. Based on an examination of the first three issues, dated Xinhai 2, 3, and 4 (Spring 1911), in FPL.

112. Zhang Pengyuan, *Lixian pai yu xinhai geming,* p. 165.

113. Huang Naishang, *Qishi zishu,* p. 200. Huang tells of his sorrow at the suicide of the governor-general, whom he respected for not seeking to uncover his revolutionary activities and for not investigating the families of the Fuzhou revolutionaries captured and killed in the Huanghuagang uprising; see pp. 198, 200.

114. Wang Tiefan, "Fujian diyi mian 'shiba xing qizhi,' " pp. 14–15.

115. Zheng, *Fujian xinhai guangfu shiliao,* pp. 67–68, 142–145.

116. Ibid.; cf. USDS, *Records,* 893.00/1046, Amoy Consul Arnold to Secretary of State, Jan. 6, 1912.

117. PRO FO 228/1800/35, Nov. 20, 1911.

118. Zheng, *Fujian xinhai guangfu shiliao,* pp. 143–145.

119. See Boorman and Howard, *Biographical Dictionary,* p. 369. Lin fell out with the revolutionary representatives because he supported Li Yuanhong over Huang Xing for provisional president of the Republic; and Lin Sen, leader of the Fujianese revolutionaries in Shanghai (and an alumnus of Anglo-Chinese College and friend of Huang Naishang), allegedly tried to have Lin Changmin assassinated; see Esherick, "Founding a Republic, Electing a President," pp. 136–139, 151 n. 48.

120. YMCA Archives, Box 23/52, Brockman to Lyon, Dec. 4, 1911.

121. Methodist Archives, Miss. I/1, 1259–5–2:36, Bashford to Dr. Homer Stuntz, Dec. 22, 1911. For other accounts of this reception, see *Fuzhou Meiyimei nianhui lu* 35 (1911), pp. 9–11; *Minutes of the Foochow Conference* (1911), p. 24.

122. *Minutes of the Fifth Session of the Central Conference* (1911), pp. 11, 20.

4. Protestants and the Symbols of Nationalism

Epigraph: *Foochow Messenger* (May 1912), pp. 14–15.

1. Ono, "Deliberate Rumor."

2. The president was Chen Peikun; for a biography see Xu Youchun, *Minguo renwu da cidian,* p. 1045.

3. YMCA Archives 23–48, Eddy letter to supporters, Apr. 20, 1911; L. E. McLachlin Annual Report, 1911.

4. YMCA Archives 23–48, Eddy circular letter to supporters, Apr. 20, 1911. On Mazzini, cf. Liang Qichao's use of him discussed in Tang, *Global Space,* pp. 88–102.

5. *Fuzhou qingnian hui bao* 3:2 (Xuantong 3/4/10 [May 8, 1911]), pp. 12–16.

6. Judge, *Print and Politics;* Tang, *Global Space;* Schwartz, *In Search of Wealth and Power;* Liu, *Translingual Practice;* cf. Harris, "Chinese Nationalism."

7. Anagnost, *National Past-Times,* p. 1.

8. Kertzer, *Ritual, Politics, and Power,* p. 6.

9. Hobsbawm, *Nations and Nationalism,* p. 3, quoting Walter Bagehot, *Physics and Politics* (London, 1887), p. 83.

10. Hobsbawm, *Nations and Nationalism,* p. 19 and passim.

11. Good recent surveys of this literature include Anderson, "Introduction"; Eley and Suny, "Introduction"; Calhoun, *Nationalism.*

12. Duara, "De-Constructing the Chinese Nation," pp. 6–9, 9; emphasis in original; cf. Pomeranz, "Ritual Imitation," for a concise summary of China's place in the nationalism literature.

13. Pye, "How China's Nationalism Was Shanghaied," pp. 107–133; Townsend, "Chinese Nationalism," pp. 97–130.

14. Schwartz, "Culture, Modernity, and Nationalism — Further Reflections," pp. 207–225.

15. Anderson, *Imagined Communities,* esp. pp. 4, 79, 81, 115–116.

16. Drake, "Protestant Geography," pp. 100–101; Paul Cohen, "Christian Missions and Their Impact," p. 580.

17. Huang, preface to Wei Ligao, *Da meiguo shilüe.* The preface is dated early November 1898, about six weeks after the suppression of the reforms on September 21.

18. Huang Naishang, *Qishi zixu,* pp. 189–190. Cf. Zhan, *Huang Naishang zhuan,* pp. 207–209.

19. Telegram texts published in *Zuohai gongdao bao* 1:20 (Jan. 3, 1912), p. 15.

20. *Foochow Messenger* (May 1912), pp. 14–15.

21. *Meiguo quanli zhi fada,* in Ohlinger Papers, YDS RG 23-13-231.

22. In fact, Methodist leaders petitioned the State Department repeatedly on this subject, from as early as January 1912; see USDS, *Records,* 893.00/634, 635, and subsequent records for several lengthy communications from Bishop J. W. Bashford to the secretary of state, President Taft, and President-elect Woodrow Wilson urging the speedy recognition of the Republic; see also 893.00/1057 from Homer Stuntz of the Methodist mission board, dated Jan. 2, 1912.

23. Letter of endorsement for Huang in Ohlinger Papers, YDS RG 23. For more on Huang's U.S. tour see University of Oregon Library, Skinner Papers, Ax 209, Box 1, James E. Skinner to Susan L. Skinner, Apr. 2, 1912; May 18, 1912; May 21, 1912.

24. *Journal of the General Conference* (1912), pp. 389–391, 398, 417; USDS, *Records,* 893.00/635, Bashford to Philander C. Knox, Secretary of State, May 24, 1912.

25. Esherick, "Founding a Republic, Electing a President," pp. 138, 140–141.

26. ABCFM Archives 16-3-5, Ella Kinnear to friends, Feb. 1, 1912; H. N. Kinnear to J. Barton, Oct. 23, 1912; L. Hodous to friends, Mar. 3, 1912.

27. "Xinmin shuo"; cf. Hao, *Liang Ch'i-ch'ao,* pp. 149–219.

28. Schwartz, *In Search of Wealth and Power,* esp. pp. 69–73.

29. Reprinted in *Fujian qudu zongshe jibao* 12 (Minguo 3, Summer [1914]), *zazhi* section, p. 1.

30. See, e.g., *Shangye zazhi* 2 (1909), front advertising section.

31. *Fuzhou Meiyimei nianhui lu,* 33 (1909), part 1, p. 6b.

32. Liang, "Xinmin shuo," p. 212; Yan, "Yuan qiang," p. 51. Schwartz, *In Search of Wealth and Power,* p. 59, traces Yan's tripartite conception of the human person to Spencer's "famous triad of physical, intellectual, and moral energies," but does not specify where in Spencer's thought the concept originates; Pusey, *China and Charles Darwin,* p. 65, alludes to it also, but only cites Schwartz.

33. Lodwick, *Crusaders Against Opium,* p. 174; Sun, *Prescriptions for Saving China,* p. 88. Interestingly, given Sun's American ties, Hobsbawm notes that citizenship in America has had a behavioral or moral dimension not seen in European countries — it is possible to be "un-American," but not "un-English"; Hobsbawm, "Mass-Producing Traditions," p. 280.

34. On this campaign and Protestant responses to it, see Keller, "Nationalism and Chinese Christians."

35. Kertzer, *Ritual, Politics, and Power*, p. 6, quoting Michael Walzer, "On the Role of Symbolism in Political Thought," *Political Science Quarterly* 82 (1967), p. 194; cf. pp. x, 1–7.

36. Lukes, *Essays in Social Theory*, chap. 3. The publication in 1983 of Hobsbawm and Ranger's *Invention of Tradition* was a milestone in making historians interested in the general topic, and recent works in American history have begun to explore the role of public ceremonies in the formation of nationalism; for a review of some see Brooke, "Reason and Passion in the Public Sphere."

37. Levenson, "Suggestiveness of Vestiges"; cf. Pomeranz, "Water to Iron, Widows to Warlords."

38. Esherick, "Founding a Republic, Electing a President," pp. 131, 146–148; cf. Harrison, "Martyrs and Militarism," p. 42; Liping Wang, "Creating a National Symbol," p. 23; Fitzgerald, *Awakening China*, chap. 5. An exception to the stress on novelty is Pomeranz, "Ritual Imitation," who argues for continuity between late imperial ritual practices and modern nationalism.

39. Esherick and Wasserstrom, "Acting Out Democracy," pp. 46–47.

40. "Out of the American welter came these imagined realities: nation-states, republican institutions, common citizenships, popular sovereignty, national flags and anthems, etc., and the liquidation of their conceptual opposites: dynastic empires, monarchical institutions, absolutisms, subjecthoods, inherited nobilities, serfdoms, ghettoes, and so forth." Anderson, *Imagined Communities*, p. 81.

41. Partha Chatterjee critiques Anderson for portraying nationalism as a model fixed by the West that could only be adopted or not by colonial populations; *Nation and Its Fragments*, pp. 4–6. I find it more persuasive to see imitation and transformation as inseparable processes — much as Christian conversion involved the simultaneous adoption and transformation of an alien doctrine, as argued in Chapter 1.

42. Cf. Pomeranz, "Ritual Imitation."

43. *Foochow Messenger*, ABCFM Centennial Number (1910), pp. 4–8, 21–22. The program is in the Emily S. Hartwell Papers, YDS RG 8–93; it lists as guests another eighteen important officials aside from the governor-general and Tartar general, among them prominent educators and the president and vice-presidents of the Provincial Assembly.

44. *Minutes of the Foochow Conference* (1908); *Minutes of the Foochow Conference* (1910), pp. 22–23.

45. Esherick describes this ceremony and notes the Western inspiration of most of its elements; "Founding a Republic, Electing a President," pp. 146–148.

46. *China Year Book* 2 (1913), p. 659.

47. *Foochow Messenger* (March 1913), p. 31.

48. YMCA Archives 23–52, Brockman to Lyon, Dec. 4, 1911.

49. ABCFM Archives, 16.3.5, Ella Kinnear to friends, Feb. 1, 1912.

50. Quoted in Esherick, "Founding a Republic, Electing a President," p. 146.

51. Esherick, "Founding a Republic, Electing a President," p. 147

52. Zheng, *Fujian xinhai guangfu shiliao*, pp. 67–68.

53. *Zuohai gongdao bao* 1:17 (Xinhai 10/1 [Nov. 21, 1911]), p. 15b. The serial dropped the imperial year designation Xuantong 3 from its cover with this issue (the first after the revolution), replacing it with the cyclical year designation Xinhai.

54. *Minutes of the Foochow Conference* (1911), p. 37.

55. See essays in Hobsbawm and Ranger, *Invention of Tradition,* esp. pp. 7, 11–12, 114, 130, 261, 266, 277.

56. Hobsbawm, "Mass-Producing Traditions," pp. 265–268.

57. Wang Yinnan, *Zhongguo de guoqi, guohui, he guoge,* p. 81; cf. Rawski, "Creation of an Emperor."

58. The music (without lyrics) for the first Qing attempt at a national anthem is in *Illustrated Catalogue of the Chinese Collection,* pp. 158–159.

59. Kamachi, *Reform in China,* pp. 252–255.

60. Chen Guohong, *Zhonghua minguo guogeshi,* pp. 15–20; on Yan's role see Lo, *Correspondence of G. E. Morrison,* vol. 1, pp. 768–769.

61. Chen Guohong, *Zhonghua minguo guogeshi,* pp. 23–48; cf. Hobsbawm, "Mass-Producing Traditions."

62. Chen Guohong, *Zhonghua minguo guogeshi,* pp. 23–48, chap. 5; Fitzgerald, *Awakening China,* p. 184; Chen Hengming, *Zhonghua minguo zhengzhi fuhao,* pp. 182–188.

63. *Fujian qudu zongshe jibao* 1 (1907), *lishi* section, p. 2.

64. Chun Bi, "Fuzhou guangfu de 'shishi geyao,'" pp. 99–101; Zheng Lisheng, "Minguo yuannian Fuzhou minjian bianyin."

65. *Minutes of the Foochow Conference* (1909), p. 14.

66. Scholes, *God Save the King!* pp. 7–12, 54–58.

67. McCutchan, *Our Hymnody,* pp. 471–473.

68. Cannadine, "Context, Performance and Meaning of Ritual," p. 125 n. 88, quoting Percy A. Scholes, *"God Save the Queen": The History and Romance of the World's First National Anthem* (London, 1954), p. 141.

69. *Zongzhu shizhang* (1871/HY), Hymn 74, entitled "Shangdi baohu zhonghua shi" (God preserve China).

70. *Zongzhu shizhang* (1884, rev. 1891/HY), Hymns 171–172; for the same hymns in the Fuzhou dialect, see *Shengshi yuepu* (1906/HY), Hymns 171–172. The Methodist renditions are in *Jiushijiao shige* (1892/HY), Hymns 133–135. For Huang's editorial role see *Fuzhou Meiyimei nianhui shi,* p. 210.

71. *Songzhu shengshi* (1915), Hymn 408 (to a new tune, but still scanning to "God Save the King"), in Belcher Papers, YDS RG 8–23; also Hymn 38 in an abridged edition of the same hymnal (n.p., n.d.) in Smith Papers, YDS RG 5–15–53.

72. Respectively, Hymn 389 in Blodgett and Goodrich's *Songzhu shige* (1895/HY) and Hymn 36 in *Youtu shige* (1904), in World Student Christian Federation Archives, YDS RG 46–217–1660. These are two variants of the one hymn, purportedly written by a Chinese theological student.

73. *Songzhu shige* (1907/HY), Hymn 268. This hymn is cited as worthy of recognition as a patriotic song, despite its Christian flavor, in Chen Guohong, *Zhonghua minguo guogeshi,* pp. 67–68.

74. Wang Shenyin, *Zanmeishi (xinbian) shihua,* pp. 295–296.

75. *Qingnian shige* (1909) Hymn 84, in World Student Christian Federation Records, YDS RG 46–217–1660. For still more patriotic Chinese songs set to this tune, used outside Protestant circles, see Chen Guohong, *Zhonghua minguo guogeshi,* pp. 59–60; and the rather ornate version written by Y. S. Tsao for the Chinese Students' Alliance in

America (which also had an alternative tune), in *Directory of the Chinese Students' Alliance,* pp. 49–51, World Student Christian Federation Papers, YDS RG 46–82–669.

76. Franklin Ohlinger, "Christian Hymns in Missionary Work," *Northwestern Christian Advocate* (June 1886), clipping in "Ideal" scrapbook, Ohlinger Papers, YDS RG 23–12.

77. *Rongcheng Gezhi shuyuan biyedan,* p. 2, in YDS CL 001–33.

78. Commencement program for 1901, in Hartwell Papers, YDS RG 8–93; *Foochow Messenger* (1910), p. 7.

79. ABCFM Archives 16.3.5, H. Kinnear to friends, May 2, 1913; cf. USDS, *Records,* 893.00/1752, Fowler to Department, May 26, 1913.

80. *Rongcheng Gezhi shuyuan biyedan,* pp. 1, 2b; commencement programs for 1901 and 1910, in Hartwell Papers, YDS RG 8–93. Some of the essays were delivered in English, others in Chinese.

81. Commencement program for 1901, in Hartwell Papers, YDS RG 8–93. A class song in Chinese was also performed during the ceremony, but its text is not printed in this (English) copy of the program.

82. Note that ninety out of the ninety-one graduates of this college up to 1913 were church members by the time they graduated; *Foochow Messenger* (June 1913), p. 27.

83. Cf. Anderson, *Imagined Communities,* p. 145.

84. Hobsbawm suggests that the growing popularity in England of "God save the King" — the sentiment and the song — "implied a demotion of social hierarchy, a strengthening of the subject's direct bonds to the central ruler who, whether this was intended to or not, increasingly came to represent a new kind of state." Hobsbawm, "Mass-Producing Traditions," p. 266.

85. *Jiushijiao shige* (1892; repr. 1897), Hymn 235, translated here without retaining the meter.

86. The term can also mean simply "commoner" in Qing administrative documents, but in this context the ancient meaning of law-abiding persons seems a better fit.

87. Dikotter, *Discourse of Race in Modern China,* pp. 116–122.

88. Thus, documents sent by the new military governor to the British consul on Nov. 12 and 13, 1911, were dated the year 4609 from the accession of the Yellow Emperor; PRO FO 228–1811, pp. 31, 42. On the Fujianese revolutionaries in Shanghai using this dating, see Zheng, *Fujian xinhai guangfu shiliao,* p. 9.

89. *Fuzhou Meiyimei nianhui lu* 34 (1911), *juan shang,* p. 9b.

90. Firth, *Symbols,* pp. 336–367, 352; Hobsbawm, "Mass-Producing Traditions," p. 280.

91. This flag is in the Ohlinger collection at the Rutherford B. Hayes Presidential Center in Fremont, Ohio, according to Crouch, *Christianity in China,* p. 317; Ohlinger resided in Shanghai for most of this period, however. On U.S. missionary patriotism see Hunter, *Gospel of Gentility,* pp. 148–157.

92. Photograph in Beard Papers, YDS RG 8–254–39.

93. Feuerwerker, *Foreign Establishment,* p. 57. Feuerwerker cites no documentation for the statement. The U.S. flag was flown on the "gospel boat" of the American Board mission in Fuzhou, but this was probably due to the international practice of identifying the nationality of shipping rather than a conscious assertion of U.S. nationalism; see photographs in Hunter, *The Gospel of Gentility,* pp. 20, 125.

94. Smith, *Flags Through the Ages,* pp. 108–109; cf. Chen Hengming, *Zhonghua minguo zhengzhi fuhao,* p. 175.

95. *Fujian qudu zongshe jibao* 1 (1907), *lishi* section, p. 2; see also a Chinese artist's rendition of an anti-opium parade in Fuzhou, with two men bearing Qing flags in front, in Ohlinger Papers, YDS RG 23–14–239. It is not clear to me whether this developing public use of the flag to express or invoke patriotism was a top-down development initiated by the court or sprang from the increasing familiarity of Chinese people (through study abroad and in various ways through the Western presence in China) with the importance of national flags to the Western powers and Japan. The question is an interesting one.

96. Fitzgerald, *Awakening China,* pp. 180–185.

97. For pictures of this flag, see a calendar of the first year of the Republic, published in Shanghai early in 1912, showing this flag and the five-bar flag crossed over portraits of Sun Yatsen and Li Yuanhong, in the Ohlinger Papers, YDS RG 23–11–214; see also a medal presented by Sun Yatsen to a Fuzhou revolutionary in early 1912 showing the two flags crossed, in a plate at the front of *Fujian wenshi ziliao* 27 (1991). Cf. Fitzgerald, *Awakening China,* p. 181.

98. Wang Tiefan, "Fujian diyi mian 'shiba xing qimao,'" pp. 14–15. A significant Fuzhou contingent had participated in the botched Huanghuagang uprising in Guangzhou in April of 1911, and twelve of them, including some young men from prominent scholar-official families in the city, died in the battle or were executed after it; their widows were the ones who made the flag. For the Fuzhou role in the uprising, see essays in *Jinian Sun Zhongshan xiansheng wenzhang xuanji.*

99. Sun favored the flag of the Revolutionary Alliance, a white sun on blue sky in the upper corner of a red field, later the national flag of the Republic of China under the Nationalists; see Chen Hengming, *Zhonghua minguo zhengzhi fuhao,* p. 177–178; Fitzgerald, *Awakening China,* pp. 182–185.

100. This passage contains a fascinating mixture of rational and superstitious reflection on the symbolism of flags; see Sun, *Prescriptions for Saving China,* pp. 223–225.

101. From Beard Papers, YDS RG 8–254–44; for another early instance showing the Qing flag, see a picture of elementary-age students marching, with one carrying a Qing flag on a pole, in Methodist Archives, China O.P. #2, loose before p. 43 (this may not be from Fujian, however).

102. See also a 1922 picture of Trinity Church Volunteer School flag exercises, showing young children doing calisthenics with national and church flags, in album in the Institute of Religion, Fujian Teachers' University; picture of the "1st Foochow Girl Guides," leader carrying the flag, in CMS Archives, Acc. 8 F1/7; 1921 shot of students of CMS Girl's School (Taoshu) on the school parade ground, each, in alternation, holding either a Chinese flag or a Union Jack, CMS Archives, Acc. 8 F1/16.

103. Huang Naishang, *Qishi zixu,* p. 202, reports that 150–160 of the 500-strong force were Christians; see also articles in *Fujian wenshi ziliao* 27 (1991); Sites, *Nathan Sites,* p. 206; ABCFM Archives 16.3.5, Irene Dornblasser letter extract, Jan. 20, 1912.

104. Hobsbawm, *Nations and Nationalism,* pp. 91–92; Hobsbawm, "Mass-Producing Traditions," p. 280; cf. Anderson, *Imagined Communities,* p. 121, for a slightly different perspective on colonial education.

105. For a fascinating exploration of these themes, see Macleod, *Building Character in the American Boy,* esp. pp. 81–82 on drill building character; p. 87 on the "military rhetoric [which] permeated late Victorian Protestantism"; pp. 178 ff. on the Boy Scouts' "appropriation of the symbols of American nationhood."

106. See photograph captioned "Flag raising, Foochow Older Boys Camp," in Gold Papers, YDS RG 8–85–8; cf. photograph of Foochow YMCA School Boy Scout Troop (1915–1920), Gold Papers, YDS RG 8–85-Envelope 10.

107. *Mianlihui jiangyi baihua* (1915), (1916), (1918–1920), in Three-Self Patriotic Movement / China Christian Council library, Shanghai; see esp. English introduction to 1915 edition.

108. *Jidujiao xialing ertong yiwu xuexiao* (1921), pp. 19–23, 142, appendix, in Three-Self Patriotic Movement / China Christian Council library, Shanghai.

109. Egan, *Latterday Confucian,* p. 43.

110. Ding Xiancheng, "Xinhai geming qianhou," pp. 63–64.

111. See Methodist Archives, China O.P. #1, pp. 137, 124.

112. In Gold Papers, YDS RG 8–86. A handwritten caption on the back gives the year tentatively as 1914.

113. YMCA Archives, E. H. Munson Annual Report, 1915, pp. 15–17.

114. *Fuhkien Witness* 4:10 (1908), p. 3, in Beard Papers, YDS RG 8–255–32.

115. For other examples of this use of the flags of the nations in ceremonial decoration, see photograph captioned Grade School Boys Clubs Joint Meeting, in Gold Papers, YDS RG 8–85-Envelope 8; and photographs in Methodist Archives, China O.P. #3, pp. 59, 105; China O.P. #8, p. 17.

116. This point has been missed in most treatments of the YMCA in China, which have looked at it purely as another American mission organization.

117. *Cycle of Prayer,* pp. 13–15, in YMCA Archives, Printed material, "Student work," Box 1–1.

118. L. E. McLachlin to E. C. Jenkins, Oct. 6, 1915, in YMCA Archives 27–75. The "sacrifice" referred to is the loss to China of the gifted national general secretary, Fletcher Brockman, who had been called by Mott to join him in the international work.

119. For the background to McLachlin's masculine imagery here, see the insightful analysis of the relationship between gender and civilization in American discourse in this period in Bederman, *Manliness and Civilization,* esp. pp. 31–41, 187–190.

120. Hutchison, *Errand to the World,* pp. 125–138.

121. Duara, "De-Constructing the Chinese Nation," p. 9; Anderson, *Imagined Communities,* p. 81; Hobsbawm, *Nations and Nationalism,* p. 19.

122. See photograph of artist's impression of Nanking Exposition, in Methodist Archives, China O.P. #1, p. 101.

123. Cf. another picture of Koh in Methodist Archives, China O.P. #6, p. 24.

124. Ding Xiancheng, "Xinhai geming qianhou," p. 66; for a photograph see *Fujian wenshi ziliao* 27 (1991), front plates.

125. Chen Wen Yuen, "Why and How I Became a Christian," one-page typed account dated 1947, in Smith Papers, YDS RG 5–13.

126. Methodist Archives, Miss. I/1, 1259–5–3:35, Cole to Carson, Nov. 24, 1911.

127. ABCFM Archives 16.3.5, Hodous to friends, Mar. 30, 1912.

128. Madancy, "Revolution, Religion, and the Poppy"; Methodist Archives, Miss. III/1, 1043–3–2:41, Carson to North, Feb. 26, 1913.

129. USDS, *Records,* 893.00/1589, Fowler to State, Feb. 12, 1913, encl.; 893.00/ 1590, Fowler to State, Feb. 18, 1913, encl.; 893.00/1779, Fowler to State, June 14, 1913, encl.

130. Cf. Madancy, "Revolution, Religion, and the Poppy," pp. 3, 26–27. Madancy believes that the anti-Christian side of the rebellion became pronounced only after government troops recaptured Xianyou city from the rebel forces in May 1913, causing considerable destruction. Missionary accounts indicate rebel attacks on Chinese church members and preachers going back at least to late 1912, however.

131. *Minutes of the Foochow Conference* (1911), p. 37.

132. Drawn from accounts in *Zuohai gongdao bao* 1:18 (Xinhai 10/15 [1911]), p. 20; USDS, *Records,* 893.00/965, Thompson to Department, Dec. 7, 1911; Sites, *Nathan Sites,* p. 206; YMCA Archives 23–52, Brockman to Lyon, Dec. 4, 1911; E. H. Munson letter to friends, Dec. 8, 1911; YMCA Archives, Box 2, A. Q. Adamson Quarterly Report, Sept. 30, 1911.

133. Hobsbawm and Ranger, *Invention of Tradition,* pp. 7, 266.

134. Anderson, *Imagined Communities,* pp. 4, 81.

5. Kingdom Come? The Protestant Heyday in Fuzhou, 1912–1922

Epigraphs: (1) See figure 5.3. The motto is a paraphrase of the words of Jesus Christ in Mark 10:45: "The Son of Man did not come to be served, but to serve, and to give his life as a ransom for many." (2) YMCA Archives, Box 11, T. C. McConnell Annual Report, 1920, p. 3.

1. Cf. Pusey, "On Liang Qichao's Darwinian 'Morality Revolution.' "

2. ABCFM Archives 16.3.5, Kinnear to Dr. James L. Barton, Nov. 12, 1912. One of the first patients in the new facility was Lin Bingzhang (the pre-1911 head of the Anti-Opium Society).

3. *Foochow Messenger* (February 1917), p. 1. The church, now known as Guanxiang tang, was returned to church use in the early 1990s, but the pipe organ is long gone.

4. *Minutes of the Foochow Conference* (1920), p. 89. The CMS schools were Trinity School (*Sanyi xuexiao*), now Fuzhou Number Nine Middle School, opened in 1912, and Taoshu Girl's School, opened in 1900; Gwynn, *"T.C.D." in China,* pp. 50–51; Chen Dequan, "Yi 'jiu dianxian shushu,' " p. 94.

5. For the history of this school, see Scott, *Fukien Christian University.*

6. Wallace, *Hwa Nan College,* pp. 7–16. The building now houses the administration division of the Fujian Teachers' University.

7. See pictures and captions in Methodist Archives, China O.P #1, p. 260, and loose at front. The rate of exchange was then about two Chinese dollars to one U.S. dollar.

8. Smith Family Papers, YDS RG 5–8–5, "Village Chapels," one-page undated MS.

9. *Gutian Jidujiao zhi,* pp. 1–5. These numbers refer to new church buildings only, not to the much greater number of new congregations that were established in rented premises or converted dwellings.

10. Board members listed in *Fuzhou qingnian hui bao* 2:3 (Xuantong 2/12/25 [Jan. 25, 1911]), inside front cover. On Lin Changmin, see YMCA Archives 23–52, Brockman to Lyon, Dec. 4, 1911.

11. A. Q. Adamson, Quarterly Report, Sept. 30, 1911, p. 2, in YMCA Archives, Box 2; for identifications cf. Zhang Pengyuan, *Lixianpai yu Xinhai geming*, p. 166.

12. Ibid.; see also *Fuzhou qingnian hui bao* 5:2 (July 16, 1913), p. 2; YMCA Archives, T. C. McConnell Annual Report, 1920, p. 3.

13. Sun Daoren, Zhang Yuanqi, and Xu Chongzhi; *Fuzhou qingnian hui bao* 5:3 (Aug. 16, 1913), p. 9. All of these men were replaced in the aftermath of the Second Revolution that year, but their successors were equally well disposed toward the YMCA.

14. YMCA Archives, L. E. McLachlin Annual Report, 1916, p. 2.

15. Examples: educators, Wang Xiu, Chen Zuntong, Shi Jingchen; National Assembly delegates, Song Yuanyuan, Lin Wanli (Baishui); veteran revolutionaries, Zheng Zuyin, Lin Shizhao; bankers and industrialists, Lin Yushi, Liu Chonglun, Liu Chongwei, Liu Chongding; pastors, Ding Yuming, Lin Zehua; postal and Customs employees, Wu Guanchun, Ni Wenxiu; physician, Lin Tao'an; mission school graduate, Cheng Gongchen; see lists in *Fuzhou qingnian hui bao* 5:3 (Aug. 16, 1913), pp. 9–20; 5:6 (Nov. 16, 1913), pp. 16–17; 5:7 (Dec. 16, 1913), pp. 13–14; 6:5 (May 16, 1914), pp. 13–14; 6:6–7 (July 1, 1914), pp. 15–16. On the "Electric Light Liu" family, see Chen Wenzhong, *Fuzhou shi Taijiang jianshe zhi*, p. 105; Chen Zhilin's friend Liu Chongyou of the pre-1911 Provincial Assembly, who was at this time (1913) representing Fujian in the national parliament in Beijing, was the eldest brother in this family. For Lin Baishui, see *Fuzhou lishi renwu* 2 (1989), pp. 100–108.

16. YMCA Archives, L. E. McLachlin Annual Report, 1914, pp. 3–4; 27–79, David Z. T. Yui report letter, Apr. 7, 1916; L. E. McLachlin Annual Report, 1916, p. 5.

17. Hartwell Papers, YDS RG 8–94-Envelope 2. On clearing the streets for officials, see Doolittle, *Social Life of the Chinese*, vol. 1, pp. 299–300.

18. *Twenty-One Years' Work Among the Blind in Foochow*, YDS Missions Pamphlets 63–471; Hartwell Papers, YDS RG 8–92-6; RG 8–92-Papers 1906–1918; RG 8–93 (printed bilingual program); RG 8–94-1; RG 8–94-Envelope 1.

19. L. E. McLachlin gives a colorful description of the 1913 campaign, which was decided in the very last moments when one team member came running in with four hundred dollars in fees; YMCA Archives, 25–63, one-page typescript.

20. YMCA Archives, E. H. Munson Annual Report, 1915, pp. 15–16, 6.

21. YMCA Archives, E. H. Munson Annual Report, 1917, pp. 2–3; L. E. McLachlin Annual Report, 1917, pp. 5–6; 30–100, E. H. Munson letter, July 15, 1919; YMCA Archives, Box 17, *Mingri zhi Fuzhou* (1919), front matter.

22. YMCA Archives, Box 2, A. Q. Adamson, Report for Second Quarter, 1911, p. 6; the pledge amounts and sources are listed on an undated excerpt in Box 23–50 (probably originally the last section of Adamson's report) headed "A Positive Testimony." One family signing their pledge is pictured in *Foreign Mail Annual* (1912), p. 37.

23. YMCA Archives, Annual Reports for 1919 of E. H. Munson, p. 11, and R. G. Gold, p. 1.

24. YMCA Archives 23–50, "A Positive Testimony."

25. YMCA Archives 23–48, Brockman to McLachlin, Mar. 15, 1911.

26. *Fuzhou qingnian hui bao* 3:3 (Xuantong 3/4/29 [May 27, 1911]), p. 4; see also pp. 1–10; 3:2 (Xuantong 3/4/10 [May 8, 1911]), p. 7.

27. Interview with Xu Lebin and Xu Shihui, Fuzhou, Apr. 22, 1994. A missionary-trained "Dr. Hu" of Fuzhou (probably Xu Zeya) in resplendent official costume is pictured in *Mercy and Truth* 16 (1912), p. 110.

28. YMCA Archives, Box 2-Reports, A. Q. Adamson, Report for Second Quarter, 1911, p. 5; cf. Box 23–49, A. Q. Adamson to friends, May 1, 1911, p. 4; L. E. McLachlin Annual Report, 1911.

29. Hersey, *The Call.*

30. YMCA Archives, A. Q. Adamson Annual Report, 1911, p. 1.

31. YMCA Archives, L. E. McLachlin Annual Report, 1911; YMCA Archives, Box 23–49, Adamson to friends, May 1, 1911, p. 4.

32. YMCA Archives, Box 23–49, Adamson to friends, May 1, 1911, pp. 4–5.

33. *Fuzhou qingnian hui bao* 3:3 (Xuantong 3/4/29 [May 27, 1911]), pp. 7–10.

34. *Fuzhou qingnian hui bao* 3:3 (Xuantong 3/4/29 [May 27, 1911]), p. 16.

35. Chen Wenzhong, *Fuzhou shi Taijiang jianshe zhi,* p. 52; YMCA Archives, L. E. McLachlin Annual Report, 1916, pp. 6, 9. The building is now used as a residence for staff of the Fuzhou Number Thirteen Middle School.

36. YMCA Archives, E. H. Munson Annual Reports, 1918, pp. 1–2; 1917, p. 9. Non-Protestant officials and educators shared Munson's concern over the efflorescence of prostitution in the city and its influence on their students; see, e.g., the discussion of ending the practice of students living off campus in *Fujian sheng diyi ci jiaoyu xingzheng huiyi baogao* (1916), vol. 2, pp. 6–7.

37. For a similar parallel, see Garrett, "Chambers of Commerce and the YMCA"; in structure and activities the YMCA was more akin to the reform societies than it ever was to the quasi-official chambers of commerce.

38. *Minhou nongchan gongjinhui, shenghui shizheng* section, p. 9. Interestingly, the Provincial Assembly is listed not as a government organ but as an "association." On professional associations in the Republican period, see Xiaoqun Xu, "Between State and Society."

39. Quoted in YMCA Archives, R. G. Gold Annual Report, 1919, p. 7.

40. Recent work by Bryna Goodman has countered the image of these bodies as "traditional" institutions, stressing the degree to which they served as vehicles for modern nationalism in Shanghai; see Goodman, "Locality as Microcosm of the Nation?"; and Goodman, *Native Place, City, and Nation.*

41. YMCA Archives, L. E. McLachlin Annual Report, 1917, p. 5.

42. YMCA Archives, R. G. Gold Annual Report, 1919, p. 3; L. E. McLachlin Annual Report, 1916, p. 6.

43. YMCA Archives, Box 17, *Mingri zhi Fuzhou,* p. 6; E. H. Munson Annual Report, 1919, p. 5. As provincial governor in 1924, Sa conferred a plaque on the family honoring Huang's deceased brothers, Naimo and Naiying, and he contributed the cover calligraphy for the initial edition of Huang's autobiography, published after Huang's death in 1924; Zhan, *Huang Naishang zhuan,* p. 226; Huang, *Qishi zixu* (1925), cover.

44. YMCA Archives, T. C. McConnell Annual Report, 1919, pp. 11–12; for biogra-

phies of Sa, see *Fuzhou lishi renwu* 1 (1988), pp. 65–75; Xin Ping, *Minguo jiangling lu,* p. 272.

45. YMCA Archives, E. H. Munson Annual Report for 1910–1911, p. 2; cf. 23–50, McLachlin to Beard, June 21, 1911; L. E. McLachlin Annual Report for 1910–1911; A. Q. Adamson Annual Report for 1910–1911.

46. Cf. photograph of another elderly gentry contributor, in Gold Papers, YDS RG 8–86, "Conferences" folder.

47. For Habermas's use of the term "public sphere" and its application to modern China, see Rowe, "Public Sphere." Rowe's position is critiqued in Wakeman, "Civil Society."

48. Hutchison, *Between the Times,* esp. the conclusion.

49. The story of the "White House conference" was related to Fuzhou readers in *Fuzhou qingnian hui bao* 3:3 (Xuantong 3/4/29 [May 27, 1911]), pp. 6–7.

50. This link in China was not exclusive; the same men continued to patronize Buddhist temples, non-Christian philanthropic institutions and schools, etc. The significant change is that Protestant institutions entered the ranks of those bodies toward which men of standing in Fuzhou displayed their benevolence.

51. *Foreign Mail Annual* (1915), p. 10.

52. YMCA Archives 25–61a, Eddy to friends, Apr. 1, 1913; cf. Egan, *Latterday Confucian,* p. 43.

53. *Foochow Messenger* (June 1913), pp. 17–21; Mott Papers, YDS RG 45–117–1946, 171–2927; YMCA Archives 25–61a, Robertson to friends, Apr. 21, 1913.

54. YMCA Archives, L. E. McLachlin Annual Report, 1913, p. 4; E. H. Munson Annual Report, 1914, pp. 1–2. The latter summarizes the weak points of the 1913 campaign, among them the fact that the addresses of inquirers were often unclear, so that only about 900 of the 1,530 names could be located by the follow-up team after the meetings.

55. YMCA Archives, L. E. McLachlin Annual Report, 1913, p. 3; *Foochow Messenger* (June 1913), p. 18.

56. YMCA Archives 25–61a, Eddy to friends, Apr. 1, 1913.

57. YMCA Archives, L. E. McLachlin Annual Report, 1913, p. 3.

58. YMCA Archives 25–61a, Eddy to friends, Apr. 1, 1913. The cities were Fuzhou, Funing, Xinghua, Fuqing, Yongfu, Minqing, Gutian, Yanping, Jianyang, Jianning, and Shaowu in the north and Xiamen, Quanzhou, and Zhangzhou in south Fujian.

59. The Chinese speakers were Wang Ganhe and Huang Zhiji of Fuzhou, David Yui (Yu Rizhang) and C. T. Wang (Wang Zhengting) of the national YMCA, and the Rev. Ding Limei, evangelist for the Student Volunteer Movement in China; see *Call to Prayer,* pamphlet in YMCA Archives 26–70 and in Beard Papers, YDS RG 8–21–1. C. T. Wang took the place of Fletcher Brockman; see *Report of Province-Wide Evangelistic Campaign,* p. 6.

60. *Report of Province-Wide Evangelistic Campaign,* p. 16; YMCA Archives 25–66, W. E. Taylor to Eddy, Mar. 2, 1914; 28–86, E. H. Munson, "Need of a Student Conference Site for North Fukien," n.d., p. 2; L. E. McLachlin Annual Report, 1914, p. 1.

61. *Report of Province-Wide Evangelistic Campaign,* pp. 10, 5, 7.

62. Eddy, *How China's Leaders Received the Gospel,* pp. 18–19, in Eddy Papers, YDS

RG 32–17–146; YMCA Archives, E. H. Munson Annual Reports, 1914, p. 10, 1915, p. 15; L. E. McLachlin Annual Report, 1914, pp. 1–2.

63. YMCA Archives 26–70, Robertson report letter, Dec. 18, 1914.

64. YMCA Archives, E. H. Munson Annual Reports, 1914, p. 7, 1915, pp. 2–3.

65. *Report of Province-Wide Evangelistic Campaign*, pp. 5–11, 16; YMCA Archives, L. E. McLachlin Annual Report, 1914, p. 3. On mission efforts to start work in Jianning, see Ye Jianyuan, *Zhonghua shenggonghui Fujiansheng jiaoqu*, pp. 36–38.

66. YMCA Archives, L. E. McLachlin Annual Report, 1913, p. 4.

67. YMCA Archives, L. E. McLachlin Annual Report, 1914, p. 1; cf. *Foreign Mail Annual* (1915), p. 45.

68. C. T. Wang letter of Nov. 10, 1914, quoted in *Report of Province-Wide Evangelistic Campaign*, p. 6.

69. Eddy, *How China's Leaders Received the Gospel*, p. 19; ABCFM Archives 16.3.5, H. Kinnear to friends, May 2, 1913. The identification is not certain, because the official is not named in either source, but one person, Zhou Han, headed the provincial Department of Education continuously from March 1913 through 1914; see Liu Shoulin, *Xinhai yihou shiqinian zhiguan nianbiao*, pp. 342–43.

70. YMCA Archives, E. H. Munson Annual Reports, 1914, p. 8.

71. Eddy Papers, YDS RG 32–6–129, eight-page typescript headed "Lecture No. 3 — The Hope of China — by Sherwood Eddy," undated, but, from internal evidence, probably 1914. The two countries with a "national religion" were not specified; presumably Japan was one.

72. Hutchison, *Errand to the World*, pp. 91–95; cf. Hutchison, "Modernism and Missions."

73. YMCA Archives, L. E. McLachlin Annual Report, 1914, p. 2.

74. Cf. Zürcher, "Jesuit Mission in Fujian."

75. YMCA Archives 22–43, L. E. McLachlin to John R. Mott, Mar. 31, 1910

76. National committee members are listed in the annual reports in English published under various titles by the National Committee of the YMCAs of China.

77. Fairbank, *Liang and Lin*; Spence, *Gate of Heavenly Peace*, pp. 154–174; Boorman and Howard, *Biographical Dictionary*, p. 370.

78. Beard Papers, YDS RG 8–21–1, Willard L. Beard to mother, Nov. 17, 1913.

79. See Fairbank, *Liang and Lin*; Boorman and Howard, *Biographical Dictionary*, pp. 368–372; *Who's Who in China* (1920), pp. 112–113; Xu Youchun, *Minguo renwu da cidian*, p. 467.

80. Lin did send his children to mission schools, however; see biography of Lin Huiyin in *Fuzhou shi jianzhu zhi*, pp. 360–362.

81. He Gonggan, "Min yan gongyou douzheng ji," esp. pp. 13 ff., 55; YMCA Archives, E. H. Munson Annual Report, 1916, p. 4. Liu's alternate name was Buxi, and he is referred to in YMCA sources in English as Lau (or Law) Buo Ka, reflecting the dialect pronunciation of Buxi.

82. He Gonggan, "Min yan gongyou douzheng ji," p. 14.

83. YMCA Archives, E. H. Munson Annual Report, 1914, p. 3; 26–72, McLachlin to Eddy, Apr. 16, 1915; E. H. Munson Annual Report, 1915, p. 5.

84. YMCA Archives, L. E. McLachlin Annual Report, 1916, p. 3; 27–75, McLachlin

to Eddy, Oct. 6, 1915; E. H. Munson Annual Report, 1916, p. 4; Beard Papers, YDS RG 8–21–1, Beard letter, May 23, 1915

85. Biographies in *Fuzhou lishi renwu* 6 (1992), pp. 54–59, and 1 (1990), pp. 55–59; Hummel, *Eminent Chinese*, pp. 813–814. On the status of the *zhuangyuan,* see Miyazaki, *China's Examination Hell*, pp. 85, 90–93.

86. Wang Xiaoqi, *Xiqing Wangshi chongxiu zupu* (1935), vol. 2, Shengmou branch, pp. 14b–17b, 16b. The high status of this family is reflected in this genealogy, which includes tributes to family members from such luminaries as Liang Qichao, Chen Baochen, Lin Shu, and Xu Shichang.

87. Gao Rong, "Fujian sheng tushuguan jianshi."

88. YMCA Archives 28–87, Munson to Eddy, Apr. 25, 1917. The YMCA sources in English refer to him as Uong Ngieng Gung, from the Fuzhou dialect pronunciation of his alternative name Yangong.

89. YMCA Archives, R. G. Gold Annual Report, 1919, pp. 5–6.

90. YMCA Archives 28–87, Munson to Eddy, Apr. 25, 1917; *Fuzhou qingnian hui bao* 9:3 (Oct. 1, 1916), inside front cover, listing Wang Yangong on the board of directors.

91. YMCA Archives, R. G. Gold Annual Report, 1919, pp. 5–6; E. H. Munson Annual Report, p. 8.

92. YMCA Archives, E. H. Munson Annual Report, 1921, p. 8; 28–87, Munson to Eddy, Apr. 25, 1917; R. G. Gold Annual Report, 1919, pp. 5–6; on his daughter Wang Shirong, see *Xiqing Wangshi zupu* (1993), p. 167.

93. Wang Xiaoqi, *Xiqing Wangshi chongxiu zupu,* vol. 2, Shengmou branch, pp. 16b–17; *Xiqing Wangshi zupu* (1993), p. 443.

94. YMCA Archives, T. C. McConnell Annual Report, 1920, p. 14. YMCA sources in English refer to Wang Xiaoxiang as Uong Ngieng Hung, from his alternative name Yanyun.

95. YMCA Archives, Box 17, Fuzhou YMCA, *Mingri zhi Fuzhou* (1920), pp. 1, 12; YWCA campaign brochure (1920), in YDS HR 164–1; *Shangyou* (FPL) 1:1 (1922) p. 66; the YWCA began work in Fuzhou around 1915.

96. *Minutes of the Foochow Conference* (1920), p. 89. On the "institutional church" movement, see Reid, *Dictionary of Christianity,* p. 576, Hudson, *Religion in America,* pp. 302 ff.

97. *Minutes of the Foochow Conference* (1924), pp. 53–54; Stauffer, *Christian Occupation,* p. 379. On YMCA reactions see YMCA Archives 27–75, McLachlin to Eddy, Oct. 6, 1915; Box 11, T. C. McConnell Annual Report, 1922, p. 4. For the educational exposition see *Shangyou* 1:1 (1922) pp. 4, 66, inside front cover; FPA *ziliao* 9–7–247, *Fujian jiaoyu xingzheng yuekan* 3:1 (1922), final section, pp. 1–6.

98. *Xiqing Wangshi zupu* (1993), pp. 168–170, 443–444.

99. Called Uong Hau Ciong in YMCA sources in English. In lineage terms he was a cousin to the sons of Wang Renkan and an uncle to their children, but one would have to trace back six generations to find a common forebear.

100. Wang Xiaoqi, *Xiqing Wangshi chongxiu zupu* (1935), vol. 1, Shengmo branch, pp. 8b–9; Wallace, *Hwa Nan College,* pp. 44–45, 52–55, 126, 132; FPA *Jiaoyuting* archives 2–1–8, Hwa Nan registration application, p. 460; *Fujian ziyiju . . . yilan biao,* p. 17; *Minhou jiaoyu yanjiu* (1917), *xueshu zhuanjian* section, p. 30.

101. YMCA Archives, T. C. McConnell Annual Report, 1917, p. 3; *Fuzhou jidujiao qingnian hui nianbao* (1932) p. 16, (1933) pp. 28–29.

102. YMCA Archives, Box 11, T. C. McConnell Annual Report, 1920, p. 13.

103. YMCA Archives, T. C. McConnell Annual Report, 1917, p. 3; Box 11, E. H. Munson Annual Report, 1920, pp. 11–12; Box 17, *Mingri zhi Fuzhou* (1920), p. 1; annual report in Chinese, 1921, pp. 1, 8; *Shangyou* 1:1 (1922), p. 66

104. Wang Xiaoqi, *Xiqing Wangshi chongxiu zupu* (1935), vol. 1, Shengmo branch, pp. 8b–9, vol. 2, postfaces; vol. 3, postfaces; interview with Wang Shishen (eldest daughter of Wang Xiaoquan), Fuzhou, May 1994.

105. Wang Shishen interview, Fuzhou, May 1994; *Wangshi zupu* (1993), pp. 144–148, esp. biographies of Wang Shijun (1927–1964), Shikeng (born in 1929).

106. Interviews with Li Shuren (alumna and former teacher, Hwa Nan College, aged over ninety), Fuzhou, Apr. 21, 1994, and Xu Shihui (alumnus and former teacher, Anglo-Chinese College, aged over eighty), Fuzhou, Apr. 21, 1994; on the Wang sisters and the Anglo-Chinese College, see Dunch, "Mission Schools and Modernity."

107. Wang Zhenxian, "Ershi shiji zhi jiaoyuguan"; Wang Fuchu, "Women zenyang zuo jiaoyuzhe."

6. Why China Did Not Become a Christian Republic

Epigraphs: *Juejiao* 1 (8/1925); Mao, " 'Friendship' or Aggression?" p. 448; Beard, "Missionary's Thoughts."

1. *Minutes of the Foochow Conference* (1902), p. 40; cf. ibid. (1912), p. 34; ibid. (1906), p. 79.

2. *Minutes of the Foochow Conference* (1908), p. 99.

3. Books on both the "conquest of paganism" and the Wesleyan revival were published by Fuzhou Methodists: *Luoma zongjiao jizhan shi* by Wu Di'an (Ohlinger) with Huang Zhiji; and *Weili zhuan* by Xue furen (Sites) with Huang Naishang.

4. Except for the role of Christianity, this reading of the nineteenth century as the age of world progress was similar to that in vogue in the new government schools in Fujian after 1901; see the history textbook of the Fujian Military Preparatory School, *Fujian lujun wubei xuetang kecheng*, in FPL, esp. pp. 58–68, covering the eighteenth and nineteenth centuries.

5. The classic study is Young, *Presidency of Yuan Shih-k'ai*.

6. Schoppa in *Blood Road*, chap. 2, discusses a similar tension in the neighboring province of Zhejiang in the 1910s; unlike Fujian, however, Zhejiang was under the control of the Zhejiang elite until the entry of northern troops in early 1917.

7. Huang Naishang, *Qishi zixu*, pp. 205–206; Zhan, *Huang Naishang zhuan*, pp. 167–174; ABCFM Archives, ABC 16.3.5, Kinnear to Rev. Enoch Bell, May 4, 1912; Kinnear to Dr. Barton, Aug. 19, 1912; Hodous to Bell, Oct. 19, 1912.

8. Zheng Lansun, *Fujian xinhai geming shiliao*, pp. 315–336; ABCFM Archives 16.3.5, Hodous to Bell, Oct. 19, 1912; Madancy, "Ambitious Interlude," pp. 281–282.

9. Zhan, *Huang Naishang zhuan*, pp. 179–182.

10. Biographies in *Fuzhou Meiyimei nianhui shi*, p. 90; Gaimusho, *Kaitei gendai Shina*

jimmeikan, pp. 219–220; Gaimusho, *Gendai Chuka minkoku jimmeikan,* p. 391; Fan Yinnan, *Dangdai Zhongguo mingren lu,* p. 284. On Chen's leadership in opium suppression in the early Republic, see Madancy, "Ambitious Interlude," pp. 290 ff.; *Fuzhou qingnian hui bao* 5:5 (10/16/1913), p. 9.

11. Zou, "Fujian gua'er yuan," p. 177; *Fuzhou qingnian hui bao* 5:4 (9/16/1913), p. 6.

12. Biographies in Gaimusho, *Kaitei gendai Shina jimmeikan,* pp. 199; Gaimusho, *Gendai Chuka minkoku jimmeikan,* p. 380; Perleberg, *Who's Who in Modern China,* p. 25.

13. YMCA Archives, Box 11, E. H. Munson Annual Report for 1920, p. 11 ("Ding Ci Ting" is Chen Zhiting, Chen Zhilin's alternate name); Box 64, Charles W. Harvey to E. C. Jenkins, Aug. 8, 1924.

14. YMCA Archives, E. H. Munson Annual Report, 1917, pp. 5, 9–10.

15. YMCA Archives, E. H. Munson Annual Report, 1920, p. 2; Box 11, E. H. Munson Annual Report, 1921, p. 1; T. C. McConnell Annual Report, 1922, p. 5.

16. On Li Houji's administration in Fujian, see Fan Shouzheng, "Li Houji zai Fujian."

17. YMCA Archives, L. E. McLachlin Annual Report, 1916, p. 11; E. H. Munson Annual Report, 1916, p. 10.

18. The provincial government in Fuzhou began to lose effective control of parts of the province in the late 1910s, and even after the nominal reunification of China under the Nationalist Party in 1927 much of the province remained outside the government's control until the defeat of the anti-Chiang "Fujian Rebellion" and the appointment of Chen Yi as provincial governor in 1934.

19. YMCA Archives, Box 12, T. C. McConnell Annual Report, 1923, p. 6.

20. Hung, *Flaming Evangel of Kutien,* pamphlet in YDS A166.05, p. 3

21. G. D. Ciu to Bishop Keeney, July 21, 1921, in Bissonnette, *Donald Ciu of Kutien,* p. 27.

22. Ciu to Keeney, Aug. 11, 1921, in Bissonnette, *Donald Ciu of Kutien,* pp. 28–29.

23. On Zhou Daojian's life and death, see in addition *Gutian jidujiao zhi,* pp. 71–73.

24. On Bashford's life and ministry in China, see Grose, *James W. Bashford,* esp. pp. 111–160.

25. On Chinese images of America, see Arkush and Lee, *Land Without Ghosts.*

26. Ding Xiancheng, "Xinhai geming qianhou," p. 64.

27. YMCA Archives 25–63, L. D. Cio to F. S. Brockman, July 19, 1913, in Brockman to Mott, Oct. 2, 1913; cf. *Fuzhou qingnian hui bao* 6:4 (4/1914), p. 3. In 1915, David Z. T. Yui of the national YMCA led an official commercial delegation from China on a two-month tour of the United States, during which he personally took up the immigration issue with the U.S. secretary of labor, who traveled with the delegation, and was able to secure an official order clarifying that Chinese with valid student visas should be landed without further examination; see YMCA Archives 26–73, Yui to Mott, July 30, 1915; 26–74, J. B. Densmore (acting secretary of labor) to "my dear friend David" (Yui), Aug. 3, 1915.

28. See translations from U.S. papers in *Fuzhou qingnian hui bao* 5:6 (11/1913), pp. 11–15. The Scranton YMCA was the home association of L. E. McLachlin, the senior YMCA secretary in Fuzhou.

29. *Fuzhou qingnian hui bao* 6:2 (2/1914), pp. 12–14; cf. 5:7 (12/1913), pp. 4–5; 6:4

(4/1914), p. 3. Zhu's comments are reminiscent of Liang Qichao's earlier observations after his trip to America in 1903, excerpted in Arkush and Lee, *Land Without Ghosts*, pp. 84–95.

30. The adoption of the terminology of imperialism is discussed in Chow, *May Fourth Movement*, pp. 354–55 n. g.

31. For earlier critiques, see Schwartz, *In Search of Wealth and Power*, pp. 38–39, discussing Yan Fu's *Zhina jiaoan lun* (1892).

32. This is not the place to undertake an extended critique of the term; for a useful recent overview tracing four different genealogies of usage (all dating no earlier than the 1960s and none mentioning missionaries in China), see Tomlinson, *Cultural Imperialism*.

33. Latourette, *History of Christian Missions*, pp. 694–699, 812–815. The fullest treatment of the anti-Christian movements of the 1920s is Lutz, *Chinese Politics and Christian Missions*.

34. YMCA Archives, Box 11, T. C. McConnell Annual Report, 1922, p. 3.

35. YMCA Archives, Box 11, E. H. Munson Annual Letter to the Foreign Department of the International Committee, 1920; T. C. McConnell Annual Report, 1920, p. 3. See also Peter, *Broadcasting Health*, esp. pp. 1–10.

36. See flyer in Chinese issued by the Fujian Student Federation commending the health campaign and other patriotic causes (domestic industry and mass education), in YMCA Archives, Box 10.

37. See *Taijiang shijian;* Fukien Student Federation, *Recent Japanese Outrage in Foochow,* pamphlet in Hartwell Papers, YDS RG 8–93; *Waijiao wendu.*

38. YMCA Archives, T. C. McConnell Annual Report, 1923, p. 2. For a similar incident in St. John's University in Shanghai in 1919, see Chow, *May Fourth Movement*, p. 323 n. f.

39. YMCA Archives, Box 12, T. C. McConnell Annual Report, 1923, p. 5.

40. YMCA Archives, Box 12, R. G. Gold Annual Report, 1925, p. 1; E. H. Munson Annual Report, 1925, p. 2.

41. YMCA Archives, Box 12, R. G. Gold Annual Report, 1925, p. 2.

42. Welch, *Buddhist Revival*, cites concern about the challenge of Christian missions and their methods as one factor behind Buddhist activism in the Republican period; see pp. 21, 27–28, 129, 185–186.

43. *Fujian sheng weisheng zhi*, pp. 258–259; *Fuzhou diwu zhongxue xiaozhi*, p. 9.

44. *Juejiao* 1 (8/1925); these and other slogans were printed vertically down the margins on each page. Communist Party involvement is noted in Zhang Zhenqian, "Shouhui jiaoyu quan," p. 155.

45. *Juejiao* 1 (8/1925), p. 3.

46. Fitzgerald, *Awakening China*, chap. 5.

47. The military campaign is outlined in Jordan, *Northern Expedition*, pp. 93–96.

48. *Minutes of the Foochow Conference* (1927), p. 55; *Foochow News* 2:4 (1927), p. 2; *Annual Report of the Board of Foreign Missions* 109 (1927), p. 101.

49. Statistics for 1925, in YMCA Archives, Box 12, R. G. Gold Annual Report, 1925, encl.

50. YMCA Archives, Box 12, E. H. Munson Annual Report, 1927, pp. 1–2.

51. See Zhang Zhenqian, "Shouhui jiaoyu quan," and following articles in *Fujian*

wenshi ziliao 13 (1986); *Minutes of the Foochow Conference* (1927), pp. 69–80. On Lin Buji, cf. University of Oregon Special Collections, Idabelle Lewis Main Papers, Ax 216, Box 1, Idabelle Lewis to mother, Mar. 29, 1929; Dorothy Walters Collection of Idabelle Lewis Main, 29–2–5, typed memoir by Idabelle Lewis Main, pp. 9 ff; Gwynn, *"T.C.D."* *in China*, p. 61.

52. *Annual Report of the Board of Foreign Missions* 109 (1927), pp. 101–102; Hsueh, *Foochow College Up to Date*, pamphlet in YDS HR 189, p. 1.

53. S. Sites, *Hu King Eng, M.D.*, pamphlet in Methodist Archives, Acc. 1979–16, 1467–1–2:19; Burton, *Notable Women*, pp. 15–70; interview with Xu Daofeng, Hwa Nan College, Fuzhou, Feb. 17, 1994.

54. *Uk Ing: The Pioneer*, p. 81. The orphanage was forcibly entered by a mob on January 14 after a rumor spread of vile things being done to the Chinese infants inside; Chinese doctors in the city were called upon to inspect the children and the exhumed corpses of dead ones to confirm the charge. For an account viewing the incident as a principled attack on imperialism by the masses, see Jiang Boying, *Fujian geming shi*, vol. 1, pp. 194–195.

55. *Uk Ing: The Pioneer*, pp. 75–84; interview with Xu Daofeng, Hwa Nan College, Fuzhou, Feb. 17, 1994; *Fuzhou Meiyimei nianhui shi*, pp. 111, 188.

56. Official recognition is shown in the many congratulatory messages from officials printed in anniversary volumes of the Protestant schools; see, e.g., those from Lin Sen in *Sili Fuzhou Heling yinghua zhongxue liushi*, p. 3; and in *Sili Fujian xiehe daxue ershiwu*. For more on the Protestant schools under the Nationalists, see Dunch, "Mission Schools and Modernity."

57. See *Fuzhou Jidujiao qingnian hui nianbao*, issues for 1931–1935, in FPL. Some of the YMCA's non-Christian patrons from the 1910s appear in these reports, such as Sa Zhenbing, who sponsored the 1933 membership campaign (1933, pp. 10–12), and the old gentry educator Chen Peikun, who wrote the calligraphy (reading *shude shuren,* "Establish virtue, build up young men") for the cover of the 1932 report.

58. For surveys on the church situation reflecting the demoralization of the 1930s, see Beard, "Missionary's Thoughts"; Bissonnette, "Methodist Church in North Fukien," pp. 256–268.

59. On these developments, see Bays, "Growth of Independent Christianity"; Zha, *Zhongguo Jidujiao renwu xiaozhuan*; Kinnear, *Against the Tide*.

60. Some of these issues are explored in Dunch, "Protestant Christianity in China Today."

61. Examples are legion—particularly those by YMCA authors, e.g., Lewis, *Educational Conquest*; Eddy, *Students of Asia*, chap. 4.

62. On the latter point, cf. Chatterjee's reproach of Anderson in *Nation and Its Fragments*, chap. 1; on the application of Western theory to China, see Bin Wong, *China Transformed*, pp. 163–166.

63. On the interpenetration of "traditional" and "modern" elements in Chinese nationalism, see Goodman, *Native Place, City, and Nation*; Pomeranz, "Ritual Imitation."

64. Cf. Liu, *Translingual Practice*, chap. 1.

65. The definition is from Larry Diamond, "Toward Democratic Consolidation," *Journal of Democracy* 5 (1994), p. 5, quoted in Brook, "Auto-Organization," p. 22.

66. Habermas, *Structural Transformation of the Public Sphere.*

67. For a survey of the literature see Brook and Frolic, "Ambiguous Challenge of Civil Society."

68. Kuhn, "Civil Society and Constitutional Development."

69. Brook and Frolic, "Ambiguous Challenge of Civil Society"; Wakeman, "Civil Society."

70. Compare Wakeman's extensive rejection of Rowe's use of the terms "public sphere" and "civil society" for late imperial Hankou to his more limited critique of Strand's application of them to 1920s Beijing; Wakeman, "Civil Society."

71. Others, as noted in Chapter 2, were more directly tied to official patronage, such as the Anti-Opium Society; cf. Madancy, "Ambitious Interlude," p. 372.

72. Fincher, "Political Provincialism"; Wong, *China Transformed,* p. 175; cf. Duara, *Rescuing History,* p. 178.

73. Kuhn, "Civil Society," p. 301.

74. Duara, "State and Civil Society," p. 304.

75. Duara, "State and Civil Society," pp. 315–324; Duara, *Rescuing History,* chap. 6; cf. Kuhn, "Civil Society," p. 306; Wakeman, "Models of Historical Change."

76. Fitzgerald, *Awakening China,* pp. 273–274.

77. Cohen, "Being Chinese," esp. p. 105.

Glossary

aiguo	愛國
aiguo zhi daode xin	愛國之道德心
aiqun	愛群
Anglo-Chinese College	福州鶴齡英華書院
Anxi	安溪
bagong	拔貢
bai Shangdi	拜上帝
bai Shangdi shan shi ye, wubei wu bu shi zhe	拜上帝善事也吾輩無不是者
Banzhong	阪中
baolan	包攬
benchu chuandao	本處傳道
bu xiu zhi shengming	不朽之生命
bu yu su tuo	不于俗托
Caizheng bu/si	財政部、司
Cangqian	倉前
canyiyuan	參議員
chang you liangmin	常有良民
Changle	長樂
Chating gongyishe	茶亭公益社
Chen Baochen (Tao'an, Boqian)	陳寶琛（弢庵，伯潛）

Chen Hengmei	陳恒美
Chen Hongyi	陳鴻沂
Chen Mengren	陳孟仁
Chen Minwang	陳敏望
Chen Nengguang (Bingtai)	陳能光（丙台）
Chen Peikun (Yunshan)	陳培錕（韻珊）
Chen Wenchou (Ding Ung Tiu)	陳文疇
Chen Wenyuan	陳文源
Chen Yi	陳儀
Chen Zhilin (Zhiting, b. 1878)	陳之麟（芷汀）
Chen Zuntong	陳遵統
Cheng Gongchen	程拱宸
Chenghuang	城徨
chenshi	塵世
chuandao	傳道
chuzhong	初中
dan	擔
dao	道
dao yi zhi men	道義之門
daode	道德
de	德
deyu, zhiyu, tiyu	德育，智育，體育
Dili tu	地理圖
Ding Limei	丁立美
Ding Xiancheng	丁先誠
Ding Yuming	丁玉名
dou	斗

fan renshen	範人身
fan renxin	範人心
fazheng	法政
Fazheng xuetang	法政學堂
fu gongsheng	附貢生
Fu'an	福安
Fubao	福報
fugong	副貢
fumu	父母
Funing (Xiapu)	福寧（霞浦）
Fuqing	福清
fusheng	附生
Fuzhou (Foochow)	福州
gailiang shehui, zengjin guomin daode, kaitong guomin zhishi	改良社會，增進國民道德，開通國民智識
ganxie dudu	感謝都督
Gao Dengli	高登鯉
gaozhong	高中
genbenshang zhi zhifa	根本上之治法
Gonglihui	公理會
gongsheng	貢生
gongyi	公益
gongyi tuanti	公益團體
gongyishe	公益社
guafen	瓜分
Guandi	關帝
guangfu hui	光復會
Guangxu	光緒

guanjie	官界
Guanxiang tang	觀巷堂
Guanyin	觀音
Guifeng (Kwoi Hung)	貴峰
Gulangyu	鼓浪嶼
Guling	鼓嶺
Guo Youpei	郭幼培
guojia shehui	國家社會
guojia sixiang	國家思想
guomin	國民
guomin chengdu zhi gaoxia	國民程度之高下
guomin jiaoyu	國民教育
Gutian	古田
Hanzu dulihui	漢族獨立會
hao	號
He Xiuying (1901–1931)	何秀瑩
Heling Yinghua shuyuan (Anglo-Chinese College)	鶴齡英華書院
Hinghwa (Xinghua)	興化
Hong Hongru	洪鴻儒
Hong Ye (William Hung)	洪業
Houguan	侯官
houyi	後裔
Huang Bihong (Yongquan)	黃必宏（湧泉）
Huang Fuju	黃福琚
Huang Jiacheng	黃家成
Huang Jixing	黃紀星
Huang Mingwang	黃明望
Huang Naimo (1863–1894)	黃乃模

Huang Naimu (b. 1870)	黃乃穆
Huang Naishang (Jiumei, Bichen, Fucheng; Uong Nai Siong, 1849–1924)	黃乃裳（九美、蔽臣、紱丞）
Huang Naiying (1859–1893)	黃乃英
Huang Qiude (Wong Kiu Taik, 1834?–1893)	黃求德
Huang Zhiji (Ai'an; Uong De Gi, 1866–1928)	黃治基（艾庵）
Huang Zhongfeng (Zhizhai)	黃鍾灃（質齋）
Huangyi	黃裔
Huaxiang	花巷
Hufeng	湖峰
Hwa Nan Women's College	華南女子文理書院
jian yi bu wei wu yong ye	見義不爲無勇也
jiandu/huidu	監督，會督
Jianning	建寧
Jian'ou	建甌
Jianyanbao	建言報
Jianyang	建陽
jiao linguo you dao hu	交鄰國有道乎
jiao'an	教案
jiaohui zhi chanwu ye	教會之產物也
jiaoyuhui	教育會
jieyanju	戒煙局
jinbu pai	進步派
Jingxing bao	警醒報
Jingxing she	警醒社
jinshi	進士
jiuren jishi	救人濟世
juan	卷

junyue	軍樂
juren	舉人
Kang Yong	康詠
Ke	柯
li	里
Li Changshui (Li Diong Cui)	李長水
Li Funan (Yuzhai)	李馥南（郁齋）
Li Hongzhang	李鴻章
Li Houji	李厚基
Li Meizhu (Dr. Li Bi Cu)	李美珠
Li Qifan (Li Chi Van)	李啓藩
Li Rongfan	李榕藩
Li Shuren	李淑仁
Li Yuanhong	藜元洪
Li Zhongye (Cihou)	李仲鄴（次侯）
Liancheng	連城
Lianfeng jushi (Xie Xi'en)	蓮峰居士（謝錫恩）
liangmin	良民
liangyi	糧役
Lianjiang	連江
lieqiang	列強
Lin Baishui (Wanli)	林白水（萬里）
Lin Bingzhang (Huiting)	林炳章（惠亭）
Lin Buji	林步基
Lin Changmin (Zongmeng, 1876–1925)	林長民（宗孟）
Lin Fucun	林馥村
lin gongsheng	廩貢生

Lin Hanguang	林瀚光
Lin Huiyin (Lin Whei-yin)	林徽因
Lin Jianyan (b. 1892)	林劍言
Lin Lucun	林輅存
Lin Rushan (Ling Oi Seng)	林如山
Lin Sen (Zichao)	林森（子超）
Lin Shizhao	林師肇
Lin Shu	林舒
Lin Shufen	林樹棻
Lin Tao'an (Ling To Ang)	林叨安
Lin Wenqing (Dr. Lim Boon Keng)	林文慶
Lin Yushi	林雨時
Lin Zehua	林則話
Lin Zexu	林則徐
Lin Zhenzhen (Ling Ching Ting, 1825?–1879)	林振珍
ling	靈
linsheng	廩生
Liu Chongding	劉崇鼎
Liu Chonglun	劉崇倫
Liu Chongwei	劉崇偉
Liu Chongyou	劉崇佑
Liu Hongshou (Buxi; Lau Buo Ka, d. 1916)	劉鴻壽（步溪）
Liu Huiru (Youwen)	劉惠如（有文）
Liu Meicun (Xieyuan)	劉梅村（爕元）
Liu Shufan	劉書藩
Liu Tong	劉通
Liu Xuebin	劉學彬
Liu Yaoyang	劉耀揚
Liu Yuandong	劉元棟

Liudu	六都
Lu Chuhuang	盧初璜
Lu Guantai	盧觀泰
Lujiao	鹿角
Luo Wenzao	羅文藻
Luofeng	羅峰
Luoyuan	羅源
Meihui liwen	美會禮文
Meiyimei hui	美以美會
Meiyimei hui ganglie	美以美會剛列
Min County	閩縣
Min River	閩江
min wu aihu guojia sixiang	民無愛護國家思想
minde	民德
ming	名
Minjing	閩警
Minnan	閩南
Minqing	閩清
Minsheng huibao	閩省會報
Minxin	民心
Minzheng bu	民政部
minzu, minquan, minzhu	民族，民權，民主
mixin	迷信
Mozi	墨子
mushi	牧師
Nanping	南平
Nantai	南台

Ni Tuosheng (Watchman Nee, 1903–1972)	倪柝聲
Ni Wenxiu	倪文修
Ningde	寧德
Niukeng (Ngu Kang)	牛坑
nonghui	農會
Peng Shousong	彭壽松
pingdeng	平等
Pingnan	屏南
Pushou	樸壽
Qi Xuan	祈暄
qiang	槍
Qiaonan gongyishe	橋南公益社
Qingnian hui	青年會
qita gongyi shiwu	其他公益事務
Quan Min daxuetang	全閩大學堂
quanshi	勸士
Qudushe	去毒社
ren	仁
rexin gongyi fu you xiangwang renshi	熱心公益負有鄉望人士
Rongcheng gezhi shuyuan (Foochow College)	榕城格致書院
Sa Zhenbing (1859–1951)	薩鎮冰
Sanqingtuan	三青團
Shangdi	上帝
shangjie	商界
Shangshu	尚書

Shangyou tang	尚友堂
Shaowu	邵武
shehui	社會
sheng zonghui	省總會
shengyuan	生員
shenjie	紳界
shetuan	社團
Shi Jingchen	施景琛
shijia	世家
shiye	實業
shiyong chuandao	試用傳道
shouhui jiaoyu quan yundong	收回教育權運動
shude shuren	樹德樹人
shuji zhang	書記長
Shun	舜
Shuobao she	說報社
Si you fen	死有分
Song Shangjie	宋尚節
Song Yuanyuan	宋淵源
sui	歲
sui gongsheng	歲貢生
Sun Daoren	孫道仁
Tang Shaoyi	唐紹儀
Taoshu Girls' School	淘淑女子書院
Taotai	道台
Tating	塔亭
Tianantang	天安堂
tianguo zhi jinbu	天國之進步

tiansheng yingcai zhong wei you yong	天生英材終爲有用
tianzhi	天職
tianzu hui	天足會
tiyu	體育
tiyu hui	體育會
tongbao	同胞
Tongmenghui	同盟會
Tongzhi	同治
Trinity College (Sanyi xuexiao)	三一學校
tuanlian	團練
tudi	土地
tuochou minjiao xiangan banfa tiyi an	妥籌民教相安辦法提議案
tuoshi	托事
waiguo you xin ren	外國有心人
Wang Ganhe (Uong Guang Huo)	王淦和
Wang Qingyun (1797–1862)	王慶雲
Wang Qiuding	王求定
Wang Renkan (1849–1893)	王仁堪
Wang Shijing	王世靜
Wang Shijun (1927–1964)	王世鈞
Wang Shikeng (b. 1929)	王世鏗
Wang Shishen	王世深
Wang Xiaoquan (Zhenxian, Fuchu; Uong Hau Ciong, 1882–1967)	王孝泉（振先，複初）
Wang Xiaoxiang (Yanyun; Uong Ngieng Hung, 1891–1992)	王孝緗（彥芸）
Wang Xiaozong (Yangong; Uong Ngieng Gung, b. 1889)	王孝總（彥功）

Wang Xiu	王修
Wang Zhengting (C. T. Wang)	王正廷
Wei fuwu ye, fei yi yi ren	為服務也非以役人
Wei Jinzhong (Ngoi Cheng-Tung)	魏盡忠
Wei Yuan	魏源
Wo ai Zhonghua meidi	我愛中華美地
wo benguo Zhonghua	我本國中華
woguo weixin zhi zumu	我國維新之祖母
Wu Guanchun	吳觀椿
Wu Guanluan	吳觀鑾
Wu Liande (Wu Lien Teh, Gnoh Lean Tuck)	伍連德
Wu Tingcheng (Guangchen)	吳庭根（光臣）
wusuo chengming	無所成名
wuzhi xiaomin	無知小民
xiangfei	鄉匪
xiansheng	先生
Xianyou	仙游
Xie Tianbao (Dr. Sia Tieng Bo)	謝天保
Xie Xi'en (Sia Sek Ong, 1839–1897)	謝錫恩
xiedou	械鬥
xin Zhongguo	新中國
Xinde tonglun	信德統論
Xinghua (Putian)	興化（莆田）
xinhai	辛亥
Xinmin shuo	新民說
xinzheng	新政
xiong	胸
xiyue	西樂

Xu Bomei (Hu Bo Mi, 1828–1907)	許播美
Xu Chengmei (Hu Sing Mi, 1840–1898)	許承美
Xu Chongzhi	許崇智
Xu Daofeng	許道峰
Xu Daowu	許道武
Xu Dishan	許地山
Xu Hanguang	許漢光
Xu Jinhong (Hu King Eng, 1865–1929)	許金匐
Xu Jixiang	許繼祥
Xu Jiyu	徐繼畬
Xu Lebin	許樂賓
Xu Rulei	徐如雷
Xu Shichang	徐世昌
Xu Shifang	許世方
Xu Shiguang (Hu Sie Guong)	許世光
Xu Shihui	許世暉
Xu Shiying	許世英
Xu Shuhong (Hu Seuk Eng, 1870?–1962)	許淑匐
Xu Tianfu	許天福
Xu Wenming (Hu Ung Ming, b. 1876)	許文明
Xu Yangmei (Hu Yong Mi, 1837–1893)	許揚美
Xu Zehan (Hu Caik Hang, 1860–1920)	許則翰
Xu Zeya (Wenzhi, Zian)	許則雅（文智，子安）
Xu Zezhou (Hu Caik Ciu)	許則周
Xu Zhimo	徐志摩
xuanju	選舉
Xuantong	宣統
Xue Chengen (Nathan Sites)	薛承恩
Xue Fenshi (Alfonso Sycip)	薛芬士

Xue Minlao (Hsueh Min-lao, Albino Sycip)	薛敏老
Xue Tingmo (Donald T. M. Hsueh)	薛廷模
Xunshan shizhe	旬山使者
yamen	衙門
Yan Fu	嚴複
Yan Qu (Boyu)	嚴璩（伯玉）
Yang Tinglun	楊廷綸
Yangwu ju	洋務局
Yanping	延平
yanshuo yuan	言說員
Yao	堯
Ye Duanmei (Iek Duang Me)	葉端美
Ye Shoumei (Yek Siu Mi)	葉守美
Ye Yingguan (Iek Ing Guang, 1839–1923)	葉英官
yi	義
yiduan	異端
Yin Xuecun (Dr. S. C. Yin)	殷雪邨
Yiwenshe	益聞社
yongbao Huamin	永保華民
Yongfu	永福
Yongtai	永泰
you fusheng	優附生
you gongsheng	優貢生
you ju gongshengyuan yishang zhi chushenzhe	有舉貢生員以上之出身者
you linsheng	優廩生
You Zhaoyuan (Shaoquan)	游肇源（少泉）
youmin	莠民
youzhi shishang	有志士商

youzhi zhi shi	有志之士
Yu Rizhang (David Z. T. Yui)	余日章
Yu Shuxin (Chuanzhen; U Seuk Sing)	余淑心（傳眞）
Yu Zhongying	余鍾英
Yuan Shikai	袁世凱
zeng gongsheng	增貢生
Zeng Shaoqing	曾少慶
zengsheng	增生
Zhang Heling (Diong Ahok, d. 1890)	張鶴齡
Zhang Yuanqi	張元奇
zhangcheng	章程
zhanglao	長老
Zheng Chenggong (Koxinga)	鄭成功
Zheng Jiming	鄭季明
Zheng Lansun (Zuyin)	鄭蘭蓀（祖蔭）
Zheng Lie	鄭烈
Zheng Quan (Zhongjin)	鄭權（仲勁）
Zheng Xiguang	鄭錫光
Zheng Zhonglin	鄭鍾麟
Zheng Zuyin (Lansun)	鄭祖蔭（蘭蓀）
Zhenshen tang	眞神堂
zhenxing shiye	振興實業
zhishi	執事
zhiyu	智育
zhizao liang guomin	制造良國民
Zhongguo wansui	中國萬歲
Zhonghua wenming dabang	中華文明大邦
Zhou Daojian (Donald Ciu Do Gieng, 1891–1921)	周道見

Zhu Lide (Cio Lik Daik)   朱立德

zhuangyuan   狀元

zi   字

ziyou   自由

zongli   總理

Zongli yamen   總理衙門

Zou Rong   鄒容

Zuo Zongtang   左宗堂

Zuozhuan   左傳

Bibliography

Archival Collections

American Board of Commissioners for Foreign Missions Archives. Harvard University. (Microfilm.)

Church Missionary Society Archives. University of Birmingham, England.

Fujian Provincial Archives. Fujian Jiaoyuting (Education Office) Archives, *zong* 2.

———. Fukien Post Office Archives, *zong* 56.

———. *Ziliao* (Historical Materials) Collection.

Great Britain. Foreign Office Archives. Public Records Office, London.

Methodist Episcopal Church Board of Foreign Missions Archives. Archives Division, General Commission on Archives and History of the United Methodist Church. Drew University, Madison, New Jersey.

United States. Department of State. *Despatches from the United States Consuls in Amoy, China, 1844–1906.* (Microfilm.)

———. *Despatches from the United States Consuls in Foochow, China, 1849–1906.* (Microfilm.)

———. *Despatches from United States Ministers in China, 1843–1906.* (Microfilm.)

———. *Records of the United States Department of State Relating to the Internal Affairs of China, 1910–1929.* (Microfilm.)

University of Oregon Library, Special Collections. Dorothy Walters Collection of Idabelle Lewis Main, Coll. 29.

———. Ida Belle (Lewis) Main Papers, Ax 216.

———. James E. and Susan L. Skinner Papers, Ax 209.

Yale Divinity School Library, Special Collections. Willard Livingstone Beard Papers, Record Group 8.
——. Harold and Marian Belcher Papers, Record Group 8.
——. Christian Literature in Chinese Collection.
——. George Sherwood Eddy Papers, Record Group 32.
——. Ralph G. Gold Papers, Record Group 8.
——. Charles Hartwell and Emily Susan Hartwell Papers, Record Group 8.
——. Missions Pamphlet Collection.
——. John R. Mott Papers, Record Group 48.
——. Franklin and Bertha S. Ohlinger Papers, Record Group 23.
——. Smith Family Papers, Record Group 5.
——. World Student Christian Federation Archives, Record Group 46.
Yale University Library, Manuscripts and Archives. George H. Hubbard Papers, MS 965.
YMCA of the USA Archives. University of Minnesota.

Books and Periodicals

A Ying, ed. *Fan Mei huagong jinyue wenxueji* (Collected texts on the opposition to the American coolie exclusion treaty). Beijing: Zhonghua shuju, 1960.
Ai'an xiansheng [Huang Zhiji]. *Jiandaoji* (Discovered truths compiled). 12 *juan*. Fuzhou: Methodist Seminary, 1903.
Anagnost, Ann. *National Past-Times: Narrative, Representation, and Power in Modern China*. Durham: Duke University Press, 1997.
Anderson, Benedict. *Imagined Communities: Reflections on the Origins and Spread of Nationalism*. London: Verso, 1983; revised edition 1991.
——. "Introduction." In Gopal Balakrishnan, ed., *Mapping the Nation*, pp. 1–16. London: Verso, 1996.
Anlijian jiaohui Fujian sheng zonghui (Provincial council of the Anglican church in Fujian). Manuscript minutes of the annual meetings, 1883–1909. Institute of Religion, Fujian Teachers' University.
Annual Report of the American Board of Commissioners for Foreign Missions. Boston, 1860–1930.
Annual Report of the Board of Foreign Missions of the Methodist Episcopal Church. New York, 1860–1930.
Annual Report of the Church Missionary Society. London, 1860–1930.
Annual Report of the Young Men's Christian Associations of China. Shanghai, 1908–1917.
Arkush, R. David, and Leo O. Lee, eds. *Land Without Ghosts: Chinese Impressions of America from the Mid-Nineteenth Century to the Present*. Berkeley: University of California Press, 1989.
Arnold, Julean H. "Educational Activity in Foochow, China." In United States Bureau of Education, *Report of the Commissioner of Education for the Year Ended June 30, 1907*. Vol. 1, pp. 191–220. Washington, D.C.: U.S. Government Printing Office, 1908.
Baldwin, S. L. *Ling Ching Ting: The Converted Opium Smoker*. New York: Self-Supporting Missionary Publication Department, [Board of Foreign Missions, Methodist Episcopal Church], n.d. Pamphlet in YDS, A167.13.

Baoling fuyin shuyuan (Catalogue of the Baldwin Seminary). [Fuzhou]: n.p., 1905.

Barnett, Suzanne Wilson, and John King Fairbank, eds. *Christianity in China: Early Protestant Missionary Writings*. Cambridge: Harvard University Press, 1985.

de Bary, Wm. Theodore, et al., eds. *Sources of Chinese Tradition*. New York: Columbia University Press, 1960.

Bays, Daniel H. "The Growth of Independent Christianity in China, 1900–1937." In Bays, ed., *Christianity in China*.

Bays, Daniel H., ed. *Christianity in China: From the Eighteenth Century to the Present*. Stanford: Stanford University Press, 1996.

Beard, W. L. "A Missionary's Thoughts After Thirty-Eight Years in China." *Chinese Recorder* (1933). Offprint in Beard Papers, YDS Record Group 8–251.

Bederman, Gail. *Manliness and Civilization: A Cultural History of Gender and Race in the United States, 1880–1917*. Chicago: University of Chicago Press, 1995.

Bernhardt, Kathryn. *Rents, Taxes, and Peasant Resistance: The Lower Yangzi Region, 1840–1950*. Stanford: Stanford University Press, 1992.

Bissonnette, W. S. *Donald Ciu of Kutien: A Brief Sketch of His Life and Work*. N.p., n.d. Pamphlet in University of Oregon Library, Special Collections, Ida Belle Main Papers, Ax 216, Box 2.

———. "The Methodist Church in North Fukien." In International Missionary Council, *The Growing Church*, pp. 256–268. New York: International Missionary Council, 1939.

Bloch, Ruth. "Religion and Ideological Change in the American Revolution." In Mark A. Noll, ed., *Religion and American Politics: From the Colonial Period to the 1980s*. New York: Oxford University Press, 1990.

Boorman, Howard L., and Richard C. Howard, eds. *Biographical Dictionary of Republican China*. 4 vols. New York: Columbia University Press, 1967–1971.

Borthwick, Sally. "Students and Revolutionary Culture in Late Qing Schools." *Papers on Far Eastern History* 19 (March 1979), pp. 91–109.

Brokaw, Cynthia. *The Ledgers of Merit and Demerit: Social Change and Moral Order in Late Imperial China*. Princeton: Princeton University Press, 1991.

Brook, Timothy. "Auto-Organization in Chinese Society." In Brook and Frolic, eds., *Civil Society in China*.

Brook, Timothy, and B. Michael Frolic. "The Ambiguous Challenge of Civil Society." In Brook and Frolic, eds., *Civil Society in China*.

Brook, Timothy, and B. Michael Frolic, eds. *Civil Society in China*. Armonk, N.Y.: M. E. Sharpe, 1997.

Brooke, John L. "Reason and Passion in the Public Sphere: Habermas and the Cultural Historians." *Journal of Interdisciplinary History* 29:1 (1998), pp. 43–67.

Buck, David D. *Urban Change in China: Politics and Development in Tsinan, Shantung, 1890–1949*. Madison: University of Wisconsin Press, 1978.

Burns, Islay. *Memoir of the Rev. Wm. C. Burns, M.A., Missionary to China from the English Presbyterian Church*. London: James Nisbet, 1885.

Burton, Margaret. *Notable Women of Modern China*. New York: Fleming H. Revell, 1912.

Butler, Jon. *Awash in a Sea of Faith: Christianizing the American People*. Cambridge: Harvard University Press, 1990.

Calhoun, Craig. *Nationalism.* Minneapolis: University of Minnesota Press, 1997.

Call to Prayer in Behalf of the Fukien Provincial Evangelistic Campaign, October 22– December 1st, 1914. N.p., [1914].

Cangshan wenshi (Cangshan history). Fuzhou, 1988–.

Cannadine, David. "The Context, Performance and Meaning of Ritual: The British Monarchy and the 'Invention of Tradition,' c. 1820–1977." In Hobsbawm and Ranger, eds., *Invention of Tradition.*

Carlson, Ellsworth C. *The Foochow Missionaries, 1847–1880.* Cambridge: East Asian Research Center, Harvard University, 1974.

Catalogue of Foochow College, College Year Feb. 1915–Jan. 1916. Fuzhou: n.p., 1915. Beard Papers, YDS Record Group 8–255–28.

Chan, Wing-Tsit, ed. *A Source Book in Chinese Philosophy.* Princeton: Princeton University Press, 1963.

Chang, Chung-li. *The Chinese Gentry: Studies on Their Role in Nineteenth-Century Chinese Society.* Seattle: University of Washington Press, 1955.

Chang, P'eng-yuan [Zhang Pengyuan]. "The Background of Constitutionalists in Late Qing China." In Eto and Schiffrin, eds., *China's Republican Revolution.*

———. "The Constitutionalists." In Wright, ed., *China in Revolution.*

Chatterjee, Partha. *The Nation and Its Fragments: Colonial and Postcolonial Histories.* Princeton: Princeton University Press, 1993.

Chen Dequan. "Yi 'jiu dianxian shushu'" (Recollections of the "Old Telegraph Office School"). *Fujian wenshi ziliao* 20 (1988), pp. 89–94.

Chen Guohong. *Zhonghua minguo guogeshi* (History of national anthems of the Republic of China). Tainan: Quanguo geda shuju, 1961.

Chen Hengming. *Zhonghua minguo zhengzhi fuhao zhi yanjiu* (Research on the political symbols of the Republic of China). Taipei: Taiwan Commercial Press, 1986.

Chen Wenzhong, ed. *Fuzhou shi Taijiang jianshe zhi* (Construction history of the Taijiang area of Fuzhou). Fuzhou: Fujian Science and Technology Publishing House, 1993.

Chen Yan, comp. *Fujian tongzhi* (Fujian gazetteer). Fuzhou: n.p., 1938.

Chew, Daniel. *Chinese Pioneers on the Sarawak Frontier, 1841–1941.* Singapore: Oxford University Press, 1990.

China Mission Year Book. Shanghai, 1910–1925.

The China Year Book. London, 1912–1939.

Chow Tse-tsung. *The May Fourth Movement: Intellectual Revolution in Modern China.* Cambridge: Harvard University Press, 1960; repr. Stanford: Stanford University Press, 1967.

Ch'u, T'ung-tsu. *Law and Society in Traditional China.* Paris: Mouton, 1961.

———. *Local Government in China Under the Ch'ing.* Cambridge: Harvard University Press, 1962; repr. Stanford: Stanford University Press, 1969.

Chun Bi. "Fuzhou guangfu de 'shishi geyao'" (Topical songs during the 1911 revolution in Fuzhou). *Fuzhou wenshi ziliao xuanji* 1 (1981), pp. 99–101.

Church Missionary Intelligencer and Record. London, 1870–1890.

The Church Missionary Record. London, 1830–1875.

Church Missionary Society. *Mr. Wigram's Tour to the Missions of the Church Missionary*

Society in 1886–87: Letters from Mr. Edmund F. E. Wigram, Descriptive of the Society's Work in the Countries Visited. London: Church Missionary Society, 1887.

———. *Register of Missionaries (Clerical, Lay, and Female), and Native Clergy, from 1804–1904.* [London]: [Church Missionary Society,] printed for private circulation, 1904.

The C.M.S. Gazette. London, 1909–1917.

Codrington, F. I. *Hot-Hearted: Some Women Builders of the Chinese Church.* London: Church of England Zenana Missionary Society, n.d.

Cohen, Myron L. "Being Chinese: The Peripheralization of Traditional Identity." In Tu Weiming, ed., *The Living Tree: The Changing Meaning of Being Chinese Today.* Berkeley: University of California Press, 1995.

Cohen, Paul A. *Between Tradition and Modernity: Wang T'ao and Reform in Late Ch'ing China.* Cambridge: Harvard University Press, 1974.

———. *China and Christianity: The Missionary Movement and the Growth of Chinese Antiforeignism, 1860–1870.* Cambridge: Harvard University Press, 1963.

———. "Christian Missions and Their Impact to 1900." In Denis Twitchett and John K. Fairbank, eds., *Cambridge History of China,* vol. 10, *Late Ch'ing,* part 1. Cambridge: Cambridge University Press, 1978.

———. *Discovering History in China: American Historical Writing on the Recent Chinese Past.* New York: Columbia University Press, 1984.

———. "Littoral and Hinterland in Nineteenth Century China: The 'Christian' Reformers." In Fairbank, ed., *Missionary Enterprise.*

Constitution of the Anglo-Chinese College. Foochow: n.p., 1887. Methodist Episcopal Church Board of Foreign Missions Archives.

Crouch, Archie R., et al., eds. *Christianity in China: A Scholar's Guide to Resources in the Libraries and Archives of the United States.* Armonk, N.Y.: M. E. Sharpe, 1989.

Cycle of Prayer of the College Young Men's Christian Association of China. N.p., 1896. YMCA of the USA Archives.

Dikotter, Frank. *The Discourse of Race in Modern China.* Stanford: Stanford University Press, 1992.

Ding Shouhe, ed. *Xinhai geming shiqi qikan jieshao* (Introduction to periodicals at the time of the Xinhai revolution). Beijing: People's Publishing House, 1983.

Ding Xiancheng. "Xinhai geming qianhou Fuzhou jiaohui xuexiao de aiguo yundong yu geming zhanzheng de huiyi" (Recollections of the patriotic movement in Fuzhou church schools around the time of the 1911 revolution, and of the revolutionary battle). *Fuzhou wenshi ziliao xuanji* 1 (1981), pp. 63–68.

Directory of the Chinese Students' Alliance in the Eastern States of the United States. N.p., 1911. YDS.

Dobson, W. A. C. H., trans. *Mencius.* Toronto: University of Toronto Press, 1963.

Doolittle, Justus. *Social Life of the Chinese: With Some Account of Their Religious, Governmental, Educational, and Business Customs and Opinions, with Special but Not Exclusive Reference to Fuhchau.* 2 vols. New York: Harper, 1865; repr. Singapore: Graham Brash, 1986.

Douglas, Ann. *The Feminization of American Culture.* New York: Alfred A. Knopf, 1978.

Drake, Fred W. "Protestant Geography in China: E. C. Bridgman's Portrayal of the West." In Barnett and Fairbank, eds., *Christianity in China.*

Drake, Fred W., ed. *Ruth V. Hemenway, M.D.: A Memoir of Revolutionary China, 1924–1941.* Amherst: University of Massachusetts Press, 1977.

Duara, Prasenjit. *Culture, Power, and the State: Rural North China, 1900–1942.* Stanford: Stanford University Press, 1988.

———. "De-constructing the Chinese Nation." *Australian Journal of Chinese Affairs* 30 (July 1993), pp. 1–26.

———. "Knowledge and Power in the Discourse of Modernity: The Campaigns Against Popular Religion in Early Twentieth-Century China." *Journal of Asian Studies* 50:1 (1991), pp. 67–83.

———. *Rescuing History from the Nation: Questioning Narratives of Modern China.* Chicago: University of Chicago Press, 1995.

———. "State and Civil Society in the History of Chinese Modernity." In Frederic Wakeman, Jr., and Wang Xi, eds., *China's Quest for Modernization: A Historical Perspective.* Berkeley: Institute of East Asian Studies, University of California, Berkeley, 1997.

Dunch, Ryan. "Mission Schools and Modernity: The Anglo-Chinese College, Fuzhou." In Glen Peterson, Ruth Hayhoe, and Yongling Lu, eds. *Education, Culture, and Identity in Twentieth-Century China.* Ann Arbor: University of Michigan Press, 2001.

———. "Protestant Christianity in China Today: Fragile, Fragmented, Flourishing." In Stephen Uhalley, Jr. and Xiaoxin Wu, eds., *China and Christianity: Burdened Past, Hopeful Future.* Armonk, N.Y.: M. E. Sharpe, 2000.

Eastman, Lloyd E. *Family, Fields, and Ancestors: Constancy and Change in China's Social and Economic History, 1550–1949.* New York: Oxford University Press, 1988.

Eddy, G. Sherwood. *How China's Leaders Received the Gospel.* New York: Foreign Department, YMCA International Committee, n.d.

———. *The Students of Asia.* New York: Student Volunteer Movement for Foreign Missions, 1915.

Egan, Susan Chan. *A Latterday Confucian: Reminiscences of William Hung (1893–1980).* Cambridge: Council on East Asian Studies, Harvard University, 1987.

Eley, Geoff, and Ronald Grigor Suny. "Introduction: From the Moment of Social History to the Work of Cultural Representation." In Geoff Eley and Ronald Grigor Suny, eds., *Becoming National: A Reader,* pp. 3–37. Oxford: Oxford University Press, 1996.

Elman, Benjamin A. "Political, Social, and Cultural Reproduction via Civil Service Examinations in Late Imperial China." *Journal of Asian Studies* 50:1 (1991), pp. 7–28.

Esherick, Joseph W. "Founding a Republic, Electing a President: How Sun Yat-sen Became *Guofu.*" In Eto and Schiffrin, eds., *China's Republican Revolution.*

———. *The Origins of the Boxer Uprising.* Berkeley: University of California Press, 1987.

———. *Reform and Revolution in China: The 1911 Revolution in Hunan and Hubei.* Berkeley: University of California Press, 1976.

Esherick, Joseph W., and Jeffrey N. Wasserstrom. "Acting Out Democracy: Political Theater in Modern China." In Jeffrey N. Wasserstrom and Elizabeth J. Perry, eds., *Popular Protest and Political Culture in Modern China: Learning from 1989.* Boulder, Colo.: Westview Press, 1992.

Eto Shinkichi and Harold Z. Schiffrin, eds. *China's Republican Revolution*. Tokyo: University of Tokyo Press, 1994.

Fairbank, John K., ed. *The Missionary Enterprise in China and America*. Cambridge: Harvard University Press, 1974.

Fairbank, Wilma. *Liang and Lin: Partners in Exploring China's Architectural Past*. Philadelphia: University of Pennsylvania Press, 1994.

Faithfull-Davies, Margaret E. *The Banyan City*. London: Church of England Zenana Missionary Society, 1910.

Fan nietai lilin qudu zongshe kai huiyi an (A meeting of the Anti-Opium League honored by the attendance of Provincial Judge Fan). Fuzhou: n.p., 1909.

Fan Qilong. "'Shiyi/jiu' qiyi—xinhai geming zai Fujian" (The "11/9" Uprising—the Xinhai revolution in Fujian). In Tang Wenji, ed., *Fujian shi luntan: Jinian Zhu Weigan jiaoshou lunwenji* (Discussions on Fujian history: essays in memory of Professor Zhu Weigan). Fuzhou: Fujian renmin chubanshe, 1992.

Fan Shouzheng et al. "Li Houji zai Fujian" (Li Houji in Fujian). *Fujian wenshi ziliao* 9 (1985), pp. 1–23.

Fan Yinnan, comp. *Dangdai Zhongguo mingren lu* (Directory of prominent persons in contemporary China). Shanghai: Liangyou tushu Publishers, preface 1932.

Feuerwerker, Albert. *The Foreign Establishment in China in the Early Twentieth Century*. Ann Arbor: Center for Chinese Studies, University of Michigan, 1976.

Fincher, John H. *Chinese Democracy: The Self-Government Movement in Local, Provincial and National Politics, 1905–1914*. Canberra: Australian National University Press, 1981.

———. "Political Provincialism and the National Revolution." In Wright, ed., *China in Revolution*.

Finke, Roger, and Rodney Stark. "How the Upstart Sects Won America: 1776–1850." *Journal for the Scientific Study of Religion* 28 (1988), pp. 27–44.

Firth, Raymond. *Symbols: Public and Private*. Ithaca, N.Y.: Cornell University Press, 1973.

Fitzgerald, John. *Awakening China: Politics, Culture, and Class in the Nationalist Revolution*. Stanford: Stanford University Press, 1996.

Foochow Messenger. Fuzhou, 1903–1940s.

Foochow News. Fuzhou, 1920–1930s.

Ford, Eddy Lucius. *The History of the Educational Work of the Methodist Episcopal Church in China: A Study of Its Development and Present Trends*. Foochow: Christian Herald Mission Press, 1938.

The Foreign Mail Annual. New York, 1906–1912.

Freedman, Maurice. *Chinese Lineage and Society: Fukien and Kwangtung*. London: Athlone Press, 1965.

———. *Lineage Organization in Southeastern China*. London: Athlone Press, 1958.

Fryer, John D., ed. *The Educational Directory for China* 1 (1895).

Fubao (Fujian news). Fuzhou, 1896–1897.

The Fuhkien Witness. Fuzhou, 1902–1908.

Fujian jiaoyu xingzheng yuekan (Fujian educational administration monthly). Fuzhou, 1920s.

Fujian jiaoyu zonghui yilan (Overview of the Fujian Educational Association). Fuzhou: n.p., [1907?].

Fujian lujun wubei xuetang kecheng: Lishi xue (Fujian Military Preparatory School curriculum: History). N.p., n.d.

Fujian qudu zongshe jibao (Fujian Anti-Opium League quarterly report). Fuzhou, 1907–1914.

Fujian sheng diyi ci jiaoyu xingzheng huiyi baogao (Report of the first meeting of the Fujian Provincial Conference on Educational Administration). Fuzhou: n.p., 1916.

Fujian sheng weisheng zhi (Gazetteer of public health in Fujian Province). Ed. Fujian sheng weisheng zhi Editorial Committee. Fuzhou, n.p., 1989.

Fujian wenshi ziliao (Materials on Fujian history). Fuzhou, 1981–.

Fujian ziyiju chouban chu di yici baogao shu (First report of the Preparatory Office for the Fujian Provincial Assembly). N.p., [1909].

Fujian ziyiju diyi jie quanti yiyuan yilan biao (Complete list of representatives to the inaugural Fujian Provincial Assembly). N.p., [1910].

Fujian ziyiju diyi jie yi'an zhaiyao (Fujian Provincial Assembly, first session: Summary of resolutions). N.p., [1909].

Fujian ziyiju yishi suji lu (Minutes of the Fujian Provincial Assembly). Fuzhou, 1909–1910.

Fukien Student Federation. *The Recent Japanese Outrage in Foochow.* N.p., n.d. Pamphlet in Hartwell Papers, YDS Record Group 8–93.

Fuzhou diwu zhongxue xiaozhi (School history of Fuzhou Number 5 Middle School). Ed. Fuzhou diwu zhongxue xiaozhi Editorial Committee. Fuzhou: mimeo., 1992.

Fuzhou Jidujiao qingnian hui nianbao (Annual report of the Fuzhou YMCA). Fuzhou, 1930s.

Fuzhou lishi renwu (Figures in Fuzhou history). Fuzhou, 1990–.

Fuzhou Meiyimei nianhui lu (Record of the Foochow Annual Conference of the Methodist Episcopal Church). Fuzhou, 1877–1949.

Fuzhou Meiyimei nianhui shi (History of the Foochow Conference of the Methodist Episcopal Church). Ed. Lin Xianfang et al. Fuzhou: [Methodist Church], 1936.

Fuzhou qingnian hui bao (Fuzhou young men). Fuzhou, 1909–1919.

Fuzhou shi jianzhu zhi (Fuzhou construction gazetteer). Ed. Fuzhou Construction Gazetteer Editorial Committee. Beijing: China Construction Industry Publishing House, 1993.

Fuzhou shuobao she zhangcheng (Constitution of the Fuzhou Explain-the-News Society). N.p., n.d.

Fuzhou wenshi ziliao xuanji (Selected materials on Fuzhou history). Fuzhou, 1981–.

Fuzhou Ying lingshi hunzheng Tianansi jishi (A factual record of the confused claim of the British consul in Fuzhou to the property of the Tianan Monastery). Fuzhou: Minnan Fire Brigade, 1909.

Gaimusho, Johobu [Information Division, Ministry of Foreign Affairs, Japan]. *Gendai Chuka minkoku Manshu teikoku jimmeikan* (Biographical dictionary of the modern Republic of China and the Empire of Manchuria). Tokyo: Gaimusho, 1937.

———. *Kaitei gendai Shina jimmeikan* (Revised biographical dictionary of contemporary China). Tokyo: n.p., 1928.

Gao Rong. "Fujian sheng tushuguan jianshi" (Brief history of the Fujian Provincial Library). *Gulou wenshi* (Gulou history) 2 (1991), pp. 75–81.

Garrett, Shirley S. "The Chambers of Commerce and the YMCA." In Mark Elvin and G. William Skinner, eds., *The Chinese City Between Two Worlds.* Stanford: Stanford University Press, 1974.

———. *Social Reformers in Urban China: The Chinese Y.M.C.A., 1895–1926.* Cambridge: Harvard University Press, 1970.

Gernet, Jacques. *China and the Christian Impact: A Conflict of Cultures.* Trans. Janet Lloyd. Cambridge: Cambridge University Press, 1985.

Goertz, Peter S. "A History of the Development of the Chinese Indigenous Christian Church Under the American Board in Fukien Province." Unpublished Ph.D. dissertation, Yale University, 1933.

Goodman, Bryna. "The Locality as Microcosm of the Nation? Native Place Networks and Early Urban Nationalism in China." *Modern China* 21:4 (1995), pp. 387–419.

———. *Native Place, City, and Nation: Regional Networks and Identities in Shanghai, 1853–1937.* Berkeley: University of California Press, 1995.

de Groot, J. J. M. *Sectarianism and Religious Persecution in China.* Amsterdam: Johannes Muller, 1903–1904; repr. Taipei: Ch'eng Wen, 1970.

Grose, George Richmond. *James W. Bashford: Pastor, Educator, Bishop.* New York: Methodist Book Concern, 1922.

Gutian Jidujiao zhi (Gazetteer of [Protestant] Christianity in Gutian). Ed. Gutian xian Jidujiao sanzi aiguo yundong weiyuanhui (Gutian County Committee of the Protestant Three-Self Patriotic Movement). [Gutian]: n.p., n.d.; preface 1989.

Gutian xian xiangtu zhilüe (Abridged local gazetteer of Gutian County). Comp. Zeng Guangxi et al. N.p., 1906.

Gutian xianzhi (Gutian County gazetteer). Comp. Huang Chengyuan et al. N.p., 1942.

Gwynn, R. M., E. M. Norton, and B. W. Simpson. *"T.C.D." in China: A History of the Dublin University Fukien Mission, 1885–1935, Compiled for the Mission's Jubilee.* Dublin: Church of Ireland Printing and Publishing, 1936.

Habermas, Jürgen. *The Structural Transformation of the Public Sphere: An Inquiry into a Category of Bourgeois Society.* Trans. Thomas Burger. Cambridge: MIT Press, 1989.

Hane, Mikiso. *Modern Japan: A Historical Survey.* Boulder, Colo.: Westview Press, 1986; second edition 1992.

Hao, Chang. *Liang Ch'i-ch'ao and Intellectual Transition in China.* Cambridge: Harvard University Press, 1971.

Harper, Susan Billington. "Ironies of Indigenization: Some Cultural Repercussions of Mission in South India." *International Bulletin of Missionary Research* 19:1 (1995), pp. 13–20.

Harris, Peter. "Chinese Nationalism: The State of the Nation." *The China Journal* 38 (July 1997), pp. 121–137.

Harrison, Henrietta. "Martyrs and Militarism in Early Republican China." *Twentieth-Century China* 23:2 (1998), pp. 41–70.

Hartwell, E. S. "The Story of the Christian Herald Industrial Homes in Foochow." *Woman's Work in the Far East* 32 (1911), pp. 64–70.

Hatch, Nathan O. *The Democratization of American Christianity*. New Haven: Yale University Press, 1989.

He Gonggan. "Min yan gongyou douzheng ji" (The struggle for public ownership of salt in Fujian). *Fujian wenshi ziliao* 17 (1987), pp. 1–74.

Heling Yinghua shuyuan zhangcheng (Catalogue of the Foochow Anglo-Chinese College). [Fuzhou]: n.p., 1917.

Hersey, John. *The Call*. New York: Alfred A. Knopf, 1985; repr. New York: Penguin, 1986.

Hevia, James L. "Leaving a Brand on China: Missionary Discourse in the Wake of the Boxer Movement." *Modern China* 18:3 (1992), pp. 304–332.

A History of the Dublin University Fuh-Kien Mission, 1887–1911. Dublin: Hodges, Figgis and Co., 1912.

Ho, Ping-ti. *The Ladder of Success in Late Imperial China: Aspects of Social Mobility, 1368–1911*. New York: Columbia University Press, 1962.

Hobsbawm, Eric J. "Mass-Producing Traditions: Europe, 1870–1914." In Hobsbawm and Ranger, eds., *The Invention of Tradition*.

——. *Nations and Nationalism Since 1780: Programme, Myth, Reality*. Cambridge: Cambridge University Press, 1990; second edition 1992.

Hobsbawm, Eric, and Terence Ranger, eds. *The Invention of Tradition*. Cambridge: Cambridge University Press, 1983.

Hook, Marion. *"Save Some": CEZMS Work in Fuh-Kien*. London: Church of England Zenana Missionary Society, n.d.

Hsueh, Donald T. M. [Xue Tingmo]. *Foochow College Up to Date*. N.p., n.d. Pamphlet in YDS, HR 189.

Huang Jiumei [Naishang]. "Xue Mushi zhuanlüe" (Brief biography of the Rev. Nathan Sites). *Minsheng huibao* (Fukien church gazette) 253 (June 1895), pp. 2139b-2140; 254 (July 1895), pp. 2157b-2158; 255 (August 1895), pp. 2172b-2173.

Huang Naishang. *Fucheng qishi zixu* (Autobiography at age seventy). Composed in 1919, published in 1925. Reprinted in Liu Zizheng [Lau Tzy Cheng], *Huang Naishang yu Xin Fuzhou* (Huang Naishang and the "New Fuzhou"). Singapore: Nanyang xuehui, 1979.

——. "Pigui pian shang: Pi chaojian" (In refutation of spirits, part one: Refuting [Buddhist and Taoist] otherworldliness). *Fubao* 27 (July 28, 1896).

——. "Pigui pian xia: Pi yinci" (In refutation of spirits, part three: Refuting base shrines). *Fubao* 29 (Aug. 5, 1896).

——. Preface to Wei Ligao [Myron C. Wilcox], *Da meiguo shilüe* (History of America). Fuzhou: Methodist Publishing House, 1899.

[Huang Naishang]. "Zongjiao guan" (My religious outlook), part 1. *Zuohai gongdao bao* (Fuzhou Christian journal) 1:9 (1911), pp. 7–8.

Huang, Philip C. C. *Civil Justice in China: Representation and Practice in the Qing*. Stanford: Stanford University Press, 1996.

Huang Zhiji. *Ye Mo henglun* (Comparison of Jesus and Mozi). Fuzhou: Methodist Publishing House, 1912.

Hudson, Winthrop S. *Religion in America*. New York: Charles Scribner's Sons, 1965; third edition 1981.

Hummel, Arthur W. *Eminent Chinese of the Ch'ing Period*. Washington, D.C.: U.S. Government Printing Office, 1943; repr. Taipei: Ch'eng Wen, 1975.

Hung, William [Hong Ye]. *The Flaming Evangel of Kutien*. N.p., n.d. Pamphlet in YDS, A166.05.

Hunter, Jane. *The Gospel of Gentility: American Women Missionaries in Turn-of-the-Century China*. New Haven: Yale University Press, 1984.

Hutchison, William R. *Errand to the World: American Protestant Thought and Foreign Missions*. Chicago: University of Chicago Press, 1987.

——. "Modernism and Missions: The Liberal Search for an Exportable Christianity, 1875–1935." In Fairbank, ed., *Missionary Enterprise*.

——. *The Modernist Impulse in American Protestantism*. Cambridge: Harvard University Press, 1976.

Hutchison, William R., ed. *Between the Times: The Travail of the Protestant Establishment in America, 1900–1960*. Cambridge: Cambridge University Press, 1987.

Illustrated Catalogue of the Chinese Collection of Exhibits for the International Health Exhibition, London, 1884. Comp. Imperial Maritime Customs of China. London: William Clowes and Sons, 1884.

Jiang Boying, ed. *Fujian geming shi* (History of the revolution in Fujian). 2 vols. Fuzhou: Fujian renmin chubanshe, 1991.

Jidujiao xialing ertong yiwu xuexiao jiaoyuan zhinan (Teacher's manual for Chinese Daily Vacation Bible Schools). Comp. Bao Zheqing [Bau Tsih Ching]. N.p., 1921.

Jin Jiandu zhilüe (Biography of Bishop Kingsley). Fuzhou: Methodist Publishing House, 1871.

Jingxing bao (Awakening). Fuzhou, 1910–1911.

Jinian Sun Zhongshan xiansheng danchen 125 nian, xinhai geming 75 zhou nian xueshu taolun hui, Huanghuagang qiyi Fuzhou diqu lieshi shiyi yantaohui wenzhang xuanji (Selected papers from the conference commemorating the 125th anniversary of Sun Yatsen's birth and the 75th anniversary of the 1911 revolution, and from the symposium on the Fuzhou martyrs in the Huanghuagang uprising). Ed. Fuzhou shi shehui kexue suo (Fuzhou Municipal Institute of Social Sciences) and Fuzhou shi lishi xuehui (Fuzhou Municipal Historical Association). Fuzhou: n.p., [1986].

Jiushijiao shige (Songs of salvation). Fuzhou: Methodist Publishing House, 1897; preface 1892.

Jordan, David. *Gods, Ghosts, and Ancestors: The Folk Religion of a Taiwanese Village*. Berkeley: University of California Press, 1972.

Jordan, Donald. *The Northern Expedition: China's National Revolution of 1926–1928*. Honolulu: University of Hawaii Press, 1976.

Journal of the General Conference of the Methodist Episcopal Church. New York, 1855–1936.

Judge, Joan. *Print and Politics: "Shibao" and the Culture of Reform in Late Qing China*. Stanford: Stanford University Press, 1996.

Juejiao (Sever relations). Fuzhou, 1925.

Kamachi, Noriko. *Reform in China: Huang Tsun-hsien and the Japanese Model*. Cambridge: Council on East Asian Studies, Harvard University, 1981.

Keller, Charles A. "Nationalism and Chinese Christians: The Religious Freedom Campaign and Movement for Independent Chinese Churches, 1911–1917." *Republican China* 17:2 (1992), pp. 30–51.

Kertzer, David I. *Ritual, Politics, and Power*. New Haven: Yale University Press, 1988.

Kinnear, Angus I. *Against the Tide: The Story of Watchman Nee*. Fort Washington, Pa.: Christian Literature Crusade, 1973.

Ko, Dorothy. "Thinking About Copulating: An Early-Qing Confucian Thinker's Problem with Emotion and Words." In Gail Hershatter, Emily Honig, Jonathan N. Lipman, and Randall Stross, eds., *Remapping China: Fissures in Historical Terrain*. Stanford: Stanford University Press, 1996.

Korson, Thomas E. "Congregational Missionaries in Foochow During the 1911 Revolution." *Chinese Culture* 8:2 (1967), pp. 44–107.

Kuhn, Philip A. "Civil Society and Constitutional Development." In Léon Vandermeersch, ed., *La Société Civile face à l'Etat dans les traditions chinoise, japonaise, coréenne et vietnamienne*. Paris: Ecole Française d'Extrême-Orient, 1994.

Kwok Pui-lan. *Chinese Women and Christianity, 1860–1927*. Atlanta: Scholars Press, 1992.

Lacey Sites, C. M., ed. *Educational Institutions of the Methodist Episcopal Church in China*. Shanghai: Methodist Publishing House, 1907.

Lacy, Walter N. *A Hundred Years of Chinese Methodism*. New York: Abingdon-Cokesbury Press, 1948.

Lamley, Harry J. "*Hsieh-tou*: The Pathology of Violence in Southeastern China." *Ch'ing-shih wen-t'i* 3:7 (1977), pp. 1–39.

Larson, Pier M. "'Capacities and Modes of Thinking': Intellectual Engagements and Subaltern Hegemony in the Early History of Malagasy Christianity." *American Historical Review* 102:4 (1997), pp. 966–1002.

Latourette, Kenneth Scott. *A History of Christian Missions in China*. London: Society for Promoting Christian Knowledge, 1929; repr. Taipei: Ch'eng-wen, 1973.

Lau, D. C., trans. *Mencius* (Bilingual edition). 2 vols. Hong Kong: Chinese University Press, 1984.

Lee, K. K. [Li Jinqiang]. "Revolution in Treaty Ports: Fujian's Revolutionary Movement in the Late Qing Period, 1895–1911." Unpublished Ph.D. dissertation, Australian National University, 1992.

Legge, James, trans. *The Chinese Classics*, vol. 2: *The Works of Mencius*. 1895; repr. Hong Kong: Hong Kong University Press, 1960.

Leung, Yuen Sang. "Religion and Revolution—The Response of the Singapore Chinese Christians to the Revolutionary Movement in China." In Lee Lai T'o, ed., *The 1911 Revolution: The Chinese in British and Dutch Southeast Asia*. Singapore: Heinemann Asia, 1987.

Levenson, Joseph R. "The Suggestiveness of Vestiges: Confucianism and Monarchy at the Last." In Arthur F. Wright, ed., *Confucianism and Chinese Civilization*. Stanford: Stanford University Press, 1964.

Lewis, Robert Ellsworth. *The Educational Conquest of the Far East*. New York: Fleming H. Revell, 1903.

Li Jinqiang [K. K. Lee]. "Qingji Fuzhou geming yundong xingqi ji geming tuanti yanjin chutan" (The emergence of the revolutionary movement and the evolution of revolutionary organizations in Fuzhou in the Qing—initial findings). In Modern History Institute, Academica Sinica, ed., *Xinhai geming yantaohui lunwenji* (Collected papers from a symposium on the Xinhai revolution). Taipei: Modern History Institute, Academica Sinica, 1983.

[Li, Persis]. *The Seeker: The Autobiography of a Chinese Christian*. Trans. and comp. M. M. Church. London: Church of England Zenana Missionary Society, n.d.

Lianfeng jushi [Xie Xi'en]. *Yesu shi shei lun* (Who is Jesus?). Fuzhou: Methodist Publishing House, 1872.

Liang Qichao. "Xinmin shuo" (On the renovation of the people). In Li Huaxing and Wu Jiaxun eds., *Liang Qichao xuanji* (Selected works of Liang Qichao). Shanghai: Shanghai renmin chubanshe, 1984.

Lieming kenqing Min-Zhe zongdu Songyuan zhao xinyue jin yun yangyao jin Fujian kou chengwen (Text and signatures of a petition imploring the Min-Zhe governor-general Songyuan to prohibit the importation of foreign opium into Fujian ports in accordance with the new treaty). N.p., [1907?].

Lin Denghao. "Liu Yuandong lieshi xiaozhuan" (Brief biography of the martyr Liu Yuandong). *Fuzhou wenshi ziliao xuanji* 6 (1986), pp. 137–140.

Lin Wenhui. *Qingji Fujian jiaoan zhi yanjiu* (Research on the missionary cases in Fujian in the Qing period). Taipei: Taiwan Commercial Press, 1989.

Litzinger, Charles A. "Rural Religion and Village Organization in North China: The Catholic Challenge in the Late Nineteenth Century." In Bays, ed., *Christianity in China*.

Liu, Lydia H. *Translingual Practice: Literature, National Culture, and Translated Modernity—China, 1900–1937*. Stanford: Stanford University Press, 1995.

Liu Shoulin. *Xinhai yihou shiqinian zhiguan nianbiao* (Yearly tables of officeholders for seventeen years after 1911). Beijing: Zhonghua shuju, 1966.

Liu Tong. "Ji *Jianyan bao*" (Recollections of the newspaper *Jianyan bao*). *Fujian wenshi ziliao* 6 (1981), pp. 46–52.

———. "Xinhai Fujian guangfu huiyi" (Recollections of the 1911 revolution in Fujian). In *Xinhai geming huiyi lu* (Memoirs of the Xinhai revolution), vol. 4. Beijing: Zhonghua shuju, 1962.

Liu Zizheng [Lau Tzy Cheng]. *Huang Naishang yu Xin Fuzhou* (Huang Naishang and the "New Fuzhou"). Singapore: Nanyang xuehui, 1979.

Lo Hui-min, ed. *The Correspondence of G. E. Morrison*. 2 vols. Cambridge: Cambridge University Press, 1976.

Lodwick, Kathleen L. *Crusaders Against Opium: Protestant Missionaries in China, 1874–1917*. Lexington: University Press of Kentucky, 1996.

Lukes, Steven. *Essays in Social Theory*. London: MacMillan, 1977.

Lutz, Jessie G. *Chinese Politics and Christian Missions: The Anti-Christian Movements of 1920–1928*. Notre Dame, Ind.: Cross-Cultural Publications, 1988.

Lutz, Jessie G., and Rolland Ray Lutz. *Hakka Chinese Confront Protestant Christianity, 1850–1900, with the Autobiographies of Eight Hakka Christians, and Commentary*. Armonk, N.Y.: M. E. Sharpe, 1998.

Macauley, Melissa Ann. "The Civil Reprobate: Pettifoggers, Property, and Litigation in

Late Imperial China, 1723–1850." Unpublished Ph.D. dissertation, University of California, Berkeley, 1993.

Maclay, R. S. *Life Among the Chinese, with Characteristic Sketches and Incidents of Missionary Operations and Prospects in China*. New York: Carlton and Porter, 1861.

Macleod, David I. *Building Character in the American Boy: The Boy Scouts, YMCA, and Their Forerunners, 1870–1920*. Madison: University of Wisconsin Press, 1983.

Madancy, Joyce A. "Ambitious Interlude: The Anti-Opium Campaign in China's Fujian Province, 1906–17." Unpublished Ph.D. dissertation, University of Michigan, 1996.

———. "Revolution, Religion, and the Poppy: Opium and the Rebellion of the 'Sixteenth Emperor' in Early Republican Fujian." *Republican China* 21:1 (1995), pp. 1–41.

Mann, Susan. "Widows in the Kinship, Class, and Community Structures of Qing Dynasty China." *Journal of Asian Studies* 46:1 (1987), pp. 37–56.

Mao Tse-tung. " 'Friendship' or Aggression?" In *Selected Works of Mao Tse-tung*, vol. 4, pp. 447–450. Beijing: Foreign Languages Press, 1961.

Maspero, Henri. *Taoism and Chinese Religion*. Trans. Frank A. Kierman, Jr. Amherst: University of Massachusetts Press, 1981.

Mathews, Donald G. *Religion in the Old South*. Chicago: University of Chicago Press, 1977.

McCutchan, Robert Guy. *Our Hymnody: A Manual of the Methodist Hymnal*. New York: Abingdon-Cokesbury Press, second edition, 1937.

McElroy, Sarah Coles. "Transforming China Through Education: Yan Xiu, Zhang Boling, and the Effort to Build a New School System, 1901–1927." Unpublished Ph.D. dissertation, Yale University, 1996.

McIntosh, Gilbert. *The Mission Press in China, Being a Jubilee Retrospect of the American Presbyterian Mission Press, with Sketches of Other Mission Presses in China, as well as Accounts of the Bible and Tract Societies at Work in China*. Shanghai: American Presbyterian Mission Press, 1895.

Meiguo huagong jinyue jishi erbian (Continued account of the American treaty excluding Chinese laborers). N.p.: Pingdeng she (Equality Society), 1905. Fujian Provincial Archives, *Ziliao* Collection, 2–8–18.

Meiguo quanli zhi fada (America, a world power). Trans. Franklin Ohlinger (with Huang Zhiji). Shanghai and Fuzhou: Methodist Publishing House, 1907. Ohlinger Papers, YDS Record Group 23–13–231.

Meihui liwen (Methodist Church discipline). Fuzhou: Methodist Publishing House, 1869.

Meihui liwen (Methodist Church discipline). Fuzhou: Methodist Publishing House, 1872.

Meihui nianlu (Methodist Church annual record) (1868). Bodleian Library, Oxford University.

Meiyimei hui ganglie (Discipline of the Methodist Episcopal Church). Fuzhou: Methodist Publishing House, 1895; preface 1892.

Meiyimei hui nianhui dan, fu Li mushi deng shuxin (Record of the annual conference of the Methodist Episcopal Church, with appended letters from the Rev. Li and others). [Fuzhou]: [Methodist Publishing House], 1874.

Mercy and Truth: A Record of CMS Medical Mission Work. London, 1879–1927.

Metzger, Thomas. *Escape from Predicament: Neo-Confucianism and China's Emerging Political Culture*. New York: Columbia University Press, 1977.

Mianlihui jiangyi baihua (Hints and helps on Christian Endeavor prayer meeting topics). 1915–1920.

Miller, Perry. *The Life of the Mind in America: From the Revolution to the Civil War*. New York: Harcourt, Brace, and World, 1965.

Min Tu-ki. "The Late-Ch'ing Provincial Assembly." In Min Tu-ki, *National Polity and Local Power: The Transformation of Late Imperial China*, trans. and ed. Philip A. Kuhn and Timothy Brook. Cambridge: Council on East Asian Studies, Harvard University, and the Harvard-Yenching Institute, 1989.

Mingri zhi Fuzhou (The Fuzhou of tomorrow). 1919. YMCA of the USA Archives.

Minguo Fujian gexian shi (qu) hukou tongji ziliao 1912–1949 (Population statistics for the counties, cities, [and administrative districts] of Fujian in the Republican period, 1912–1949). [Fuzhou]: Fujian sheng danganguan, n.d.; preface 1988.

Minguo Fujian sheng xingzheng qu hua (Administrative divisions in Republican Fujian). Fuzhou: Fujian Provincial Archives, 1988.

Minhou jiaoyu yanjiu (Minhou County [Fuzhou] educational research) 1 (1917).

Minhou nongchan gongjinhui canguanren bianlan (Guide for visitors to the Minhou Agricultural Produce Promotional Fair). Ed. Support Committee for the Minhou Agricultural Produce Promotional Fair. Fuzhou: n.p., 1917.

Minhou yishi gonghui nianjian (Minhou Physicians' Association yearbook) 3 (1937).

Minjing (Fujian, be warned!). N.p., [1904–1905].

Minnan jiuhuohui di yici baogao shu (First report of the Minnan Fire Brigade). Fuzhou, 1908.

Minsheng huibao (Fukien church gazette). Fuzhou, 1876–1898.

Minutes of the Central Conference of the Methodist Episcopal Church in China. Shanghai, 1897–1911.

Minutes of the Foochow Conference of the Methodist Episcopal Church. Fuzhou, 1877–1949.

Miyazaki, Ichisada. *China's Examination Hell: The Civil Service Examination of Imperial China*. Trans. Conrad Schirokauer. New York: Weatherhill, 1976.

Naquin, Susan. *Millenarian Rebellion in China: The Eight Trigrams Uprising of 1813*. New Haven: Yale University Press, 1976.

Nathan, Andrew J. *Peking Politics, 1918–1923: Factionalism and the Failure of Constitutionalism*. New York: Columbia University Press, 1976.

Nind, J. Newton, et al. *Mary Clarke Nind and Her Work, by Her Children: Her Childhood, Girlhood, Married Life, Religious Experience and Activity, Together with the Story of Her Labors in Behalf of the Woman's Foreign Missionary Society of the Methodist Episcopal Church*. Chicago: J. Newton Nind for the Woman's Foreign Missionary Society, 1906.

Ono Shinji. "A Deliberate Rumor: National Anxiety in China on the Eve of the Xinhai Revolution." In Eto and Schiffrin, eds., *China's Republican Revolution*.

Overmyer, Daniel J. "Alternatives: Popular Religious Sects in Chinese Society." *Modern China* 7:2 (1981), pp. 153–190.

——. "Attitudes Toward Popular Religion in the Ritual Texts of the Chinese State: The *Collected Statutes of the Great Ming.*" *Cahiers d'Extrême Asie* 2 (1991), pp. 225–255.

——. "Dualism and Conflict in Chinese Popular Religion." In Frank E. Reynolds and Theodore M. Ludwig, eds., *Transitions and Transformations in the History of Religions: Essays in Honor of Joseph M. Kitagawa.* Leiden: E. J. Brill, 1980.

Ownby, David. *Brotherhoods and Secret Societies in Early and Mid-Qing China: The Formation of a Tradition.* Stanford: Stanford University Press, 1996.

Pakenham-Walsh, W.S. *Some Typical Christians of South China.* London: Marshall Bros., 1905.

Pan Shouzheng. "Xinhai geming zai Fuzhou" (The Xinhai revolution in Fuzhou). *Fuzhou wenshi ziliao xuanji* 1 (1981), pp. 1–33.

Pan Zuchang. "Xinhai geming Tengshan renwu yiwen" (Random anecdotes on Tengshan personalities in the 1911 revolution). *Cangshan wenshi* 6 (1991), pp. 39–49.

Peel, J. D. Y. "'For Who Hath Despised the Day of Small Things?' Missionary Narratives and Historical Anthropology." *Comparative Studies in Society and History* 37:3 (1995), pp. 581–607.

Perleberg, Max. *Who's Who in Modern China.* Hong Kong: Ye Olde Printerie, 1954.

Peter, W. W. *Broadcasting Health in China: The Field and Methods of Public Health Work in the Missionary Enterprise.* Shanghai: Presbyterian Mission Press, 1926.

Pomeranz, Kenneth. "Ritual Imitation and Political Identity in North China: The Late Imperial Legacy and the Chinese National State Revisited." *Twentieth-Century China* 23:1 (1997), pp. 1–30.

——. "Water to Iron, Widows to Warlords: The Handan Rain Shrine in Modern Chinese History." *Late Imperial China* 12:1 (1991), pp. 62–99.

Pu Hanzi. "Sanbo geming zhongzi de Qingmo Houguan liangdeng xiaoxuetang" (The late Qing revolutionary catalyst, Houguan Intermediate School). *Fuzhou wenshi ziliao xuanji* 1 (1981), pp. 58–62.

Pusey, James Reeve. *China and Charles Darwin.* Cambridge: Council on East Asian Studies, Harvard University, 1983.

——. "On Liang Qichao's Darwinian 'Morality Revolution,' Mao Zedong's 'Revolutionary Morality,' and China's 'Moral Development.'" In Richard W. Wilson, Sidney L. Greenblatt, and Amy Auerbacher Wilson, eds., *Moral Behavior in Chinese Society.* New York: Praeger, 1981.

Pye, Lucian W. "How China's Nationalism Was Shanghaied." *Australian Journal of Chinese Affairs* 29 (January 1993), pp. 107–133.

Qiaonan gongyishe zhengxinlu (Financial statement of the Qiaonan Public Welfare Society) 2–3 (1908–1909).

Qingnian (China's young men). Shanghai, 1905–1912.

Qingnian hui bao (China's young men). Shinghai, 1901–1905.

Qingnian shige (YMCA hymnal). Shanghai: YMCA National Committee, 1911; foreword 1909.

Qishi nianlai zhi Minqing Meiyimei hui (Seventy years of the Methodist church in Minqing). Ed. Editorial Department of the Minqing Methodist Church Seventieth Anniversary Commemoration Preparatory Committee. Minqing, Fujian: Minqing Methodist Church, 1938.

Quanjie yapian lun (Exhortation to abandon opium). Fuzhou: n.p., 1853. In *China and Protestant Missions: A Collection of Their Earliest Missionary Works in Chinese,* Microfiche collection filmed from Harvard-Yenching Library, published by IDC Publishers, Leiden.

Rankin, Mary Backus. *Elite Activism and Political Transformation in China: Zhejiang Province, 1865–1911.* Stanford: Stanford University Press, 1986.

Rawski, Evelyn Sakakida. *Agricultural Change and the Peasant Economy of South China.* Cambridge: Harvard University Press, 1972.

——. "The Creation of an Emperor in Eighteenth-Century China." In Bell Yung, Evelyn S. Rawski, and Rubie S. Watson, eds., *Harmony and Counterpoint: Ritual Music in Chinese Context.* Stanford: Stanford University Press, 1996.

——. *Education and Popular Literacy in Ch'ing China.* Ann Arbor: University of Michigan Press, 1979.

——. "Elementary Education in the Mission Enterprise." In Barnett and Fairbank, eds., *Christianity in China.*

Reed, Bradly W. "Money and Justice: Clerks, Runners, and the Magistrate's Court in Late Imperial Sichuan." *Modern China* 21:3 (1995), pp. 345–382.

Reid, Daniel G., Robert D. Linder, Bruce L. Shelley, and Harry S. Stout, eds. *Dictionary of Christianity in America.* Downer's Grove, Ill.: InterVarsity Press, 1990.

Report of Province-Wide Evangelistic Campaign, Fukien, China, October 22–December 1st, 1914. [Fuzhou]: Fukien Provincial Evangelistic Committee, [1914].

Robert, Dana L. "The Methodist Struggle over Higher Education in Fuzhou, China, 1877–1883." *Methodist History* 34:3 (1996), pp. 173–189.

Rongcheng Gezhi shuyuan biyedan (Foochow College commencement program). Fuzhou: Methodist Publishing House, 1897. YDS CL 001–33.

Rowe, William T. "The Public Sphere in Modern China." *Modern China* 16:3 (1990), pp. 309–329.

Sanneh, Lamin. *Translating the Message: The Missionary Impact on Culture.* Maryknoll, N.Y.: Orbis, 1989.

Schneider, Laurence A. *Ku Chieh-kang and China's New History: Nationalism and the Quest for Alternative Traditions.* Berkeley: University of California Press, 1971.

Scholes, Percy A. *"God Save the King!": Its History and Its Romance.* London: Oxford University Press, 1942.

Schoppa, R. Keith. *Blood Road: The Mystery of Shen Dingyi in Revolutionary China.* Berkeley: University of California Press, 1995.

Schwartz, Benjamin I. "Culture, Modernity, and Nationalism—Further Reflections." *Daedalus* 122:3 (1993), pp. 207–225.

——. *In Search of Wealth and Power: Yen Fu and the West.* Cambridge: Belknap Press of Harvard University Press, 1964.

Scott, Roderick. *Fukien Christian University.* New York: United Board for Christian Colleges in China, 1954.

Shangye zazhi (Commerce magazine). Fuzhou, 1910–?.

Shangyou (Shangyou church magazine). Fuzhou, 1920–?.

Shengshi yuepu (Sacred songs with music). Fuzhou: Foochow College Press, 1906.

Sili Fujian xiehe daxue ershiwu zhounian jinian ce (Commemorative volume of the twenty-fifth anniversary of Fukien Christian University). N.p., 1941.

Sili Fuzhou Heling yinghua zhongxue liushi zhou xiaoqing jinian kan (Commemorative volume for the sixtieth anniversary of the Anglo-Chinese College, Fuzhou). N.p., 1940.

Sili Fuzhou qingnian hui zhongxue ershiwu zhou jinian tekan (Souvenir volume for the twenty-fifth anniversary of the Fuzhou YMCA private high school). Fuzhou: Fuzhou YMCA, 1930.

Sites, S. Moore. *Hu King Eng, M.D.* N.p., n.d. Methodist Episcopal Church Board of Foreign Missions Archives.

———. *Nathan Sites: An Epic of the East.* New York: Fleming H. Revell, 1912.

Smith, Whitney. *Flags Through the Ages and Across the World.* Maidenhead, England: McGraw-Hill, 1975.

Song Ong Siang. *One Hundred Years' History of the Chinese in Singapore.* 1923; repr. Singapore: Oxford University Press, 1984.

Songzhu shengshi (Union hymnal). Fuzhou: Methodist Publishing House, 1915.

Songzhu shige (Songs of worship). N.p., 1895.

Songzhu shige (Songs of worship). Yokohama: n.p., 1907.

Spence, Jonathan D. *Chinese Roundabout: Essays in History and Culture.* New York: W. W. Norton, 1992.

———. *The Gate of Heavenly Peace: The Chinese and Their Revolution, 1895–1900.* New York: Viking, 1981.

———. *God's Chinese Son: The Taiping Heavenly Kingdom of Hong Xiuquan.* New York: W. W. Norton, 1996.

Standaert, Nicolas. *Confucian and Christian in Late Ming China: The Life and Thought of Yang Tingyun (1562–1627).* Leiden: E. J. Brill, 1988.

Stauffer, Milton T., ed. *The Christian Occupation of China.* Shanghai: China Continuation Committee, 1922.

Stock, Eugene, with revisions by T. McClelland. *For Christ in Fuh-Kien: The Story of the Fuh-Kien Mission of the Church Missionary Society.* 4th ed. London: Church Missionary Society, 1904.

Sun, Yat-sen. *Prescriptions for Saving China: Selected Writings of Sun Yat-sen.* Ed. Julie Lee Wei, Ramon H. Myers, and Donald G. Gillin. Stanford: Hoover Institution Press, 1994.

Sweeten, Alan Richard. "Catholic Converts in Jiangxi Province: Conflict and Accommodation, 1860–1900." In Bays, ed., *Christianity in China.*

Tahara Teijiro, comp. *Shinmatsu minsho Chugoku kanshin jimmeiroku* (Biographies of Chinese officials and gentry of the late Qing and early Republic). Dalian: Chugoku kenkyukai, 1918.

Taijiang shijian (The Taijiang incident). Ed. Jianbao Editorial Board. Fuzhou: Jianbao Publishers, 1920.

Tang, Xiaobing. *Global Space and the Nationalist Discourse of Modernity: The Historical Thinking of Liang Qichao.* Stanford: Stanford University Press, 1996.

Thompson, Roger R. *China's Local Councils in the Age of Constitutional Reform, 1898–1911.* Cambridge: Council on East Asian Studies, Harvard University, 1995.

———. "The Political Impact of Students Returned from Law and Administration Courses in Japan." *Republican China* 16:1 (1990), pp. 1–17.

Tianantang bashi zhou jinian kan (Church of Heavenly Peace eightieth anniversary commemorative volume). Ed. Wei Jianxiang. Fuzhou: Methodist Church, 1936.

T'ien Ju-k'ang. *Peaks of Faith: Protestant Mission in Revolutionary China*. Leiden: E. J. Brill, 1993.

Tomlinson, John. *Cultural Imperialism: A Critical Introduction*. Baltimore: Johns Hopkins University Press, 1991.

Townsend, James. "Chinese Nationalism." *Australian Journal of Chinese Affairs* 27 (January 1992), pp. 97–130.

Tseng, Timothy. "Chinese Protestant Nationalism in the United States, 1880–1927." *Amerasia Journal* 22:1 (1996), pp. 31–56.

Tsin, Michael. "Imagining 'Society' in Early Twentieth-Century China." In Joshua A. Fogel and Peter Zarrow, eds., *Imagining the People: Chinese Intellectuals and the Concept of Citizenship, 1890–1920*. Armonk, N.Y.: M. E. Sharpe, 1997.

Twenty-One Years' Work Among the Blind in Foochow. N.p., n.d. YDS Missions Pamphlets 63–471.

Uk Ing: The Pioneer—Historical Beginnings of Methodist Woman's Work in Asia and the Story of the First School, a Compilation. Foochow: Christian Herald Mission Press, 1939.

Waijiao wendu-Fuzhou Zhong Ri renmin dou'ou an (Diplomatic correspondence relating to the Foochow fracas). Beijing: Foreign Ministry, 1921.

Wakeman, Frederic, Jr. "The Civil Society and Public Sphere Debate: Western Reflections on Chinese Political Culture." *Modern China* 19:2 (1993), pp. 108–138.

——. *The Fall of Imperial China*. New York: Free Press, 1975.

——. "Models of Historical Change: The Chinese State and Society, 1839–1989." In Kenneth Lieberthal, Joyce Kallgren, Roderick MacFarquhar, and Frederic Wakeman, Jr., eds., *Perspectives on Modern China: Four Anniversaries*. Armonk, N.Y.: M. E. Sharpe, 1991.

Wallace, L. Ethel. *Hwa Nan College: The Woman's College of South China*. New York: United Board for Christian Colleges in China, 1956.

Wang Fuchu [Xiaoquan]. "Women zenyang zuo jiaoyuzhe" (How should we go about being educators?). *Shangyou* 1:1 (1922), pp. 29–32.

Wang, Liping. "Creating a National Symbol: The Sun Yatsen Memorial in Nanjing." *Republican China* 21:2 (1996), pp. 23–63.

Wang Shenyin, ed. *Zanmeishi (xinbian) shihua* (Historical sketches on *Hymns of Praise* [new edition]). Shanghai: China Christian Council, 1993.

Wang Tiefan. "Fujian diyi mian 'shiba xing qizhi'" (Fujian's first "eighteen-star flag"). *Cangshan wenshi* 6 (1991), pp. 14–15.

——. "Fujian Tongmenghui zai Cangshan mimi zhizao zhadan" (The secret manufacture of bombs in Cangshan by the Fujian Revolutionary Alliance). *Cangshan wenshi* 6 (1991), pp. 16–18.

Wang Xiaoqi, comp. *Xiqing Wangshi chongxiu zupu* (Revised genealogy of the Wangs of Xiqing). N.p., n.d.; preface 1935.

Wang Yinnan, ed. *Zhongguo de guoqi, guohui, he guoge* (China's national flag, national emblem, and national anthem). Beijing: Renmin chubanshe, 1987.

Wang Zhenxian [Xiaoquan]. "Ershi shiji zhi jiaoyuguan" (The educational outlook of the twentieth century). *Minhou jiaoyu yanjiu* (1917), *xueshu zhuanjian* section, pp. 1–30.

Watson, Burton. *Early Chinese Literature*. New York: Columbia University Press, 1962.

Welch, Holmes. *The Buddhist Revival in China*. Cambridge: Harvard University Press, 1968.

Who's Who in China. Shanghai, 1920.

Wiest, Jean-Paul. "Lineage and Patterns of Conversion in Guangdong." *Ch'ing-shih wen-t'i* 4:7 (1982), pp. 1–32.

Wiley, I. W. *China and Japan*. Cincinnati: Hitchcock and Walden; New York: Phillips and Hunt, 1879.

Williamson, Alexander [Wei Lianchen]. *Gewu tanyuan* (Natural theology). Shanghai: Christian Literature Society, 1910; first edition 1876.

Wolf, Arthur P. "Gods, Ghosts, and Ancestors." In Arthur P. Wolf, ed., *Studies in Chinese Society*. Stanford: Stanford University Press, 1978.

Wong, R. Bin. *China Transformed: Historical Change and the Limits of European Experience*. Ithaca, N.Y.: Cornell University Press, 1997.

Wright, Mary Clabaugh, ed. *China in Revolution: The First Phase, 1900–1913*. New Haven: Yale University Press, 1968.

———. "Introduction: The Rising Tide of Change." In Wright, ed., *China in Revolution*.

Wu Di'an [Linji-Franklin Ohlinger], with Huang Zhiji. *Luoma zongjiao jizhan shi* (History of the religious conflict in Rome). Shanghai: Methodist Publishing House, 1906.

Wu Jiaqiong. "Lin Bingzhang shengping gaishu" (Biographical sketch of Lin Bingzhang). *Fujian wenshi ziliao* 19 (1988), pp. 98–104.

Wu Jiayu and Lin Jiazhen. "Fujian jinyan yundong 'Qudushe'" (The Fujian anti-opium movement Qudushe). *Fuzhou wenshi ziliao xuanji* 2 (1983), pp. 15–18.

Wylie, Alexander. *Memorials of Protestant Missionaries to the Chinese: Giving a List of Their Publications, and Obituary Notices of the Deceased, with Copious Indexes*. Shanghai: American Presbyterian Mission Press, 1867.

Xie Xi'en. *Jiuling shiyao* (Ten essentials for salvation). Fuzhou: Methodist Publishing House, 1874.

[Xie Xi'en]. *Sia Sek Ong and the Self-Support Movement in Our Foochow Mission: The Story of His Life and Work Related by Himself*. New York: [Methodist Episcopal Church Board of Foreign Missions], n.d. Pamphlet in YDS.

Xin Ping, ed. *Minguo jiangling lu* (Biographies of Republican military officers). Shenyang: Liaoning renmin chubanshe, 1991.

Xiqing Wangshi zupu, renshen dong disici xukanben (Genealogy of the Wangs of Xiqing, fourth updated edition, winter 1992). Privately published in Taiwan, 1993.

Xu Bomei. *Xinde tonglun* (Essay on virtue by faith). Fuzhou: Methodist Publishing House, 1872.

———. Untitled manuscript memoir. 100 pages. Ca. 1900.

Xu Hanguang [Dr. Katharine H. K. Hsu], comp. *Gaoyang Xushi zupu* (Genealogy of the Xu family of Gaoyang). N.p., n.d.; privately printed in Houston, Tex., 1995.

Xu, Xiaoqun. "Between State and Society, Between Professionalism and Politics: The Shanghai Bar Association in Republican China, 1912–1937." *Twentieth-Century China* 24:1 (1998), pp. 1–29.

[Xu Yangmei]. *The Way of Faith Illustrated: Autobiography of Hu Yong Mi of the China Mission Conference*. Cincinnati: Curts and Jennings; New York: Eaton and Mains, 1896.

Xu Yangmei. *Xu Mushi xinxiaolu* (The Rev. Xu's record of the results of faith). Shanghai and Fuzhou: Methodist Publishing House, 1917; prefaces 1897.

Xu Youchun, ed. *Minguo renwu da cidian* (Dictionary of Republican biography). Shijiazhuang: Hebei renmin chubanshe, 1991.

Xu Zezhou [Hu Caik Ciu], ed. *Mengzi (Fuzhou tuhua zhujie)* (Mencius, in the Fuzhou colloquial language, with commentary). Fuzhou: Zhonghua Printing Co., 1919.

Xue furen [Mrs. S. Moore Sites], with Huang Naishang. *Weili zhuan* (Life of John Wesley). Fuzhou: Methodist Publishing House, 1878.

Xunshan shizhe (Zion's herald). Fuzhou, 1874–1876.

Yan Fu. "Yuan qiang" (On strength). In Jian Bozan et al., *Wuxu bianfa ziliao congkan* (Collected documents of the 1898 reform movement), vol. 3 of 4. Shanghai: Shanghai renmin chubanshe, 1953.

Yang, C. K. *Religion in Chinese Society*. Berkeley: University of California Press, 1961.

Ye Jianyuan. *Zhonghua shenggonghui Fujiansheng jiaoqu ge zhiqu jianshi: Lianjiang, Pingnan, Ningde, Jianning* (Brief history of the districts of the Fujian diocese of the Chung-hua Sheng-kung-hui: Lianjiang, Pingnan, Ningde, and Jianning). N.p., [1933].

Ye, Weili. " 'Nu Liuxuesheng': The Story of American-Educated Chinese Women, 1880s–1920s." *Modern China* 20:3 (1994), pp. 315–346.

Yen Ching Hwang. *The Overseas Chinese and the 1911 Revolution: With Special Reference to Singapore and Malaya*. Kuala Lumpur: Oxford University Press, 1976.

Young, Ernest P. *The Presidency of Yuan Shih-k'ai: Liberalism and Dictatorship in Early Republican China*. Ann Arbor: University of Michigan Press, 1977.

[Young Men's Christian Associations of China and Korea]. *Among Young Men in the Middle Kingdom: A Report of the Work of the Young Men's Christian Associations of China and Korea*. Shanghai: YMCA, 1912.

———. *Record of the Seventh Annual Conference of the Secretaries of the International Committee, July 23–29, 1909*. Shanghai: YMCA, 1909.

———. *The Work of the Young Men's Christian Associations of China and Korea During 1908: A Report to the General Committee by the General Secretary*. Shanghai: YMCA, 1909.

[Young Men's Christian Associations of China]. *The 1930 Special Study Report of the Young Men's Christian Associations of China (Summarized Edition)*. Shanghai: National Committee of the YMCAs of China, 1931.

———. *The Year Nineteen Sixteen*. Shanghai: YMCA, 1917.

Youtu shige (YMCA hymnal). Shanghai: YMCA, 1904. World Student Christian Federation Archives, YDS Record Group 46–217–1660.

Zarrow, Peter. "Introduction: Citizenship in China and the West." In Joshua A. Fogel and Peter Zarrow, eds., *Imagining the People: Chinese Intellectuals and the Concept of Citizenship, 1890–1920*. Armonk, N.Y.: M. E. Sharpe, 1997.

Zha Shijie. *Zhongguo Jidujiao renwu xiaozhuan* (Brief biographies of Chinese Protestants). Taipei: China Evangelical Seminary Press, 1982.

Zhan Guanqun. *Weixin zhishi, tuohuangzhe, geming dangren: Huang Naishang zhuan*

(Reform advocate, emigration pioneer, and revolutionary: A biography of Huang Nai-shang). Fuzhou: Fujian renmin chubanshe, 1992.

Zhang Pengyuan [P'eng-yuan Chang]. *Lixianpai yu xinhai geming* (Constitutionalists and the Xinhai revolution). Taipei: Zhongguo xueshu zhuzuo jiangzhu weiyuanhui, 1969.

Zhang Zhenqian. "Shouhui jiaoyu quan yundong de huiyi" (Recalling the movement to recover educational sovereignty). *Fujian wenshi ziliao* 13 (1986), pp. 154–161.

Zheng Lansun [Zuyin] et al., eds. *Fujian xinhai guangfu shiliao* (Historical materials on the Xinhai revolution in Fujian). Liancheng, Fujian: Jianguo chubanshe, 1940.

Zheng Lisheng. "Minguo yuannian Fuzhou minjian bianyin de 'Huanying Sun xian-sheng' quben" (Popularly published songbooks welcoming Sun Yatsen to Fuzhou in the first year of the Republic). In *Jinian Sun Zhongshan xiansheng*.

Zhonghua Jidujiao qingnian hui wushi zhou nian jinian ce (Commemorative volume for the fiftieth anniversary of the Chinese YMCA). Shanghai: YMCA Press, 1936.

Zhonghua minguo kaiguo wushi nian wenxian (Collected documents on the fiftieth anniversary of the establishment of the Republic of China). Taipei: Editorial Commis-sion of the Collected Documents on the Fiftieth Anniversary of the Establishment of the Republic of China, 1964.

Zhou Bangdao. *Jindai jiaoyu xianjin zhuanlüe* (Biographies of modern educational pio-neers). Taipei: Zhongguo wenhua daxue chubanbu, 1982.

Zongzhu shizhang (Hymns of worship). Fuzhou: American Board Mission, 1871.

Zongzhu shizhang (Hymns of worship). Fuzhou: American Board Mission, 1884; revised edition 1891.

Zou Tianhuan. "Fujian gua'er yuan huiyi" (Memories of the Fujian Orphanage). *Fuzhou wenshi ziliao xuanji* 2 (1983), pp. 176–181.

Zuohai gongdao bao (Cau hai kung dao pao / Fuzhou Christian Journal). Fuzhou, 1911–1912.

Zürcher, Erik. "The Jesuit Mission in Fukien in Late Ming Times: Levels of Response." In E. B. Vermeer, ed., *Development and Decline of Fukien Province in the Seventeenth and Eighteenth Centuries*. Leiden: E. J. Brill, 1990.

Index

ABCFM. *See* American Board of Commissioners for Foreign Missions

Ahok, Mr. *See* Zhang Heling

Allen, Young J., 58

American Board of Commissioners for Foreign Missions (ABCFM): growth in Fujian, 3–4, 17–18, 149; church government, 17–19, 22–23, 24; schools, 35, 40, 41, 43, 130–131, 135, 136; hymns, 129, 130; official patronage of, 153–154; mentioned, 64, 144, 171

Anagnost, Ann, 115

Anderson, Benedict, 116–117, 147

Anderson, George (U.S. consul in Xiamen), 59–60

Anglicans. *See* Church Missionary Society

Anglo-Chinese College, Fuzhou: founding, 22, 34, 38–40; careers of graduates, 41–43, 46, 102, 183–184; and U.S. exclusion laws, 56–58, 60; politics of students and alumni, 62–68, 92–93, 99, 104, 106–110, 139–143, 181–182, 228*n105*; and YMCA, 69, 74; prominence of, 78, 245*n56*; mentioned, 82, 176

Anti-Opium Society: founding and activities, 50–54, 68; Protestants in, 54–55, 66, 77, 78, 157–158; and Qiaonan Society, 62–64; and YMCA, 72, 74, 75; and nationalism, 116, 121–122, 134, 199, 200; functions assumed by state after *1911*, 162; mentioned, 89, 124, 167, 172

Baldwin, Stephen L., 21, 33

Bashford, James W., 110, 111, 149, 151, 184, 208*n73*, 230*n22*

Boy Scouts, 137, 191, 235*n105*

Bridgman, Elijah C., 118

Britain: Chinese Protestants educated in, 35, 42, 47; and opium, 49, 53–55; YMCA in, 69; national anthem, 128–129, 131, 146; and nationalist ritual, 130, 134; mentioned, 3, 49